Claes Oldenburg: An Anthology

Claes Oldenburg: An Anthology

Essays by Germano Celant, Dieter Koepplin, Mark Rosenthal

Guggenheim Museum / National Gallery of Art

Claes Oldenburg: An Anthology
Curated by Germano Celant

This exhibition is co-organized by the National Gallery of Art,
Washington, D.C., and the Solomon R. Guggenheim Museum, New York, and is
presented in association with The Museum of Contemporary Art, Los Angeles,
the Kunst- und Austellungshalle der Bundesrepublik Deutschland, Bonn, and the
Hayward Gallery, London.

National Gallery of Art, Washington, D.C.
February 12–May 7, 1995

The Museum of Contemporary Art, Los Angeles
June 18–September 3, 1995

Solomon R. Guggenheim Museum, New York
October 7, 1995–January 21, 1996

Kunst- und Austellungshalle der Bundesrepublik Deutschland, Bonn
February 15–May 12, 1996

Hayward Gallery, London
June 6–August 19, 1996

ISBN 0-89207-139-7

Printed in Germany by Cantz

Guggenheim Museum Publications
1071 Fifth Avenue
New York, N.Y. 10128

Contents

Foreword

The National Gallery of Art and the Solomon R. Guggenheim Museum are extremely pleased to present *Claes Oldenburg: An Anthology*, the first exhibition jointly organized by our two institutions. Surveying the career of one of America's most distinguished artists, this major exhibition presents a remarkably diverse body of work that spans the last three-and-one-half decades. Throughout these years Oldenburg has created a rich and provocative visual language that is the result of an intense engagement with and keen observation of the world around him. That language takes many forms, from performances to writings, from drawings to sculpture, the latter ranging in scale from the intimate to the monumental.

For subject matter, Oldenburg has consistently turned to the commonplace. For example, the plaster objects for his early installation *The Store* are based on merchandise glimpsed through the shop windows of downtown New York, the city that the artist has inhabited, with periodic absences, for nearly forty years. Since the 1960s, Oldenburg has been transforming the mundane objects of our world into mysterious and sensuous works of art. By making hard forms soft or small things large, and by refusing to accept the nature of objects as static, immutable, or self-evident, Oldenburg gives us cause to reexamine many of our fundamental perceptions about the world. This exhibition and the monograph published on its occasion present the full range and tremendous diversity of Oldenburg's creative production and thereby illuminate the formal logic and consistency of thought that characterize his work as a whole.

Beginning with the Happenings of the early 1960s, and continuing through the most recent large-scale, outdoor sculpture, Oldenburg has often worked in fruitful collaboration with other artists, and, occasionally, architects. Since 1976, he has joined forces with the art historian and writer Coosje van Bruggen to produce twenty-five large-scale projects that have been installed in urban centers across America and Europe. Together, Oldenburg and van Bruggen have helped to redefine the very nature of public sculpture in works such as the colossal *Crusoe Umbrella* in Des Moines, the fifty-one-foot *Spoonbridge and Cherry* at the Walker Art Center in Minneapolis, and most recently, four giant shuttlecocks on the lawn of the Nelson-Atkins Museum of Art in Kansas City. This exhibition documents many of these projects through drawings, maquettes, and models.

The curator of the exhibition is Germano Celant, the Guggenheim Museum's Curator of Contemporary Art, who has been intensely involved with Oldenburg's work for more than a decade. He has written two essays for this monograph, an introduction that addresses Oldenburg's affair with objects, and an overview of Oldenburg's and van Bruggen's large-scale projects. He is joined by Mark Rosenthal, Curator of Twentieth-Century Art at the National Gallery, who considers the critical issue of monumentality in Oldenburg's work, and Dieter Koepplin, head of the Department of Prints and Drawings at the Kunstmuseum Basel, who looks in depth at a monumental indoor project, *The Entropic Library*, created for the 1989 Paris exhibition *Magiciens de la Terre*. In addition to these essays, this book documents Oldenburg's entire career through a chronological presentation of the work, in many cases rephotographed under the artist's direction, archival photographs of rarely-seen performances, and a selection of the artist's writings.

We are especially pleased that the exhibition will be traveling to the Museum of Contemporary Art, Los Angeles, the Kunst- und Austellungshalle der Bundesrepublik Deutschland, Bonn, and the Hayward Gallery, London. To our colleagues at those institutions as well as to the lenders who have so generously parted with their works of art for this show go our most sincere thanks.

Throughout the preparation of the exhibition and publication Claes Oldenburg and Coosje van Bruggen have worked closely with the staffs of our two museums. They have not only given generously of their time and expertise, but have also lent a large number of works from their own collection to the exhibition. For their great patience, insight, and generosity we are extremely grateful.

Earl A. Powell III
Director
National Gallery of Art, Washington, D.C.

Thomas Krens
Director
Solomon R. Guggenheim Museum, New York

Acknowledgments

This exhibition and the monograph published on its occasion were realized with the generous collaboration of many individuals and institutions. First and foremost, I would like to express my profound gratitude to Claes Oldenburg and Coosje van Bruggen. They have been instrumental throughout every phase of this project, dedicating ample portions of their time and counsel and generously offering the resources of their studio and archives to assist with the effort. Their total enthusiasm and unwavering friendship have made it a privilege to work with them.

A project of this magnitude could not have been realized without the cooperation of the private collectors and institutions whose works comprise this show. I wish to acknowledge their generosity; in parting with their works, they have contributed immeasurably to the project's success. A special debt of gratitude goes to Kimiko and John Powers, who have enthusiastically supported the artist's work for many years, and who have lent numerous works to this exhibition.

The many staff members of the artist's studio, the National Gallery of Art, and the Solomon R. Guggenheim Museum who have coordinated the various aspects of the exhibition and catalogue deserve much praise. At Oldenburg's studio, David Platzker has expertly overseen the project since its inception and has contributed new and invaluable research on the artist's work and career. My thanks to Viki Rutsch, Carla Grosse, and Diana Jackier, assistants to Claes Oldenburg, for their contribution to this project.

At the National Gallery, I would like to thank Earl A. Powell III, Director, and Alan Shestack, Deputy Director, for their enthusiastic support of this project. I am especially indebted to Marla Prather, Associate Curator of Twentieth-Century Art, who oversaw all curatorial matters for this exhibition from Washington, working closely with the artist from the planning stages through the installation. Jessica Stewart provided administrative support with utmost efficiency. In the Department of Exhibitions, headed by D. Dodge Thompson, exhibition officer Naomi Remes capably handled the many complexities of organization and administration for the show. She was assisted by Stephanie Fick. Chief Registrar Sally Freitag and her staff did an excellent job shipping and installing this exhibition, which is composed of many large and fragile objects. The care of those objects was conscientiously overseen by exhibition conservators Mervin Richard and Michael Pierce, as well as by Shelley Sturman, head of the Department of Sculpture Conservation, and her staff. Nancy R. Breuer, Associate General Counsel, saw to the many legal matters involved in an exhibition of this scope. Finally, my thanks to the design and installation department, namely Gaillard Ravenel, Mark Leithauser, Gordon Anson, John Olson, and Jane Rodgers, for their help in realizing a spectacular installation.

At the Guggenheim Museum, I am grateful to Thomas Krens, Director, for his support. Special thanks are due to Lisa Dennison, Curator of Collections and Exhibitions, and Michael Govan, former Deputy Director, both of whom were instrumental in the planning stages of this exhibition. Clare Bell, Assistant Curator, has managed the coordination of the catalogue from the curatorial end. Carole Perry, Curatorial Assistant, and Julia Blaut, Research Associate, have painstakingly resolved many issues associated with the research and documentation of the publication.

My gratitude is also extended to other members of the Guggenheim's staff, including Judith Cox, General Counsel; Amy Husten, Manager of Budget and Planning; Maryann Jordan, Director of External Affairs; Pamela Myers, Administrator for Exhibitions and Programming; and Aileen Silverman, Assistant to the Registrar.

This monograph was produced by the Guggenheim's Publications Department. I am sincerely grateful to Anthony Calnek, Director of Publications, whose thorough attention to all matters concerning the volume has ensured its successful realization. Elizabeth Levy, Production Editor, brought her considerable expertise to bear in addressing the intricate details involved with its production; Jennifer Knox White, Assistant Editor, gave careful editorial attention to the documentation found at the end of this book; Michelle Martino, Graphic Designer, contributed her talent and skill to the design and layout of the book; and David Heald, Manager of Photographic Services, contributed important new photography to the book.

My deep appreciation goes to Mark Rosenthal, Curator of Twentieth-Century Art at the National Gallery; and Dieter Koepplin, head of the Department of Prints and Drawings at the Kunstmuseum Basel, for their original essays for the catalogue. I would like to acknowledge the essential contribution made by Massimo Vignelli, who designed the publication. My appreciation is extended as well to Stephanie Salomon for her astute editing of parts of this book.

Finally, I wish to extend my thanks to the various other individuals who have so amiably helped in different phases of this project. My utmost appreciation to PaceWildenstein, especially Mark Glimcher and Douglas Baxter, for their assistance. Special thanks also to Ellen Page Wilson and Douglas S. Parker for photographing many of Oldenburg's pieces under difficult deadlines. And I extend sincere appreciation to Stefan Illing-Finné of Cantz, who once again has exhibited his exceptional technical wizardry in the production of a Guggenheim publication.

This project has been supported by the labor of a number of interns and researchers at the Guggenheim Museum, whose assistance and skill have been instrumental in bringing this exhibition and catalogue to fruition. I would like to thank Jonathan Applefield, Benjamin Barzune, Kathy Drasher, Inma Escobar, Abigail Esman, Lara Ferb, Josette Lamoureux, Liane Radel, Clare Rogan, and Zelfira Tregulova.

For the efforts on the part of all those who contributed to this project, my heartfelt thanks and gratitude.

Germano Celant

Claes Oldenburg and the Feeling of Things

Germano Celant

The object feels. This is the great discovery that Claes Oldenburg has introduced to Modern art. In creating a feeling object, and presenting it as art, Oldenburg intertwines the organic and the inorganic; human feeling and the physical presence of the object are joined in such a way that detached, impersonal objectness is no longer distinguishable from sensuality and sexuality, and one can therefore "speak of the sexuality of an object."[1]

The intertwining of objects and senses produces a suspension of feeling, leading to a neuter terrain where the human body supplants the object. The object then becomes fraught with perturbations and passions, becomes swollen and agitated, rises and falls, becomes despondent or sad. It takes its place alongside human beings with its own personal history.

Similarly, if feeling is something situated on the threshold between life and the object, the human being is also transformed, becoming a feeling object. If we look at Oldenburg's soft sculptures and performances of the 1960s, we see that this absurd condition—a feeling object moving and palpitating like a human, or a human being becoming an object—is the crux of his understanding and procedure: his sculptures are anthropologized while human beings are rendered utterly alien and unrecognizable. The object is given new life, while life itself is annulled in the object.

Thus, Oldenburg reveals the similarities and differences, the affinities and divergences that have sustained, in art, the confrontation between man and object. The relationship between the thing and its maker had always been assumed to be vertical: either the artist looked down from above— literally, in the case of Jackson Pollock and his drip paintings—or vice versa, as with Man Ray's aerial objects. With Oldenburg, the relationship becomes horizontal. The object is no longer something under or above us, but next to us, beside us: an object with a life of its own.

What I want to do is to create an independent object which has its existence in a world outside of both the real world as we know it and the world of art. It's an independent thing which has its own power, just to sit there and remain something of a mystery. I don't want to prejudice the imagination. I want the imagination to come and make of it what it wants to make of it, but the object will always slip out of whatever definition it may be given. If someone says it looks satirical, the next day it may look very unsatirical. It may look like an ordinary thing. My intention is to make an everyday object that eludes definition.[2]

An object/being animated by physical, vital ferment, which throbs and rumples, fits softly into any context, looks like a "real thing" yet has a character and "identity," an actor that elicits laughter and sadness, surrenders to others yet aspires, with all its might, to an existence of its own: "How near can a thing come to being it and not be it?"[3]

In similar fashion the object/being, indirectly, falls to the zero-point of feeling, becomes bum and thing, waste and scrap, neuter entity at the very limit of the artificiality of the object. Sexual differences, form, visible appearance, and age cease to be of any importance, as if he/she had been denied all living identity and could be frozen in time or space.

Loving life and movement I am always seeing movement even in the inanimate. I wish simply to create life, which is impossible as I go about it and the result is with my materials the illusion of life, comic or ironic or absurd. It becomes stopped movement or just the opposite of movement.

   This happens even when my materials are living things, people f.ex.

   To freeze in space is of course the very character of art, my method.[4]

But how did this transition take place, where humanity is transferred onto a piece of cardboard or fabric, a bit of paint or plaster, and the object begins to live and feel like a "body" with its own dynamics and pulsations, a thing with a varied, unpredictable existence, both fantastic and usual? What is the origin of the artist's desire to realize a project that pretends to existential autonomy? What historical and artistic conditions brought this to bear?

We are fortunate to have a photographic record of a pivotal moment in this evolution. In 1950, Hans Namuth captured on film images of Pollock covering large canvases spread across the floor with his drippings, even entering into the painting's space. Through the act of dripping, an impersonal, industrial technique, the difference between the human being and the object (in this case a painting) was suddenly and irrevocably obliterated. Feeling became concentrated in the end of the paintbrush or in a tube of color. No longer was anything human of any importance, and all experience and knowledge became concentrated in the contact between pigment and canvas. All knowing and seeing now revolved around feeling oneself as tube or color, paintbrush or stick. The bending of Pollock's body over the canvas describes an extension whereby the body is a mechanism dependent on the object; it becomes a thing projected over a thing. The frontal distinction between painter and canvas collapses, and each becomes a *common* object, each laying claim to its own existence, as though the subject were no longer required to feel but rather to identify with the thing, and it were more fitting that the object feel and identify with the subject.

Looking at this relationship in an erotic light, one might take the canvas as a "partner" with which the human being seeks to commingle, bending over it, joining with it. Yet painting by dripping leads to a sexuality that is *neuter*. It opens up a dimension of inorganic pleasure where the orgasm is chromatic and industrial, satiating a libido that is no longer viscidly expressive but objective. In this sense, Pollock invests the canvas with a sexuality that is infinite, absolute, but ultimately without life or soul, vital only in the realm of things. In the drip paintings, there is an absence of vitalistic and spiritualistic representations of human feeling, with a consequent distancing of the artist from the organismic energism that marked the sexually charged art of the first half of the twentieth century in favor of a neutral unrestrainedness realized entirely on the surface, the skin of the object or canvas.

   This is the first manifestation of an *erotic partnership* between artist and object. Oldenburg's notes of 1962 reveal that he was well aware of this relationship at that time:

The erotic or the sexual is the root of "art;" its first impulse. Today sexuality is more directed, or here where I am in Am. at this time, toward substitutes, f.ex. clothing rather than the person, fetishistic stuff, and this gives the object an intensity, and this is what I try to project.[5]

He had already considered the sexuality of Action Painting:

Jackson Pollock, photographed in his studio in 1950 by Hans Namuth.

Jasper Johns, Target with Four Faces, *1955. Assemblage: encaustic and collage on canvas with objects, surmounted by four tinted plaster faces in wood box with hinged front; with box open: 33 ⅛ x 26 x 3 inches (85.4 x 66 x 7.6 cm) overall. The Museum of Modern Art, New York, Gift of Mr. and Mrs. Robert C. Scull.*

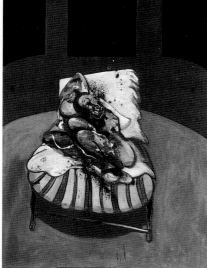

Piero Manzoni with one of his "living sculptures," 1961.

Francis Bacon, Three Studies for a Crucifixion *(detail), March 1962. Oil with sand on canvas, three panels, 78 x 57 inches (198.1 x 144.8 cm) each. Solomon R. Guggenheim Museum, New York.*

Lately I have begun to understand action painting, that old thing, in a new, vital and peculiar sense—as corny as the scratches on a NY wall and by parodying its corn I have (miracle) come back to its authenticity! I feel as if Pollock is sitting on my shoulder, or rather crouching in my pants.[6]

If art's sexuality is neuter, inert and infinite, bound to the union with an inorganic body, the desire of every artist is to create a tactile, sensual rapport with an object, painting, or sculpture that is "human," that is, capable of feeling and arousing the senses. Wrote Oldenburg:

My struggle has been to return painting to the tangible object, which is like returning the personality to touching and feeling the world around it, to offset the tendency to vagueness and abstraction. To remind people of practical activity, to suggest the sense and not to escape from the senses.[7]

From 1955 to 1961, the tradition of presenting subject and object as differentiated and parallel entities was violated anew. In works such as *Target with Four Faces* (1955), Jasper Johns makes the universe of the body coincide with the world of things. Similarly, Yves Klein and Piero Manzoni, starting in the late 1950s, began to take the experience of the body-object to extremes, using the body as paintbrush or simply recognizing it as a "living sculpture."

In other cases it is painting itself that takes on an autonomous existence and shares the wanderings and excesses of a will of its own—as in Robert Rauschenberg's *Combines*, with their inclusion of real objects that often pulsate in reality, or Piero Manzoni's *Achromes*, in which colorless kaolin crystallizes into a painting, while the artist stands aside in deference to the pure life of the material. The general attitude of the post-Pollock period is characterized both by a feeling of the body as a thing, and by a withdrawal of art from the cycle of action and rest.

At the same time, in the fields of dance, music, and literature, different modes of feeling the body as thing emerged in the work of Merce Cunningham, John Cage, and Samuel Beckett, who attempted to liberate the gesture, sound-text, and writing from all functional dependency on the body. They sought to give it an autonomous sensibility, one whose subject would know nothing, as if it were an insensate organ, a sensitive but artificial limb endowed with perceptions independent of its ego: machine or thing, separate from the human self.

With Cage and Cunningham, dance and music dissolve in the ordinariness and banality of everyday activity, where all gesture, action, sound, and noise are equivalent, lacking all linearity and plan. Of greater concern than technical transformation and motor efficiency is self-expression, which can be found in everything, including the panting, undisciplined body. Indeed, the undisciplined, the indeterminate, the unintentional, are all rich in expressive energy and fully used and embraced in Cage's music and Cunningham's performances. What matters is revealing the event in all its logical and illogical autonomy, avoiding the risk of imputing to reality a characteristic that doesn't belong to it. From this arises the use of *chance method* and the insertion of common people and sounds into the work. In particular, the bodily apparatus of the performer, in not being subjected to any discipline whatsoever, remains unruly and responds not only to the ear and eye, but to the encumbrance and disjointed force of the entire body. In a certain sense the body, as an object, is *indifferent* to commands and thus rebels, with its heaviness and passivity, against all nonbodily, technical manipulation. The intention is to let the performers develop a total reception of the stimuli that without distinction arouse motor and auditory desires. The urge to dance and to produce sounds is sought in itself, which is like saying that all elements of expression and communication can enter the field to form, with their collective presence, organic and inorganic, a danced, musical whole, where the parts emerge both identical and complimentary as meaningful things, forces and images, actions and spaces.

Beckett, on the other hand, finds a path for his writing by giving speech to the organic or inorganic object linking the human and the inhuman. He invents no mask for it, but merely lets it speak, in a monologuing, neutral flow, because it corresponds to no one in particular. Writing, for him, is the final, extreme attempt to do away with the I—as in *Not I*—in order to safeguard the word as material and thing.

With Beckett, writing is enacted, and the world is seen. There is nothing to explain. The point is therefore not to produce literature or poetry, but to show what is written: the existence and vitality of the written thing. The attitude is the same as Oldenburg's toward art and its result, the art object.

Why should I even want to create "art"—that's the notion I've got to get rid of. Assuming that I wanted to create some thing, what would that thing be? Just a thing, an object. Art would not enter it. I make a charged object ("living"). An "artistic" appearance or content is derived from the object's reference, not from the object itself or me.[8]

Historically, moreover, the complementary relationship between depersonalization or suspension of subjectivity and the development of the vital presence of the object arose in a period when literary and artistic production was greatly marked by the splendors and miseries of alcohol and drug consumption, which resulted in an identification between body and thing. Art's entry into this excess of impersonality is an essential key to understanding the great linguistic leap best exemplified in the adventure that runs from Pollock to the Beat Generation. The sublimity and degradation spurred by artificial substances have always been viewed with suspicion and at times condemned and criminalized, and yet they form the basis of many artistic transformations, such as the liberating, cathartic vision marking such movements as Cubism and Surrealism. The vision afforded by drug intertwines the godly universe and the animal universe, eliciting perception of the animate world of things.

The annihilation and failure of every relationship leads to paralysis, inaction, and lack of communication with others. An irremediable loneliness then arises, leading to something extreme: the animation of something immobile. In Beckett, dead things begin to scream, becoming open mouths spouting torrents of words. An uncontrolled agony of an object-mouth that never stops talking and inveighing against the world. Things in Beckett echo the body, its arising in the space of life, except that they are neuter and impersonal, fated to an incessant repetition. One can say that the writer, once he has entered a realm of immobility and nothingness—*The Unnameable*—sets himself the task of letting us know this.

This intention is evident in the paintings of Francis Bacon, who, in succumbing to the ineffable, uses the failure of human existence to visualize loneliness and silence, inanity and annihilation—as witnessed by the break-up of the figure in the surroundings —in a confusion of body and furniture where it becomes difficult to tell where the figure ends and the inanimate object begins.

Oldenburg likewise radicalizes a *bodily thingness*, which is already present in his early works, the portraits and landscapes executed between 1956 and 1959. The only difference is that the mimesis of reality, obvious and immobile, does not come by way of representation but rather through *availability*. The artist makes the things of the world available, presenting them in their existential virtuality, ready to excite and be excited. Letting the object feel like a body, with its soft skin and internal lymphatic systems, Oldenburg invests the object with sexuality, provides it with an autonomous "sensitivity." The object-body is a sensate limb, an artificial device endowed with an independent perception all its own; it is no longer the surface trace of Bacon, but something tactile that swells and dilates, fattens and bends, withdraws and expands, an *inorganic landscape* into which one can sink one's hands, mouth, or sexual organ, as one might into any body, human or animal.

I have had repeated the vision of human form, which is much more than that "trace" spoken by Bacon. It is the forms that the living human being can take, in all its parts, mental and physical, and this is the subject, in the fullest sense possible, of my expression—the detached examination of human beings through form. Myself, other individuals, and the expressions of human beings collectively, as in the city or the newspaper or advertising, or in any of the anonymous forms of naive art—street drawing, "mad" art, comics. I render the human landscape, and for me there exists no other, and this is a pimple or a body or a street or a city or the earth, because the human imagination does not obey any proprieties, as of scale and time, or any proprieties whatsoever.[9]

Such form, devoid of properties and organs, belongs to no will, obeys no plan, is free of all constraint, seeming to liquefy or crystallize in a whole that has nothing vital or spiritual about it: a *thing*. Nevertheless, one cannot say whether this thing is *animate* or *anthropomorphic*, since it has no autonomy with regard to human beings. It exists only if we lend it our bodies. And in this lending, this giving of ourselves to it, we become inorganic and the object becomes human. In Oldenburg's sculptures and Happenings, it is the thing or object itself that represents the maximum of reification, that celebrates the triumph over all intention-bearing subjects. It asserts a new kind of social relationship that is no longer intersubjective; rather, it takes place between two *quasi-things*.

Ecce Thing

Assimilating the thing into the human being and stubbornly seeking out its sexual specificity does not mean degrading and abasing humanity. It means, rather, shattering the boundary separating the thing from the human being—no longer accepting having, on the one hand, the thing in all its intangible remoteness, and on the other, the human being as self-conscious subject. It is a movement in the direction of radicality and excess, in that on the one hand it undermines and berates all pretense to subjectivity and favors neuter, impersonal impulses that make one experience one's own body as thing, and on the other hand it sustains a tortuous passion

Milkweek Pods, 1959. Milkweed pods, nail, and wire on wood base, painted with latex and casein, 8½ x 4¼ inches (21.6 x 10.8 cm). Collection of Claes Oldenburg and Coosje van Bruggen, New York.

Elephant Mask, 1959 (worn by Pat Muschinski). Newspaper soaked in wheat paste over wire frame, painted with latex, 37 x 27 x 24 inches (76.2 x 68.6 x 61 cm). Collection of Claes Oldenburg and Coosje van Bruggen, New York.

for things destined to deteriorate and disappear, instilling them with a strong sex appeal. Thus is born the *thingness* of sex.[10]

In 1959, after creating, in drawings and collages, a series of enigmatic, ambiguous images ranging from a surreal griffin to figureheads, monstrous metaphorical figures with disturbing features somewhere between machines and flowers, between human figures and objects, Oldenburg traced the contours of *"Empire" ("Papa") Ray Gun* (fig. 2), a cross between a toy ray gun and a male genital organ, in which the dualism between body and object is addressed and reconciled. It is a being of neuter sexuality epitomizing the conflict between such opposites as object and subject, thing and person (or part of the person). *Ray Gun* is not, in fact, condemned to deny, forget, or annul its vital and sensual borrowings; it is a sexual organ carried over to the dimension of thing: it "shoots, but doesn't kill," as Oldenburg put it in his notes. It is an element of balance that freezes life and vitalizes the object. A phallic self-exposing that eternalizes arousal. An endless love bestowed upon the impersonal, neuter being of the object, which becomes the surface of contact between beings giving and taking one another. A stratagem of subjectivity which neutralizes personal feeling, exorcizing it by making it impersonal.

By bestowing his own sexuality upon the object, the external support and locus of transfer, the artist ensures himself a continual bodily sensation. The thing—indeed the tendency not to carry out the sex act, to suspend it, without letting it fall into a gratification that would suddenly end the experience—actually makes it temporally lasting. This continuity, situated in the context of the gesturalism of Abstract Expressionism, is an initial response by Oldenburg to the ephemerality of sensory experience as expressed by Pollock and Willem de Kooning. His intention is not to resolve art in a swift, fleeting act confined to the desolation of conferring the life-force of one's body to the thing; rather, it is to consign experience to a thing possessing a latent, collected force, a thing that is not the product of a fragmentary, tortuous mode of fulfillment, but a continuous "fleshly" presence. The element must live, have weight, rise and settle. This is why Oldenburg is interested in the brutality of things. He is a great realist, who aspires to a passionate, antimetaphysical realism that might rekindle the flames of desire around "brute" things: *Ray Gun* thus becomes "an assertion of a new and rude potency" as well as "the necessity of composing true and vulgar art."[11]

Oldenburg's early works present an obvious demystification of beauty. They are composed of rough materials in search of a primordial figural power devoid of any ideal appearance. Their surfaces consist of naked, lowly materials—newspaper soaked in wheat paste and wrapped around wire—which convey no sense of a finished surface whatsoever. They are crude forms inseparably linked in appearance to urban scraps, and are therefore rough, naked, and plebeian. As things, however, they *have weight*. It is a weight connected to gravity, which makes them hang downward, like dead bodies or meat carcasses—Bacon and Beckett, again—liquifying or decomposing.

The coarseness of the materials is of interest in itself, as a truth of the object. Their crudeness challenges the sublimity of art. It makes us accept things as they are, rejecting all mystification.

Milkweed Pods (1959), one of Oldenburg's earliest sculptures, projects a *shadow* that is the complement of the suspended body, a weight of existence and contingent, chance incarnation.

Shadow, in all the artist's work, is *a priori* a perceptible, physical part of the object, as well as part of his own personality. It confers a mysterious presence upon the mass, acts in space, becomes part of the total geometry of the body. It participates in the total configuration of human existence, presenting itself, indeed, as the opposite of life. Assumed as part of the personality, it becomes instead an image of absence. That is, it represents an unconscious component of the thing. In its combining of coarse, crude elements—derived from lowly materials—with shadow, *Milkweed Pods* can be considered an early allegory of the *presence* of an object with a complex, intricate personality made up of positive and negative, conscious and unconscious. It floats and grows in the world, is something *other* than itself. Even the choice of plant, the milkweed, gives the sense of an organic autonomy, and underscores the presence of an inner latex, a kind of lymph that makes autonomy and survival possible. As his first act, Oldenburg chooses life—not as becoming, however, but as desiccation and death. What interests him is the sense of a being's ephemerality, as the destiny hanging over all things: "How near can a thing come to being it and not be it?"[12]

In 1959, Oldenburg began experimenting with the two poles of body as shell and body as dead entity, that is, as epidermic, worthless object. His sculpture at this time was made to be worn—the *Elephant Mask*, for example—which established an initial relationship between the impersonal, neuter object and the body. Once donned, the mask calls one's attention to the opposition between life and garment. It covers the wearer's face and torso—it was worn by Pat Muschinski in 1960, the year she and Oldenburg were married—and simply becomes a continuation of his/her sensuality. It asserts itself simultaneously as garment and body, site of the encounter and interpenetration of material and being. Once it has appeared, gender and age distinctions lose their importance. All that matters is to be wrapped in layers of material.

If one looks at the few portraits and self-portraits that Oldenburg executed in 1959–60, one will note the artist's predilection for the clothing covering the bodies of the subjects portrayed. What interests him are the shirt and tie in *Self-Portrait* (1959), and the fur collar worn by the subject in *Girl with Furpiece (Portrait of Pat)* (1959–60). It is almost as though Oldenburg sees the clothing as fleshly tissues that have ceased being inorganic and are now therefore indistinguishable from the skin of the subjects' faces. In the portraits there is no longer any distinction made between garment and body, or rather, between the experience of skin and fabric, between exterior and interior, between organic and inorganic. In this sense *Sausage* (1957), which consists of a stuffed stocking, prefigures the vision of the object as fleshly clothing. As "soft sculpture," hung and endowed with shadow, *Sausage* is flesh that can live, die, and move about, and can therefore be thought of as something excitable (its sexual connotation is quite obvious), even while confining sexuality to the neutral, impersonal realm of soulless, bodiless sex. It is an entity imbued with an expressivity that, while it doesn't experience pleasure, remains poised at the threshold of an extreme experience, that of possessing a corporeal, organic, ambient, and vital destiny as sculpture.

In soft objects, the expressionism is built in. But the effect need not be seen as expressionistic. Once the room space is established, the mass of air and light is taken into account, and the "skin" of the subject is

Girl with Furpiece (Portrait of Pat), *1959–60. Oil on canvas, 41 x 31 inches (104.1 x 78.7 cm). Destroyed.*

Self-Portrait, *1959. Oil on canvas, 68 x 47½ inches (172.7 x 120.7 cm). Collection of Claes Oldenburg and Coosje van Bruggen, New York.*

thinned to give the illusion of participating in the whole space (though the effect is gravity). The model of the animate body, with its interchange through the skin with its surrounding, is combined with the inanimate subject. The soft sculptures are therefore not objects in the sense of the hard isolated objects of the Dada or Surrealist period.[13]

The sex appeal of soft sculpture (the stocking is both a tool and an ornament for seduction) serves to take one past the threshold of pleasure in the organic and the banal. This is the first step toward the autonomous feeling of the thing itself—genderless, faceless, ageless: *ecce thing.*

But where does this thing live? In the world of urban scraps, that universe of ruins and finds, the old and the discarded, through which anyone may rummage in hopes of finding something that might reflect one's own feeling. The predilection for used, worn-out, pre-existing things expresses a sort of metaphysical stinginess that drives Oldenburg, in keeping with the most classical of Freudian paradigms, to look for gold not so much in his own excrement as, with greater ambition and social vision, in that of humanity.

The excitement of throwing oneself on the refuse and decay of everyday life—the flip side of the luster and efficiency of consumer goods—is a way to avoid making yet another "creative" addition to the universe, a typical desire of the avant-garde. In contrast to this indirectly consumeristic impulse, Oldenburg prefers finding the object already made, in all its complexity and autonomy.

This attraction to pre-existing things extraneous to the artist's own identity (and therefore sexuality) allows Oldenburg to escape the creative self-centeredness of Abstract Expressionism, which exalts the human being in all his rational and irrational, gestural and behavioral manifestations, and to take cognizance of the life of things that offer themselves to our gaze and touch. The intention is to convert the destructive and dramatic energy of the rejection of the image, as effected by the Action Painters, into a faith in the world just as it appears, in all its brutality and meanness. In this way, the period of anguish and fear, of silence and loneliness, of self-destruction and negation, is transformed into a training process for integration, however critical, into reality. Aware that the insufficient, existential rebellion typical of Pollock brings with it only a *spectacularization* of the artist's critical attitude toward the world, Oldenburg seeks to extract a value and dignity from the world existing before the artist's gesture. He creates no new images fashioned in a blaze from nothingness, but offers pre-existing visual entities, so that the individual will find himself in front of a subject that is his equal—"already born": *thing vs. thing, body vs. body.*

The orientation is inclusive in nature, impelling the art to *swallow*, rather than invent, the maximum amount of iconic data, with an open, conscious attitude. The idea is to situate art in a "real" circumstance, so that it will be disposed to accepting all possible instances of expression and communication. Thus the artist uses art not as a potential form of personal salvation or protective screen, but as an *area* in which to isolate the conditions of organic and inorganic existence. The artist chooses a sampling of life and presents it.

The need is that of *throwing oneself into the world* in order to take upon oneself its banal conditions and bring out the logic of the everyday. Art and life become interchangeable poles of an investigation that wavers between the aesthetic and the

sociological, the anthropological and the artistic. In the same way, if the opposition between beings and things ceases to exist, then the boundaries between languages also cease to exist, and a mixed-media "interlanguage" emerges that, in having all media at its disposal, is the only language capable of expressing this state of artistic communication.

Apparently, this process of prosaicization and recourse to banalities and scraps, which, like the *con-fusion* of languages, arises in an urban setting, has its roots in Futurism and Dada. If, however, it is possible to trace a history of the linguistic and behavioral influences on this period, one cannot, based on what we know about the most prominent artists in all fields, from art and music to dance and theater, fail to grasp the catalytic effect that the rediscovery of Marcel Duchamp had in general. Indeed, in reading about Cage, Cunningham, Maya Deren, Johns, Allan Kaprow, Oldenburg, and Rauschenberg, the Living Theater and the Judson Group, one notices that their basic operating assumptions all changed as soon as they became aware of Duchamp's work.[14] It was above all during the two-year period from 1957 to 1959—which corresponds to the publication and international diffusion of Duchamp's works and writings[15] as well as the appearance of the first monographic study of his oeuvre[16]—that one witnessed a clear change of linguistic sign in the arts.

But before going any further, let us examine briefly what was different about Duchamp's attitude, since with Duchamp what is of interest is not so much the work as the manner of being.[17] Duchamp was an individual who, rather than continue his visual lucubrations on the relationship between art and life, left art and entered wholly into life. Rather than continue to develop techniques aimed at keeping alive the fantasy of life in art, he adopted the simplest solution of all: he gave art the meaning of his own life and in a sense affirmed its dissolution in his person and his choices in the world.

Duchamp presents himself as an "homme comme un autre," as one who acts and has direct contact with things and "ready-mades." Indeed, he places himself on the same level as them, situating his body among things themselves. The intention is to satisfy its needs, without any dream of revealing absolute truths: "In the first place," he asserts, "never believing in truth"[18] or in social messages, "I do not think that that the work I've done could have any importance whatsoever in the future, from a social point of view."[19]

Duchamp thus follows primary impulses and urges, and does not present solutions ("there are no solutions because there are no problems").[20] He simply lives his life. All this sets him apart from those who claim to give answers to work and life, without following their courses. "My art, if you will, is that of living," he says; "every second, every breath is a work that is inscribed nowhere, that is neither visual nor cerebral."[21] And since the person and the art become one and the same, the manifestations of Duchamp's artistic being are expressed in his body, outward choices of objects, states of consciousness and unconsciousness, paradoxes and witticisms.

It is therefore possible, for Duchamp, to *be reflected* in a thing, a ready-made or nonartistic object, or to be continually *comprised* in the transformation of the body, which can become object or image, and in the vitality of word-play, where the word becomes object, body, and thought.

Moreover, his commitment to the signic elevation of reality attests to his need to escape the sectarian, mythic discourse of art. The goal is to annul art in life, or if one wishes to consider the problem from another perspective, to recognize the arbitrariness of art. However one may look at it, art loses value, since the Duchampian experience proves that art is useless and "hated" by life. If this is true, only by standing the terms on their heads can we give new life to art. Thus are the useless and the discarded recuperated—the very things that art has always tended to imitate and represent. And if the thing becomes art, then it also becomes creative: it feels and expresses itself. The circle is closed.

The range of artistic modes of behavior derived from Duchamp is too vast to define here. Restricting ourselves to the period in question, however, we can say that in New York, the understanding of his work stems primarily from the key figure of the 1950s, John Cage, Duchamp's close friend and chess student, whose musical debt to the visual artist is summed up in this phrase: "a way to write music: study Duchamp."[22]

For Cage, music comes very close to life.[23] Indeed, Cage is convinced that everyday life, with its things, sounds, noises, actions, and events is able, *if one pauses to listen*, to provide us with a vast quantity of musical elements. In a sense the musical, visual, and active whole can be constructed with the artist taking a *passive* stance, with passivity thus opening up a vast area for the *active* intervention of the things themselves.

This inversion of sign does not degrade or abase the humanity of the creative person, but rather liberates it from the constraints of a world of needs and desires that must be satisfied at all cost. The object is no longer taken up as tool or means, but becomes instead the opposite, an end. The same can be said for the body, which must be adopted more for its orgasmic functionality, its "dripping," but can also be used as a neuter, autonomous, feeling thing in itself.

What is most striking about the creative approaches of Duchamp and Cage is their impersonal, neuter character, the utter lack of concern for pleasure or pain, desire or fear, anguish or happiness. This manner of being is not only part of being as thing in itself, with its own motivation, but is also spurred by autonomous sentiments entirely independent of subjective emotions and expressive desires. One might say that it is almost the opposite of self-love and pretentiousness, of success and failure.

As of this moment, the mutual belonging of beings and things no longer in opposition to one another makes it possible to pass from one to the other, that is, to have an *amorous, erotic* relationship between them. And since eros is something intermediary between opposites, the *conjunctio maritalis* between organic and inorganic, between body and surrounding, between human being and city, guarantees new relationships and new filiations.

From 1956, when Oldenburg first came to New York, to 1959, the date of his first solo show at Judson Gallery, the repercussions of the jolt produced by the *totalizing* aesthetics of Duchamp and Cage (totalizing because it makes the *whole* available) yielded their first results in triggering a reconciliation and confusion between the arts and the world. Visual art, like theater, dance, and music, began to transcend its limits, to take up positions in the *excess* of the extreme experience. A proliferation of socio-linguistic structures, from Environmental art to Happenings, was set in motion, guaranteeing the circulation of eros between bodies and things, motion and architecture, voids and wholes, silence and noise, and thus establishing an erotic practice between subjects and objects freed from distinctions derived from ethical or

Sausage, *1957. Stocking, stuffed and tied with string, 35 inches (88.9 cm) high. Museum Ludwig, Cologne, Ludwig Donation.*

Marcel Duchamp, Bicycle Wheel, *1913. Bicycle wheel mounted on painted wood stool, 49 inches (124.5 cm) high. Philadelphia Museum of Art, Gift of Galleria Schwarz, Milan.*

Rehearsal of Allan Kaprow's A Spring Happening, *performance at Reuben Gallery, New York, March 22–27, 1961. Photo by Robert R. McElroy, New York*

Merce Cunningham and John Cage, ca. 1965.

metaphysical value-judgements. It was a shift that conceived of eros not as an end but as the *neuter* contemplation of one thing to another, of one body to another. A visual, physical eros that is not an assertion of self but the opposite, a loss of self. The new consciousness of art did not lie only, as for Pollock, in linking subjective experience to things, but also in *bringing together* already existing, effective, present terms. The negative character of this experience sets in motion a different passion between things, with the result that art, as Kaprow writes in his seminal piece "The Legacy of Jackson Pollock," "become[s] preoccupied with and even dazzled by the space and objects of our everyday life, either our bodies, clothes, rooms, or, if need be, the vastness of Forty-Second Street."[24]

The disappearance of differences, and the affirmation of equivalences, leads to the formulation of an *aesthetics of in-between*, which occupies an intermediate area of actions and behaviors, of spaces and architecture, a dialectic among indifferent things. This approach, which no longer seeks to define beautiful or ugly, good or evil, art or anti-art, implies a continual adaptation to circumstances, to occasions, to the given, to the discernment and conscious use of self, pleasure, and things.

All these elements establish a situation that is *erotic* in the most profound sense of the word, for it seeks intermediate relations between the opposite poles of the real. In this sense art, by situating itself on the middle line, unfolds in the interval between things and bodies, finding its foundation in the presupposition that the will of the lover and that of the beloved are secretly the same. The transition, or the movement that makes it possible, serves to recount and create the event, the happening: a quest for temporal and spatial dislocations of visual and performance *occasions* that live on transformations and shifts, transfers and discharges of energy. The detour of art from "suggestion of life" to "Happening" first took place, in New York, in October 1959, when Kaprow produced his *18 Happenings in 6 Parts*; Red Grooms took the Happening in another direction with his presentation of *The Burning Building* in his Delancey Street studio in December 1959. Both works call attention to the fact that art, in its tending toward life, actually exists for death. Its being-in-the-world is connected to the ephemeral, the throwaway—it contemplates death as a possibility bearing down on its present.

If we put all the spoils of the world—from the organic, vital elements to the inorganic, lifeless ones—on the same level, we arrive at a much more serene perspective of life and death, one based on a circular, reversible conception of time and things. Circularity among equivalent elements implies a contempt-free, thoughtworthy relationship with death and the inorganicness of things. And since in their existence, as in that of living things, circularity is either an imminent future or a continuous and present reality, the generation that came after the orgasmic, gestural cult of life of the Abstract Expressionists became interested in the loci of death—that is, in those areas where life consumes itself and the object dissolves and becomes obsolete: the city. Here human beings, like objects, belong to an in-between realm, crossing between life and death, suspended between being and nonbeing, in a realm where the present is only a *passing*. And if there is any truth to this process, past and future cease to be of any importance and should be ignored, because experience knows only one time: *presence* and the *present*, which take place here and now. All beings and things are masters and prisoners of this present, which cannot be evaluated subjectively. It is, and is full of, presences, hence there is no more time for the past or the future, just as there is no room for absence. There is only the passage from one presence to another, a passing from sameness to sameness, from fullness to fullness, from thing to thing. As it is impossible to transcend it, one must therefore immerse oneself therein, so as to experience its simultaneous presence and texture. This movement does not, however, constitute a journey; it is not a displacement from one point to another, from a gesture to a thing or vice versa. It has nothing to do with utopia or dream, and thus shares nothing with Futurism, Surrealism, or the other vanguard movements of the century; rather, it is an immersion in a universe that knows no distinction, a pit that is full and complete. One is neither outside it nor inside it, neither in the physical nor in the spiritual, neither in the city nor in nature, neither in the street nor at home; one is only immobile in the present, a world that is complete yet always completing itself, always living and dying, where what matters is to pass from one presence to another, from one status to another, *indifferently*.

A Gray Babel

The embrace of the present results in an immersion in the situation in which human beings and things find themselves. At the same time it means acceding to the fact of death, whether organic or artificial—or cultural. All preclusion is suspended to let life cross over into death and vice versa. The ritual of art can then appropriate the death-life nexus for itself, establishing a passage from one to the other so that the creation of life may sink into, or draw sustenance from, dead matter.

In 1959, after two years of reading and study, of gaining consciousness of self and place,[25] Oldenburg went into the street and spent hours drawing transitory scenes and events, depicting, day after day, "the black-grey face of things, modern and cityfied."[26] He chose the urban panorama and the territory of the street as entrance into a black hole into which everything falls: "the street is death," or better yet, placed in context it is "a set on American death."[27] With its beggars and bums surrounded by garbage and the throwaway objects of industrial society, the street is the perfect field for testing the existential durability of bodies that become things and things that regenerate in order to become energetic presences, of life cyclically passing into death.

From the urban panorama the artist does not, however, extract specific objects; rather, he takes an interest in the vast ocean of things and bodies, the tide of their common flow, which makes all their flesh, with their organic and inorganic skins, the same. They give and take one another, affirm and negate one another, as one takes the place of the preceding one, without taste or distaste, since they are all marked by a movement and passage that transcends the individual given. The street presents itself as a reproduction in miniature of the entire world; it is a highly inorganic, irregular nature where the continuous shouts, silences, immobility, movement, garbage, and life transfer objects and bodies from one place to another, without any meaning whatsoever, following a path that depends only on the place, on the here and now. In the street one can no longer claim that things and bodies have stable, durable qualities; rather, they participate together in the multiform world of life and its endless excitation.

I am especially interested in mapping out the forms that hold man together, regardless of conscious thought. Involuntary universality of forms, I dig them out of myself and find them everywhere.[28]

The city is a labyrinth in which distinctions and directions dissolve, where a multiplicity of events and contents arises yet remains unknown and ungraspable, because their identities are bound to the passage and movement taking place between beings and things. The city is alive with people and crowds, with things that stick to one another, connected by rituals that are pulverized, relativized, repeated, and articulated.

The experience of the labyrinth, in Oldenburg, first passes through the random, pasted material of *C-E-L-I-N-E, Backwards* (1959, fig. 3); in this early relief, the name of the French writer (author of *Death on the Installment Plan*, which Oldenburg had read in 1959 for its urban subject matter) is molded in newspaper and wheat paste, with the letters somewhat broken up and arranged backwards. The impasto of letters evokes the chaotic lava of humans and things that make up the city, a molecular universe impossible to depict without resorting to an image of "magma." It is an anarchic macrosystem based, like Céline himself, on the mutual contamination and confusion of relations.

The clutter and reversal of the name transform it, in Beckettian fashion, into a barrier rendering communication impossible. Its absurdity and incommunicability are necessary for the word to assert its autonomy, to project and resonate in space like a body. It invades space and shares it with others. For this reason its failure to communicate is a triumph: the word reaches the maximum level of exposure, no longer protected by anything but its bodily appearance. As existence, it is marked by a fast tempo, the present, as attested by the sudden movement of color, splashed on and spread about with rapid gestures.

The whole, even in its squalor and meagerness, has something sensual and tactile about it: it is a *voluminous* word that becomes a mouth or a body, a *surging forth* of a perceptible fragment of the human being, an image of its present, as it moves about the city, passes through the streets, enters stores and houses.

At the bottom of everything I have done, the most radical effects, is the desire to touch and be touched. Each thing is an instrument of sensuous communication.[29]

The link holding opposites together is *intimacy*, which unites and binds—not intimacy, however, in the sense of a particular feeling of warmth, but as an energy or context holding things together. *The Street* (pages 44–59), installed first at the Judson Gallery in winter 1960 and redone later that year at the Reuben Gallery, brings together figures and characters, bodies and things, all intimately interconnected by their common belonging to a single universe of material and atmosphere, a world inspired by the Lower East Side of Manhattan and its landscape. It broadens and deepens the molecular coexistence of *C-E-L-I-N-E, Backwards*, taking it to a volumetric, environmental, almost architectural level. The vowel-figure here assumes a more comprehensive position: it exists, but is negated in its dialogue with the other figures or in the vortex with its opposite or complement. Made up of flat figures in corrugated cardboard cut into silhouettes bordered in black and either hung from the ceiling, spread out on the floor, or jutting from the gallery's walls, *The Street* is based on the movement of these shapes toward and away from one another, with the result that, although they are placed at different points or superimposed, they dissolve in and among one another. Their chaos and disorderliness serves to eliminate their distance and isolation, so that nothing is absolute. We are not, however, at the point of the disappearance and dissolution of the single subject; rather, the subject here unfolds in a game that denies the end in itself. The figures are not subjects, but part of a dialogue that embraces opposites within itself. In this sense the cut-and-black outline defining the figures should not be thought of as a limit but as a point of virtual contact between body and shadow. They are free, scattered pieces of a three-dimensional mosaic, a crowd of things and bodies seeking a compromise in order to survive with one another. They live *together*. And as their mutual belonging is the logic of their existence, it also explains their *double* presentation, in different spaces with different installations, or as internal and external spaces that form an *enclosed outside* (the white walls of the Judson Gallery were thought of as an open landscape, while the arrangement at the Reuben Gallery was based on the idea of an open circulation). This rapport of mutual belonging is also behind the interrelationship existing between the series of events comprising *Snapshots from the City* (fig. 8), a performance held in *The Street*. It revolved around the primitivism of the body as human, organic wreckage alongside the ephemeral refuse of cardboard and burlap garbage bags full of newspapers that constitutes the harsh universe of *The Street*.

In *Snapshots from the City*, Oldenburg and Muschinski obliterate themselves, fighting on the same level as the refuse and garbage, becoming their mirror, a bogus image of them, an earthly, thingly instance. His body comes layered with bandages and burlap bags and covered with dirt, and at unexpected moments makes gestures and emits guttural sounds as sudden and unpredictable as street scenes themselves. In this medley, in which everything is different, what matters is the interweaving of things no longer transcended but merely confused.

Unlike the chaotic universe of Jean Dubuffet, which lives on the *representation* of the urban universe and the material landscape, *The Street* does not use artistic language to describe, and thus to comment on, the city, its culture of ephemerality and scraps, anonymity and impersonality; rather, it brings the city, and its language, to us.

Jean Dubuffet influenced me to ask why art is made and what the art process consists of, instead of trying to conform to and extend a tradition. My work is not a social commentary, decoration and entertainment, and I do not accept any one definition of nature enough to devote myself to its description. Such attitudes may be present in my work, but only because they are present in society and therefore condition my way of seeing and touching at one particular instant.[30]

Compared to traditional painting (experienced frontally) or sculpture (which is taken in from all sides), *The Street* moulds a dynamic model in which feeling things, human figures and objects, converge in a single context. They inhabit a landscape, an architecture, which they maintain simultaneously as a reference to the outside *and* the inside. They do not, however, form a rigid, petrified system, as is usually the case with sculptural and environmental plastic arts; rather, in their

organic and inorganic definitions, ranging from the fleshliness of the performer to the cardboard of the various elements, they move about, are *active*. They lead one to think that their difference is not definitive, stable and perfect, but penetrates a space that is wholly continuous, without voids. In this sense, one may draw comparisons between *The Street* and the architectural poetics of Expressionism, since in Bruno Taut and Erich Mendelsohn, as in Oldenburg, the walls of the building and the inside rooms are like the skin of the human body and the urban surroundings, scattered with stalactites and stalagmites, obelisks and phallic columns, caryatids and shells, in a blend of organic and inorganic sensibilities.

To recover vital forces one must start from the bottom up, from the point of contact between body and shadow. In 1960, after having constructed a totality, a combination of urban crowd and urban landscape, Oldenburg moved from the whole to the fragment, with the result that now the figure is no longer found but raised and constructed from pieces, scraps, and details. This shift from the two-dimensionality of the shadow-characters of *The Street* to the physical figuration of an image—as in *Kornville Flag (Provincetown)*, and *Landscape with Lighthouse (Provincetown)*, both 1960—arose from the artist's desire to give greater presence and sensuality to his figures. Aware that "primitivism" must pass through such things as totems and fetishes, Oldenburg began to work on "sacred" images, such as the flag, which do not depict anything but themselves. The flag is an abstract entity that eschews all connection to an image; it is a cipher of nothing but itself.

And since anything can become a fetish—a piece of wood or cardboard, a stone, a smell, a piece of food, a word—in 1960, Oldenburg began looking for "every trite and quickly rejected idea" in pursuing "every vulgarity that technique is capable of,"[31] even while continuing to make art: "I want these pieces to have an unbridled, intense, satanic vulgarity unsurpassable, and yet be art."[32]

The fetish's power lies in the outward, superficial elements of religion. It is a magical object with a seductive charge, a secret power always entrusted to outward practices. It is a thing in itself, marginal and out of the ordinary, living an anomaly. For Marx, the commodity was a fetish; for Freud, it was equivalent to sex. To the former, the object, when commodified, undergoes a metamorphosis, becoming the receptacle of human sensations; it becomes more sexual, assuming a sensory nature independent of man, with the result that society becomes based on relations between things, not subjects. Marx thus intuits the seductive and erotic process of the object. Freud, on the other hand, sees the fetish as a surrogate for sexual interest that makes it possible to negate the difference between masculine and feminine. The fetish implies a relationship of partial extraneousness in regard to the feminine sex, something similar to a neuter and impersonal sexuality that is projected onto things and sees them as substitutions for its own libido. In this sense a shoe, a cake, a glove, an ice-cream cone, a black girdle, a tie, a pistol, and a Good Humor bar become the vehicles of a misplaced sexuality, things that excite not because of their symbolism, nor because they represent some part of the male or female body, but because they are additions, appendixes that engulf sensation and experience. The fetishist, a solitary individual full of fantasies (the artist?), is aroused by an erotic relationship with the thing, which he experiences as his lover.

In Oldenburg's imagination, the city is the locus of the

artist's complicity. It is his echo; it responds to him from a distance. It is the sum total of all his paths, of all virtual and real events. Its exploration commands his language. In *The Street*, the city is the meeting-place of a crowd of ghosts and shadows in black and white, seen from the outside, as from a photographic imagination—a snapshot—that turns shapes into silhouettes. Here the street is read as a map or a book. The figures seen are registered *on the surface*; they profile a pure otherness. The subjectivist hypothesis is absent: here the point is to talk about the world, about one's encounter with its crowds, where one's own being is lost. It is no accident that in *Snapshots from the City*, performed within the landscape of *The Street*, the fate of the body, and the artist, is to be perceived as an external thing, illegible or at least lost in the urban chaos. The bum—a social being, but also a second-class citizen—is totally integrated in the definition of an objective, "thingly" space, part of a social, material whole that forces him to exist in the labyrinth of anonymity as a neuter, impersonal entity. In *The Street*, the artist continues his wanderings, reduced to being an elementary physical designation: an opaque, dirty being that lets the events of everyday life accumulate on his person, with so little control over them that he cannot distinguish them from the other cardboard phantoms.

From the chink opened up by this existence as thing among things springs the deciphering, or at the very least the consciousness, of a being-in-the-world—one replete with an analysis of its own meaning. Having found himself among things, the artist is now forced to give shape to his own psychology, which when translated into *The Store* (1961, pages 74–127) becomes "psychophany."

The Labyrinth of Desires

The Store is an interior that suggests the unconscious, an intimate, personal "elsewhere." It is enclosed upon itself, like a body and its organs. To experience it, one must anatomize it, proceeding by cuts and snips, in order to define its heterogeneous whole in all its details. One must enter its cavity to discover its spectacular, dramatic external articulation. In this sense, it is the container of a strange human anthropology enacted by the scraps and figures which lay bare the artist's obsessions.

I have always felt the need of correspondence between one's art and one's life. I feel my purpose is to say something about my times . . . for me this involves a recreation of my vision of the times . . . my reality, or my drama-reality, and this demands a form of a theatrical nature . . . like the film or theatre. It is not a challenge to or a development of painting, but another form. . . . I am making symbols of my time through my experience . . . and do not really recognize a rest period or a period out of my experience, as most do . . . i.e., a period for raising children or establishing a home or whatever might be done as if outside the vision . . . for me there is no "outside vision" except this special undefined outside of myself as spectator of myself . . . every instant is the drama and my art is the record or evidence.[33]

It is an attempt to see and live the city, and oneself, without detachment—not sociologically, but psychologically, as a collection of all the dregs of a sensual, sexual imaginary realm: as the labyrinth of desires.

In 1961, Oldenburg, with his Ray Gun Mfg. Co., moved into a store on 107 East Second Street. In December, he opened *The*

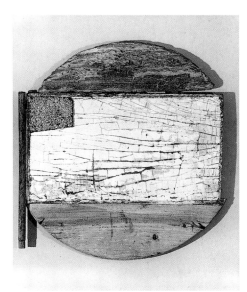

Kornville Flag (Provincetown), *1960. Driftwood, 19¼ x 17 inches (48.9 x 43.2 cm). Musée National d'Art Moderne, Centre Georges Pompidou.*

Store, in which he presented his objects in a new *incarnation*. What mattered now was no longer the incorporeal—that is, the silhouette and its shadow, the phantom, drawing, two-dimensionality, and lightness—but materiality and gravity, carnality and sensuality, plasticity and tactility, the envelopes covering and feeding the body. *The Store* is full of things like clothes and food, things related to libidinal practices, tools of a subjectivity oriented toward the assumption of the sexual other.

The store is born in contorted drawings of the female figure and in female underwear and legs, dreams of the proletarian Venus, stifled yearnings which transmute into objects, brilliant colors and grossly sensuous surfaces.[34]

The transition from the ghostly appearance of *The Street*—in which the figures, though cardboard, look like sheets or veils and thus like two-dimensional, painterly representations—to three-dimensional elements made of muslin strips soaked in wet plaster, wrapped around chicken-wire structures, and painted in violent, artificial colors, thus creating more recognizable images *that look like* real things, superimposes art and eroticism, which both move through a *mimetic* dimension. Both, in fact, offer a dressing, a simulacrum, an envelope devoid of reality; they give presence to absence, make visible the invisible. Both *dress up the real*, by imputing their own desires to it.

The Store is filled with pieces of clothing, from stockings, pants, and garter belts to shoes, shirts, and panties. It is a hymn to the confusion between body and object, between drapery and the nude. Through color, the artist reveals the impetuous, vibrant thrill of visual desire, making the clothing shine like bodies in the sun. And while the artist rejects any connection with the mystical passage from fabric to flesh in Gianlorenzo Bernini, one can surely deduce a relation here to Peter Paul Rubens—who heightens the chromatic effects of skin and creates erotic passages between skin and fur and between clothing and surroundings—or to Diego Velázquez and Nicolas Poussin, who are obsessively concerned with the beauty of clothing, fabrics, and furs in their work. The difference is that Oldenburg mediates these lessons with the contemporary experience of the mass media.

Another statement of this participation of thing with its surrounding is found in the Store reliefs, whose torn edges indicated removal from a larger shape. Vision at the time, for me, was assumed flatter, and what was seen, taken as a plane surface, like a film, mirror, or newspaper. Thus an advertisement or part of one, ripped from a newspaper, was taken to correspond to a glance at the plane of vision.[35]

The analogy to painting becomes even more appropriate when we consider that Oldenburg is interested in the image of the body and its *veil* as it appears two-dimensionally in advertising and mass communications. He is not interested in statuary, but in the *representation* of clothing, which in art is as vibrant and alive as the body.

From clothing to fragments, Oldenburg cuts out his images, translates them to plaster, folding them softly outward like a breast or gluteus muscle, then offers them one beside the other—first at the Martha Jackson Gallery, and later at *The Store* on East Second Street. Mutilation and cutting serve to bring out the inside of the object's *skin*, lifting the lips of the anatomy's wounds. It brings onto the same level the object, which is cadaverous because inserted in the universe of advertising ghosts, and the throbbing, trembling body. The parallel between the artificial world and the organic world confirms the premises of a vision in which *bodies* are united in being things, *inorganic entities* which nevertheless can feel.

Moreover, the obsession with translating the object into a bodily whole is evident in the artist's urgent desire to fill up all the wall space. This is a way to emphasize the importance of the *anatomy* of the image; it is not a negative process, but a way of extending and *interconnecting* all experiences of the visible:

The fragmentation is the concrete realization of vision, passing from one item to another in a multitude.[36]

For the entire period that *The Store* occupied its Lower East Side quarters, Oldenburg was present among his products, presenting himself as manufacturer and shopkeeper, a body attesting to the continuity between desire and commodity, flesh and plastic. An object moving among other objects, he travels about in the cavity of the impersonal as if wanting to underscore the fact of having given up his own organic nature. The artist devitalizes himself because he is aware that the human being is no longer capable of seeing and feeling himself as a "landscape," now that he has become part of the general landscape. He is an insert in a cavity that knows nothing of lived experience. He no longer belongs to himself, but only to the world, empty or full, in which he moves. He and it are one same thing:

The store may be better understood if it is considered not itself a psychological statement, but a collection of psychological statements, which exist concretely in the form of the signs and advertisements. . . . An imitation of nature or nature in the city, but nature altered toward psychology, which is to say: the true landscape of the city.[37]

A hallucination where bodies are part of stores, the street, buildings. Indeed, they are mute figureheads of the epic of the inorganic:

Torn-birth-fragments. I think of space as being material like I think of the stage as being a solid cube or hollow box to be broken, so an hallucination basic to my work is of the continuity of matter, that air and the things in it are one, are HARD, and that you can RIP a piece of air and the thing in it out of it, so that a piece of object and a whole object and just air, come as one piece.[38]

The Store is a plastic landscape in which feeling has been estranged, displaced, broken, dehumanized, because it has achieved total autonomy. This is why the boundaries between the artist and his products, between being and objects, is abolished in it. Unrelated objects are brought together, objectivity and subjectivity merge. *The Store* is a *womb* one may enter through glass, or rather through the cold gaze of sight, the mental erotic: there is an equivalency with Duchamp's *Black Widow*. *The Store* is not only part of the history of art, but of the history of the city as well. It is a three-dimensional painting inscribed in the corridor of paintings that is East Second Street and its shop-windows. It is a *tangible* space; its perspective is not illusory, but real. It is one shop window/painting among the rest. But it is also one shop among the rest, a parody of an art gallery.

Seeing and being seen, swallowing and being swallowed: the sexual metaphors are always open, so much so that growth and arousal proceed from art's continual borrowing from eros, and vice-versa. Thus does *The Black Girdle* (1961, fig. 36)—like *Blue and Pink Panties* (1961, fig. 28) and *Two Girls' Dresses* (1961, fig. 30)— become "the pointer in the direction of erotic imagery involving both merchandise and the female body."[39]

Arousal, however, is not only connected to femininity. There is also food, upon which the same humors and lusts, the same impulses and perversities are unleashed. In *The Store*, an intimate, closed space, compact block of (neuter) imagination and pleasure, sensual fulfillment passes through eyesight and touch and its endless libidinous obsessions. Here things saturate and interpenetrate one another, are articulated in each other, because they strive for the same voluptuous, fecal density. The artist feeds on them, and this is why food too is one of the fields in which his imagination operates. Like Marcel Proust, Oldenburg brings out the neuralgic condition of food (though Proust makes food an oral possession), which constitutes the riverbed and habitat of intimacy and erotic fixations, his passion. In the cavity of 107 East Second Street, a slice of *Small Yellow Pie* (1961, fig. 60) and an *Ice Cream Sandwich* (1961, fig. 40) mingle with a *Times Square Figure* (1961, fig. 64) and *Bride Mannikin* (1961, fig. 66) as living proof of the erotic *marriage* between savoring food and savoring flesh.

Food's emotional and libidinal charge mirrors the excess of the body's lusts, so much so that in *The Store* it is a stimulus to intimacy and can be assimilated and penetrated. The artist insinuates himself in it the way he insinuates himself in intimacy, with the result that his sculpture and painting in relief become his very own flesh. This feeling of fullness is reflected in the object, which begins to mingle, to grow, to become covered with violent, striking colors. It visually overflows, showing how, through food, the outside is transformed into the inside: thing and body cease to be distinguishable. All is part of a single whole, which presents the same story.

If in *The Street*, the presentation of cardboard scraps and drawings coincide with the fleshly presentation of the movements and guttural noises of Oldenburg and Muschinski—and with the lightness of the crowd and its evanescent shapes—in *The Store*, the use of *history* continues, both on the level of things and on that of human beings. Most importantly, if the portions of food and clothes are *fragments of experience*, past and present, then the whole store and its inhabitant are *historical*.

And it is to *history*, to a past present, that the performances, executed inside and outside *The Store*, continually make reference. *Snapshots from the City* attempts to shift the relationship of affinity between objects and modes of behavior. The later *Circus (Ironworks/Fotodeath)* (pages 64–71), presented at the Reuben Gallery in February 1961, attests to the definitive *transformation* of the one into the other, so much so that the performance can be defined as a "farce for objects in bright colors."[40]

Farce, like science fiction, goes against reality; in this case, the human being goes against his own subjectivity. This creates an osmosis that produces alienation and estrangement, to the point where the performances can be defined as *tableaux vivants*, since their effect is not dramatic so much as *enigmatic*, as though the figures in a painting had suddenly begun talking and moving about on their own. It is a transformation of flesh into plastic form, both mobile and immobile, which does not present any imitation of reality or nature, but offers humanized objects—human sphinxes endowed with feeling.

In *Circus*, the simultaneous presentation of several "tableaux" gave the piece—which was divided into two parts, *Ironworks* and *Fotodeath*—a primary role in the triumph of the exchange between life and death, between hardness and softness, between photography and reality. Also based on the stereotypes of everyday life, *Circus* makes the action of its five tableaux vivants occur coincidentally, as in the ring of a real circus. Intersecting and overlapping with one another, these tableaux form images which, because of their accidental nature, seem to happen unexpectedly. They are not narrative; rather, they occur *incidentally*. In *Circus*, the images present themselves like objects; they seem like obstacles. A levelling occurs between them, based on the tremendous silliness of the ceaseless flow of gestures and actions that don't distinguish between thing and human being. The subtitle *Ironworks* itself implies notions of industrial rigidity and mass production typical of a factory, while *Fotodeath* establishes an analogy between the fixed, crystallized image in photography and reproduced bodies and figures, an exchange between life and death that moves in both directions, the last one being to keep alive those human beings who will pass away.

Through the combination of levels—which defies explanation—a transmission and accumulation of information take place, likening the performance to the chance arrangement of pasted newspaper in Oldenburg's early reliefs.

The mingling of different bits of information or of different images is something like a lucid delirium here. It is based on the dualism of extremes: the rational coincides with the irrational, calm intertwines with frenzy, violence mingles with gentleness. The theme of the *double* then re-emerges in the series of performances produced by Oldenburg, under the rubric of *Ray Gun Theater*, at 107 East Second Street from February 23 to May 26, 1962. There were two different "versions" or "scripts" for each of the subjects, which were, in chronological order: *Store Days*, *Nekropolis*, *Injun (N.Y.C.)*, *Voyages*, and *World's Fair*.

Drawing inspiration from the space and the architecture, as well as from the time-span and the city in which they were performed, these pieces reflect, in yet another doubling, both the story of the place and the seasons. They resort to such New York emblems as the Statue of Liberty and the mass of immigrants and strange people living in the city, with their odd period dress from past and present, melodious songs and layers of sounds and colors; at the same time, in keeping with the tradition of the Nordic sagas, they represent the seasons from life to death, pain to pleasure, day to night, conscious to unconscious, north to south, and winter to summer.

These cyclical moments of life are made perceptible through the use of light, the colors black and white, and the transformation of clothing from heavy to light, as well as by social events that together make up the epic of inorganic life.

These are plastic landscapes in which the performers as well as the public are included and of which they become a part, which transforms them into lived situations in which people no longer belong to themselves but to the place—*The Store*—in which they move about. Among the mobile elements are the ever-recurring titles and figures in whom gestures always take on a meaning that place the person on the same level as an inanimate object. In particular, the enigmatic figures enacted by Lucas Samaras in all of the performances can be read as splendid illustrations of this osmosis. Samaras plays the stereotype of the fetishist, the narcissist, the person obsessed with something that takes the place of the beloved's body; he sheds light on the condition of the person who identifies with an object. In *Store Days I* he has a morbid relationship with a glove; in *Store Days II* he becomes a serial killer who, aroused by the color of blood and by battered bodies, is soothed by the rip of toilet paper, which sublimates violence into fecal matter. Muschinski is the lyrical, romantic Street Chick, who dances and moves lightly about; and Oldenburg is the witness, the man who looks on: photographer, newspaper vender, and voyeur.

These figures, these object-bodies, find themselves immersed in a continuous space between store and audience or between materials and gestures: an unbroken, tangible space. The fullness proceeds without breaks, but always by opposite signs: extroverted and introverted, mental and emotional, constructive and destructive.

The performances, however, shun narration, always maintaining an indeterminate appearance and development. They are events of *transition* in which unity dissolves in favor of organicity. At times the deconstructive theme concerns aspects of the city, as in *Nekropolis*, the city in which life and death co-exist in and under the streets. The human beings in *Nekropolis I*, which is presented in dark colors, move about like mice in cellars, with their dark bodies and violent, swift movements, while in *Nekropolis II*, the movement of the performers no longer represents underground constriction but the lifestyle of the international traveler: in fact, the characters come from all over the world, from Argentina, Czechoslovakia, Greece, Poland, and Sweden. It is a carnival of cultures.

At times the theme is instead the transition from the country to the city, as in *Injun*. Here the subject is the violence and fear expressed toward "other" cultures, which in New York becomes a conflict between urban culture and rural culture. There are no winners in this clash: one culture kills the other, and even the witness, played again by Oldenburg, ends up killing himself.

The apocalyptic vision of these pieces, their being-for-death, is challenged as spring approaches. The personification of the seasons creates correspondences with life and its fullness. In *Voyages*, seductive sirens suddenly appear, reflected in the water-mirror; vortices of energy, created by the actors' gestures, begin to form, and the finale is a great pile of paper, still a metaphor for the body, which in the end fills up the entire landscape of *The Store*.

Lastly, in *World's Fair*, Spring finally arrives, and with it, life. In *World's Fair I*, it comes in the figure of a little girl surrounded by characters moving about in water, like fish; in *World's Fair II*, it appears with the birth of objects sprouting from a human body, supine and therefore dead, and with the *expulsion* of the audience from the landscape, to make room for *Upside-Down City* (1962, fig. 69). The circle closes with this inversion. It is a vision of the world in which reality is turned upside down: human beings and buildings are likened to things, organic entities become inorganic, rigid structures turn soft, becoming endowed with a reactive ability.

With the closing of *The Store* in 1962, the proximity and exploration of space moves out of an interior urban space to an exterior one. With *Injun*, performed in Dallas in 1962, and the presentation of *Gayety*, *Stars*, and *Autobodys* in, respectively,

Chicago, Washington, D.C., and Los Angeles in 1963, the experience of the tableaux vivants is extended to include the cultures and histories of individual cities, places, and situations.

Rooted in the city, the performances become civic in nature, reflecting sociocultural conditions: climate, geography, poetry, crime, monumentality, decentralization. Symptomatic of this urban reflection is *Autobodys* (pages 176-81), in which the proximity of bodies and automobiles translates into a scene illuminated by car headlights and consisting of the gestures of people directing traffic or moving about on wheelchairs.

In 1965, Oldenburg made *Washes* (fig. 140), which took place in a pool, and *Moveyhouse* (fig. 141), performed at the Forty-first Street Theater in New York, two pieces in which the landscape or field of vision has two different consistencies. In water, the field is deep, and one may float or sink, enter or exit; with the passage of time, the water may turn flat and immobile, or become agitated, until it turns into a stormy sea. *Washes* is thus a *tangible* image in which people, in bathing suits, and objects—dinghies and life-preservers—move about as in a landscape, on and under the water. In *Moveyhouse*, on the other hand, a light projector transforms the players, who have been directed to move about the theater seats, into silhouettes on a screen. These immaterial images—mirroring the nonexistent spectators, for the members of the audience were not allowed to sit down—are but black-and-white tableaux vivants. Only one audience member, the aged Marcel Duchamp, makes his body felt, and only because he pleads fatigue and is granted permission to sit down.

Presence in absence, in the total immersion in a nothingness, like water or shadow—this is the significance of the being-for-death of *Washes* and *Moveyhouse*, in which the emphasis is on the nothingness of presence in the face of plastic and images. The performances—like the ensembles of *The Street* and *The Store*—express an anguished projection of death, as the starting point for a human being on the way to becoming an object. In their innocence, the performances take part in the *initiation* process that obliterates boundaries as well as differences, so that death may become life and vice versa. As in *Fotodeath*, where the camera captured images alive and then rendered them dead, managing to give them eternal life in the future, here the performances become the apotheosis of an uncontrolled, unplanned *vitality* in which *all* opposites mingle and become confused, though the finale is still dissolution, proving that the destiny of everyone is being-for-death.

Objects, like photographs, are simulacra of death. Among these one must also include monuments and history, which document time's eternity, as well as the traces of a past sinking into a nothingness with no return.

The dissolution of all narration thus does not express a vandalistic transgression of communication, art or theater, but on the contrary aims to express the continuity existing among entities. It serves to contain them in a single time and space.

The union between a Swiss Army Knife and the city of Venice was immortalized in *Il Corso del Coltello* (pages 419–39), a performance conceived by Oldenburg, Coosje van Bruggen, and Frank O. Gehry and realized in Venice in September 1985. Unlike the early performances, which had "free scores" and were based on the notion of a frame formed by various obstacles suggested by gestures and objects, *Il Corso del Coltello* expresses the incomparable beauty and strangeness of things, but it also, as in a real theater, puts real actors on the stage, who in Beckettian fashion tell a fantastic story sprouted from van Bruggen's imagination. Here we witness the maturity of the object, which has become a *speaking being*, whereas before, in earlier performances, it emitted only gutteral noises. It is as though the object were regenerated in the story, suggesting a creative will to cut and break the umbilical links between past and present, between Happenings and theater, thanks to a new richness stemming from a mobility between the languages of art, literature, and architecture (which in 1976 would lead to a new dimension in sculpture, carried over in the large-scale projects that Oldenburg has made in collaboration with van Bruggen). The task of personifying the knife is assigned to the great ship and to Oldenburg himself, almost as though his art were leading to a dramatic meeting between history and kitsch, nobility and mass tourism. Or as though it were in any case responsible for the two edges of a *cut* whose lips represented society's opposites and contradictions.

From *Voyages* to *Washes* to *Il Corso del Coltello*, the theme of water, metaphor of a life-giving womb, runs through all of Oldenburg's work. It gives birth to a *soft* city that is palpable, enjoyable, elusive, sweet, pasty, penetrable, acquiescent, slippery, billowing, erectable, flaccid, and turgid, a city that cannot be inhabited except by soft beings and things, which are equivalent to one another:

I've expressed myself consistently in objects with reference to human beings rather than through human beings.[41]

The Thing Feels and Thinks

At the closing of *The Store*, the desire of things to exist *together* with human beings has been satisfied. The obstacles between organic and inorganic bodies have been eliminated, since Oldenburg, the artist, publicly *lives*—visible to all the passersby looking in through the window—with subjective feelings that transform into food, clothing, mannikins, and fragments of objects. The *conjunction* between the two forms of existence, reinforced by the ritual of the Happenings, which develops a further indeterminacy between the poles of lived experience and artificiality, definitively opens the street up to an object that lives, has feelings of its own, becomes soft and malleable, and moves about. In autumn 1962, at the Green Gallery (directed by Dick Bellamy), Oldenburg exhibited a series of new works, "soft sculptures" such as *Giant Ice-Cream Cone* (1962, fig. 81) and *Floor Cake* (1962, fig. 72). These marked the artist's entrance into a new dimension through the use of size, the painted canvas surface of the object, and the dimension of movement:

Every image in my work implies a body activity both on a physical and an imaginative level . . . and the play element which is essentially dynamic, is always present. . . . Essentially, all moves as long as the body is capable, unlike a tree, of relatively unlimited ambulance.[42]

Thus,

the possibility of movement of the soft sculpture, its resistance to any one position, its "life," relate to the idea of time and change.[43]

After contemplation come action and mobility, which satisfy

the arousal of the object; now it becomes abnormal, soft, swollen. The object part, food or clothing, that was petrified in plaster in 1962 is now offered in soft, sensual guise, as though an influx of flesh had generated its substance, brought it out from within without breaking. The swollenness announces an intense interiority, a thrust toward impatient fullness. It gives vent to an impulse of expansion, as though the richness contained within the object had found an outlet, thus *emancipating* it. The energy field conveyed into the flesh of the object captures a dynamism, a kind of growth where its precious skin, like that of a young girl, actually grows and expands. Carried over into food, the effervescence makes the object pasty and leavened, hence cooked and thus enjoyable and edible. Erotically consumable.

Exploring Oldenburg's path through the tumescence and maturity of the object, we see that this phase coincides with two kinds of images, food and sails. The former, in the form of meat, banana, cheeseburger, and potatoes, registers an energy that has developed over a period of time. Each food contains and protects within itself the richness of a consumption/consummation, a moment of life. Moreover, the coloring expresses the happy end of maturation, while the swollenness preserves the charm of the precarious, the ephemeral life of the thing.

Alongside these meanings, swelling is the work of breath: it makes the object like a sail, and presupposes wind:

Soft sculpture is in a primitive state but with the aid of plastics and latex and things to come, there will be soon the completely articulated (instead of balloonlike symmetrically joined) pneumatic sculpture. . . . I imagine outdoor sculptures, responsive to the wind.[44]

From *Freighter and Sailboat* (1962, fig. 70) and *Battleship: Centerpiece for a Party* (1962, fig. 82) to *Leaf Boat with Floating Cargo* (1992, fig. 300), the motif of the boat has been perpetuated in Oldenburg's work. The sail of a boat pulls, it acts in the future. The swelling of a sail also underscores the desire for lightening. A swollen sail is round, much like a woman's body. Analogies between the swelling of the object and the female body are continuous; it is most plainly articulated in a collage, *Notebook Page: Dormeyer Mixer* (1965, fig. 133). The object in its roundness is also a womb that encircles and protects, restoring a prenatal condition and revealing a new life.

In 1963, the recognition of the corporeality of the object leads the artist to turn to industrial products, as if he felt the need to sensitize a universe that by its very nature has nothing soft about it at all. Thus, after having expanded the softness and scale of food and clothing, Oldenburg tries his hand with *Soft Typewriter* (1963, fig. 102) and *Soft Pay-Telephone* (1963, fig. 100), which were first created in "ghost" versions—canvas painted with acrylic—before being realized in vinyl, at which point they were "real."

The transition from canvas to vinyl is a telling one, bringing out an epidermal thickness possessing a number of different characteristics. Canvas is opaque, conveys warmth, and is bound to the tradition of painting, while vinyl is industrial, smooth and cold, with light and reflections sliding along its surface—it is almost like a metal. Its appearance in Oldenburg's work instills objects with the consciousness of an accumulation, which might be related to food, as in *Giant BLT (Bacon, Lettuce and Tomato Sandwich)* (1963, fig. 96), or might be

associated with the accumulation of information and communications, as in *Soft Typewriter* and *Soft Pay-Telephone* and the later *Giant Soft Fan* (1966–67, fig. 166).

The shininess of the skin also points to a rejection of the gaze and assumes the consistency of flesh that is desired but forbidden, hard, inaccessible to the touch. It is as though the object were slipping from the artist's hand, and he were now limited only to *designing*:

Manufactured Object: Object made by conventional industrial procedure according to plans by artist serving his purposes and not the purpose for which objects made by this procedure normally are intended.[45]

This shifting of functions is made clear by the fundamental roles assumed, starting in 1963, by the artist's various personal and professional partners (from Muschinski and Samaras to Gemini G.E.L. and Lippincott, Inc.) as well his later collaborators (van Bruggen, Gehry, and others), who gave shape to things *designed* by Oldenburg, such as *Bedroom Ensemble* (1963, fig. 112), *Lipstick (Ascending) on Caterpillar Tracks* (1969, fig. 194), *Giant Ice Bag* (1969–70, fig. 189), and the various *Large Scale Projects*. It is as though the artist, after abandoning Abstract Expressionist gesturality and embracing a three-dimensional construction art based on the malleability of plaster and canvas, had felt the need, once he had confronted the industrial object, to put himself on the same level as it. To become, by osmosis, cold and linear, to be part of a *colossal* project favoring the absence, or rather the availability, of the human being in relation to the object.

The search for an *impersonal* hand finds concrete expression in the Home, the central piece of which is *Bedroom Ensemble*, in which the artist begins to deny the impulse to superabundance implicit in the act of painting and sculpting. He neutralizes Pollock by transforming him into a decoration, cut up into little squares that entirely negate the idea of the *arena* (to use Harold Rosenberg's metaphor) of Action Painting, even as he reduces sculpture to a state of inertia by transforming it into furniture. The transition from *The Street* to the Home, from drawing to sculpture, is expressed thus:

Newspaper equals drawing (Street), Food equals painting (Store), Furniture equals sculpture.[46]

The silence of the object is achieved through the rejection of softness and sensuality. Things become paralyzed, suspending desire, as if subjected to an erotic anaesthesia. *Bedroom Ensemble* attests to the failure of desire, its congealment, its impotence. The sculpture and furniture cannot be *used*; they are pure presence, neuter and impersonal. Their fleshliness has been clearly negated, hidden beneath a cloak of plastic and artificial materials: synthetic leopard-skin, fake fur, and vinyl. Underlying their neutrality, however, is a strong concept: impersonal planning and design, which makes the object *full of ideas*, thus charged with thought. It is, thus, a moment of development. The suppression of fleshliness and sensuality leads to the privileging of intellect and conceptualization. Oldenburg is on the same wavelength as the Minimalists, but his position tends to push the object toward a logical and rational "consciousness" of itself, so that what matters is the thing reflecting the thought and project, as opposed to the object that feels and adapts to the surrounding and context.

And since the connection is between desire and seeing, sight takes the upper hand. *Bedroom Ensemble* celebrates the hegemony of the visual over the tactile, and is, in fact, constructed according to a single-perspective point of view. In its exaltation of perspective, the piece inevitably also exalts form and style, thus sinking its roots into the diffuse, integrated Platonism of everyday industrial life. And since the ideas and concepts are *independent* of the context, *Bedroom Ensemble* is a self-contained installation. That is, it is not adapted to the space, but creates and imposes its own space; there is nothing arbitrary about it. It is an absolute, and when moved from one city to another—even one country to the next—it remains independent and autonomous with respect to the architecture in which it is placed.

By 1963, with the appearance of *The Home*, Oldenburg's work begins to relate strongly to architecture and urbanism, no longer as mere contexts, but as subjects in themselves. He effects a shift toward landscape, both interior and exterior, from the house to the city, so that the object becomes charged with a subjective, social responsibility. He wants the object to enter and exit the stage of the context, only to become autonomous or disappear in a public announcement. To present itself, that is, as a *monument* of personal and social everyday life. To enact this leap, Oldenburg chooses the *automobile*, symbol of this duality between private and public.

With the *Airflow* series (1965, pages 217–25), he exhibits objects that are at once integrated and mobile in the urban context. Here the human being no longer has a body but is transformed into an industrial prosthesis: the car becomes an extension of his senses, an object now independent of the organism, moving about the city, amidst its architecture. In similar fashion, with the series of contemporaneous Home objects in painted cardboard and vinyl—including, among others, *Soft Washstand* (1966, fig. 131), *Soft Toilet* (1966, fig. 127), *Light Switches – Hard Version* (1964, fig. 106), and *Bathtub – Hard Model* (1966, fig. 128)—the subject moves "far enough away to be on the verge of disappearing from function into archetype."[47]

By this point, the only thing missing is an affirmation of the object as architecture. And indeed, Oldenburg comes close to this definition with his *Proposed Colossal Monuments* (1965–69, pages 264–83), which are characterized by an *overflowing* quality and by their transformation of the object into urban architecture. Here the traditional art object entertains a new relationship with the outside world. It is no longer an object depending on or emancipated from a context of consumption reduced to a small scale. Rather, it enters the realm of great plans, of the *Large-Scale Projects*, which reduce the gap between art and urbanism and take the disciplines of sculpture and painting to new places where they can clash with reality's resistance. We witness here the liberation of the object that asserts itself as reality, though from an anomalous point of view, that of its feeling—part sensual, part fantastic—as it is transformed into urban reality. The object overflows outside itself and thus acquires a radical, extreme exteriority. It expands and transcends its own specific occasion, the installation and Happening. It puts itself on the stage and lets itself be penetrated and possessed, like architecture, which incorporates the organic, desires it and makes it its own, welcomes it, touches it, brings it into itself and possesses it, thus enacting the definitive passage of the organic into the inorganic: sculpture versus architecture.

Translated, from the Italian, by Stephen Sartarelli.

1. Richard Kostelanetz, "Interview with Claes Oldenburg," in *The Theater of Mixed Means* (New York: RKEDitions, 1980), p. 157.
2. Jan McDevitt, "Object: Still Life; Interview," *Craft Horizons* (New York) 25, no. 5 (Sept. 1965), p. 31.
3. Claes Oldenburg, *Notes*, Los Angeles, 1963.
4. Claes Oldenburg, *Raw Notes*, ed. Kasper König (Halifax, Canada: The Press of the Nova Scotia College of Art and Design, 1973), p. 7.
5. Oldenburg, *Notes*, New York, 1962.
6. Oldenburg, *Notes*, New York, 1961.
7. Ibid.
8. Ibid.
9. Oldenburg, *Notes*, New York, 1963.
10. Mario Perniola, *Il sex-appeal del inorganico* (Turin: Einaudi, 1994), pp. 49−51.
11. Quoted in Barbara Rose, "The Origins, Life and Times of Ray Gun: All Will See as Ray Gun Sees . . . ," *Artforum* (New York) 8 (Nov. 1969), p. 52.
12. Oldenburg, *Notes*, Los Angeles, 1963.
13. Oldenburg, *Notes*, New York, 1968.
14. See Jean Biner, *The Living Theater* (Lausanne: Editions L'Age d'Homme, 1968); Merce Cunningham, *Changes: Notes on Choreography* (New York: Something Else Press, 1968); A. Forge, *Robert Rauschenberg* (New York: Abrams, 1969); Allan Kaprow, *Happenings* (New York: Abrams, 1969); Richard Kostelanetz, ed., *John Cage* (New York: Praeger, 1968); and Max Kozloff, *Jasper Johns* (New York: Abrams, 1967).
15. See Jacques Caumont, *Marcel Duchamp* (Milan: Bompiani, 1993).
16. R. Lebel, *Sur Marcel Duchamp* (Paris: Trianon, 1959).
17. For Duchamp, as for the Dadaists in general, "the point was to call into question the behavior of the artist such as people envisioned it." Quoted in Pierre Cabanne, *Entretiens avec Marcel Duchamp* (Paris: Editions Belfond, 1967), p. 100.
18. Quoted in John Tancock, "The Influece of Marcel Duchamp," in *Marcel Duchamp* (exh. cat.; New York: The Museum of Modern Art and the Philadelphia Museum of Art, 1973), p. 165.
19. Cabanne, p. 135.
20. James Johnson Sweeney, radio interview with Marcel Duchamp, WNBC, New York, 1955.
21. Cabanne, p. 135.
22. John Cage, *Silence* (Middletown, Conn.: Wesleyan University Press, 1966).
23. Kostelanetz, p. 14.
24. Allan Kaprow, "The Legacy of Jackson Pollock," *Art News* (New York) 57, no. 6 (Oct. 1958), p. 56.
25. Barbara Rose, *Claes Oldenburg* (exh. cat.; New York: The Museum of Modern Art, 1970), pp. 19−27.
26. Oldenburg, *Notes*, New York, 1960.
27. Quoted in Rose, p. 37.
28. Oldenburg, *Notes*, New York, 1963.
29. Ibid.
30. Claes Oldenburg, "Statement," in *Dubuffet and The Anticulture* (New York: Richard Feigen Gallery, Oct. 1969).
31. Quoted in Rose, p. 53.
32. Oldenburg, *Notes*, New York, 1960.
33. Ibid.
34. Oldenburg, *Notes*, New York, 1968.
35. Ibid.
36. Oldenburg, *Notes*, New York, 1961.
37. Ibid.
38. Quoted in Rose, p. 69.
39. Oldenburg, *Notes*, New York, n.d .
40. Quoted in Coosje van Bruggen, *Claes Oldenburg: Nur Ein Anderer Raum/ Just Another Room* (Frankfurt: Museum für Moderne Kunst, 1991), p. 90.
41. Jeanne Siegel, "How to Keep Sculpture in and Out of a Museum: An Interview with Claes Oldenburg on his Retrospective Exhibition at the Museum of Modern Art," in *Arts Magazine* (New York) 44, no. 1 (Sept.–Oct. 1969), p. 25.
42. Oldenburg, *Notes*, New York, May–July 1967, p. 107.
43. Oldenburg, *Notes*, New York, 1966.
44. Ibid.
45. Oldenburg, *Notes*, Los Angeles, 1963−64.
46. Ibid.
47. Quoted in Rose, p. 97.

A Note to the Reader

This anthology of works by Claes Oldenburg includes reproductions of objects included in the exhibition as well as some that are not. Many of these works of art have been rephotographed for this publication under the supervision of the artist, while others are depicted in their original or site-specific installations. In the latter case, photographs came largely from the artist's extensive archive, which was also the source for the photographs of performances staged by Oldenburg, from the Happenings that took place in the early 1960s in New York City through *Il Corso del Coltello*, a collaboration with Coosje van Bruggen and Frank O. Gehry staged in Venice in 1985. This anthology also includes photographs of every one of the twenty-five large-scale projects created by Oldenburg and van Bruggen.

The book is divided into five sections. These sections are demarcated with headings written by the artist and typed on his trusty L.C. Smith antique typewriter. Oldenburg is a prolific writer, and while this anthology provides visual documentation of his career as a sculptor, draughtsman, and performer, it also includes a small selection from his notes and from other published sources. All such writings, which appear throughout the anthology, are by Oldenburg (unless otherwise indicated) and have been adapted by him for this monograph. A selected list of Oldenburg's published writings may be found in the bibliography.

In the captions, measurements are provided in both English and metric systems; in them, height precedes width, followed by depth. Performances and exhibitions or installations are identified by title, location, and date.

1959-1963

New York City

Ray Gun
The Street
The Store

Snapshots from the City;
Blackouts; Circus: Iron-
works/Fotodeath; Ray Gun
Theater; Injun (Dallas);
Sports; Gayety (Chicago);
Stars (Washington D.C.)

Making forms out of wire covered with paper soaked in wheat paste came from a book of suggestions for children's art classes I found in the stacks of the Cooper Union Art School Library where I worked shelving books. This was 1957. Earlier I had looked at the "tents" of tentworms.

The wire and paper method enabled me to make my own form directly and cheaply. The simplicity of the technique and the look of the result satisfied my desire for primitive and organic effects. I wanted to imagine that I was inventing an art that could be followed by any "primitive" of the New York City streets, using the most ordinary available material.

The "Empire Papa Ray Gun" was done in December 1959. I had learned to exploit the tendency of the wire to go its own way and I had found a way of painting the surface by dabbing and dribbling diluted black casein paint along the spine and sides of a piece. Drops placed on the spine flowed to one side or the other. The gravity directed flow produced a vertical linear effect which counteracted the twisty, organic character of the work. I had learned also to choose certain pages in the paper, f.ex. the movie pages for their masses of blacks. I found the Times too grey and preferred the Post to the News. The News was stingy with their ink. These structures were shaped in the air out of wire hanging from the ceiling. They swung and turned while I twisted the wire into shapes. It was drawing in three dimensions. I remember the insides looked as interesting as the outsides and I hated to seal them up. The back can be seen on the "Celine Backwards" relief.

(ca. 1970)

3. C-E-L-I-N-E, Backwards, *1959*.
*Newspaper soaked in wheat paste over
wire frame, painted with casein, 30¼ x
39⅝ x 3 inches (78.1 x 100.7 x 7.6 cm).
Collection of Claes Oldenburg and
Coosje van Bruggen, New York.*

RAY GUN

1. Kid's toy. 2. Seeing through walls.
3. The universal angle. Examples: Legs,
Sevens, Pistols, Arms, Phalli--simple Ray
Guns. Double Ray Guns: Cross, Airplanes.
Absurd Ray Guns: Ice Cream Sodas. Complex
Ray Guns: Chairs, Beds. 4. Anagrams and
homophonies: Nug Yar (New York). ReuBen
(Gallery). 5. Accidental references:
A moviehouse in Harlem. A nuclear testing
site in the Sahara (Ragon). 6. What ever
is needed. A word ought to be useful.
7. Cryptic sayings: 'All will see as
Ray Gun sees.' 'The name of New York will
be changed to Ray Gun.' 'When Ray Gun
shoots no-one dies.' 8. Talismanic,
fetishistic functions.

(1961)

4. Street Ray Guns, *1959. Eight objects painted with enamel and casein, mounted in a painted wood box, 16⅛ x 13¾ x 4 inches (41.9 x 34.9 x 10.2 cm) overall. Collection of Joshua Mack and Ron Warren.*

RAY GUN

Ray gun delights in excess, extension
beyond accepted proportions, convolutions,
grotesquerie, baroquerie, movement,
proliferation, complexity of surface,
complexity of idea and image--
metamorphosis, double image, optical
illusion, image within image, infinity...
Ray gun looks to the most baroque corners
of the human experience and the human mind
for its inspiration, into madness,
hallucination, preconsciousness, children's
consciousness, present and historical
archaisms. Its aim is to <u>people</u> the world
with hallucinations, <u>make the inanimate
animate</u>, create visages everywhere, and
thus restore the excitement and meaning of
simple experience.

Time: the present

Place: the city, materials of the city,
textures of the city, expressions of the
city, of the street: asphalt, concrete,
tar, paper, metal...etc. natural and
manmade effects. Newspapers, comics,
scrawls of all sorts, anonymous passages of
materials...where we always see the face,
the visage, the spirit, looking back...
  What are my preferences in the <u>real</u>
world: the city and the poor and the
miserable; the streets...proletariat or
common people, their inventions. Popular
culture. Present-day primitives: children
madmen, the American cultureless. In
general the bleak grey face of things, not
pastoral. Modern and cityfied. This is the
setting for my mysticism.
  The erotic and the intimate, too, form
another setting...

(1959)

5. Ray Gun Poster – U.S. Death Heart,
*1960. Monoprint on newsprint, 17¾ x
11⅞ inches (45 x 30 cm). Collection of
Claes Oldenburg and Coosje van Bruggen,
New York.*

pages 44–45:
6. *Entrance to Judson Gallery, Judson
Memorial Church, New York, with posters
by Oldenburg and Jim Dine for the
Ray Gun Show, February–March 1960.*

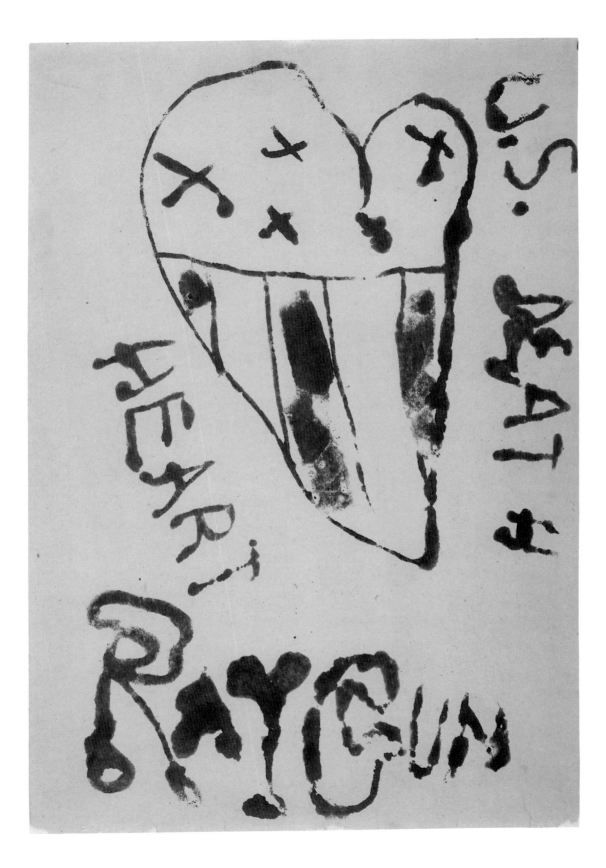

pages 46–47:
7. The Street, *Judson Gallery,*
Judson Memorial Church, New York,
February–March 1960.

left and below:
8. Snapshots from the City,
Performance at Judson Gallery, Judson
Memorial Church, New York,
February 29, March 1–2, 1960.

BRIEF DESCRIPTION OF THE SHOW

The show will consist of 1) an epic
construction in the form of a Street,
2) & 3) drawings and small sculptures and
constructions also having to do with The
Street.

The material will be mostly paper and
wood, glued paper, torn paper, paper over
wire, on wooden frames, paper hanging down,
paper jumping up, paper lying etc. etc.

The scale will vary from heroic to very
very small.

In The Street there will be suspended
figures, standing figures, lying figures,
projecting figures, falling figures, running
figures etc. etc. There will be figures on
the walls, faces on the floor and a sky made
of words and cries.

There will be signs of various sorts,
marquees, street signs etc. and various
sorts of metamorphosed objects: cigarbutts,
houses, towers, cars, medals, etc. etc.
There will be faces in windows and free
faces. Hanging heads and many heads.

There will be men and women and heroes and
bums and children and drunks
and cripples and streetchicks and boxers
and walkers and sitters and spitters
and trucks and cars and bikes and manholes
and stoplights and shadows
and cats and doggys and bright light and
darkness
fires and collisions and cockroaches and
mornings and evenings and guns
and newspapers
and pissers and cops and mamagangers and a
lot more etc.

(all components of the Street can be
purchased separately)

(1960)

9. Drawing for Announcement of
The Street at Reuben Gallery, 1960.
Pen, ink, and newspaper on paper,
13⅞ x 10 inches (35.2 x 25.4 cm).
Collection of Claes Oldenburg and
Coosje van Bruggen, New York.

pages 52—53:
10. Oldenburg and Anita Reuben at
The Street, Reuben Gallery, New York,
May 6—19, 1960.

pages 54—55:
11. Objects from The Street, 1960,
included in Blam!, Whitney Museum
of American Art, New York,
September 20—December 2, 1984.

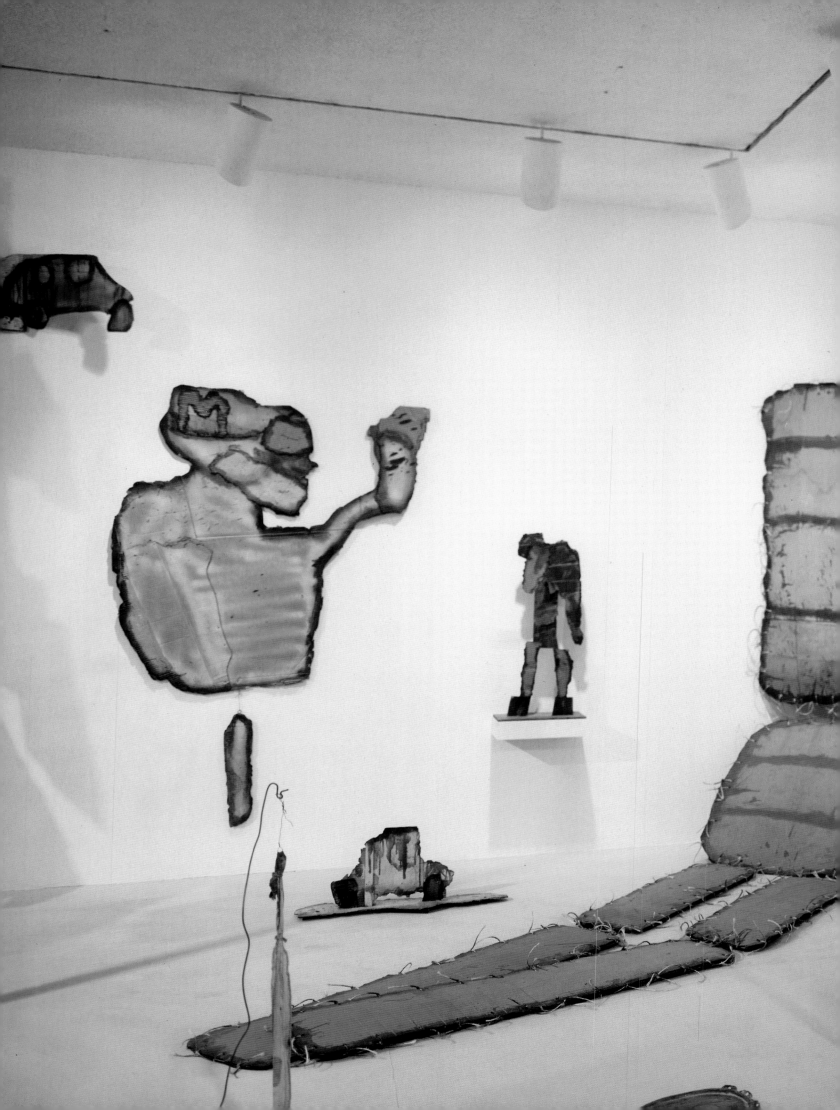

12. Empire Sign – with M and I
Deleted, *1960. Casein and spray paint on
cut-and-pasted corrugated cardboard,
54 ¼ x 23 ⅛ inches (139.1 x 60.7 cm).
The Museum of Modern Art, New York,
Gift of Agnes Gund.*

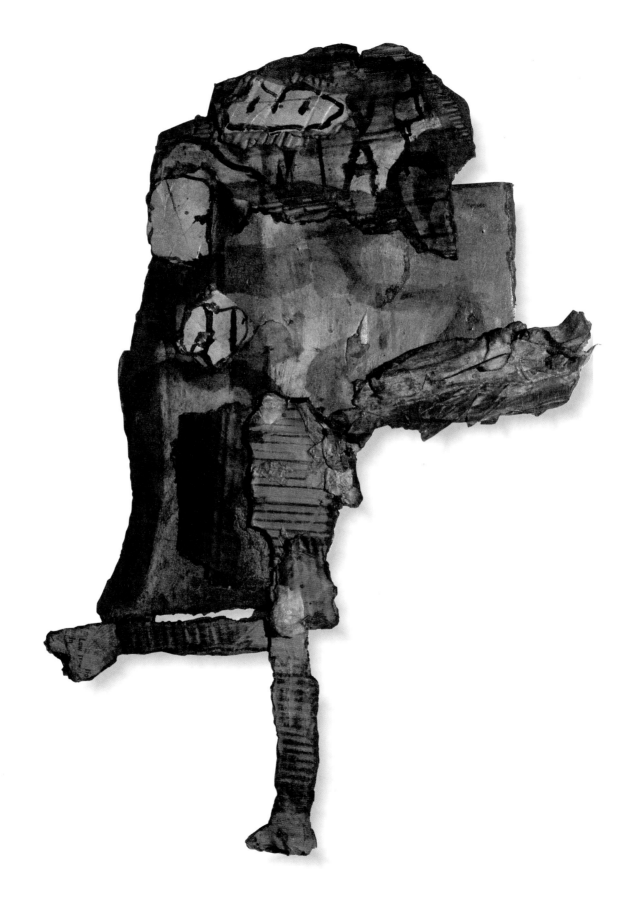

14. *Van, 1960. Cardboard, oil wash, and wood, 12¼ x 13 inches (31.1 x 33 cm); wood mount: 17½ x 18 inches (44.5 x 45.7 cm). Collection of Joseph K. Levene.*

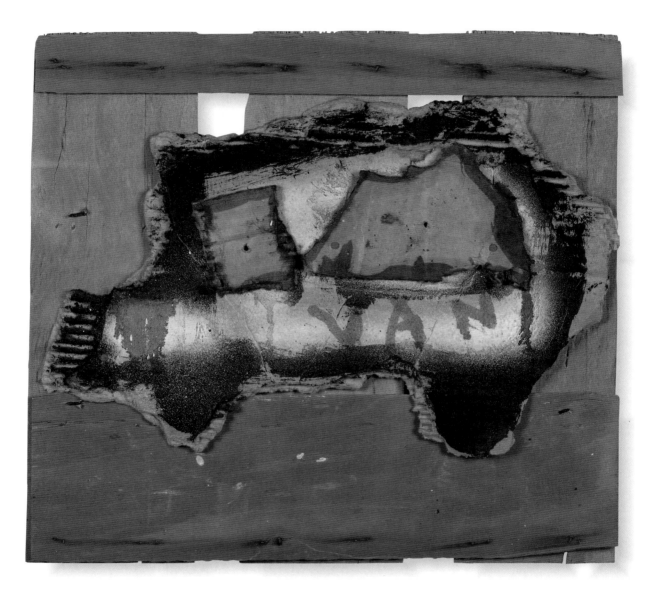

I like to work in material that is
organic-seeming and full of surprises,
inventive all by itself. For example,
wire, which has a decided life of its
own, paper, which one must obey and will
not be ruled too much, or cardboard,
which is downright hostile, or wood with
its sullen stubbornness. I am a little
afraid of metal or glass because they
have the capacity like a lion to gash and
kill, and if I gave them the freedom I
give my other materials they probably
would. As for my forms, what is most
important is that they should be very
near absolutely certain, after a long
preparation simply demand to be created.
Getting myself into that relation with a
form is most of the struggle.

   Form or the bone of a thing, its
essentialness is what matters to me the
most.

   Coming to my studio you would find my
works floating because the force I most
respect is gravity, and tethered like
dirigibles or cattle by a rope to the
walls.

   A strong sensation of if not knowledge
(no definitely not knowledge) of physical
principles is important to the artist, as
is the sharp natural eye for detail.

(1960)

Cardboard found on the street
1. is cheap. 2. makes nice coastlines.
The source of line is the street.

(1961)

16. Poster Study – "New Media, New
Forms I," Martha Jackson Gallery, *1960.*
Ink, watercolor, and newspaper collage on
paper, 24 x 18½ inches (61 x 47 cm).
Private collection.

NOTES ON THE PERFORMANCE
IRONWORKS/FOTODEATH (CIRCUS)

The original title of the piece was Circus
(referring to its structure, resembling the
multiple simultaneous action of a circus).
In two parts: Ironworks and Fotodeath, with
an intermission feature: a set of slides,
photos, and type, called Pickpocket.

Circus was given six times in the Reuben
Gallery during February, 1961. The Reuben
Gallery is a deep and wide store on
Manhattan's East Third Street. The audience
was seated as in a conventional theatre
(and stood, when there were not enough
chairs) facing a deep square stage. Over
the stage were hung four strings of weak
lightbulbs, producing when lit the sort of
dingy light one remembers from circus
tents.

In addition there were three individual
lightbulbs over different areas of the
stage, and a line of lights over a wall
which marked the back of the stage, built
across the store for the performance. There
were thirty-four events in Circus, divided
into seven sets. Ironworks was made up of
four sets, Fotodeath of three sets.
Excepting one set in Ironworks, there were
five events in each set. Each event was
assigned a zone on stage corresponding to a
lightbulb or a string of bulbs. Turning on
of the light cued the entrance of the
event. The sets were separated by periods
of darkness, during which colored
lightbulbs placed around the theatre
blinked.

The effect (from the audience's point of
view) when all events of a set were in
action was one of overlapping,
superimposition. The wall at the back of
the stage area was about seven feet high,
having two entrances, one at either side.
The entrances were hung with strips of
muslin. Muslin was bunched and draped along
the top of the wall. The wall and muslin
were sprayed red, yellow, and blue in
abstract patterns, giving a foggy color
effect.

Behind the wall, on a perch to the left,
in view of the audience, sat the Operator
(Max Baker), controlling lights and
phonograph records and projecting the slide
sequence during intermission. Above the
wall, the store receded into darkness.
Dressing rooms were behind the wall.
Excepting the entrance of a man with a bag
in Ironworks, all the players entered from
behind the wall. The floor of the stage was
of tile, broken in spots and repaired with
cement (the store had once been a
restaurant and the stage area corresponded
to the kitchen).

The left side of the stage, called "the
masculine," was painted a flat black and
dominated by blacks, greys, and neutrals.
At the meeting of the left wall and the
wall across the stage was a muslin screen
on which a shadow effect was projected. In
front of the screen was a large
construction of wood and burlap, called the
"chimney."

The right side of the stage, called "the
feminine," was by contrast brightly colored
in dominating pinks and reds. A pink form,
made of muslin around a hoop resembling a
windsock, jutted out of the wall and hung
from the ceiling.

A black wooden settee stood on the left
side against the wall and a hatrack and
long mirror hung on the right. Other
furniture and objects were brought on
stage.

Exits of events were cued by a Timer in
each set. His departure from the stage was
followed by the turning off of the lights
over the other events in a determined
sequence. When the light over an event was
extinguished, the players either went
backstage or helped in the darkness to set
up props for the next event.

A scrim was hung across the front of the
stage and so lit that the actions of
preparation for the performance were dimly
seen by the entering audience. Music was
played before and after the performance.
When the piece was ready to begin, the
scrim was taken down and slowly rolled on a
long bamboo pole in a deliberate action
functioning as an event in itself.

(1965)

FOTODEATH (EXCERPTS FROM THE SCRIPT)

pages 64—71:
17. Circus (Ironworks/Fotodeath),
Performance at Reuben Gallery, New
York, February 21—26, 1961.

A woman enters L., Pat, in long dragging
plumage and wings, very colorful and
bizarrely made up. She walks slowly and
artificially, only interested in herself.
She pulls herself up and down the ladder in
R. center taking poses, sticking her leg
out slowly, etc.

A woman in a derby hat, mannish, dressed
all in black with a patriotic band across
bodice something like a Salvation Army
woman. Gloria. Enters from R. She carries a
black bag like a sample bag and a big can
full of viscous liquid. She stops behind
table center Zone 4, and takes out of the
bag one by one, putting them on the table,
numerous different objects of many colors
but all marked clearly USA. It is as if she
is demonstrating a product, but she has no
expression on her face and says nothing.
After piling up the objects, she pours from
a huge can marked USA a viscous liquid
which runs over the objects and on the
floor. This she covers with a cloth marked
USA. She remains standing over her work
until blackout and forms a silhouette.

A photographer, Carl, in a shiny black
smock and a top hat brings out a camera and
leads in a family of three to be
photographed: Henry, Chippie and Marilyn.
Sets them on a bench and then shows them
several landscape samples. They disapprove.
Finally he finds one they will accept. He
hangs it behind them, gets under the
fotocloth but the family collapses. The
photographer sets them up again, gets under
the cloth. Again they collapse, and so on.

A man, Lucas, enters from L. in a plain
tight fastidious suit. He admires himself
in many mirrors he takes from his pockets.
He lies down with a tall mirror, posing
himself in different ways, projecting
himself upside down, etc.

A woman dressed as a man in hat, shirt,
tie, and baggy suit, Judy, enters from L.,
goes to dresser and undresses in front of
mirror. She wears extremely feminine
clothes underneath. She admires herself as
a woman then redresses as a man. She leaves
L. taking mirror with her.

(1961)

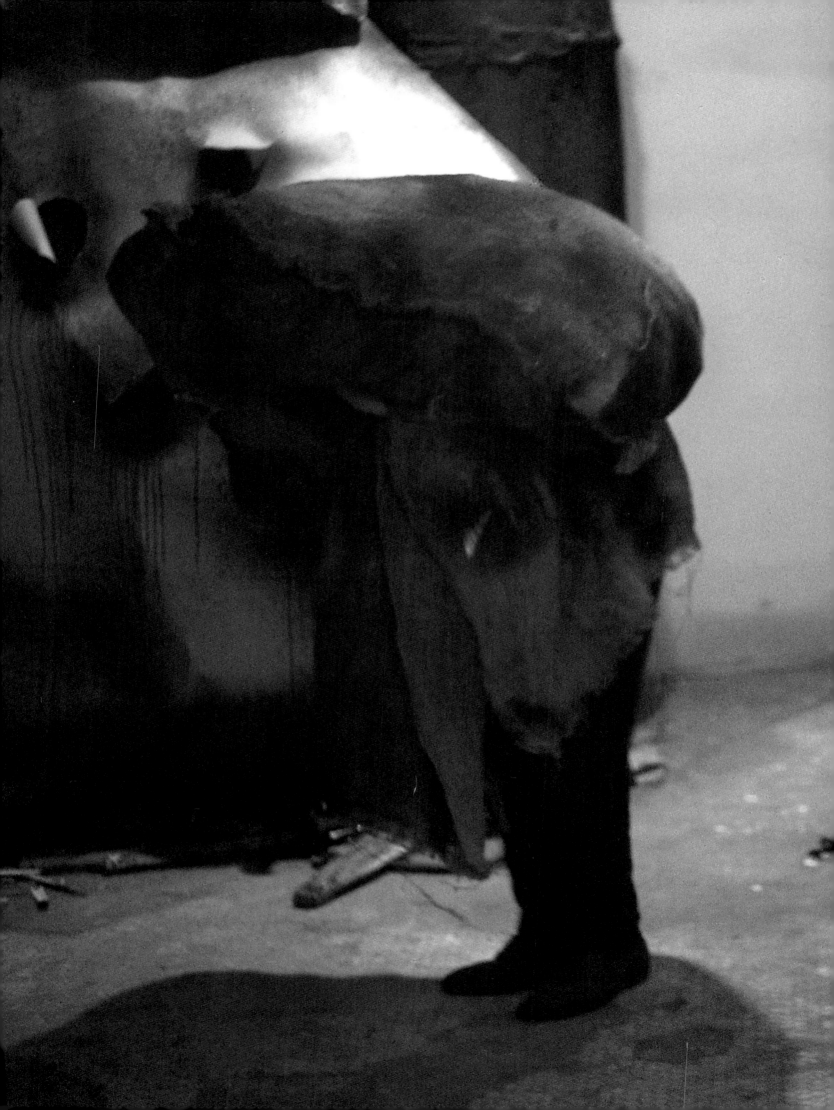

18. Striding Figure (Final Study for Announcement of a Dance Concert by the Aileen Passloff Dance Company), 1962. Dripped enamel on paper, 17¾ x 12⅛ inches (45.1 x 30.8 cm). Collection of Claes Oldenburg and Coosje van Bruggen, New York.

P......g, which has slept so long / in its gold crypts / in its glass graves / is asked out / to go for a swim / is given a cigarette / a bottle of beer / its hair is rumpled / is given a shove and tripped / is taught to laugh / is given clothes of all kinds / goes for a ride on a bike / finds a girl in a cab and feels her up / goes flying / goes driving at 100 mph.

Shy at first / soon all its dreams are realized / is stripped from its cross / straightened out, is given exercise to bring back its tired muscles / tonics to get the red back in its cheeks.

Who all its life had wished to be / is given the chance to be / a handkerchief / to go from hand to hand / from nose to nose / and in and out of pockets / over foreheads / into eyes and ears / around one set of lips and another / to be dropped and washed in a machine on a line to dry flapping in the wind.

Who all its life had wished to be / is given the chance to be / a flag / carried in the breeze up and down streets / planted on car fenders going fast / whistling in a thousand parts over a gasoline station / lazily lying on a coffin / pleased to catch the earth thrown on it / at half-mast for some famous person / lofty on a patriotic day / put away in a drawer at night nicely folded / wounded or dissolving in battle / decaying on the mast of a ship crossing the ocean.

To be a shirt / a tie / a pair of pants / a suit of clothes / going somewhere on someone / getting rumpled while dancing / having a drink spilled on it / taken off and hung up / sent to the cleaners / drawn on the body / catching hair / slicing over fingers / pressing ears.

Bolder and bolder / it becomes anything it wants to be / a hamburger / an ice cream cone / a newspaper / a sewing machine / a bicycle / impossible inexhaustible p......g.

(1960)

25. Sewing Machine, *1961. Muslin
soaked in plaster over wire frame,
painted with enamel, 46½ x 63½ inches
(118.1 x 161.3 cm). Collection of Reinhard
Onnasch, Berlin.*

26. Pepsi-Cola Sign, *1961. Muslin soaked in plaster over wire frame, painted with enamel, 58¼ x 46½ x 7½ inches (148 x 118.1 x 19.1 cm). The Museum of Contemporary Art, Los Angeles, The Panza Collection.*

27. Auto Tire with Fragment of Price,
1961. Muslin soaked in plaster over wire
frame, painted with enamel, 49 x 48 x
7 inches (124.5 x 121.9 x 17.8 cm).
Musée national d'art moderne, Centre
Georges Pompidou, Paris.

29. 7-Up, 1961. Muslin soaked in plaster
over wire frame, painted with enamel,
55⅛ x 39¼ x 5½ inches (140.7 x 99.7 x
14 cm). Hirshhorn Museum and Sculpture
Garden, Smithsonian Institution, The
Joseph H. Hirshhorn Purchase Fund and
the Joseph H. Hirshhorn Bequest Fund.

30. Two Girls' Dresses, *1961. Muslin soaked in plaster over wire frame, painted with enamel, 42 x 41 x 6 ½ inches (106.7 x 104.1 x 16.5 cm). Collection of Reinhard Onnasch, Berlin.*

31. Red Tights with Fragment 9, *1961.*
Muslin soaked in plaster over wire frame,
painted with enamel, 69⅛ x 34¼ x
8¾ inches (176.7 x 87 x 22.2 cm).
The Museum of Modern Art, New York,
Gift of G. David Thompson, 1961.

32. Mu-Mu, *1961. Muslin soaked in plaster over wire frame, painted with enamel, 64 x 41½ x 4 inches (162.6 x 105.4 x 10.2 cm). The Museum of Contemporary Art, Los Angeles, The Panza Collection.*

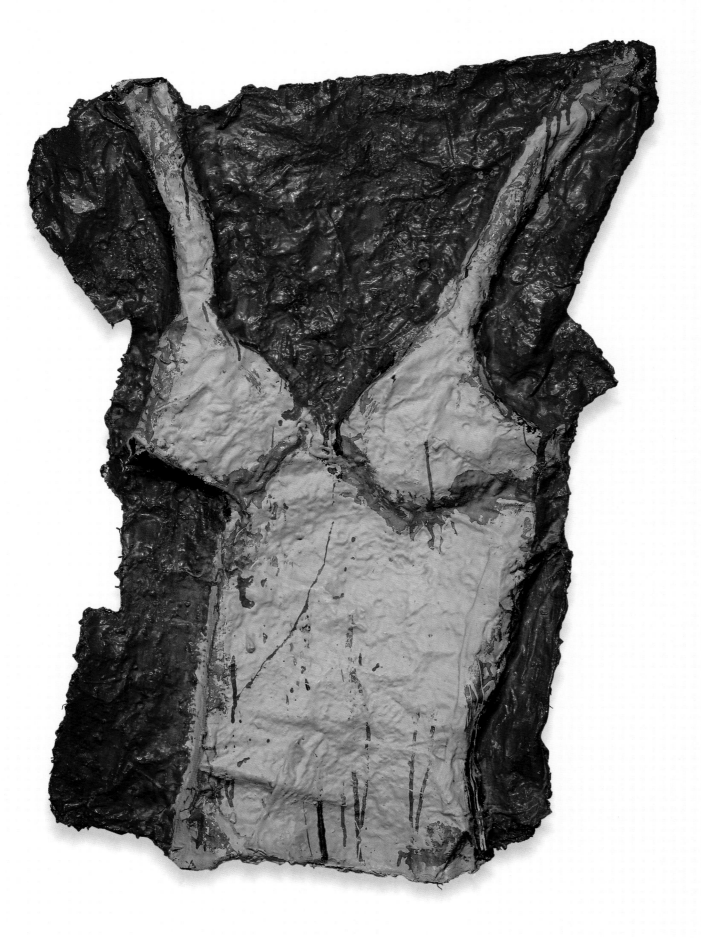

34. Braselette, 1961. *Variation:*
The White Slip. Painted plaster, muslin,
and wire, 41 x 30¼ x 4 inches
(104.1 x 76.8 x 10.2 cm). Whitney Museum
of American Art, New York, Gift of
Howard and Jean Lipman.

35. Jacket and Shirt Fragment, *1961–62.*
Muslin soaked in plaster over wire frame,
painted with enamel, 42⅛ x 30 x 6½ inches
(107 x 76.2 x 16.5 cm). Musée national
d'art moderne, Centre Georges Pompidou,
Paris.

37. Fur Jacket with White Gloves, *1961.*
Muslin soaked in plaster over wire frame,
painted with enamel, 43 ¹¹/16 *x 38* ⁹/16 *x*
5 ⁷/8 *inches (100.5 x 98 x 15 cm). Öffentliche*
Kunstsammlung Basel, Kunstmuseum.

38. Chocolates in Box (Fragment),
1961. Muslin soaked in plaster over wire
frame, painted with enamel, 44 x
32 x 6 inches (111.8 x 81.3 x 15.2 cm).
The Museum of Contemporary Art,
Los Angeles, The Panza Collection.

39. Red Sausages, *1961. Muslin soaked in plaster over wire frame, painted with enamel, 33 x 30 x 5 inches (83.8 x 76.2 x 12.7 cm). Donald Judd Estate.*

I am for an art that is political-erotical-mystical, that does something other than sit on its ass in a museum.

I am for an art that grows up not knowing it is art at all, an art given the chance of having a starting point of zero.

I am for an art that embroils itself with the everyday crap & still comes out on top.

I am for an art that imitates the human, that is comic, if necessary, or violent, or whatever is necessary.

I am for an art that takes its form from the lines of life itself, that twists and extends and accumulates and spits and drips, and is heavy and coarse and blunt and sweet and stupid as life itself.

I am for an artist who vanishes, turning up in a white cap painting signs or hallways.

I am for art that comes out of a chimney like black hair and scatters in the sky.

I am for art that spills out of an old man's purse when he is bounced off a passing fender.

I am for the art out of a doggy's mouth, falling five stories from the roof.

I am for the art that a kid licks, after peeling away the wrapper.

I am for an art that joggles like everyones knees, when the bus traverses an excavation.

I am for art that is smoked, like a cigarette, smells, like a pair of shoes.

I am for art that flaps like a flag, or helps blow noses, like a handkerchief.

I am for art that is put on and taken off, like pants, which develops holes, like socks, which is eaten, like a piece of pie, or abandoned with great contempt, like a piece of shit.

I am for art covered with bandages. I am for art that limps and rolls and runs and jumps. I am for art that comes in a can or washes up on the shore.

I am for art that coils and grunts like a wrestler. I am for art that sheds hair.

I am for art you can sit on. I am for art you can pick your nose with or stub your toes on.

I am for art from a pocket, from deep channels of the ear, from the edge of a knife, from the corners of the mouth, stuck in the eye or worn on the wrist.

I am for art under the skirts, and the art of pinching cockroaches.

I am for the art of conversation between the sidewalk and a blind mans metal stick.

I am for the art that grows in a pot, that comes down out of the skies at night, like lightning, that hides in the clouds and growls. I am for art that is flipped on and off with a switch.

I am for art that unfolds like a map, that you can squeeze, like your sweetys arm, or kiss, like a pet dog. Which expands and squeaks, like an accordion, which you can spill your dinner on, like an old tablecloth.

I am for an art that you can hammer with, stitch with, sew with, paste with, file with.

I am for an art that tells you the time of day, or where such and such a street is.

I am for an art that helps old ladies across the street.

I am for the art of the washing machine. I am for the art of a government check. I am for the art of last wars raincoat.

I am for the art that comes up in fogs from sewer-holes in winter. I am for the art that splits when you step on a frozen puddle. I am for the worms art inside the apple. I am for the art of sweat that develops between crossed legs.

I am for the art of neck-hair and caked tea-cups, for the art between the tines of restaurant forks, for the odor of boiling dishwater.

I am for the art of sailing on Sunday, and the art of red and white gasoline pumps.

I am for the art of bright blue factory columns and blinking biscuit signs.

I am for the art of cheap plaster and enamel. I am for the art of worn marble and smashed slate. I am for the art of rolling cobblestones and sliding sand. I am for the art of slag and black coal. I am for the art of dead birds.

I am for the art of scratchings in the asphalt, daubing at the walls. I am for the art of bending and kicking metal and breaking glass, and pulling at things to make them fall down.

I am for the art of punching and skinned knees and sat-on bananas. I am for the art of kids' smells. I am for the art of mama-babble. I am for the art of bar-babble, tooth-picking, beerdrinking, egg-salting, in-sulting. I am for the art of falling off a barstool.

I am for the art of underwear and the art of taxicabs. I am for the art of ice-cream cones dropped on concrete. I am for the majestic art of dog-turds, rising like cathedrals.

I am for the blinking arts, lighting up the night. I am for art falling, splashing, wiggling, jumping, going on and off.

I am for the art of fat truck-tires and black eyes.

I am for Kool-art, 7-UP art, Pepsi-art, Sunshine art, 39 cents art, 15 cents art, Vatronol art, Dro-bomb art, Vam art, Menthol art, L & M art, Ex-lax art, Venida art, Heaven Hill art, Pamryl art, San-o-med art, Rx art, 9.99 art, Now art, New art, How art, Fire sale art, Last Chance art, Only art, Diamond art, Tomorrow art, Franks art, Ducks art, Meat-o-rama art.

I am for the art of bread wet by rain. I am for the rats' dance between floors. I am for the art of flies walking on a slick pear in the electric light. I am for the art of soggy onions and firm green shoots. I am for the art of clicking among the nuts when the roaches come and go. I am for the brown sad art of rotting apples.
   I am for the art of meowls and clatter of cats and for the art of their dumb electric eyes.
   I am for the white art of refrigerators and their muscular openings and closings.
   I am for the art of rust and mold. I am for the art of hearts, funeral hearts or sweetheart hearts, full of nougat. I am for the art of worn meathooks and singing barrels of red, white, blue and yellow meat.
   I am for the art of things lost or thrown away, coming home from school. I am for the art of cock-and-ball trees and flying cows and the noise of rectangles and squares. I am for the art of crayons and weak grey pencil-lead, and grainy wash and sticky oil paint, and the art of windshield wipers and the art of the finger on a cold window, on dusty steel or in the bubbles on the sides of a bathtub.
   I am for the art of teddy-bears and guns and decapitated rabbits, exploded umbrellas, raped beds, chairs with their brown bones broken, burning trees, firecracker ends, chicken bones, pigeon bones and boxes with men sleeping in them.

I am for the art of slightly rotten funeral flowers, hung bloody rabbits and wrinkly yellow chickens, bass drums & tambourines, and plastic phonographs.
   I am for the art of abandoned boxes, tied like pharaohs. I am for an art of watertanks and speeding clouds and flapping shades.
   I am for U.S. Government Inspected Art, Grade A art, Regular Price art, Yellow Ripe art, Extra Fancy art, Ready-to-eat art, Best-for-less art, Ready-to-cook art, Fully cleaned art, Spend Less art, Eat Better art, Ham art, pork art, chicken art, tomato art, banana art, apple, art turkey art, cake art, cookie art.

add:
I am for an art that is combed down, that is hung from each ear, that is laid on the lips and under the eyes, that is shaved from the legs, that is brushed on the teeth, that is fixed on the thighs, that is slipped on the foot.

square which becomes blobby

(1961)

chair
rungs
dresses
candy
skates
buggy
kool-aid (glass)
eyeglasses (beer
stocking
vacuum
curtains

slips
lettering
tires
umbrellas
cigars
teeth·
a crossword puzzle
bulb
garterbelt?

sunshine
sunshine

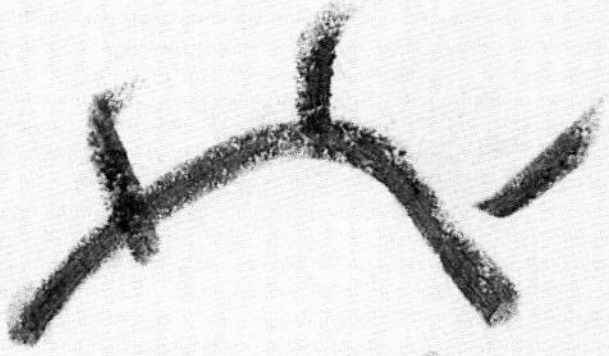

43. Pie, 7-Up, Flag, Oranges, Fifteen Cents (Studies for *Store* Objects), *1961. Collage, crayon, and watercolor on paper, 15 x 20 inches (38.1 x 50.8 cm). Private collection.*

44. Stocking Legs, Frozen Custard (Studies for *Store* Objects), *1961. Collage, crayon, and watercolor on paper, 18⅛ x 23⅞ inches (45.7 x 60.6 cm). Location unknown.*

45. A Sock and Fifteen Cents (Studies for *Store* Objects) , *1962. Collage, crayon, and watercolor on paper, 24 x 18¾ inches (61 x 47.6 cm). Collection of PaineWebber Group Inc., New York.*

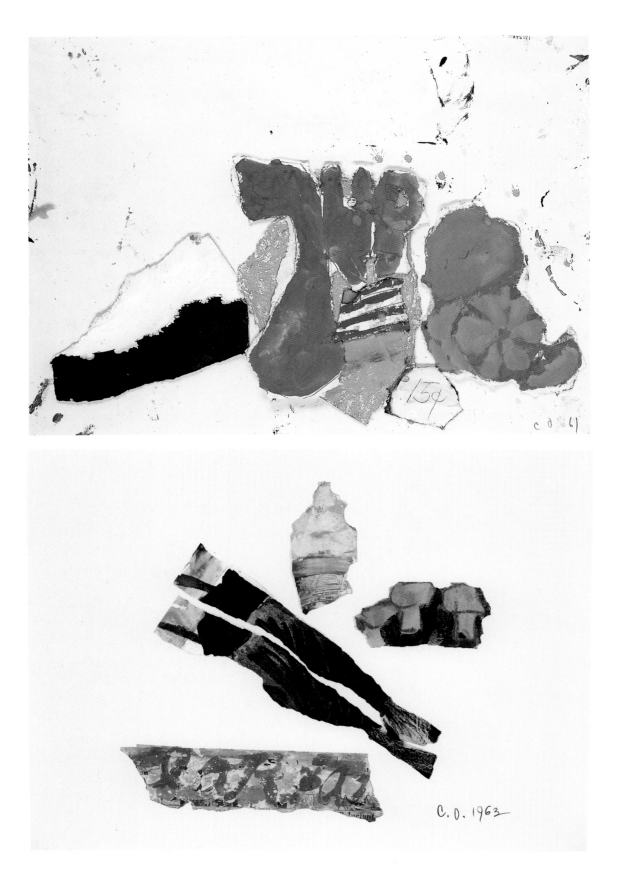

If I could only forget the notion of art
entirely. I really don't think you can win.
Duchamp is ultimately labeled art too. The
bourgeois scheme is that they wish to be
disturbed from time to time, they like
that, but then they envelop you, and that
little bit is over, and they are ready for
the next. There even exists within the b.
values a code of possibilities for
disturbance, certain "crimes" which it
requires some courage to do but which will
eventually be rewarded within the b.
scheme. B. values are human weakness, a
civilization built on human weakness, non-
resistance. They are disgusting. There are
many difficult things to do within the b.
values, but I would like to find some way to
take a totally outside position. Bohemia is
bourgeois. The beat is bourgeois--their
values are pure sentimentality--the
country, the good heart, the fallen man,
the honest man, the gold-hearted whore etc.
They would never think f.ex. of making the
city a value of good.

   Possibly art is doomed to be bourgeois.
Two possible escapes from the bourgeois are
1. aristocracy and 2. intellect, where art
never thrives too well. There again I am
talking as if I want to create art outside
b. values. Perhaps this can't be done, but
why should I even want to create "art"--
that's the notion I've got to get rid of.
Assuming that I wanted to create some thing
what would that thing be? Just a thing, an
object. Art would not enter into it. I make
a charged object ("living"). An "artistic"
appearance or content is derived from the
object's reference, not from the object
itself or me. These things are displayed in
galleries, but that is not the place for
them. A store would be better (Store--place
full of objects). Museum in b. concept
equals store in mine.

(1961)

46. Silver Torso with Brown Underwear, 1961. Enamel on newspaper, 22 x 16 inches (55.9 x 40.6 cm). Collection of Kimiko and John Powers.

THE STORE DESCRIBED & BUDGET FOR THE STORE

47. Poster for The Store, 1961. Three-color woodcut printed on cardboard, 28¼ x 22⅛ inches (71.8 x 56.2 cm). Collection of Claes Oldenburg and Coosje van Bruggen, New York.

The Store, or My Store, or the Ray-Gun Mfg. Co., located at 107 E. 2nd St., N.Y.C., is eighty feet long and varies about 10 ft wide. In the front half, it is my intention to create the environment of a store, by painting and placing (hanging, projecting, lying) objects after the spirit and in the form of popular objects of merchandise, such as may be seen in stores and store windows of the city, especially in the area where the store is (Clinton St., f.ex., Delancey St., 14th St.).

This store will be constantly supplied with new objects which I will create out of plaster and other materials in the rear half of the place. The objects will be for sale in the store.

The store will be open every day at hours I will post. F.ex. AM 10-2, PM 5-7, or the hours when I will be able to be in the store, which is also of course my studio.

The store may be thought of as a season-long exhibit, with changing & new material. It will be the center of my activities during the season.

The rent of the store is $60.00 per month, including steam heat and hot and cold water. Additional money will be needed to paint and plaster the front half and to make objects. Rent for 10 mos.--$600. Additional money to equip store--$150. Money to make objects--$250. ($24 per month). Total $1000.

(1961)

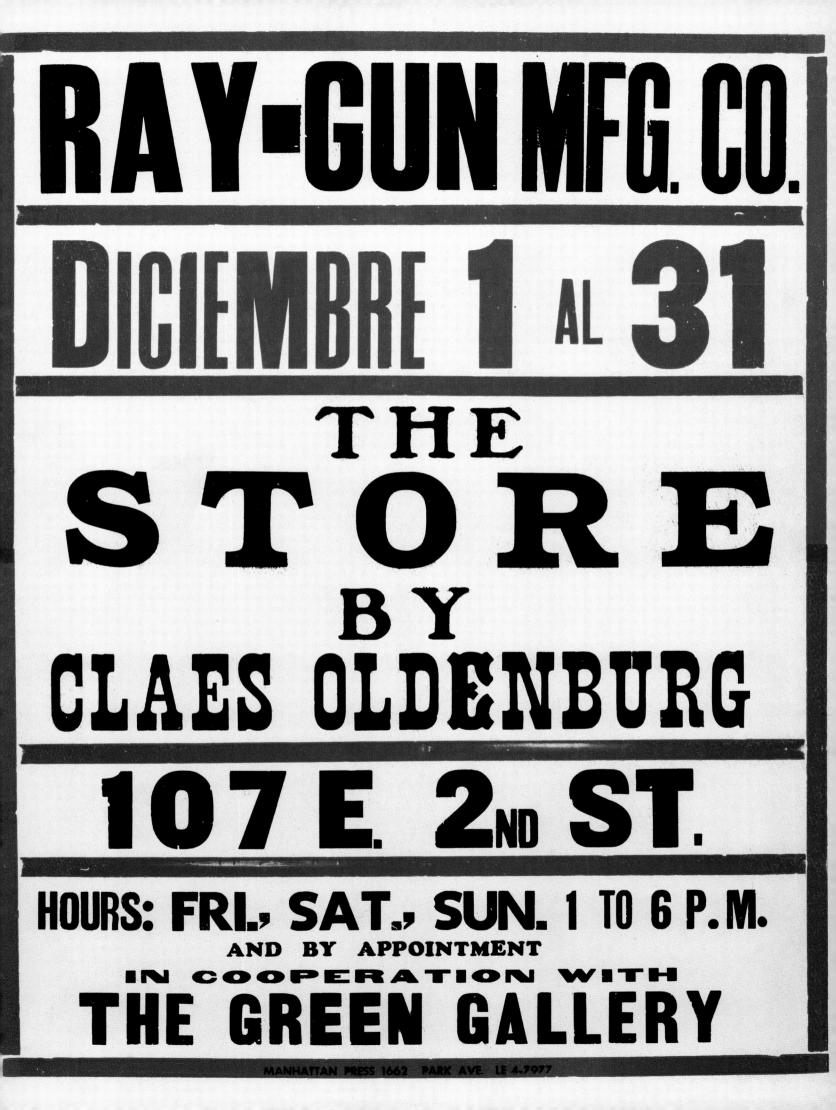

48. Interior of *The Store* (Sketch for
a Poster, Not Executed), *1961.*
Crayon and watercolor on paper,
24 x 18⅛ inches (61 x 46 cm). Collection of
Mr. and Mrs. Richard E. Oldenburg.

49. *Front window, looking into*
The Store, *107 East Second Street,*
New York, December 1961.

52. Success Plant, *1961. Muslin and burlap soaked in plaster over wire frame, painted with enamel, 28 inches (71.1 cm) high. Museum Ludwig, Cologne, Ludwig Donation.*

53. Blue Shirt, Striped Tie, *1961.*
Muslin soaked in plaster over wire frame,
painted with enamel, 36 x 20 inches
(91.4 x 50.8 cm). Location unknown.

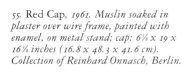

56. Blouse, 1961. Burlap soaked in plaster
over wire frame, painted with enamel,
36 x 24 x 5 inches (91.4 x 61 x 12.7 cm).
Collection of Kimiko and John Powers.

57. Men's Jacket with Shirt and Tie,
1961. Muslin soaked in plaster over wire
frame, painted with enamel, 42¼ x
31½ x 13¼ inches (107.3 x 80 x 34.9 cm).
Museum Ludwig, Cologne,
Ludwig Donation.

59. Cash Register, 1961. Muslin soaked in plaster over wire frame, painted with enamel, 25 x 21 x 34 inches (63.5 x 53.3 x 86.4 cm). Collection of Richard and Lois Plehn.

Why do I not just present the real thing instead of imitating it? Because my desire to imitate extends to the event or activity of making the thing I imitate. In one instance that is to be for a moment a sign-painter, in another, for a moment a baker of cakes, in another the cutter of suits, etc. etc. In some cases especially, but really in all, it is necessary to be for a moment nature herself, if this is possible. In handling plaster and enamel I was behaving like the painter who was at the same time painting my stairway. When I carry my plaster and paints up the stairs, the neighbors assume I am improving my home.

(1961)

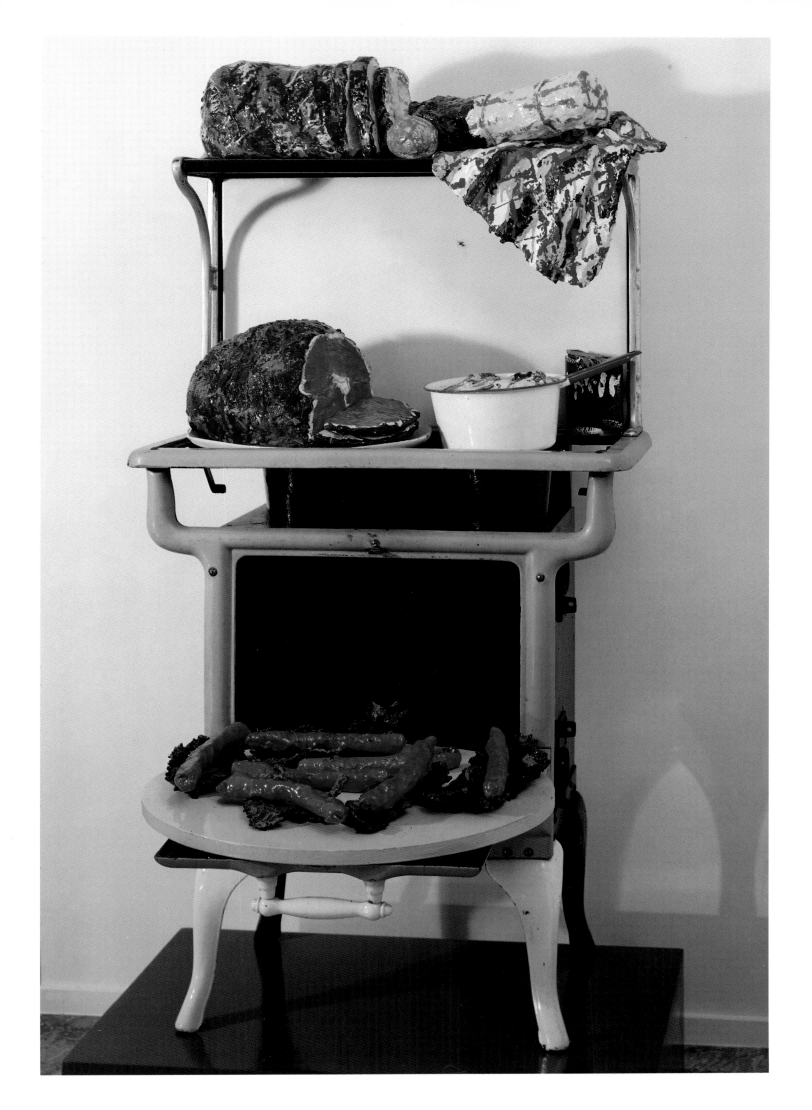

63. Roast, *1961. Muslin soaked in plaster over wire frame, painted with enamel, with rope, 14 x 17 x 16 inches (35.6 x 43.2 x 40.6 cm). Sonnabend Collection.*

64. Times Square Figure, *1961.*
Burlap soaked in plaster, painted with
enamel, 13¼ x 6 x 9¾ inches (34.9 x
15.2 x 24.8 cm). Location unkown.

65. Statue of Liberty Souvenir, 1961.
Burlap soaked in plaster, painted with
enamel on painted wood base, 6⅛ x 7⅞ x
8⅝ inches (15.6 x 20 x 21.9 cm). Courtesy
of Anthony d'Offay Gallery, London.

66. Bride Mannikin, *1961. Muslin soaked in plaster over wire frame, painted with enamel, 61 x 37½ x 35½ inches (154.9 x 95.3 x 90.2 cm). The Museum of Contemporary Art, Los Angeles, The Panza Collection.*

I am very grateful to the audience for coming each weekend. I cannot deny it is good to have an audience, though the nature of this theater is such that it would go on without an audience as a painter might go on painting with noone to watch him...This space has great limitations, I am aware of this...partly I enjoy the pressure these limitations put on me...I mean the time, the expense and the space...I hope you are not too miserable...my aim is to develop under these concentrated circumstances a sort of kernel of infinite expansion...so that at the end of this season I shall have ten extremely powerful seeds...It is becoming obvious I guess that these pieces are not unrelated...the "happening" which was in the beginning a very limited form is bearing fruit as a new physical theater, bringing to the dry puritan forms of the US stage the possibilities of a tremendous enveloping force...

Theater is the most powerful art form there is because it is the most involving...but it is forever becoming lost in trivialities...loss of power is a chronic disease of the form...realism... distance...commercial pressures...poor theater...I no longer see the distinction between theater and visual arts very clearly...distinctions I suppose are a civilized disease...I see primarily the need to reflect life...to give back, which is the only activity that gives man dignity...I am especially concerned with physicality, which is evident...only painting and sculpture have the power to give man back his physicality (which is not primitivism) when he loses it...painting and sculpture have the unique privilege of affecting the other arts in this respect...

A series of plays dealing with the US consciousness, really nonconcrete in content though expressed concretely. The content is the US mind or the US "Store". This is not understood. Despite what I say, the pieces are called happenings. I might have done happenings or may do in the future but these are not my idea of them. RG is something else, closely related to my Store pieces. It seeks to present in events what the store presents in objects. It is a theater of real events (a newsreel)...Have shorts?

Nothing is communicated or represented except through its attachment to an object (even though the object will mean different things at the same moment to different people)...It is the play of consciousness in reaction to certain objects...a play which involves the consciousness of myself my actors and my audience...This differs from conventional theater in that the communication is less fixed...more in doubt...there is a sequence but not plot or given relation of the events and objects as they occur...the sequence is purely a practical device...plot to me is sentimentality, pre-determination, an arrogance on the part of an author, a harmful fabrication which creates a residue of sentimental patterns that keep man from perceiving experience...this theater aims to make man compose experience as it changes a constant pleasure and an instrument of survival...

The theater differs from the store in that the objects of the store are reproductions, reconstructions or alterations of the actual object. This is also an anti neorealist expression. I have tried to represent my consciousness in relation to the actual object at the moment of my perception of it. This is complicated by the facts of construction...and there is only one way to handle this: to treat the materials as a complicating factor of the object, themselves objects of consciousness. On top of this I have complicated the object by introducing conventions of popular representation and artistic practise (a sort of travesty). The object is a record of passage through these complications...and must be seen as itself and not in relation to any theory. The aim of putting the store in an actual neighborhood is to contrast it to the actual object...not as might be thought in neorealist terms to point up similarities...The store title is in fact a play on words...the store means for me: my consciousness...

(1962)

pages 128–29:
67. Oldenburg speaking before a
performance of Ray Gun Theater.

pages 132–41:
68. Ray Gun Theater, a series of ten
performances at 107 East Second Street,
New York, February 23–May 26, 1962.
One scene is shown from each performance,
in the order they were presented:
Store Days I, Store Days II, Nekropolis I,
Nekropolis II, Injun (N.Y.C.) I,
Injun (N.Y.C.) II, Voyages I, Voyages II,
World's Fair I, and World's Fair II.

69. Upside-Down City, *1962. Muslin, painted with latex and spray enamel, with newspaper, wood, clothespins, and hangers, 118 x 60 x 60 inches (299.7 x 152.4 x 152.4 cm). Walker Art Center, Minneapolis, Purchased from the artist.*

RESIDUAL OBJECTS

Love objects. respect objects.
Objectivity high state of feeling.

Residual objects are created in the course of making the performance and during the repeated performances. The performance is the main thing but when it is over there are a number of subordinate pieces which may be isolated, souvenirs, residual objects.

To pick up after a performance to be very careful about what is to be discarded and what still survives by itself. Slow study & respect for small things. Ones own created "found objects." The floor of the stage like the street. Picking up after is creative. Also their particular life must be respected. Where they had their place, each area of activity combed separately and with respect for where it begins & ends.

(1962)

70. Freighter and Sailboat, *1962.*
Muslin filled with shredded foam rubber,
painted with spray enamel; freighter:
70 ¹¹⁄₁₆ x 19 ¹¹⁄₁₆ x 5 ⁷⁄₁₆ inches (179.5 x 50 x
15 cm); sailboat: 45 ¹⁄₁₆ x 28 ¹¹⁄₁₆ x 5 ⁷⁄₁₆ inches
(114.5 x 73.5 x 13.5 cm). Solomon R.
Guggenheim Museum, New York,
Gift of Claes Oldenburg and Coosje
van Bruggen, 1991.

72. Floor Cake, *1962. Canvas filled with foam rubber and cardboard boxes, painted with synthetic polymer paint and latex, 58⅛ x 114¼ x 58⅛ inches (148.2 x 290.2 x 148.2 cm). The Museum of Modern Art, New York, Gift of Philip Johnson, 1975.*

73. Floor Burger, 1962. Canvas filled with foam rubber and cardboard boxes, painted with latex and Liquitex, 52 inches (132.1 cm) high; 84 inches (213.4 cm) in diameter. Art Gallery of Ontario, Toronto, Purchase, 1967.

74. Floor Cone, *1962. Canvas filled with foam rubber and cardboard boxes, painted with synthetic polymer paint and latex, 53¼ inches x 11 feet 4 inches x 56 inches (136.5 x 345.4 x 142.2 cm). The Museum of Modern Art, New York, Gift of Philip Johnson, 1981.*

pages 150–51:
75. *Installation view of solo exhibition at the Green Gallery, New York, September 24–October 20, 1962.*

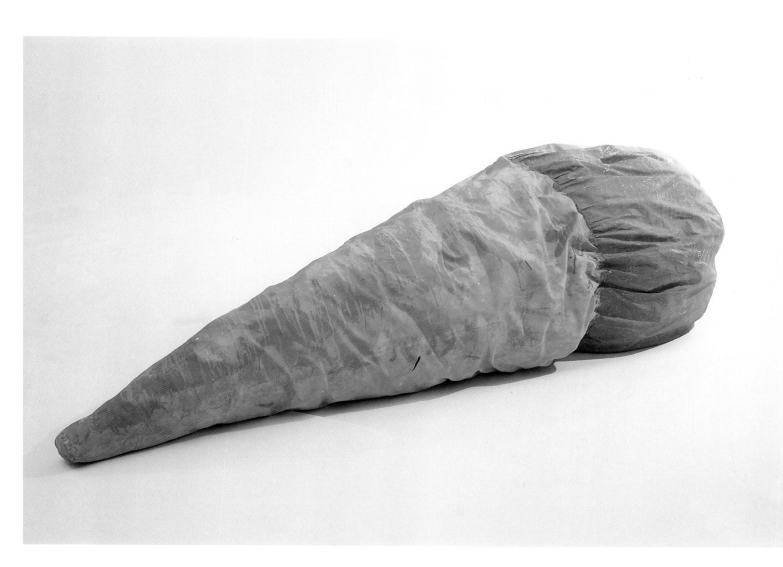

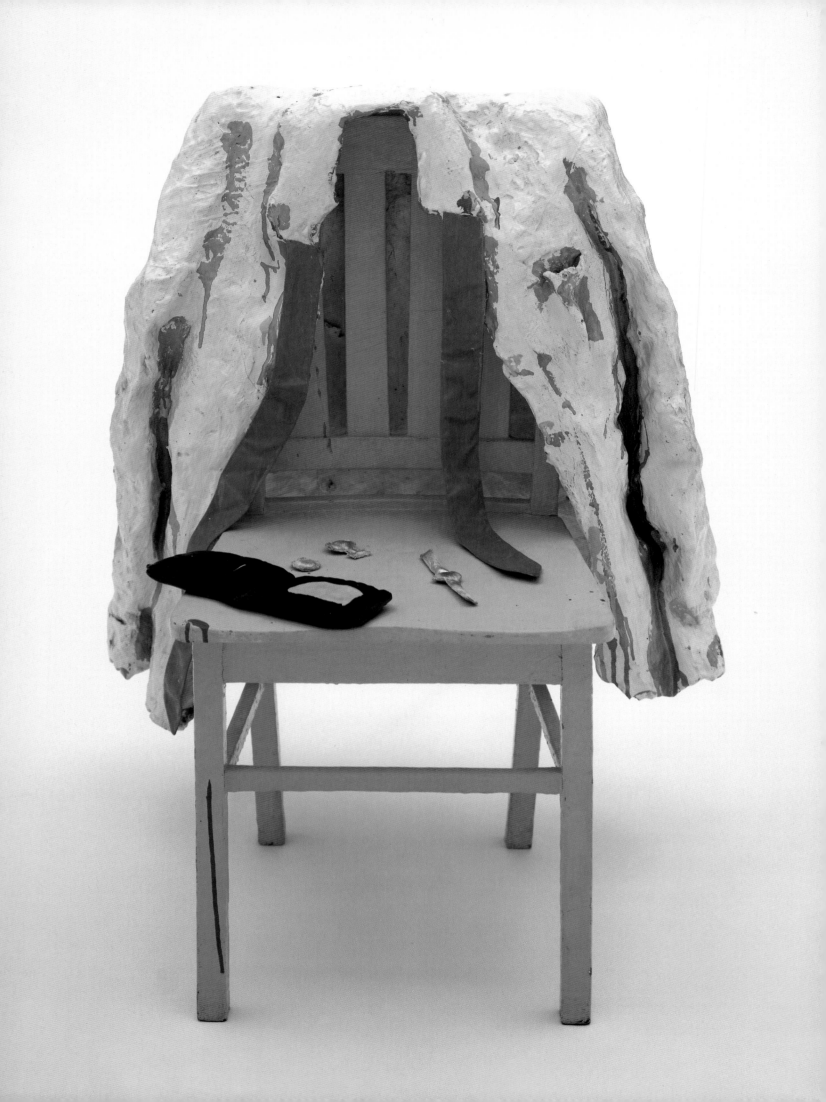

facing page:
76. Shirt with Objects on Chair, 1962. Muslin soaked in plaster over wire frame, painted with enamel, on wood chair, 39¼ x 30 x 25¼ inches (101 x 76.2 x 64.1 cm). The Museum of Contemporary Art, Los Angeles, The Panza Collection.

77. Blue Pants and Pocket Objects on Chair, 1962. Muslin soaked in plaster over wire frame, painted with enamel, on wood chair, 37 x 17 x 26¾ inches (94 x 43.2 x 68 cm). The Museum of Contemporary Art, Los Angeles, The Panza Collection.

The fact that the store represents American popular art is only an accident, an accident of my surroundings, my landscape, of the objects which in my daily coming and going my consciousness attaches itself to. An art of ideas is a bore and a sentimentality, whether witty or serious or what. I may have things to say about US and many other matters, but in my art I am concerned with perception of reality and composition. Which is the only way that art can really be useful--by setting an example of how to use the senses.--

I know that down to the last simple detail experience is totally mysterious. The only person I know that tried to prove the simplest thing in the world, like a piece of candy, was utterly mysterious was Chirico (in his early days). But I guess it's what every still-life ptr worth anything tried to show too. With me of c. well I am living in the city, a particular city, in a different time, and my subjects are as apt to be depictions of the real thing as the real things (even real pie these days does not taste like pie). Still, what I want to do more than anything is to create things just as mysterious as nature.

(1961)

81. Giant Ice-Cream Cone, *1962.*
Muslin soaked in plaster over wire frame,
painted with enamel, 13 ⅜ x 37 ½ x
13 ¼ inches (34 x 95.3 x 33.7 cm).
Sonnabend Collection.

82. Battleship: Centerpiece for a Party,
*1962. Muslin soaked in plaster over
wire frame with nails, painted with
enamel, 17 x 35⅛ x 18¼ inches (43.2 x
89.9 x 46.4 cm). Collection of Frederick W.
Hughes.*

pages 164–67:
*86. Sports, performance at Green Gallery,
New York, October 5, 1962.*

below and facing page:
*87. Prop before and during performance of
Sports, 1962. Bicycle and plastic bags
filled with shredded foam rubber, painted
with spray enamel. Destroyed.*

The "lingerie" is made from rags, plaster and enamel; the "brassieres" for example, are made of shirt sleeves, stiffened with glue before painting. The angling of the base and the use of formica is the first statement of a treatment repeated in the Bedroom Ensemble of 1963-64. As such, the Lingerie Counter is a transitional work between the Store and Home periods, with a little bit of each.

(1972)

1963-1964

New York City
Venice, California
Paris

The Home
Bedroom Ensemble
Paris Store

Autobodys (Los Angeles)

LA is many things and many things to many
people. To me it is the paradise of
industrialism. LA has the atmosphere (my
selected part of it) of the consumer, of
the home, the elegant neat result, like the
frankfurter in its nonremembered distance
from the slaughterhouse. In New York, in
Brooklyn, I see all the degradation and
slavery and terror of production as
contrasted with the floating and very
finished product on TV. Alternating dreams
and alternating themes to me are the
circumstances under which a thing is made
vs. the end product (and its circumstances
of presentation). I was attracted that is
seduced by and drawn to the Ice Age, as an
antidote to the verminous rotten but living
deaths of New York. My problem and that of
others I think is the love of mechanism
even as one flips around in the next moment
and denies it.

(1966)

89. Poster for Autobodys, 1963. Four-color
offset lithograph printed on cardboard,
22 x 14 inches (55.9 x 36 cm). Collection of
Claes Oldenburg and Coosje van Bruggen,
New York.

pages 176–81:
90. Autobodys, performance in
parking lot of American Institute of
Aeronautics and Astronautics,
Los Angeles, December 9–10, 1963.

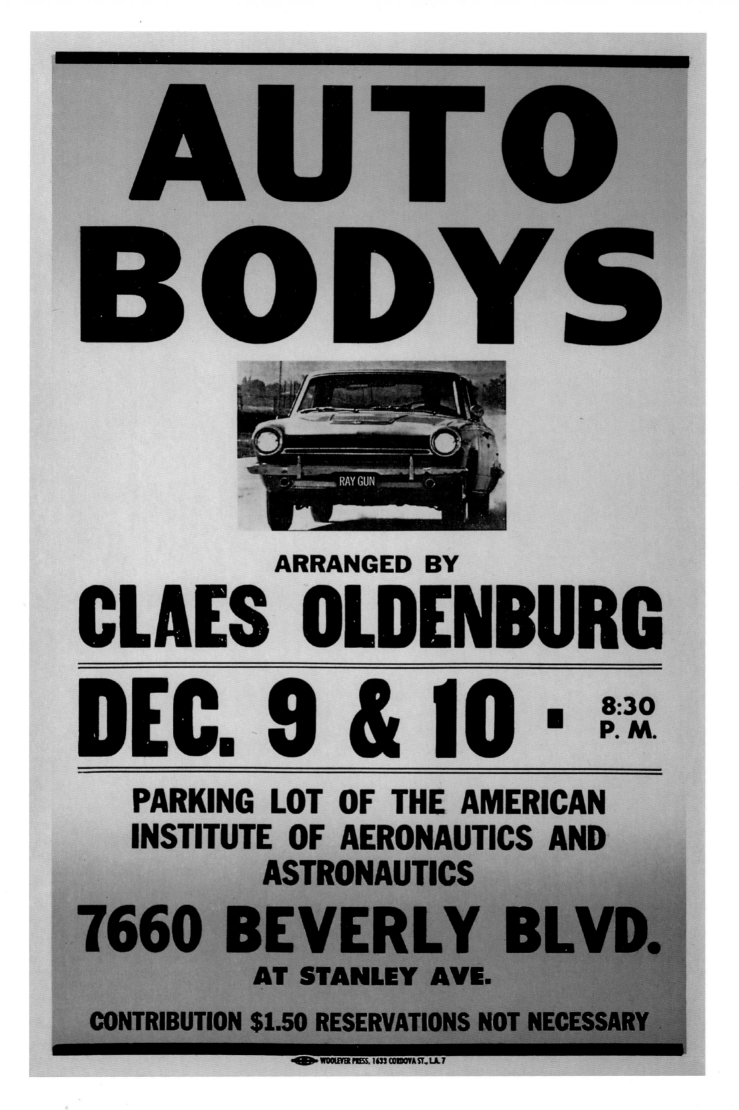

91. Giant Blue Shirt with Brown Tie,
photographed in Los Angeles in 1963 by
Dennis Hopper.

I have found myself the last two years or
so (1963) in a specific perverse relation to
my surroundings...I have combined my
unworldly fantasy in a shock wedding to
banal aspects of everyday existence...so
complete...the thing is likely to burst
either way, as it has arrived at a point
where the cohabitation is no longer
possible...either into banality or the
other way into poetry...

(1966)

93. Soft Fur Good Humors, *1963.*
Fake fur filled with kapok; and wood
painted with enamel; four units,
2 x 9⅕ x 19 inches (5.1 x 24.1 x 48.3 cm)
each. Mitchell C. Shaheen, The Brett
Mitchell Collection, Inc.

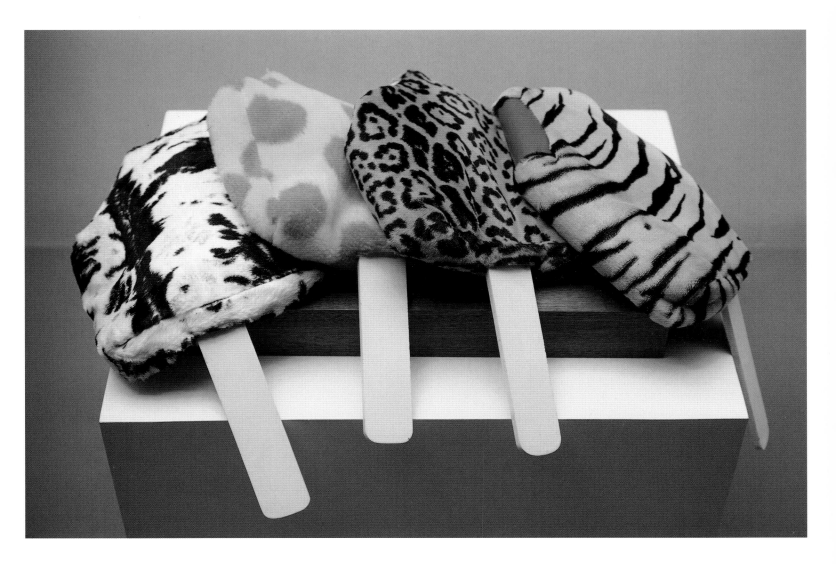

94. Baked Potato I, *1963. Burlap soaked*
in plaster over wire frame, painted
with enamel; and jersey filled with kapok;
14 x 24 x 14 inches (35.6 x 61 x 35.6 cm).
Collection of Robert H. Halff,
Promised gift to the Los Angeles County
Museum of Art.

95. Hamburger with Pickle and Tomato
Attached, *1963. Muslin soaked in plaster
over wire frame, painted with enamel,
6 inches (15.2 cm) high, 7 inches (17.8 cm)
in diameter. Collection of Carroll Janis,
New York.*

96. Giant BLT (Bacon, Lettuce and Tomato Sandwich), *1963. Vinyl filled with kapok; and wood painted with acrylic; 32 x 39 x 29 inches (81.3 x 99.1 x 73.7 cm). Collection of Maria and Conrad Janis, Beverly Hills.*

The cloth work is decidedly "sculptural,"
by which I mean that it emphasizes masses,
simple and articulated. It de-emphasizes
color. What the period of "sculptural"
painting has left is the fluidity of the
surface, which in these works is actual
because they are sculpture: the unillusory,
tangible realm. The dynamic element here is
flaccidity, where in the paint it was the
paint action and the sparkle of light--that
is, the tendency of a hard material
actually to be soft, not look soft (so it
is a concretization of a naive translation
of painting).

(1963)

97. Giant Toothpaste Tube, 1964.
Vinyl and canvas filled with kapok; and
wood and metal, painted with enamel;
25½ x 66 x 17 inches (64.8 x 167.6 x
43.2 cm). Private collection.

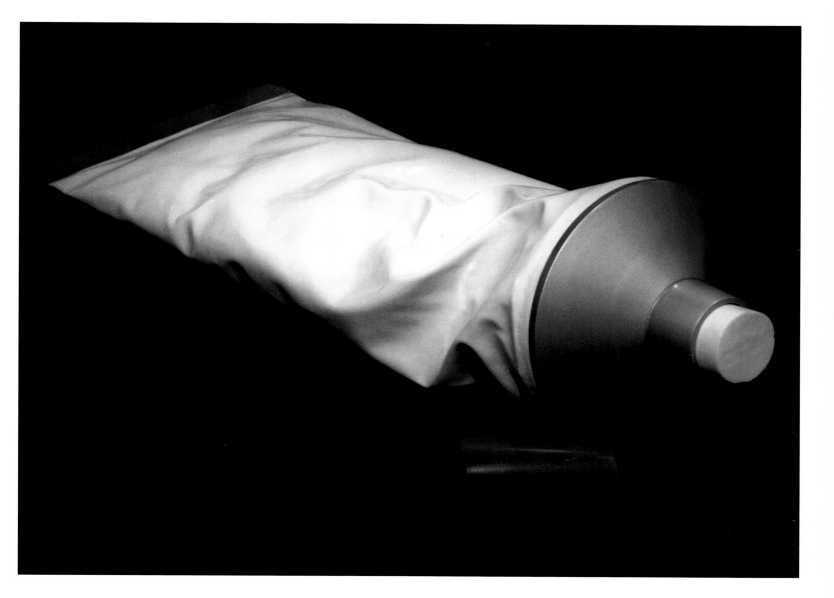

98. Study for a Soft Sculpture in the Form of a Pay-Telephone, *1963.* *Watercolor on newspaper, 42 x 28 inches (106.7 x 71.1 cm). Private collection.*

99. Soft Pay-Telephone – Ghost Version, *1963. Muslin filled with kapok, painted with acrylic, mounted on wood, 49⅛ x 22⅛ x 11¾ inches (124.8 x 56.2 x 29.9 cm). Collection of Kimiko and John Powers.*

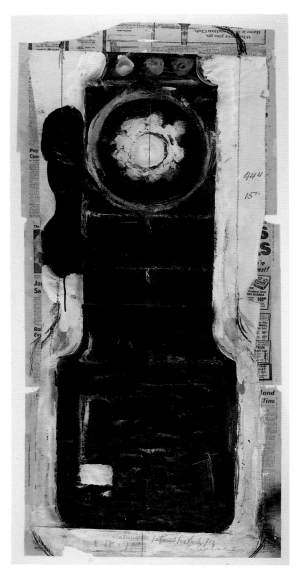

100. Soft Pay-Telephone, *1963. Vinyl filled with kapok, mounted on painted wood, 46⅛ x 19 x 9 inches (118.2 x 48.3 x 22.8 cm). Solomon R. Guggenheim Museum, New York, Gift of Ruth and Philip Zierler in memory of their dear departed son, William S. Zierler, 1980.*

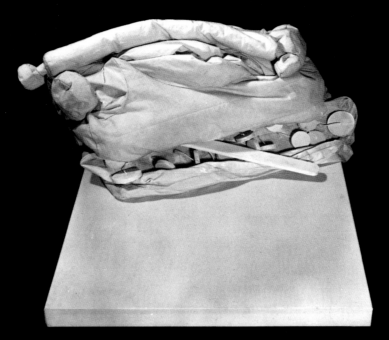

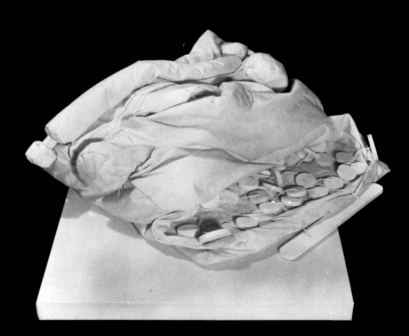

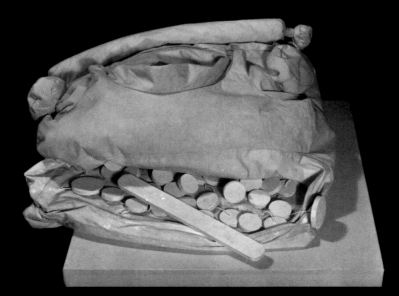

101. Soft Typewriter – Ghost Version,
1963. Three views. Canvas filled with
kapok, painted with acrylic, on wood base,
9 x 27½ x 28⅜ inches (23 x 70 x 72 cm).
Museum für Moderne Kunst, Frankfurt.

102. Soft Typewriter, 1963. Vinyl filled
with kapok; Plexiglas; and nylon cord;
9 x 26 x 27½ inches (22.9 x 66 x 69.9 cm).
Private collection.

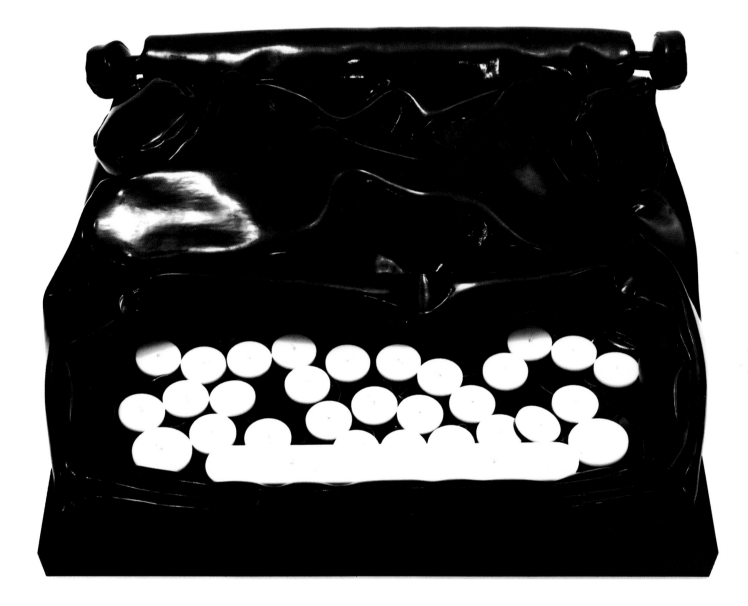

103. Study for a Sculpture in the Form of a Vacuum Cleaner – From Side, *1964. Chalk, ink, and watercolor on paper, 40 x 26 inches (101.6 x 66 cm). Private Collection.*

104. Vacuum Cleaner, *1971. Aluminum, vinyl, plastic, rubber, lightbulb, and cord, 64 x 29 x 29 inches (162.6 x 73.7 x 73.7 cm). Collection of Claes Oldenburg and Coosje van Bruggen, New York.*

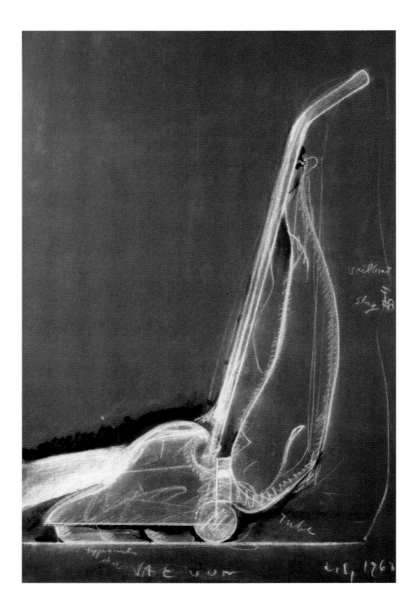

105. Electric Outlet – Hard Model, *1964.*
Cardboard, pen, ink, pencil, and spray
enamel, 48 x 29 x 5 inches (122 x 73.7 x
12.7 cm). Collection of Arne and Milly
Glimcher.

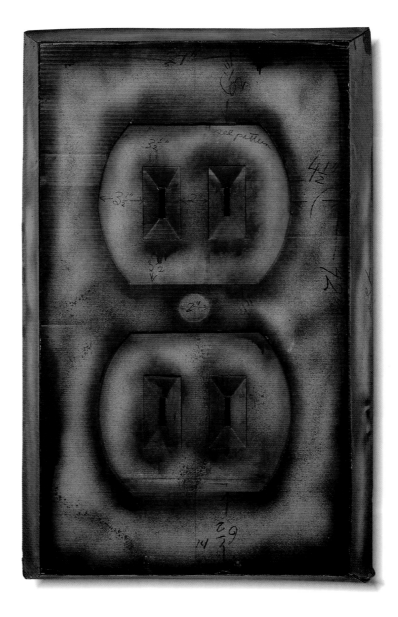

106. Light Switches – Hard Version,
1964. Painted wood and metal, 47¼ x
47¼ x 11¾ inches (121.3 x 121.3 x 29.9 cm).
Collection of Dr. Alice Kahn Ladas.

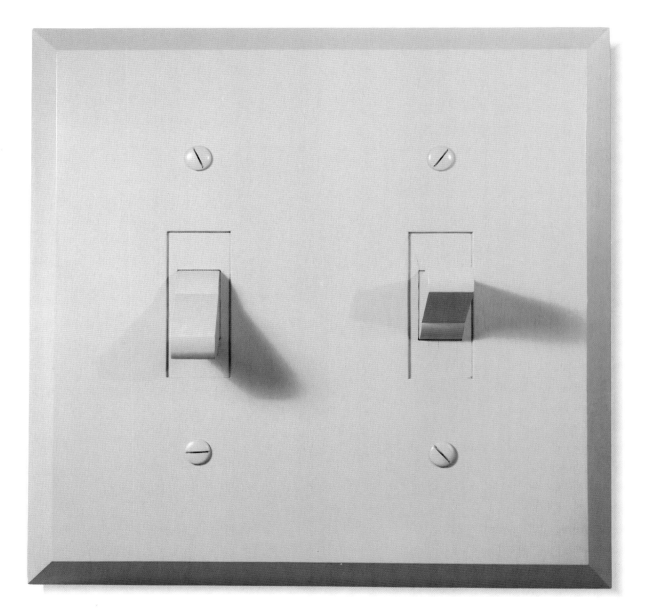

107. Soft Light Switches – Ghost
Version, *1971 version of a 1964 original.
Canvas filled with kapok; gesso; and
pencil; 47 x 47 x 12 inches (121.9 x
121.9 x 30.5 cm). Collection of Claes
Oldenburg and Coosje van Bruggen,
New York, On loan to the Museum für
Moderne Kunst, Frankfurt.*

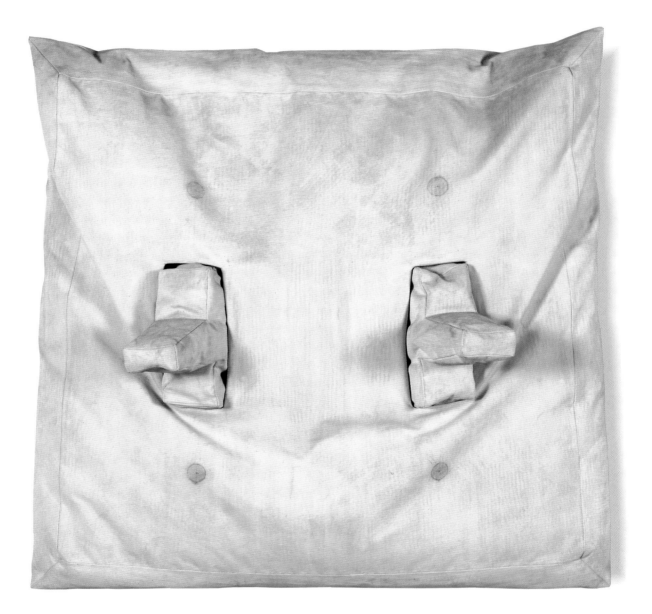

108. Soft Switches, 1964. Vinyl
filled with dacron and canvas,
47 x 47 x 3⅝ inches (119.4 x 119.4 x
9.1 cm). The Nelson-Atkins Museum
of Art, Kansas City, Missouri,
Gift of the Chapin Family in memory of
Susan Chapin Buckwalter 65-29.

Geometry, abstraction, rationality - these are the themes that are expressed formally in Bedroom. The effect is intensified by choosing the softest room in the house and the one least associated with conscious thought. The previous work had been self-indulgent and full of color, the new work was limited to black and white, blue and silver. Hard surfaces and sharp corners predominate. Texture becomes photographed texture in the surface of the formica. Noting "real" or "human." A landscape like that on the cover of my old geometry books, the one that shows the Pyramids of Egypt and bears the slogan "There is no royal road to geometry." All styles on the side of Death. The Bedroom as rational tomb, pharaoh's or Plato's bedroom...

Bedroom marked for me (and perhaps others) a turning point of taste. It aligned me (perhaps) with artists who up to then had been thought to be my opposites. But the change of taste was passed through the mechanism of my attitude, which among other rules, insists on referring to things--by imitating them, altering them and naming them.

Bedroom might have been called composition for (rhomboids) columns and disks. Using names for things may underline the "abstract" nature of the subject or all the emphasis can do this. Subject matter is not necessarily an obstacle to seeing "pure" form and color. Since I am committed to openness, my works are constructed to perform in as many ways as anyone wants them to. As time goes on and the things they "represent" vanish from daily use, their purely formal character will be more evident: Time will undress them. Meanwhile they are sticky with associations, and that is presumably why my Bedroom, my little gray geometric home in the West is two-stepping with Edward Hopper. To complete the story I should mention that the Bedroom is based on a famous motel along the shore road to Malibu, "Las Tunas Isles," in which (when I visited it in 1947) each suite was decorated in the skin of a particular animal, i.e. tiger, leopard, zebra. My imagination exaggerates but I like remembering it that way: each object in the room consistently animal.

(1976)

109. Study for a Poster for "4 Environments," Sidney Janis Gallery – THE HOME, *1963.* *Crayon and watercolor on paper,* *24 x 18 inches (61 x 45.7 cm).* *Collection of Kimiko and John Powers.*

111. Miniature Models of Furniture,
1963. Cardboard, cloth, paper, wood, spray
enamel, and acrylic paint; dimensions and
locations unknown.

pages 208–09:
112. Bedroom Ensemble, Replica I, 1969
version of a 1963 original. Wood, vinyl,
metal, fake fur, muslin, dacron,
polyurethane foam, and lacquer,
approximately 17 x 21 feet (5.18 x 6.4 m)
overall. Museum für Moderne Kunst,
Frankfurt.

114. Viandes (Meats), *1964. Plaster cast in canvas forms, painted with tempera, with porcelain plates, on marble-top base, 37 x 37 x 16 inches (94 x 94 x 41 cm). Museum Boymans-van Beuningen, Rotterdam, On long-term loan from a private collection.*

1965-1968

New York City
Stockholm
London
Chicago

Soft Sculptures: Bathroom;
Airflow; Drum Set; Juicit;
Blender; Fans; et al.

Proposed Colossal Monuments

Washes; Moveyhouse; Massage
(Stockholm)

Plan for the use of the Airflow subject:
1) Make original drawing, using photographs
of actual car.
2) Make photostat or drawing and double it
five times, resulting in six scales or modes
from which stencils may be taken and
sketches constructed.
3) Use each model differently. For example:
model 2 cut across, in half, insides
spilling out. Model 3, cut lengthwise.
Model 4, sealed, insides not visible. Model
5, insides only.

Stimulation by visit January 1966 to
original Airflow (1936) in garage of its
inventor, Carl Breer, in Detroit, where
photos were taken and drawing made of
details, interior and exterior, and actual
experience, with color texture etc.
obtained

The Airflow is imagined as a place with many
different sized object inside it, like a
gallery, a butcher shop, like The Store--
and could be just as inexhaustible a
subject.

Science/fiction. Auto-eroticism. I am a
technological liar.

(1966)

pages 214–15:
115. Oldenburg in his studio, 404 East
Fourteenth Street, New York, 1965.

116. Profile Study of the Airflow, *1965.*
Collage, pencil, and watercolor on paper,
22 x 29¼ inches (55.9 x 75.6 cm). Location
unknown.

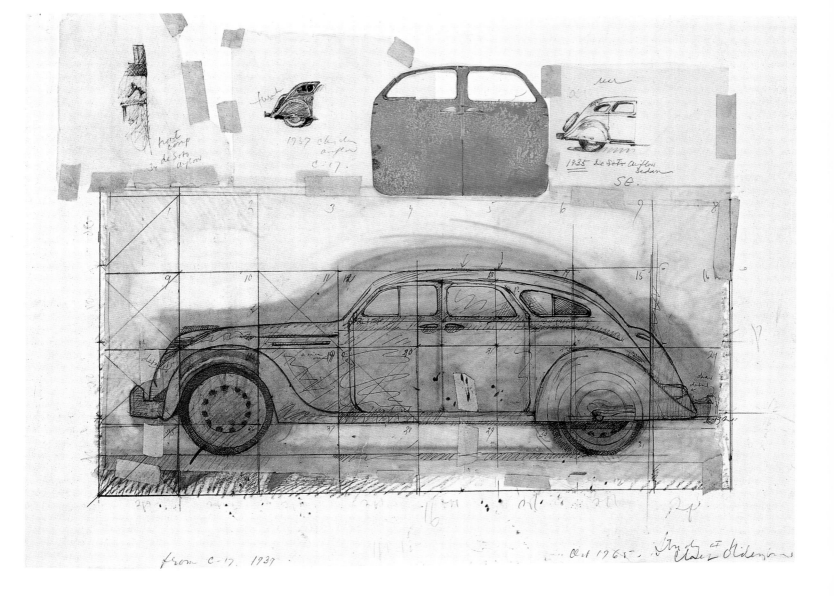

119. Soft Airflow, Scale 2 (Model), *1965.*
Canvas filled with kapok, patterned with
spray enamel; and wood; 42¼ x 25¼ x
13 inches (107.3 x 65.4 x 33 cm). Collection
of Anne and William J. Hokin, Chicago.

120. Soft Engine Parts #1, Air Flow
Model #6 (Radiator and Fan), *1965.*
Canvas filled with kapok, patterned with
spray enamel, 32 x 24 x 18 inches
(81.3 x 61 x 45.7 cm). Location unknown.

Every time I start a show I start as if I
never made a show before and absolutely
from nothing. I don't know if this is good
or bad. Whether this just means that you
repeat your mistakes or whether this is a
very good way of saving your innocence.
Because it is very important to approach a
show without really knowing what's going to
happen. And just to have the confidence that
it will happen, this is the way that I
approach the Happenings too. I, I think
it's terrifying to do it this way, but it's
always a great pleasure if it works. And it
hasn't failed entirely so far. There have
been some things that have been
disappointing. Some things I haven't been
able to bring off. But on the whole I've
met my obligations or my deadlines.

Last summer I went through two months of
what you might call inspiring myself or
priming myself by reading and buying
magazines and walking the streets of New
York and I even took off forty pounds. I
gave up smoking. I did all kinds of things
to myself to get myself stimulated or
started in some direction. And then, I went
through my notes which is always a good
stimulation--the notes from the past. There
are many pieces that I've been intending to
make, but I never get around to making. And
finally I sat down and made a list of about
fifty things I would like to make--just what
came into my mind as a result of this self-
priming. Some of those things were actually
made. But there's such a gap between
thinking of a thing and actually making it;
there's so much labour involved in carrying
a thing from the original idea to the
finished object. And a lot of these things
were a lovely idea, and I think I went
around and told people I was going to do it,
and it sounded great but I wasn't able to
make them happen in the short time that I
had. But they may happen, say, next year or
two years from now, or three years from now.

I make the list and then I start on the
list. The Bathroom happened to be something
I started in California in '63, but I was
never able to solve the toilet because I
never could find an example of the toilet,
the kind of toilet that I wanted to use.
There are so many toilets. And I also
couldn't solve the problem of the bowl
because I hadn't found styrofoam and I
wasn't able to carve this bowl in any
medium. I just didn't get around to it. So
that was hanging over from a previous time,
that was one of the things on the list--the
Bathroom. Besides, that was consistent with
my desire to continue to make the house.

Then I got involved also with the
automobile. I don't exactly know why I got
involved with the automobile. This was a
new theme, and probably has some very deep
reasons why, that I can't put my hands on

(continued on page 226)

(*continued from page 223*)

at the moment and then suddenly the
"Airflow", which was Bob Breer's father's
creation, floated into view and everything
came together in that area.

Gradually as I go along the list gets
shorter. I knock out things that don't seem
to be particularly important or that can be
saved for later or that seem just plain
silly, and the list gets shorter and
shorter and shorter and more and more
realistic. Everything progresses from the
wildest dreams to what can actually be done;
and it's surprising how little one can do
really, when you get down to it. But, it's
enough. I found that I had more than enough
for this show. And as a residue from
thinking about all the things I can do, I
have maybe a hundred ideas here for future
shows, which I don't know if I'll ever get
around to. It accumulates. There's an awful
lot of paper lying around this studio;
awful lot of sketches that will never be
realized. But, all you care about is that
out of all of this stuff, maybe there
should be fifty good ideas, because you can
really work a lifetime on <u>one</u> good idea.

When I develop a show everything usually
hangs together. After a while...one form
leads to another form and there's a kind of
consistency in the forms. There may be two
or three forms that dominate the show in
different guises. I started to work last
summer on a poster for the <u>Paris Review</u>
which took the form of a mattress, or the
corner of a mattress. And this corner of a
mattress, I think, led directly to an
absorption in the island of Manhattan,
which not only looks somewhat like this
mattress, but also by the words 'Manhattan'
suggest mattress. You could think of saying
<u>manhatress</u> for example. And <u>manhatta</u> and
<u>hatterass</u>. The resemblance between the
mattress and Manhattan then went on to
become a resemblance between Manhattan
Island and the engine, the Airflow engine.
So there's a kind of consistency in form
and you could say every show has two or
three themes with variations on themes. I
find it helpful to work that way. I strive
for a consistency which is something that's
almost never noticed by a reviewer. It's
noticed I suppose by people who see the
show. But no one ever mentions that the
show itself is a composition, like the
'happening' is a composition. We were
talking about "Moveyhouse" which was a
composition really for discs, for fans, for
the wheels of the movie camera, and the
ears of the Mickey Mouse. There are some
arcs along the side of the theatre, and
then everyone carried a circular fan, so
that there was this constant movement of
discs in the air.

(1966)

123. The Bathroom Group in a Garden
Setting, *1965. Crayon, pencil, and*
watercolor on paper, 26 x 40 inches (66 x
101.6 cm). Moderna Museet, Stockholm.

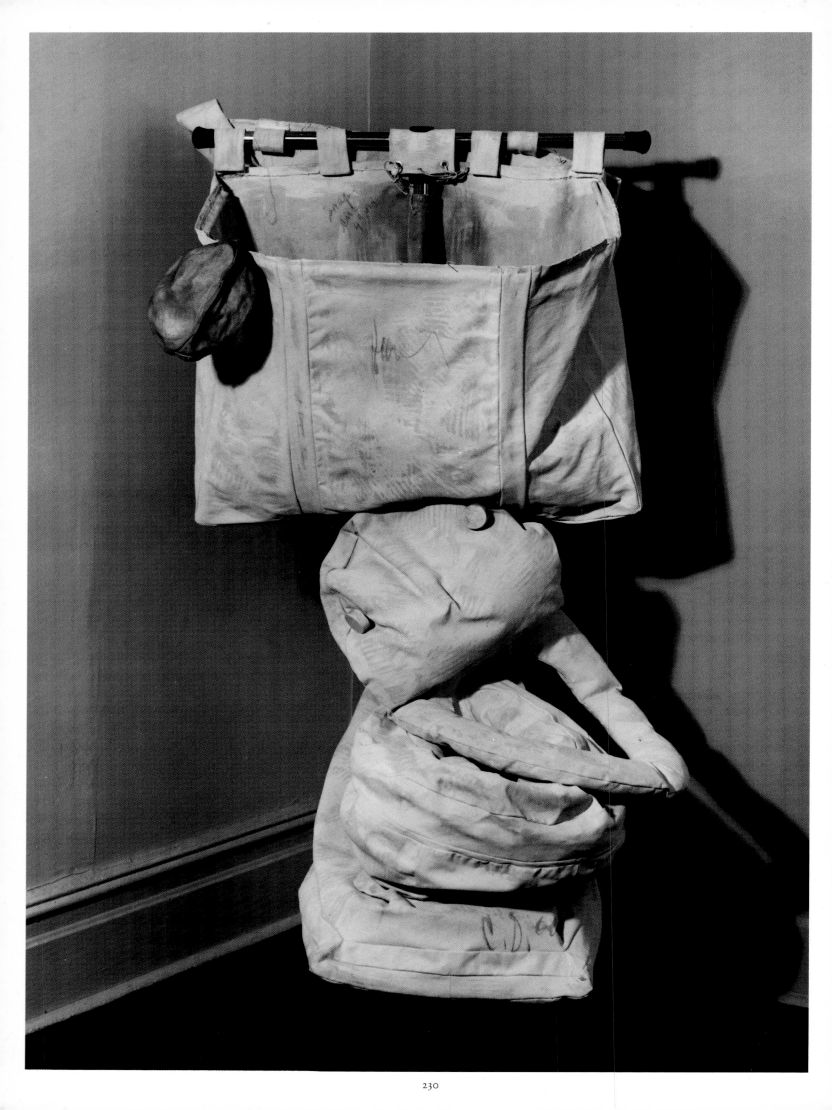

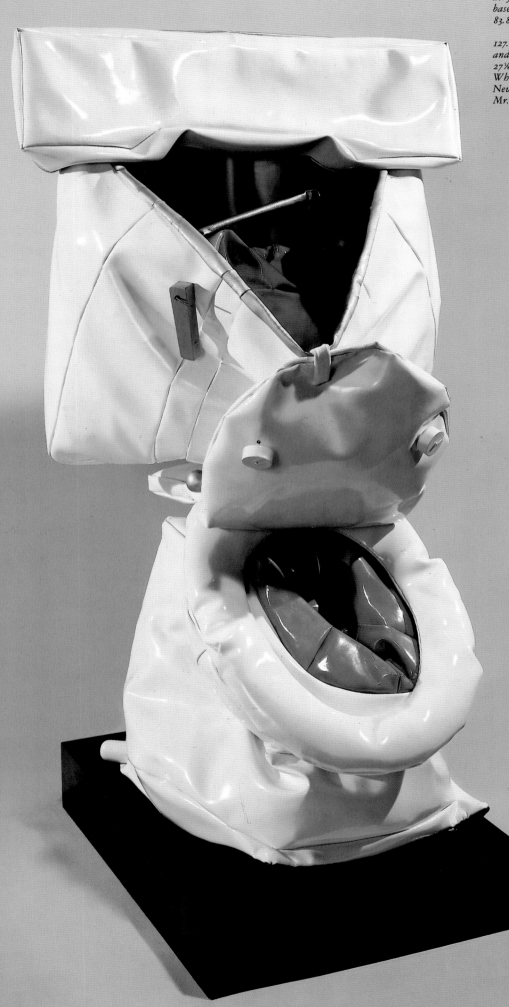

facing page:
126. Soft Toilet – Ghost Version, *1966.*
Canvas filled with kapok, painted with
acrylic, on metal stand and painted wood
base; toilet: 51 x 33 x 28 inches (129.5 x
83.8 x 71.1 cm). Private collection.

127. Soft Toilet, *1966. Vinyl, Plexiglas,*
and kapok on painted wood base, 57 1/16 x
27 7/8 x 28 1/16 inches (144.9 x 70.2 x 71.3 cm).
Whitney Museum of American Art,
New York, Fiftieth Anniversary Gift of
Mr. and Mrs. Victor W. Ganz.

facing page:
128. Bathtub – Hard Model, 1966.
Enamel, spray enamel, and felt pen on
cardboard; and wood; 81 x 33¼ x 28 inches
(205.7 x 84.4 x 71.1 cm). Museum Ludwig,
Cologne, Ludwig Donation.

129. Bathtub (Model) – Ghost Version,
1966. Canvas filled with kapok, painted
with acrylic; and wood; 80 x 30 x 30 inches
(203.2 x 76.2 x 76.2 cm). Location
unknown.

page 234:
130. Washstand – Hard Model, 1965–66.
Enamel, spray enamel, and felt pen on
cardboard; and wood; 48⅜ x 36 x
29⅜ inches (123 x 91.5 x 74.5 cm). Museum
für Moderne Kunst, Frankfurt.

page 235:
131. Soft Washstand, 1966. Vinyl filled
with kapok, on metal stand painted with
acrylic, 55 x 36 x 28 inches (139.7 x 91.4 x
71.1 cm). Museum Boymans-van
Beuningen, Rotterdam. On long-term loan
from a private collection.

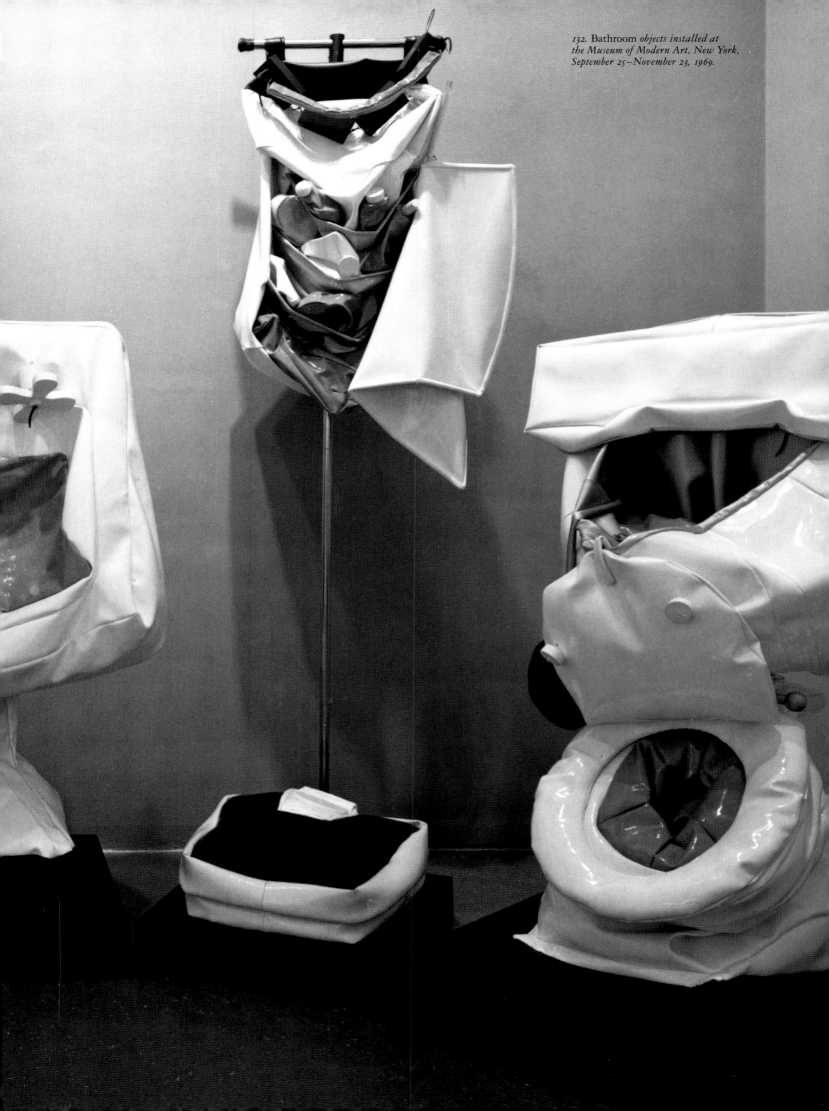

132. Bathroom *objects installed at
the Museum of Modern Art, New York,
September 25–November 23, 1969.*

My softening is not a blurring (like the
effect of atmosphere on hard forms) but <u>in
fact</u> a softening, in a clear strong light.
<u>A perception of mechanical nature as body</u>.

(1965-66)

133. Notebook Page: Dormeyer Mixer,
*1965. Ink and collage on paper, 10⅝ x
8 inches (27 x 20.3 cm). Collection of
Claes Oldenburg and Coosje van Bruggen,
New York.*

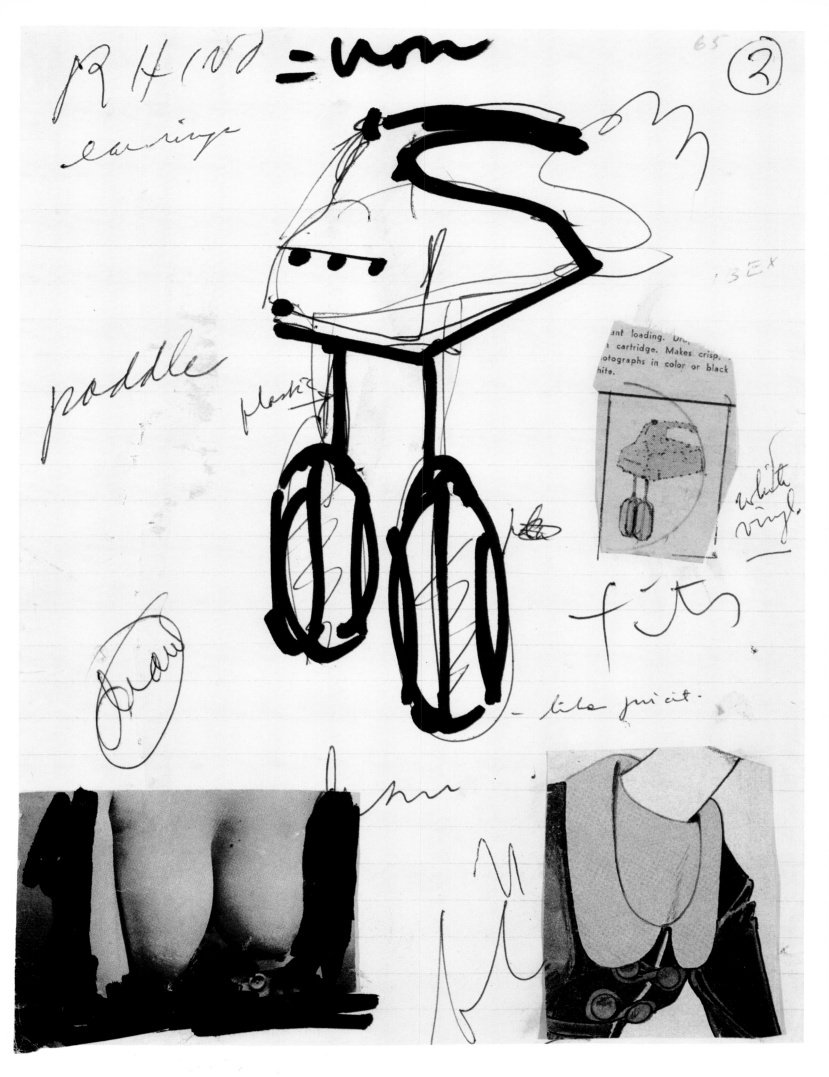

135. Giant Soft Ketchup Bottle with Ketchup, *1966–67. Canvas filled with polyurethane foam, painted, 100 x 52 x 40 inches (254 x 132.1 x 101.6 cm). Norton Simon Museum, Pasadena, California, purchased with funds granted by the National Endowment for the Arts, matched by the Pasadena Art Alliance, 1969.*

136. Shoestring Potatoes Spilling from a Bag, 1966. Canvas stiffened with glue, filled with kapok, painted with acrylic, 108 x 46 x 42 inches (274.3 x 116.8 x 106.7 cm). Walker Art Center, Minneapolis, Gift of the T. B. Walker Foundation, 1966.

137. Soft Ladder, Hammer, Saw, and Bucket, 1967. Canvas stiffened with glue, filled with polyurethane foam, painted with acrylic; and wood; 94 x 54 x 24 inches (238.8 x 137.2 x 61 cm). Stedelijk Museum, Amsterdam.

138. Soft Manhattan #1 (Postal Zones),
*1966. Canvas filled with kapok, patterned
with spray enamel, 70 x 26 x 4 inches
(177.8 x 66 x 10.2 cm). Albright-Knox Art
Gallery, Buffalo, New York, Gift of
Seymour H. Knox, 1966.*

139. Soft Manhattan #2 (Tactile Form
of the New York Subway Map), *1966.
Canvas filled with kapok, patterned with
spray enamel; and wood; 68 x 32 x 7 inches
(172.7 x 81.3 x 17.8 cm). Collection of
Mr. and Mrs. S. I. Newhouse, Jr.*

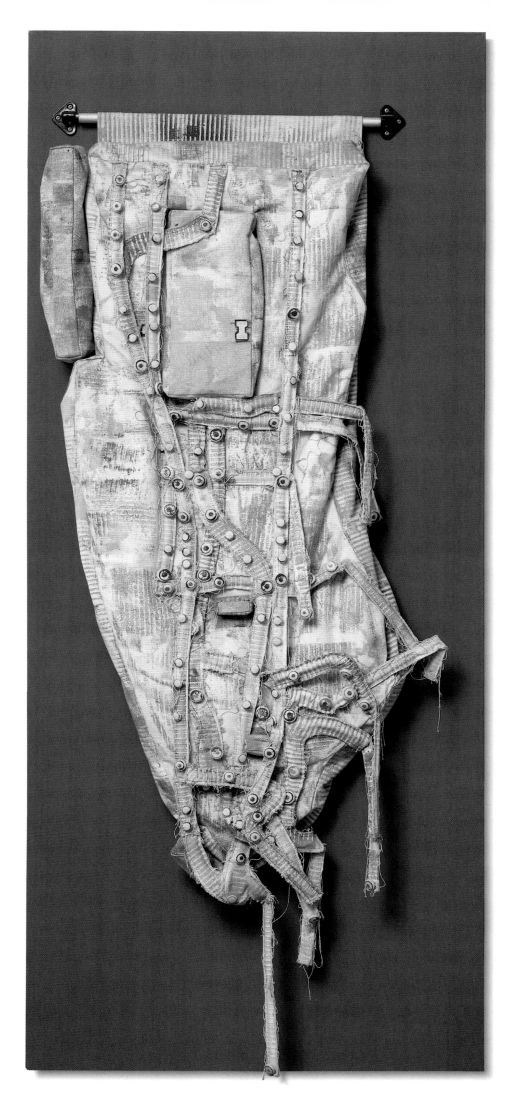

I wanted to do a piece in a swimming pool and the title suggested itself--"Washes." Then the problem was to find a swimming pool and to get the thing in motion. It took a long time to find a swimming pool. Finally Alan Solomon located the pool of Al Roon's Health Club, and that became a reality. I enrolled for classes there, and I went there and I laid around the pool, I swam, I tried all the services, I was massaged, and all the time I was just studying the possibilities of the place for a happening.

I did a lot more writing and a lot more feeling in the pool, sitting around and taking it in. And the next step is people for the happening. Like the place, they suggest very much what's going to happen. There are usually many volunteers, and I don't turn anyone down, which gets me into trouble because my cast are usually too large.

My procedure is that I meet the people one night, then the second night I invent things for them to do, and the third night I kind of cut away the things that didn't work the second night, and on the fourth night I have a run-through of the things that did work, and then comes the final piece.

It was really a color piece; it was a painting-type piece. Many of my pieces are more like dance or more like theatre, but this was a piece in which the visual was very important, like a painting. The most important element was the green water. And 'Washes' of course was reference to 'water colors.' So everything that was done was done mostly for a color effect, though there was a dance element, and the dance was shaped by the obstacle of the water-- you can only move so fast in the water. It creates a certain kind of dance. Just as in "Moveyhouse" the way you can walk across seats carrying a bike creates another kind of dance.

The best way to have seen this happening would have been from above, because the pool became equal in my mind to a canvas: a large rectangular canvas into which I could place one thing after another until I had an enormous panorama of things floating in the pool. It started with the pool absolutely still; just green water, and a little red light floating in the middle of it. Then gradually there was more and more and more matter introduced into the pool. At the end it was very full of people and of objects--there was a chair floating around, and there were pieces of clothing floating around, and newspapers--it was like Coney Island beach or a flood, and lots of color.

(1966)

"Unbridled" Monuments; or, How Claes Oldenburg Set Out to Change the World

Mark Rosenthal

I want these pieces to have an unbridled intense satanic vulgarity unsurpassable, and yet be art.[1]

Long before Claes Oldenburg attempted to reformulate the monument tradition, he conceived one of the central premises of his art. He wanted work that was at once crudely provocative, even as it maintained an identity as art. Oldenburg's statement above was made specifically in reference to *The Store* (1961, pages 105–27), a work in which the artist filled a storefront on the Lower East Side of New York with sculptures of often oversize consumer products of all kinds. He described the impetus for this installation as founded partly on the desire to build "monuments" to everyday things, which would be located in places not typically thought of as cultural.[2] His point was to make the banal into something physically imposing, as well as, possibly, beautiful.[3] As an early expression of the Pop outlook, Oldenburg's *Store* launched a process of both monumentalizing by enlarging, and making monuments—one might say follies—to the modern American experience. In effect, he was turning a serious tradition into a vehicle of antic play.

Although known throughout his career as a sculptor and a draftsman, Oldenburg has perhaps most effectively realized his aspiration as a provocateur in the arena of the monument, confounding expectations associated with the tradition and offering a new interpretation of one of the oldest and most recognizable artistic conventions. Oldenburg's first statement about public sculpture, in 1960,[4] was placed in a bit of fictional dialogue in which a certain dignitary cynically makes clear that "civic improvement" requires "bulls and greeks and lots of nekkid broads."[5] The artist himself would certainly agree that the monument is an aspect of the urban landscape, in which human activity predominates,[6] but rather than the usual assortment of subjects—men in uniform and on horseback— he wanted a more authentic version of what he called "city nature." Distinct from the natural landscape, city nature, which inspired *The Store* as well as *The Street* (1960, pages 44–59), places an emphasis on "everyday crap."[7] Reinventing the convention, the artist created the personage called Street Chick, an example of his "City Venus,"[8] who epitomizes Oldenburg's dreams of (perverse) beauty, much as earlier female figures served their makers and viewers.

The city that so fascinated Oldenburg in his early years is replete with a variety of public events, entertainments, and ceremonies. The monument, similarly, has a highly visible position in the life of the urban dweller, especially since most art is concealed within lofty, interior precincts, such as those of a museum. Not surprisingly, then, Oldenburg also enjoyed making or participating in Happenings from early on in his career,[9] for central to his overall vision is, as Coosje van Bruggen describes it, a "sense of theater,"[10] a quality that also distinguishes his work from the discrete nature of painting and sculpture. In 1961, he said:

Painting has been private and lyrical for a long time, especially when true artists are not given large and public commissions. The mural, the environment, the pageant, the masque, the larger spatial, architectural forms are forms of art not without precedent. There comes a time when the artist wants to use these forms and directly involve his audience, directly influence and involve actual experience.[11]

In that same year, Oldenburg expanded his approach to the monument by making a theoretical proposal for the 1964 World's Fair planned for New York. Inspired by the sight of a mothballed fleet of World War II freighters moored on the Hudson River, he proposed creating a reef in the bay near Ellis Island, to be titled *Monument to Immigration*. A "natural" monument in his terms, the reef would cause passing ships to crash and sink.[12] This, his first "obstacle monument,"[13] would cause general disruption and result in a growing mass of debris. For the artist, who was himself an immigrant, *Monument to Immigration* disabuses the idealistic expectations of newcomers; according to him, America proved to be a disappointment for many.[14] With his proposal, Oldenburg carried the idea of the monument, normally one of celebration, into the realm of social criticism.

While working in Washington, D.C. in 1963 on a performance piece entitled *Stars*, Oldenburg was struck by the city's concentration of imposing monuments. In the notes accompanying the performance, he frequently mentions these structures, characterizing them at one point as "sex + power in neoclassic setting."[15] In a crescendo of references, especially to the Washington Monument, he describes his work in that city finally as "ironing MONUMENTS."[16] Besides predicting a future ironing-board monument, this phrase also conveys his desire to flatten conventional notions implicit in the historic tradition, and to institute a new type of practice. His title for a 1965 drawing, *Clinical Study, Toward a Heroic-Erotic Monument in the Academic-Comics Style*, gives a good indication of this rambunctious, burlesque approach. Made during the year of the first proposed colossal monuments, the work epitomizes many of Oldenburg's subsequent edifices that undercut bourgeois pretensions. One of the first of these occurred in 1966, when he "replaced" the statue of Eros in Piccadilly Circus in London with a drill bit (fig. 147). At once a modern, formal alternative and a wonderful object in itself, the drill bit also adds a bit of lewd street humor to contrast with the stereotypical view of the high seriousness of English society.

To countervail the conventional image of a general on horseback, Oldenburg proposed, in the same year, a series of monuments that would speak for usually unheard voices. There would be a monument for lower-ranked soldiers, as well as a "Victims' monument, Indifferent monuments . . . Man-in-the-street monuments and President-just-before-he-goes-to-bed-glass-of-milk-and-pills monuments."[17] While such endeavors, Oldenburg acknowledged at first, were "impossible,"[18] they nevertheless affirmed the value of his fantasy life as well as of the "conceptual" process.[19] The monument, then, was an area in which speculative and playful exploration could occur.

Oldenburg's interpretation of the term "monument" went through a transformation following his initial forays. While he was first attracted by the large scale of such sculptures, he soon discovered and embraced the connotation of a memorial.[20] With the *Bedroom Ensemble* (1963, see fig. 112), he synthesized further meanings: "Bedroom as tomb,"[21] drawing on the traditional conjunction of eros and death while joining both in a memorial/monument structure. But it is typical of Oldenburg to be contradictory and provocative. Recalling the cynical sentiments of his fictional civic leader, he remarked, "I think of a monument as being symbolic and for the people and therefore rhetorical, not honest, not personal."[22] His future monuments would reflect this slightly duplicitous character.

In 1962, inspired by the sight of pianos in a Steinway showroom,[23] Oldenburg began making gigantically scaled objects, including such works as *Floor Cake, Floor Burger*, and

Stars, performance at the Washington Gallery of Modern Art, Washington, D.C., April 24–25, 1963.

Jean-Jacques Lequeu, Southern View
of a Cow's Stable on a Cool Meadow.
*Watercolor, 8 ⁷⁄₁₆ x 11 ⁷⁄₁₆ inches (21.2 x
29 cm). Bibliothèque Nationale de France,
Paris.*

Etienne-Louis Boullée, Newton's
Cenotaph, *1784. Ink and wash, 15 ⁷⁄₁₆ x
25 ⅝ inches (40.2 x 65.3 cm). Bibliothèque
Nationale de France, Paris.*

Pie à la Mode (all 1962, figs. 72, 73, and 83), *Baked Potato I* (1963, fig. 94), and *Shoestring Potatoes Spilling from a Bag* (1966, fig. 136). In these works, he has taken commonplace foods and given them an unexpected expression. Monumental in scale, these works are antimonumental in every traditional way. If convention dictates ostensibly eternal values and heroic figures, the artist introduces an emphasis on foods that are quickly and unceremoniously consumed, often with one's hands, and an attention to manifestations of human life, not human beings per se.

With his move in 1965 to a huge studio on East Fourteenth Street in New York City (fig. 115), Oldenburg was able to view sculptures in a commodious space and at a distance,[24] thus gaining further insights into the potential for scale manipulations. His move, together with the coincidence of being invited, also in 1965, to publish drawings for *Domus* magazine, led him to initiate a series of proposed colossal monuments. One of the first of these, the *Proposed Monument for the Intersection of Canal Street and Broadway, New York: Block of Concrete Inscribed with the Names of War Heroes* (1965, fig. 145), consisted of a block of concrete that would completely fill a major New York City intersection. This extraordinarily confrontational object would do more than merely commemorate war heroes; it would put their existence squarely into the lives of the living. Oldenburg described wanting the work "to be like a wound in the city"[25]; indeed, by obstructing traffic at a major intersection, the monument would establish a presence like no other. More so even than the Arc de Triomphe, which the driver or passerby must circumnavigate, Oldenburg's imagined sculpture disrupts daily life.[26]

Oldenburg's comments about this and other works are typically multivalent, if not contradictory. While wanting a "wound," he also observed that the war memorial "is an example of how a subject is created by circumstances. My original idea was formal only." But the form "required interpretation. The monument became very specific when I went along with a suggestion that the walls and top be covered with the names of war dead."[27] These wildly divergent ways of describing his work are perhaps deliberately obfuscatory, for it is often the case that Oldenburg's choice of subject is too replete with content not to have been arrived at deliberately. But his favorite sources in the mid-1960s do evince a sublime merging of form and content.

Pyramids, columns, and obelisks all attracted Oldenburg's attention from early on in his career, as indicated in his *Raw Notes* of 1963, the year of his performance in Washington, D.C., where a number of such structures are found. These have the power to inspire awe by virtue of their size and elemental forms,[28] even as they are dedicated to the memory of august events and historical figures. Other colossi that interested Oldenburg included, in 1963, the Statue of Liberty (photographed lying in parts around Madison Square upon her arrival),[29] and in 1968, the dramatically scaled heads found on Easter Island.[30]

Of particular significance to Oldenburg were the eighteenth-century French architectural drawings of Etienne-Louis Boullée, Claude-Nicolas Ledoux, and Jean-Jacques Lequeu, reproductions of which he first discovered while working in the library of Cooper Union College from 1956 to 1961. The imaginary structures of these artists were often conceived as having a funerary function, and suggested a sepulcher even when not specifically envisioned as such. Oldenburg echoes this somber tone in his war memorial, as well as the grandiose scale, geometric simplicity, and iconic quality of the static forms. He was drawn to the French architects' practice of employing nonfunctional yet symbolic forms, forms that announced large intentions by their very size. Although Oldenburg almost never exhibited the same seriousness or elaboration of details as Boullée, Ledoux, and Lequeu, he later matched their grandeur with his own extravagant spirit.

In contrast to works like *The Store* and *The Street*, *Proposed Monument for the Intersection of Canal Street and Broadway, New York* announces a concern for, indeed a taking note of, significant current events, including the Vietnam War.[31] It further demonstrates that an Oldenburgian monument will have a more confrontational tone than might otherwise be expected. Oldenburg wishes to replace well-behaved memorials with obstructive or obstreperous ones, and in them the typically romantic function is supplanted by a deadly serious emphasis, by something absolutely contemporary and ordinary, by explicit, lewd, or comic expressions, or by arbitrary fanciful identifications. Hence, we find a baked potato replacing the statue of Venus near the Plaza Hotel, and a fan for the Statue of Liberty (fig. 151).

Oldenburg's first realized outdoor public monument took the form of a performance/action behind the Metropolitan Museum of Art in New York on October 1, 1967. The artist hired a group of gravediggers[32] to make a six-by-three-foot hole in the ground, which was filled soon after having been made. Entitled *Placid Civic Monument*, the simple geometry of the empty rectangular hole makes for a powerful formal statement, one that repeats Oldenburg's antiwar sentiments.[33] However, he emphasized the "modesty" of his gesture, in contrast to the "pomposity" of much "civic sculpture." Indeed, he intended the hole to counter the formality of the usual base that holds a statue.[34] Also, the work graphically calls attention to the reality of death, as opposed to the pieties that inspire soldiers and sculptors. Describing his piece as a "conceptual monument," Oldenburg links himself to the incipient Conceptual movement of the later 1960s; in this regard, it is notable that *Placid Civic Monument*, while resembling a Minimal art form, is in fact a void, just as much Conceptual art had little or no physical existence.

Not surprising for Oldenburg, the hole in the ground has a sexual identity too. He had often asserted, starting at least as early as 1965, that the general content of art is erotic[35] and, in 1966, that each one of his works is, in effect, a disguise for either male, female, or both genders.[36] Thus the Central Park hole can be seen as female in character, here perversely a receptacle for the deceased, rather than being a place of birth. Oldenburg is characteristically blunt about the female identity of this hole, writing: "I felt great excitement at the moment of first incision of the shovel. The first shovelful was surprisingly red and accounted 'virgin' by the diggers."[37] He continued: "One hopes that all climaxes will not come at once."[38] If Oldenburg's performance behind the Metropolitan Museum was slightly outrageous even as it assumed a memorial function, the artist was not at all reluctant to continue in the same vein.

Starting in the mid-1960s, Oldenburg spent a large proportion of time traveling to various cities, and proposing monuments for each of them. On the first of two visits to Chicago, in 1967, he had a new insight into the effects of scale. Approaching the city by airplane, he held a clothespin in front

Placid Civic Monument, *performance behind the Metropolitan Museum of Art, New York, October 1, 1967.*

of the window, over the city below.[39] With this imaginative juxtaposition, he realized that objects scaled to a landscape could dramatically advance the potential of his art. Suddenly, though still in the realm of fantasy, he was nevertheless on the verge of colossal creations, well beyond the dimensions of any he had produced before.

Making a proposed colossal monument for a city—whether familiar or new to his experience—was similar, Oldenburg noted in 1968, to using the locale as a "studio."[40] His placement of a sculpture was effectively a formal exercise, in which he would "balance" his work with the various physical aspects of the site.[41] This responsiveness to physical and public circumstances was characteristic of Oldenburg's art as well as that of the artists of the period known for emphasizing site-specific concerns.

Most of Oldenburg's proposals, while unrealized as sculptures, took on life in a group of fanciful drawings. For London, starting in 1966, Oldenburg proposed a series of float balls, such as those used in toilet tanks, for the Thames River (fig. 148), in part because of his fascination with the fact that the city was located on water and was affected by tides.[42] He felt that an ironing board, subject of a 1965 drawing, would be an especially apt monument for Manhattan because it reflected the shape of the island and the occupation of many inhabitants of the Lower East Side.[43] And for Pasadena, he suggested *Design for a Tunnel Entrance in the Form of a Nose* (1968, fig. 159), which exhibits his usual fantasy of scale, but also his notable humor, in which logical physical appearance might have absurd results. In turning a traffic tunnel into a nose, he is at once charming, sly, perverse, and ribald.

Oldenburg's *Proposed Colossal Monument for Central Park North, New York City: Teddy Bear* (1965, fig. 143) has yet more complex intentions. The idea for the sculpture occurred during a taxicab ride on the Brooklyn-Queens Expressway. On one hand, it would formally counterbalance the Empire State Building and raise the spirits of the citizenry. ("You might feel better about living in New York," the artist said.[44]) That Oldenburg was a great aficionado of the Macy's Thanksgiving Day parade along the west side of Central Park, which featured giant balloons filled with air,[45] accords with the utopianly cheerful quality of the bear. On the other hand, the staring figure is "an incarnation of white conscience; as such, it fixes white New York with an accusing glance from Harlem. . . . I chose a toy with the 'amputated' effect of teddy paws— handlessness signifies society's frustrating lack of tools."[46] Thus Oldenburg sought to address social concerns and injustices in his art, much in keeping with the politically engaged sentiments of the time. In this regard, his *Proposed Colossal Monument to Replace the Washington Obelisk, Washington, D.C.: Scissors in Motion* (1967, fig. 153) not only represents a reconfiguration of the obelisk that dominates the District of Columbia skyline but also has complex and rich metaphoric content. According to the artist, by its open-to-closed-to-open posture over the course of twenty-four hours, the scissors alternately makes reference to a state of division and union; this connotation might refer to the state of the nation before, during, and just after the Civil War, or at the present time, or it might refer to life generally.[47]

Saying that "Egyptian colossi are recalled,"[48] Oldenburg reveals only part of the inspiration for the series called *Fagends*, which began in 1966 (figs. 174–76). This wonderfully multivalent title is typical of the artist's often nasty humor,

here concerned with what he described as the traditionally male character of London.[49] By punning on a pejorative American slang term for homosexuals, along with the English slang for cigarettes and an exhausted state ("fagged out"), he examines the fact that a word might have loaded content in one country while being relatively neutral in another. This can be thought of, the artist says, as a "Word Monument," dedicated to the power of language.[50] Further connotations are added by noting the compositional evolution of a cigarette, as described by Oldenburg. Each starts as a columnar, which is to say penis-shaped, form; after being packed together, each is freed, smoked, and finally crushed.[51]

Along with his general interest in, among other things, obelisks, columns, and "monolithic, male-oriented forms,"[52] Oldenburg was also attracted to Constantin Brancusi's *Endless Column*,[53] which was inspirational, too, for his contemporaries identified with Minimalism.[54] They took as a model Brancusi's dramatic, abstract vertical format, but Oldenburg manipulated the expectations and associations inherent in the *Column* by making representational likenesses of cigarettes, scissors, toothbrushes, screws, clothespins, and trowels. Typical is his comment about the trowel: "the form is a generalized penetrator."[55] If these objects loosely refer to a phallus, his drainpipe (figs. 160–63) might arguably be interpreted as the full genitalia, given the following: "When I refer to Brancusi's drainpipes . . . I mean no harm. . . . Only to assert . . . the inescapability of *identification*, impossibility of a clean well-lighted mind."[56] In Oldenburg's hands a cigar is not a cigar, nor is a banana simply a banana,[57] and the viewer is therefore compelled to think along the same lines. What Oldenburg does not say, but what seems apparent, is that each of these objects is essentially a self-portrait. Regarding subject matter in general, he proclaimed: "what I see is not the thing itself but—myself—in its form."[58]

Perhaps the only instances in which Oldenburg seems to have selected a personal hero for portrayal as a monument were the several drawings dedicated to Adlai Stevenson (1967, fig. 149, for example). But although the artist named the former governor of Illinois as his subject, it was, as usual, an object associated with the subject that was the artist's motif. (In this case, the object was Stevenson's hat, for which he was well known.) Stevenson was an antihero of American political history, and Oldenburg's choosing to memorialize him makes for an ironic comment on the historic convention of generals on horseback. Stevenson was the reputed intellectual who ran for the presidency and lost to a general (Eisenhower). On both counts—that of being thoughtful and being vanquished— Stevenson makes an unlikely subject. Adding further to this unlikely choice of subject is the anecdote that inspired the sculpture, of Stevenson falling dead on a London street, with his hat tumbling away nearby. Oldenburg, who described Stevenson as someone who would be "tripped over"[59] in the course of history, planned a small obstacle sculpture consisting of a group of five hats for placement on a London street, but it was never installed.

A somewhat related work is *Feasible Monument for a City Square: Hats Blowing in the Wind* (1969, fig. 177), in which Oldenburg furthers this reversal of expectations on the convention of the monument. His version is a wonderful play on Auguste Rodin's *The Burghers of Calais*, in that the human condition has been reduced from a romantic to a rather ramshackle circumstance. It also calls to mind Alberto

Giacometti's *The City Square,* Oldenburg's hats lacking even the existential dignity of Giacometti's frail beings. This, then, in Oldenburg's lexicon is a "trash monument."[60]

While *Feasible Monument for a City Square* has a modestly intrusive quality, others of Oldenburg's monuments are, as we have seen, far more an imaginary obstacle to daily life. For instance, the bowling balls for Park Avenue (1967, fig. 152) and the pool balls imagined for Central Park (1967) are more assertive than the Stevenson monument, indicating an increased level of testosterone, or "balls"; like the scissors, these are aggressive male actors in the city landscape. For the artist, the random movements of these objects represent the general anxiety of life in Manhattan, specifically the frightening traffic patterns.[61]

The first monument Oldenburg actually realized for a public setting was *Lipstick (Ascending) on Caterpillar Tracks* (1969–70, fig. 194) at Yale University. The idea for this basically phallic symbol began with the 1966 Eros statue–cum–drill bit idea for Piccadilly Square, about which the artist wrote:

It goes up
and
down[62]

Almost immediately, Oldenburg realized the potential likeness of the drill bit to a lipstick. Thus the Yale monument has a male and a female side. In the background, too, of this many-layered symbol was Oldenburg's earlier (1966) use of the lipstick specifically in relation to Marilyn Monroe. During the 1960s, when her image provided an impetus for many artists, Oldenburg was likewise intrigued, especially by Richard Avedon's photograph of the pinup icon in which she wore heavily applied lipstick.[63]

Oldenburg's tendency was almost never to show a specific person, in contrast to Andy Warhol, but to recall an individual or occasion by the use of a related object, as he had done with Stevenson.[64] About objects in general, he explained that they would

read like a list of the deities or things on which our contemporary mythological thinking has been projected. We do invest religious emotion in our objects. Look at how beautifully objects are depicted in ads in Sunday newspapers. . . . it's all very emotional. Objects are body images, after all, created by humans, filled with human emotion, objects of worship.[65]

For Oldenburg lipstick held an association of the way women were portrayed in the movies of the 1950s.[66] In relation to his sculpture *Street Chick, Lipstick* stands as a monument to another era of goddesses. Hence, although seemingly trivial, the lipstick becomes an object of some reverential interest to Oldenburg.

Oldenburg's emphasis on objects may have been influenced by his knowledge of Egyptian art and aesthetics, for to him manifestations of the material world have a spiritual dimension.[67] Curiously, whereas abstract artists had laid claim to this dimension, it was Oldenburg's goal to compete, as it were, with abstraction by suggesting that his common objects have a metaphysical, even "magical" content.[68] And just as proponents of abstract art often aspired to universality, so, too, did Oldenburg when he suggested that his found, concrete object-forms contain an "involuntary universality."[69] This, then,

Constantin Brancusi, Endless Column (version I), *1918. Oak, 6 feet 8 inches x 9⅛ inches x 9⅛ inches (203.2 x 25.1 x 24.5 cm). The Museum of Modern Art, New York, Gift of Mary Sisler.*

Auguste Rodin, The Burghers of Calais, *1886 (cast 1930s–1947). Bronze, 6 feet 7⅛ inches x 6 feet 8⅛ inches x 6 feet 5¼ inches (2.02 x 2.05 x 1.96 m). Hirshhorn Museum and Sculpture Garden, Smithsonian Institution, Washington, D.C., Gift of Joseph H. Hirshhorn, 1966.*

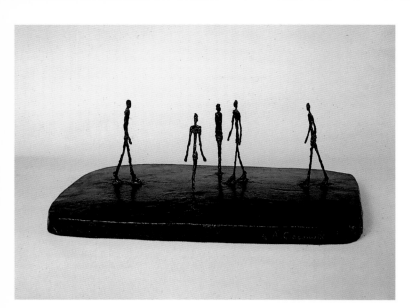

Alberto Giacometti, The City Square, *1948–49. Bronze, 9½ x 25½ x 17½ inches (24 x 64.7 x 43.4 cm). National Gallery of Art, Washington, D.C., Gift of Enid A. Haupt.*

1983 reconstruction of Vladimir Tatlin, Model of the Monument to the Third International, *1920. Hirshhorn Museum and Sculpture Garden, Smithsonian Institution, Washington, D.C.*

is the way that Oldenburg establishes a quasisacred dimension to his art of humdrum subjects.

The genealogy of *Lipstick* also contains another icon of contemporary artists, Vladimir Tatlin's *Monument to the Third International*.[70] While the Russian's emphasis on a machine-produced object was appealing to many American artists, including Oldenburg, it was Tatlin's creation of a specifically contemporary monument using technology that exemplified an exciting new direction. While one suspects that Oldenburg might have shared his colleagues' interest in Tatlin's socialist politics as well, rather than espousing those ideas, his *Lipstick* represents a more free-thinking, even anarchic point of view.[71]

Lipstick was installed at a time when protests on college campuses against the Vietnam War were prevalent, so the placement of the work on a tanklike set of tractor treads assumed considerable topical interest. A group of graduate students in architecture at Yale University had approached Oldenburg to create a monument to the "Second American Revolution"—the 1960s–70s uprisings waged on campuses against not only the war but a host of manifestations of conventional society. In this context, the tank, or the "sword," so to speak, has been turned into a plowshare by being placed beneath a gigantic lipstick; Oldenburg has made love not war, to use the vocabulary of the day.[72] He first announced this attitude when he explained that former revolutionary battlegrounds for which monuments were created were to him anachronistic, and that college campuses at which intellectual battles occur were more appropriate for his monumental work.[73]

In 1968–69, Oldenburg had turned away from soft sculptures created in a studio and toward factory-made objects. With what the artist calls his factory period, starting in 1969, the "large-scale projects" came to predominate, sculptures that were, rather than fantastical or feasible, absolutely real, and usually out-of-doors. The first urban large-scale project to be permanently placed was *Clothespin*, yet another example in the phallic vertical genre. First imagined from an airplane above Chicago in 1967, as discussed previously, the object was drawn that year as if it were a late submission to the 1922 Chicago Tribune competition (fig. 157).[74] It was subsequently made as an editioned sculpture, at four and ten feet in height, before being built in Philadelphia, in 1976 (fig. 220). Constructed to a height of six stories for a major corner across from City Hall, *Clothespin* strikes a rudely domestic, pedestrian note near the halls of authority.[75]

The scale of *Clothespin* represents Oldenburg's yet more elevated ambition, in the same vein as but even beyond the size of a typical monument or sculpture. Indeed, as he states, *Clothespin*, unlike *Lipstick*, was less important as a magical or fetishistic object than as an architectural form.[76] Thus, to the notion of what constitutes a monument is added the idea of the monument/sculpture having a structural or even architectural, and thus actual, dimension. Oldenburg's belief in this property dates from at least as early as 1963, when the monuments first began to appear; then, he matter-of-factly stated, "My work is architecture . . . personal architecture."[77] As one reviews his early monuments in light of this comment, their scale does suggest that of buildings. Moreover, it is telling that he spoke of the "architectural," rather than sculptural, form of his work.[78] Inspired by the phenomenon of buildings in the shapes of objects,[79] Oldenburg noted that his own architecture is based on "found" design,[80] that is, the given form of an object. But Oldenburg delights in the fact that his monuments/

architectural structures have no need to respond to a practical function, or even to behave as proper architecture does.[81] Instead, while being every bit as large and intrusive as buildings, his works could be assertively recalcitrant, playful, or boisterous. In effect, Oldenburg seems to want to challenge the field of architecture, which, he implies, has lost its romantic and visionary ambitions to become merely a function of computer calculations and technology.[82] While stating a challenge—"the sculptor versus the architect"[83]—Oldenburg, in fact, is seeking to reform architecture perhaps more than to defeat it.

Starting in 1976, Oldenburg made most of the large-scale projects in collaboration with his wife, Coosje van Bruggen. This team combined the introspective, personal impulses of Oldenburg with the more socially minded nature of van Bruggen.[84] In such works as *Trowel* (1976, fig. 217), *Batcolumn* (1977, fig. 221), *Crusoe Umbrella* (1979, fig. 229), *Spitzhacke* (*Pickaxe*) (1982, fig. 231), *Hat in Three Stages of Landing* (1982, fig. 232), and *Screwarch* (1983, fig. 235) they continued Oldenburg's earlier interest in the commonplace, but created a new set of monuments. Again, the emphasis is on a kind of everyman's sphere, as if the two artists wish to confront the elitist art world with the side of life it generally ignores. Compared to the Pop imagery of Andy Warhol and Roy Lichtenstein, which is usually rooted in glamorous icons and campy narratives from comic strips, these subjects are deliberately and resolutely common.

Oldenburg prefers to think of the large-scale projects as sculptures rather than monuments, however gigantic, and yet the point can be debated on various grounds. If one recalls that the pool balls appeared first as a monument drawing (1967), then as an oversize sculpture (also 1967, figs. 185–86), and finally, on a large scale in Münster, Germany (1977), the issue becomes moot. Whether indoors or out, an Oldenburgian sculpture/monument usually exhibits the same prepossessing largeness that inspires awe and wonder. Furthermore, in virtually all of his drawings for monuments, he juxtaposes two different sizes on a single plane, that of the colossal object in contrast to a diminished locale[85]; similarly, in a realized, room-sized or outdoor sculpture, the size juxtaposition is slightly grotesque, as in a painting by René Magritte.

Just as a city's planners might create a monument to an honored local son, daughter, or event, Oldenburg and van Bruggen usually have attempted in the large-scale projects to choose objects that are in some way appropriate to the site. They will consider historical connotations, along with their own free associations made on site. Sometimes, as in the case of the relationship of the *Spitzhacke* to an eighteenth-century sculpture of Hercules in Kassel, or *Free Stamp* (1991, fig. 283) vis-à-vis a Soldiers and Sailors Monument of 1894 in Cleveland, their desire is quite obviously to leapfrog the past in order to offer new monuments of a contemporary age, which, nevertheless, are somehow responsive to the specific locale. Thus, while Oldenburg may emphasize the nature of the works as sculptures, these great outdoor objects often function as monuments.

While the scale of these works of the 1980s, in addition to the *Clothespin* of the preceding decade, equals that of architecture, it still remained for the team of Oldenburg and van Bruggen to more directly indulge this interest. This was finally accomplished through a series of collaborations with the architect Frank O. Gehry. In 1983, Oldenburg and van Bruggen

Pool Balls, *1977. Reinforced concrete, three balls, each 11 feet 6 inches (3.5 m) in diameter. Aaseeterrassen, Münster.*

proposed a huge ladder toppling over in front of a law school building designed by Gehry; this structure was intended to play an architectural, if fanciful, role. Subsequently, for a performance in Venice in 1985 (pages 419–39), the three concocted a prop known as *Knife Ship I* (fig. 252), a combination of a Swiss Army knife and a ship in motion on the canals of Venice. Although *Knife Ship I* and *Toppling Ladder with Spilling Paint* (realized 1986, fig. 262) were not, strictly speaking, architectural, these predated the 1986 collaboration in which Oldenburg, van Bruggen, and Gehry planned the headquarters of the Chiat/Day advertising company in Los Angeles. Retrieving an idea conceived at the time of *Knife Ship I*, they proposed integrating a giant pair of binoculars into the façade as a doorway (realized 1991, fig. 284). However, this "sculpture" was not only an element of the architecture, it was in front of and slightly separated from the façade wall, relating to the building as a monument might. And as a testament to vision and visionariness, and an allusion to the viewing of the nearby ocean, this work achieved a new synthesis of the monument with architecture.

Although all of Oldenburg's monuments, whether real or imaginary, whether made in collaboration or on his own, have an obviously public presence because of their scale, placement, and easily accessible subject matter, they are, nevertheless highly personal. His choice of subject projects an engaging wit, warmth, and humanity that is in part childlike and in part sly and subversive. The erotic dimension is occasionally direct or on other occasions veiled, but never completely hidden or absent. Of this, he commented in 1971, "Any art that is successful in projecting positive feelings about life has got to be heavily erotic."[86] This statement is fascinating on several levels, not the least of which is Oldenburg's desire to project "positive feelings"; such an outlook appears almost anachronistic and yet it is a welcome sentiment that goes to the heart of characterizing one's reactions to his art. While being an obstructionist, then, he strikes out at forces inhibiting a more gentle world; his work projects a human plenitude that is captivating and sophisticated. In his art, there is a kind of extravagance of spirit that may at times belie a deeply searching examination of lived, contemporary life.

As with monument makers of the past, Oldenburg leaves remnants of our society behind for current and future generations to ponder. By working within this tradition, he effectively integrates his art into the culture at large, a practice not generally found among twentieth-century painters and sculptors, though much in keeping with historical art. It is, however, also an aspiration that has had some currency during the past thirty years or so in the United States, where various governmental programs have prescribed that a part of the budget for certain buildings be devoted to art; in this, there is a particularly American rush to find a large audience. The Oldenburgian spirit specifically results in the tradition of the monument being maintained and domesticated. Indeed, Oldenburg might be seen as the greatest exemplar of the monument tradition, albeit reinterpreted, in this century.

Early in his career, Oldenburg wrote that he was hostile to the convention of art being rigidly defined as an independent object but, nevertheless, he expressed the desire to maintain "the greatness of art. . . . I wish to return it [art] to a force."[87] In other words, Oldenburg went outside the space of the studio, gallery, or museum into the public domain, where he could use art's power. One comes to realize that Oldenburg's interests are slightly anarchical, that he wishes to alter the world through his artistic efforts. Herbert Marcuse recognized the potential for a sculpture by Oldenburg "to achieve a radical change," and Barbara Rose amplified the sentiment: "The erection of Oldenburg's monuments would mean that people had seen that they had the power to control their lives and modify their environment."[88] Oldenburg becomes a kind of trouble-maker, jabbing at public icons and expectations, or demonstrating a liberating degree of public eroticism. From practically the start of his career, he was conscious of the potential of disruption,[89] and happily conflated anarchic and revolutionary notions, along with idealism, sexuality, and death, as if all are inherent in the same urge. Thus he announced in 1961: "I am for an art that is political-erotic-mystical, that does something other than sit on its ass in a museum."[90]

1. Claes Oldenburg, *Store Days: Documents from The Store (1961) and Ray Gun Theater (1962)* (New York: Something Else Press, 1967), pp. 7–8.
2. Ibid., pp. 13, 60. See also p. 53.
3. See Barbara Rose, *Claes Oldenburg* (exh. cat.; New York: The Museum of Modern Art, 1970), p. 46.
4. Discussed by the artist in an unpublished interview with the author conducted in New York City, August 5, 1994 (hereafter referred to as Interview).
5. Claes Oldenburg, "A Card From Doc," 1960, published in *Injun and Other Histories (1960)* (New York: A Great Bear Pamphlet, 1966), p. 13.
6. See *Claes Oldenburg: Dibujos/Drawings 1959–1989* (Valencia, Spain: IVAM, Centre Julio González, 1989), p. 42.
7. Oldenburg, *Store Days*, p. 39.
8. Ibid., p. 142.
9. The artist discusses the Happenings in Claes Oldenburg, *Raw Notes*, ed. Kasper König (Halifax, Canada: The Press of the Nova Scotia College of Art and Design, 1973), p. 86.
10. Coosje van Bruggen, *Claes Oldenburg: Nur ein Anderer Raum/Just Another Room* (Frankfurt: Museum für Moderne Kunst, 1991), p. 10.
11. Oldenburg's 1961 notes, cited in Rose, p. 145.
12. Claes Oldenburg, *Proposals for Monuments and Buildings, 1965–1969* (Chicago: Big Table, 1969), p. 13.
13. Ibid., pp. 13–14.
14. Ibid.
15. Oldenburg, *Raw Notes*, p. 13.
16. Ibid, p. 45. See also pp. 2, 31–32, 35, 39, and 49, all regarding monuments.
17. *New Work by Oldenburg* (exh. cat.; New York: Sidney Janis Gallery, 1966), p. 2.
18. Barbara Haskell, *Claes Oldenburg: Object into Monument* (exh. cat.; Pasadena, Calif.: Pasadena Art Museum; Los Angeles: The Ward Ritchie Press, 1971), p. 62.
19. Ibid.
20. Oldenburg, *Proposals for Monuments and Buildings, 1965–1969*, p. 15. Haskell, p. 10, also discusses how the sense of a "burial vault or sepulcher" occurs frequently in Oldenburg's sculpture, even to the extent that many of his objects appear to have been toppled or fallen as in a neglected graveyard.
21. van Bruggen, p. 39.
22. Rose, p. 103.
23. Interview.
24. The artist discusses his new studio in *Claes Oldenburg* (exh. cat.; London: Arts Council of Great Britain, 1970), p. 19.
25. Oldenburg, *Proposals for Monuments and Buildings, 1965–1969*, p. 25.
26. Ibid.
27. *Claes Oldenburg: Skulpturer och teckningar* (Stockholm: Moderna Museet, 1966), [p. 52].
28. Claes Oldenburg, from 1967 São Paulo Bienal statement cited in *Claes Oldenburg* (Arts Council of Great Britain), p. 15.
29. Oldenburg, *Proposals for Monuments and Buildings, 1965–1969*, p. 14.
30. Haskell, p. 92.
31. Discussed further by the artist in ibid., p. 17.
32. Oldenburg was forced by city regulations to hire union gravediggers for this job. (Interview.)
33. Haskell, pp. 60–62. Oldenburg said of the hole that the "(G)rave is a perfect (anti) war monument, like saying no more."
34. Interview.
35. *Claes Oldenburg: Dibujos/Drawings 1959–1989*, p. 17.
36. Oldenburg discusses this aspect of his work in "Totems and Taboos," reprinted in Rose, pp. 197–98, and notes that some objects refer to masturbation, reproduction, sperm, and other sexual meanings in addition to having gender associations.
37. Haskell, p. 62.
38. Ibid.
39. Oldenburg, *Proposals for Monuments and Buildings, 1965–1969*, p. 12.
40. Ibid., p. 18.
41. Ibid., p. 20.
42. For more on the artist's associations with London, see Oldenburg, *Proposals for Monuments and Buildings, 1965–1969*, pp. 20–22; and Haskell, p. 33.
43. Oldenburg, *Proposals for Monuments and Buildings, 1965–1969*, p. 15.
44. Ibid., p. 12.
45. Also discussed in Rose, p. 103. Oldenburg also relates these balloons to

Lequeu's buildings shaped like animals (see Oldenburg, *Proposals for Monuments and Buildings, 1965–1969*, p. 14).
46. Ibid, p. 15.
47. Interview. In a related vein, Oldenburg recalled that Peter Cooper planned the words of Cooper Union College to face toward the South, as an explicit political gesture.
48. Claes Oldenburg, *Claes Oldenburg: Notes in Hand* (New York: E.P Dutton, 1971), [p.66.]
49. Haskell, p. 37.
50. Interview.
51. See Oldenburg's description in Haskell, p. 37; and his description of the many contradictory meanings of fag ends, a situation that finally yields absurdity, in "America: War & Sex, Etc." cited in Rose, p. 70.
52. Interview.
53. Ibid.
54. Oldenburg specifically mentions Brancusi's "egg," as cited in Haskell, p. 92.
55. Haskell, p. 126.
56. Rose, p. 70.
57. Oldenburg from childhood on was fond of a "great anonymous monument in the form of a banana on the pier in Oslo." See Haskell, p. 6.
58. Oldenburg, *Store Days*, p. 65.
59. Haskell, p. 12.
60. Interview.
61. Ibid.
62. Oldenburg, *Claes Oldenburg: Notes in Hand*, [p. 18].
63. Interview.
64. Discussed in Oldenburg, *Proposals for Monuments and Buildings, 1965–1969*, p. 31.
65. Haskell, p. 95.
66. Described in Oldenburg, *Proposals for Monuments and Buildings, 1965–1969*, p. 22.
67. Oldenburg speaks of the "romanticism of the objective" in *Claes Oldenburg: Dibujos/Drawings 1959–1989*, p. 56.
68. See Oldenburg, *Store Days*, pp. 9, 16, 48.
69. van Bruggen, p. 13.
70. Oldenburg, in Haskell, p. 96.
71. Barnett Newman's *Broken Obelisk* was on the premises of the Connecticut fabricator where Oldenburg worked on *Lipstick* (ibid., p. 95); but, according to the artist, Newman's *Obelisk* simply confirmed, rather than influenced, his work. (Interview.)
72. See Rose, pp. 110–11, for a discussion of how Herbert Marcuse, a New Left philosopher, supposedly inspired the students' commission to Oldenburg.
73. Oldenburg's statement on the subject of the university is cited in Ellen H. Johnson, *Claes Oldenburg* (Harmondsworth, England and Baltimore: Penguin Books, 1971), p. 46.
74. See *Claes Oldenburg: Large-Scale Projects, 1977–1980* (New York: Rizzoli, 1980), p. 48; and Oldenburg, *Proposals for Monuments and Buildings, 1965–1969*, p. 12.
75. *Claes Oldenburg   Coosje van Bruggen: Large-Scale Projects* (New York: The Monacelli Press, 1994), pp. 380–81.
76. Oldenburg, *Proposals for Monuments and Buildings, 1965–1969*, p. 33.
77. Cited in Rose, p. 192.
78. Oldenburg, *Proposals for Monuments and Buildings, 1965–1969*, p. 33.
79. van Bruggen, p. 39.
80. Haskell, p. 18.
81. Oldenburg, *Proposals for Monuments and Buildings, 1965–1969*, p. 25.
82. Ibid., pp. 24, 164. Oldenburg's observations about architecture seem largely formed by his early years in Chicago.
83. Haskell, p. 18.
84. As described by the artist in Interview.
85. Discussed by Oldenburg in *Claes Oldenburg* (Arts Council of Great Britain), p. 8.
86. Haskell, p. 10.
87. van Bruggen, p. 10.
88. Rose, p. 111.
89. In speaking about the hole behind the Metropolitan Museum of Art in New York, Oldenburg mentions *The Story of an Anarchist* by Kropotkin (Haskell, p. 62), who was a favorite author of Barnett Newman. The latter, too, fancied himself an anarchist.
90. Oldenburg, *Store Days*, p. 39.

143. Proposed Colossal Monument for Central Park North, New York City: Teddy Bear, *1965. Crayon and watercolor on paper, 23 x 17⅛ inches (58.4 x 43.7 cm). Collection of Mr. and Mrs. Richard E. Oldenburg.*

144. Proposed Colossal Monument
for Park Avenue, New York: Good
Humor Bar, *1965. Crayon and watercolor
on paper, 23⅛ x 17½ inches (59.7 x
44.5 cm). Collection of Carroll Janis,
New York.*

146. Colossal Floating Three-Way Plug,
1965. Pencil on paper, 30 x 22 inches
(76.2 x 55.9 cm). Walker Art Center,
Minneapolis, Gift of the T. B. Walker
Foundation.

148. Proposed Colossal Monument for
Thames River: Thames "Ball," *1967.*
Crayon, ink, and watercolor on postcard,
3½ x 5½ inches (8.9 x 14 cm). Collection of
Carroll Janis, New York.

149. Small Monument for a London
Street: Fallen Hat (For Adlai
Stevenson), *1967. Pencil and watercolor
on paper, 23 x 32 inches (58.4 x 81.3 cm).
Collection of Kimiko and John Powers.*

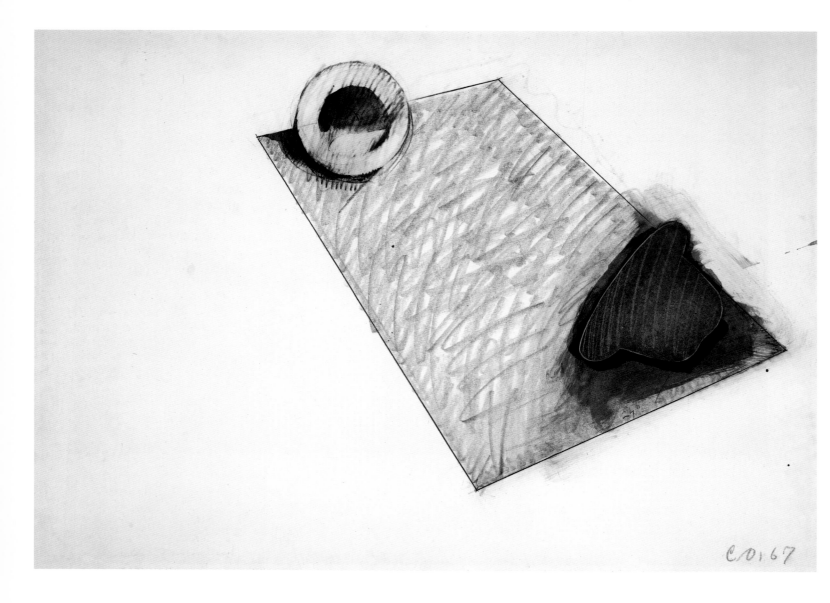

STEVENSON...

1. Two observations about London are embodied in this proposal: (a) the emphasis on detail, i.e., smallness of the landscape and the English cult of smallness; (b) the emphasis, or cultivation of obstacles. A small monument in obstacle form.

Obstacles might be most felt in the feet, so something attached to the rectangle of a street stone which could be placed by substitution for an existing stone suggested itself. A friend suggested a pigeon decoy, which would not fly away as they usually do when the feet approached. This would add an element of surprise--you would approach the pigeon and expect it to fly away, and of course it wouldn't, and you would fall on your face.

2. Specific adaptation. Death on the street entered my mind probably through such a death of a friend in 1966. He went out for a walk as he always did in the evening. He had a heart attack and died in the street. I found myself living near the spot where Adlai Stevenson died such a death, and the little monument idea took form as a modest monument to him in that spot.

This then became the empty or dropped hat of the same material as the stone, discreet but likely to be tripped on. There would be no inscription.

I think the Stevenson of legend, anyway, would have preferred this to something grandiose. I established that Stevenson wore a hat at the time of being stricken. The hat is bronze and set into one of the 24-inch paving stones, making it necessary for a passerby to watch his step, slow and be curious since the sidewalks are narrow.

In this "monument" the object retains its own size.

(1971)

151. Proposed Colossal Monument:
Fan in Place of the Statue of Liberty,
Bedloes Island, *1967. Pencil on paper,*
26 1/16 x 40 1/16 inches (66.5 x 101.8 cm).
Öffentliche Kunstsammlung Basel,
Kupferstichkabinett.

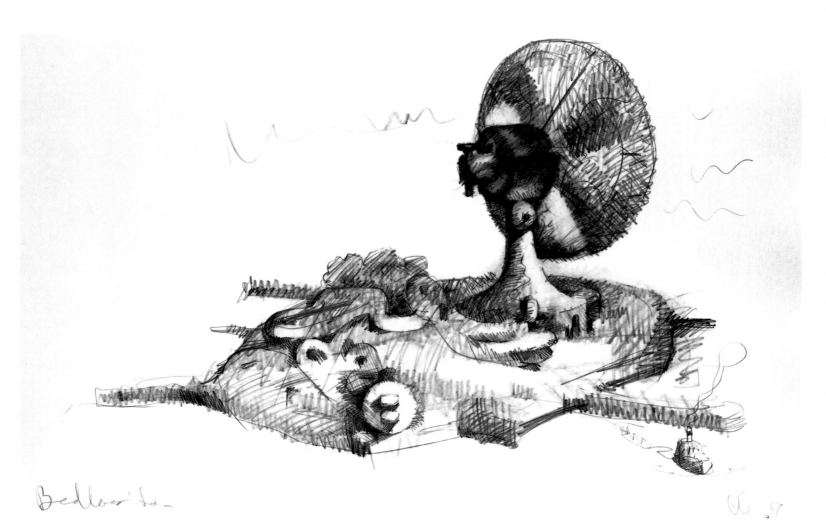

152. Proposed Colossal Monument for Park Avenue, New York: Moving Bowling Balls, *1967. Pencil and watercolor on paper, 27⅞ x 22⅛ inches (70.8 x 57.2 cm). The Menil Collection, Houston.*

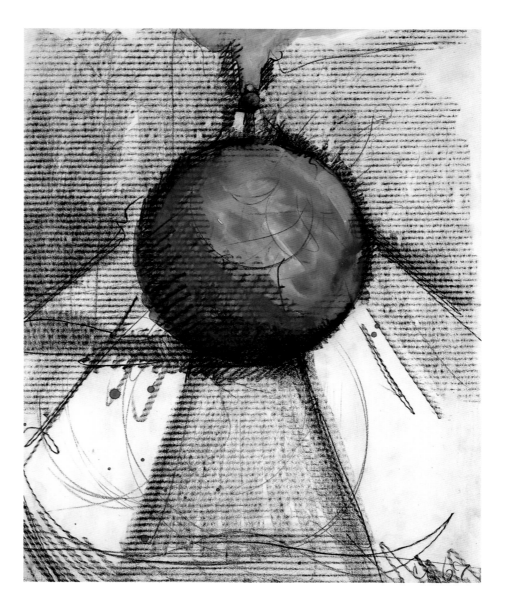

153. Proposed Colossal Monument to
Replace the Washington Obelisk,
Washington, D.C.: Scissors in Motion,
1967. Crayon and watercolor on paper, 30 x
19¼ inches (76.2 x 50.2 cm). Collection of
David Whitney.

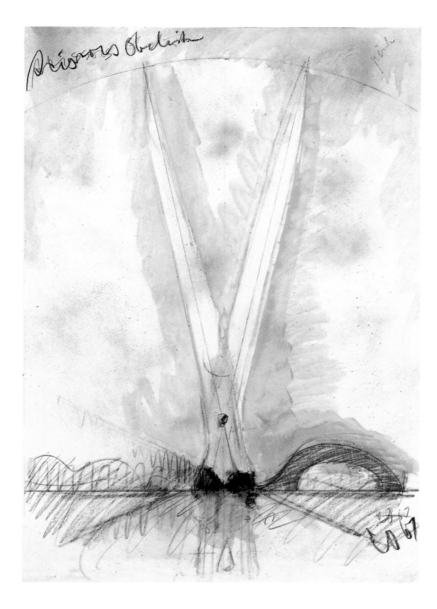

154. Proposal for a Skyscraper for
Michigan Avenue, Chicago, in the Form
of Lorado Taft's Sculpture "Death,"
1968. Pencil and ink on postcard with
collage on paper, 11¾ x 9¾ inches (29.8 x
24.8 cm). Collection of Leon and Marian
Despres.

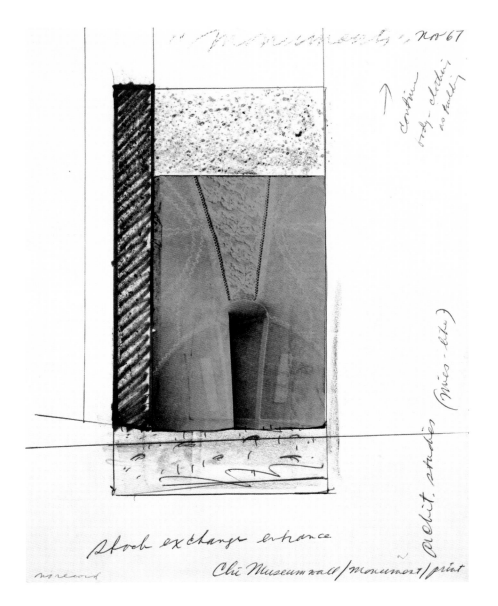

156. Notebook Page: Buildings in the
Form of Binoculars, Pelvic Region
Characters, *1969. Ballpoint pen and
collage on paper, 11 x 8½ inches (27.9 x
21.6 cm). Collection of Claes Oldenburg
and Coosje van Bruggen, New York.*

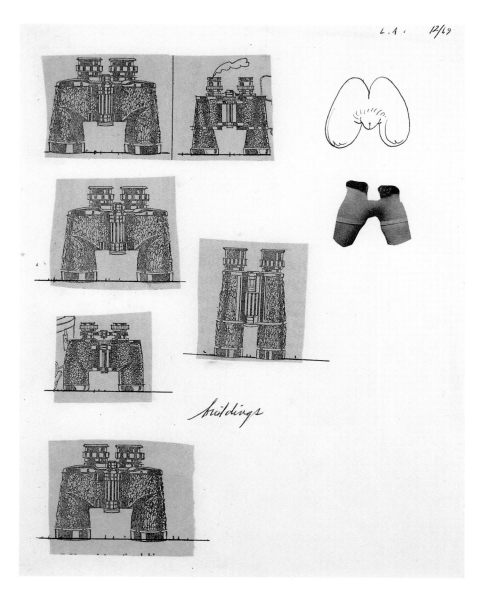

157. Late Submission to the Chicago
Tribune Architectural Competition of
1922: Clothespin (Version Two), *1967.*
Crayon, pencil, and watercolor on paper,
22 x 23¼ inches (55.9 x 59 cm). Partial
purchase with funds from Gardner Cowles
and gift of Charles Cowles, Des Moines
Art Center Permanent Collection, 1972.

158. Proposal for a Skyscraper in the
Form of a Chicago Fireplug: Inverted
Version, *1969. Crayon and watercolor
on paper, 17½ x 12 inches (44.5 x 30.5 cm).
Collection of Dr. and Mrs. Phillip T.
George, Miami.*

159. Design for a Tunnel Entrance in the Form of a Nose, *1968. Crayon and watercolor on paper, 9½ x 8 inches (24.1 x 20.3 cm). Collection of Mr. and Mrs. Robert J. Woods, Jr.*

160. Proposed Colossal Monument
for Toronto: Drainpipe, *1967. Pencil and
watercolor on paper, 40⅟₁₆ x 26⅟₁₆ inches
(102 x 66.5 cm). Art Gallery of Ontario,
Toronto, Purchased by the Trier-Fodor
Foundation with assistance from the
Klamer Family, 1989.*

161. Base of Colossal Drainpipe
Monument, Toronto, with Waterfall,
1967. Pencil and watercolor on paper,
24¼ x 22 inches (62.9 x 55.9 cm).
Collection of Kimiko and John Powers.

facing page and above:
162. Soft Drainpipe – Blue (Cool)
Version, *1967. Extended and contracted
views. Canvas painted with acrylic;
clothesline; and metal, 84 x 55½ x 15 inches
(213.4 x 141 x 38.1 cm). Tate Gallery,
Purchased 1970.*

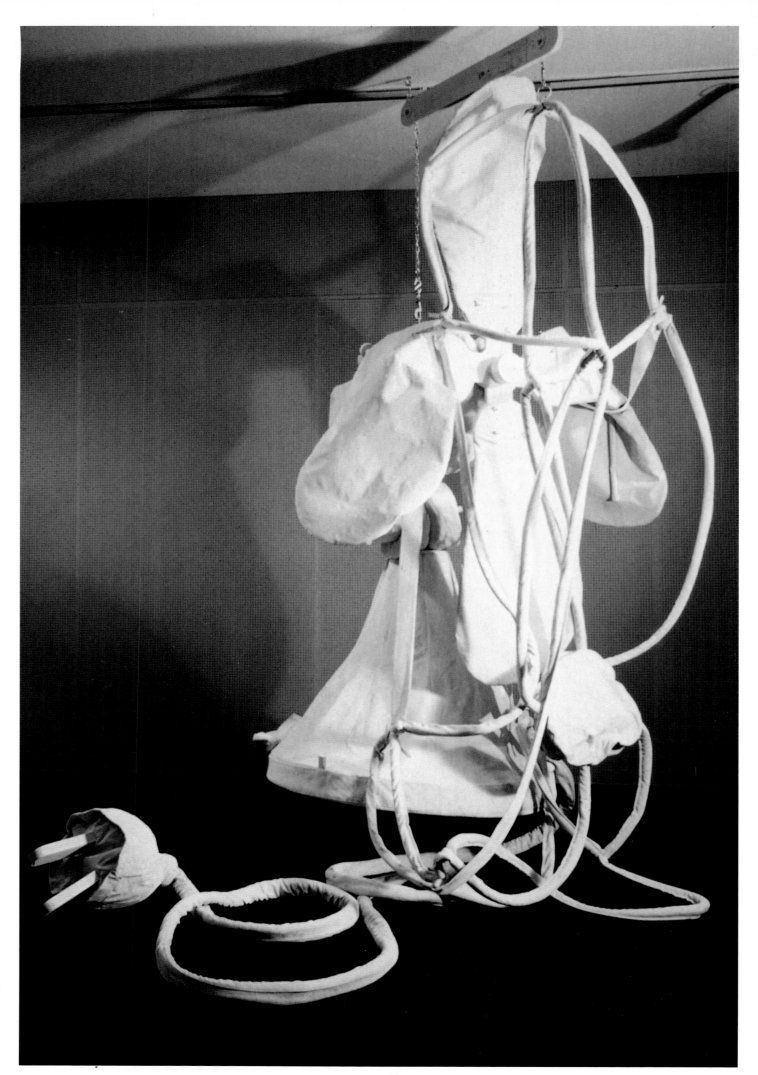

facing page:
165. Giant Soft Fan – Ghost Version,
*1967. Canvas filled with polyurethane
foam; wood; metal; and plastic; fan: 120 x
59 x 64 inches (304.8 x 149.9 x 162.6 cm);
cord and plug: 290 inches (736.6 cm) long.
The Museum of Fine Arts, Houston,
Gift of D. and J. de Menil.*

166. Giant Soft Fan, *1966–67. Vinyl
filled with polyurethane foam; wood;
metal; and plastic; fan: approximately
120 x 58⅞ x 61⅞ inches (305 x 149.5 x
157.1 cm); cord and plug: 24 feet 3¼ inches
(739.6 cm) long. The Museum of Modern
Art, New York, The Sidney and Harriet
Janis Collection, 1967.*

167. Drum Pedal Study – Schematic
Rendering, *1967. Pencil and watercolor on
paper, 30 x 22 inches (76.2 x 55.9 cm).
Collection of Kimiko and John Powers.*

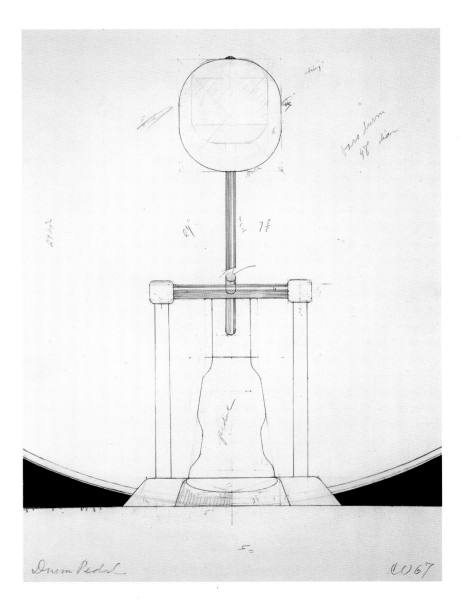

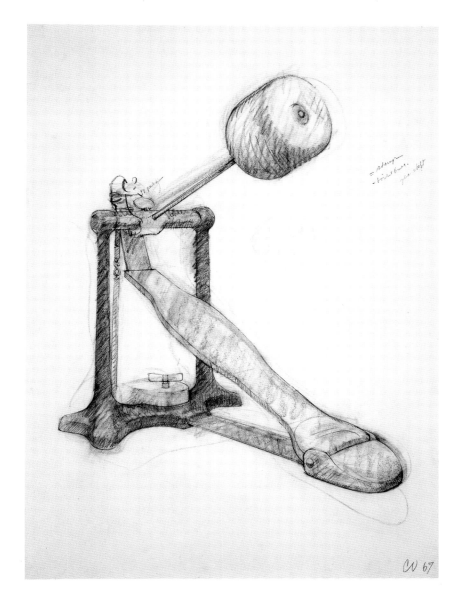

169. Study for the Giant Soft Drum Set,
1967. Pencil and spray enamel on paper,
30 x 22 inches (76.2 x 55.9 cm). Collection
of Kimiko and John Powers.

170. Drum Pedal Study – Visualization
of Collapsed Version, *1967. Pencil on
paper, 30 x 22 inches (76.2 x 55.9 cm).
Collection of Kimiko and John Powers.*

171. Giant Soft Drum Set, 1967.
Vinyl and canvas filled with expanded
polystyrene chips; metal and painted
wood parts; and wood-and-Formica base
with metal railing; nine instruments,
48 x 72 x 84 inches (121.9 x 182.9 x
213.4 cm) overall. Collection of Kimiko
and John Powers.

173. Giant Loaf of Raisin Bread, Sliced,
*1966–67. Canvas and canvas stiffened
with glue, filled with shredded
polyurethane foam, painted with acrylic;
and wood base; 46 x 96 x 40 inches
(116.8 x 243.8 x 101.6 cm). The Helman
Collection.*

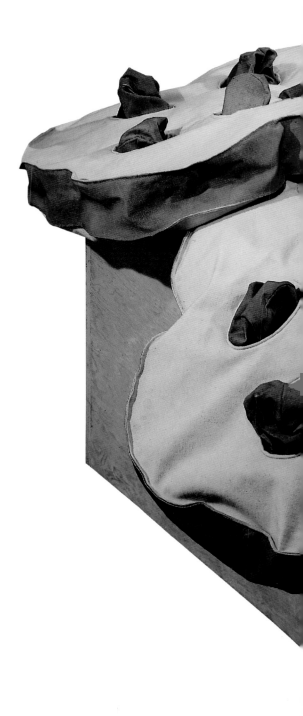

174. Colossal Fagend in Park Setting,
*1967. Pencil and watercolor on paper, 30 x
22⅛ inches (76.2 x 56.2 cm). Collection of
Robert and Jane Meyerhoff, Phoenix,
Maryland.*

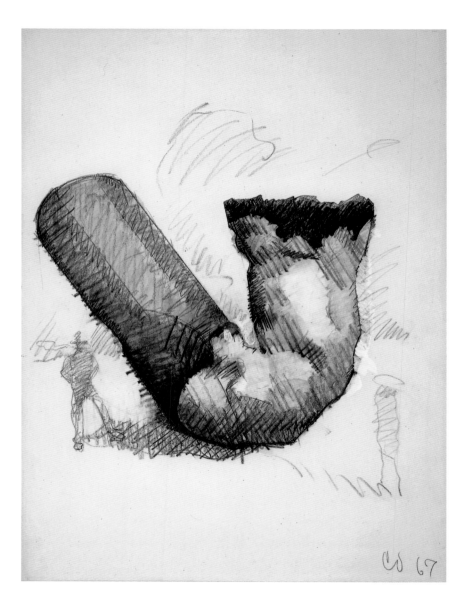

175. Colossal Fagends in Park Setting,
with Man, *1967. Pencil and watercolor on
paper, 30 x 22 inches (76.2 x 55.9 cm).
Collection of Sarah d'Harnoncourt and
Joseph Rishel, Philadelphia.*

176. Giant Fagends, 1967. Canvas,
urethane foam, and wood; 13 parts,
52 x 96 x 96 inches (132.1 x 243.8 x
243.8 cm) overall. Whitney Museum of
American Art, New York, Purchase, with
funds from the Friends of the Whitney
Museum of American Art.

FAGENDS...

The Fagends have been made in four scales.
Tubes were sewn of canvas and wire springs
placed inside. Then the tubes were tied to
chairs and urethane foam in the form of
liquid poured in. As the urethane changed
from liquid to foam, it caused the tubes to
twist into shapes determined by the ropes
and the spring. It was nearly automatic,
though of course predetermined by the
limits of the tube and expectations of what
the tube would do against the ties, etc.
   In any scale, the Fagends are a variable
and arbitrary composition, and there is no
right way to show it. There are ways that I
prefer and ways that others, who must take
the responsibility for arranging it, may
prefer. Like many of my pieces, each time
it is photographed, it is in a different
arrangement, has a different over-all
aspect.
   In colossal form, park equals ashtray.
The ashtray becomes the sculpture base.

(1971)

177. Feasible Monument for a City Square: Hats Blowing in the Wind, *1969. Canvas stiffened with glue over wire frame, painted with spray enamel and shellacked; and wood base; 10½ x 28 x 39 inches (26.7 x 71.1 x 99.1 cm). Private collection.*

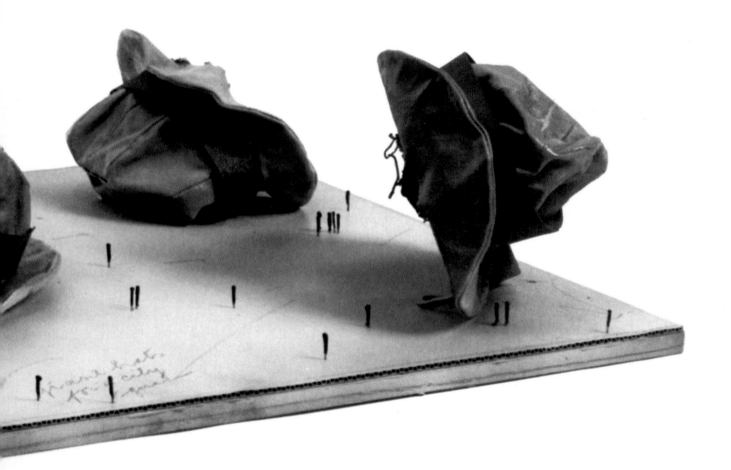

SULLIVAN TOMB...

178. Feasible Monument for Grant Park
Chicago: Memorial to Louis Sullivan
(Model), 1969. Two views. Cardboard,
painted and shellacked, 14 x 23½ x
27 inches (35.6 x 59.7 x 68.6 cm).
Collection of Kimiko and John Powers.

The legend of Louis Sullivan includes the
story that, toward the end of his life,
Sullivan was forgotten and forced to sleep
in a broom closet in a hotel on the South
Side of Chicago, cared for surreptitiously
by the employees of the hotel. When an
architect who visited him in his closet
asked if there was something he could do,
Sullivan supposedly replied, "Yes, please
turn off the light."

This broom closet in monumental scale
becomes the tomb for Sullivan, to stand in
Grant Park in front of the City of Chicago.

The structure is forbidding from the
outside. It looks like an antique bread
toaster, or an obelisk, or the Hancock
Building lengthened vertically. It is a
high steel box with sloping sides set on a
smaller box-pedestal with entrances by way
of escalators under the overhang of the big
box.

The outside walls are sleek and dark and
culminate in a peaked roof covered with a
construction that combines Sullivan's
ornament in an effect of moss or a thatched
roof, drooping over the sides. There are
several buildings in Chicago that start out
as clean skyscrapers but end in a church or
a Swiss chalet. I feel this way about
Sullivan: he's of both centuries.

The silent escalators take one up into an
enormous room completely shut off from the
light and climate of the outdoors--the only
room in the tomb, the interior of the
"broom closet," filled with a brown light
that fades into darkness at the top. One
can barely discern a vaulted ceiling
covered with copies of Sullivan's organic
designs which reach down along the walls
and dangle in the air like stalactites in a
cave.

On entering, one is standing in a walkway
about 30 feet wide, which runs around the
colossal 600-foot long figure of the
reclining Sullivan. At first, one takes it
for a mountain, especially since the body
is covered with cloth, like Lorado Taft's
Statue of Death. Only the enormous head
with beard is visible. The rest of the
body, including the arms and hands, is
conveyed by folds of the "bedcover." The
eyes are turned straight up and never will
be seen.

Gradually, one gets used to the
crepuscular light. One sees only parts of
the man, and the effect is rather abstract.
From the center of the ceiling hangs a
colossal unshaded light bulb, not lit equal
to its scale, but glowing softly from the
lights of thousands of small bulbs inside.

(1971)

179. Proposed Colossal Monument for
End of Navy Pier, Chicago: Fireplug
(Model), *1969. Cardboard, wood, and
plaster, painted with spray enamel and
shellacked, 13¼ x 17 x 23 inches (34.9 x
43.2 x 58.4 cm). Collection of Kimiko and
John Powers.*

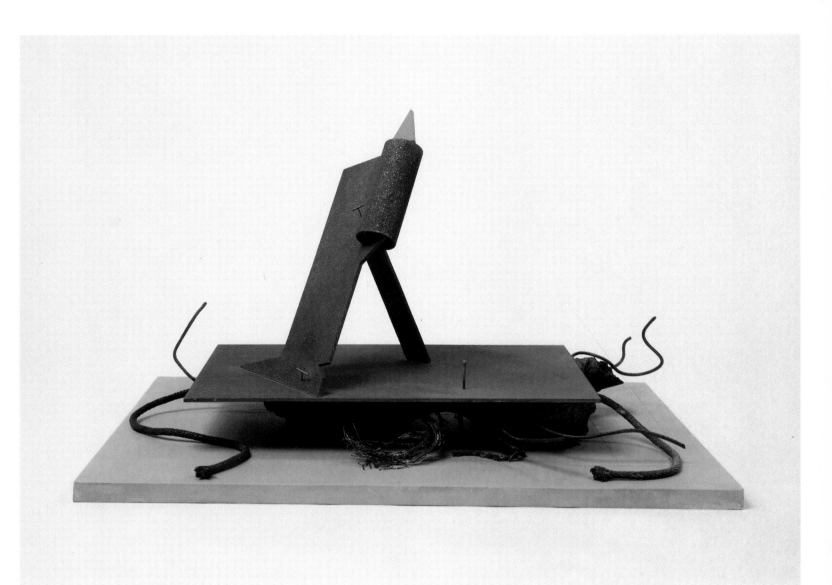

181. Chicago Picasso Adapted to a Colossal Cufflink, *1972. Pastel, colored pencil, chalk, and watercolor on paper, 29 x 22¼ inches (73.7 x 57.8 cm). Collection of Mr. and Mrs. Richard E. Oldenburg.*

183. Saw, Hard Version II, 1970. Wood,
aluminum, and polyurethane foam, 168 x
40 x 6½ inches (426.7 x 101.6 x 16.5 cm).
Stedelijk Museum, Amsterdam.

facing page:
184. Giant Three-Way Plug, Scale B,
1970. Cherry wood, 58½ x 39 x 28½ inches
(148.6 x 99.1 x 72.4 cm). Philadelphia
Museum of Art, Purchased, Fiske Kimball
Fund and funds contributed by private
donors.

pages 314–15:
185. Giant Pool Balls, *1967. Plexiglas with metal rack; sixteen balls, 24 inches (61 cm) in diameter each; 24 x 120 x 108 inches (61 x 304.8 x 274.3 cm) overall. Los Angeles County Museum of Art, Anonymous Gift through the Contemporary Art Council.*

186. Giant Pool Balls, *1967, installed at the Pasadena Art Museum, December 7, 1971–February 6, 1972.*

1969-1976

New York City
North Haven, Connecticut
Los Angeles

Fabricated Works: Geometric
Mouse; Giant Ice Bag; Lip-
stick (Ascending) on Cater-
pillar Tracks; Three Way
Plug; Alphabet/Good Humor;
Colossal Ashtray; Typewriter
Eraser; Inverted Q; Trowel;
Clothespin

Mouse Museum and Ray Gun Wing

SELF PORTRAIT...

The face is a cutout, like a mask, which is pasted on the diagram of the objects. The ice bag is also a cutout of different paper, pasted on. The face is divided in half vertically. One side shows the kindly aspect of the artist; the other, his brutal one. The body is introduced in the image of the face via the representation of the body's juices--the tongue (bringing out the insides)--which doubles as a heart and foot. The stare is partly the result of the working conditions of making a self-portrait--one hangs up a mirror and stares into it--also emphasizes the artist's reliance on the eyes. The '3 $\frac{1}{2}$' on the forehead is left on a s reminder of my concern at the time with measurements of patterns. The Ice Bag on the head signifies that subject was on my mind. It doubles as beret--attribute of the artist.

The objects are shown in the order in which they were made, reading left to right, from the Good Humor Bar of 1963 through the Geometric Mouse of 1969. They circulate about the artist's head like the representation of unconsciousness in the comics, or the astrological signs on the hat of Merlin the Magician--deflated to an Ice Bag.

I alternated between the image of a magician and that of a clown, trying to make a combination of the two. Two clown representations, I recall, which contributed are the 'Joker' from Batman comic strip and the laughing face that used to be on Tilyou's Amusement Park, 'The Funny Place', at Coney Island. I remembered, also, the self-portraits (in agony) of Messerschmidt, which were analysed by Ernst Kris.

(1971)

187. Symbolic Self-Portrait with Equals, *1969. Pencil, crayon, spray enamel, watercolor, and collage on paper, 11 x 8¼ inches (27.9 x 21 cm). Moderna Museet, Stockholm.*

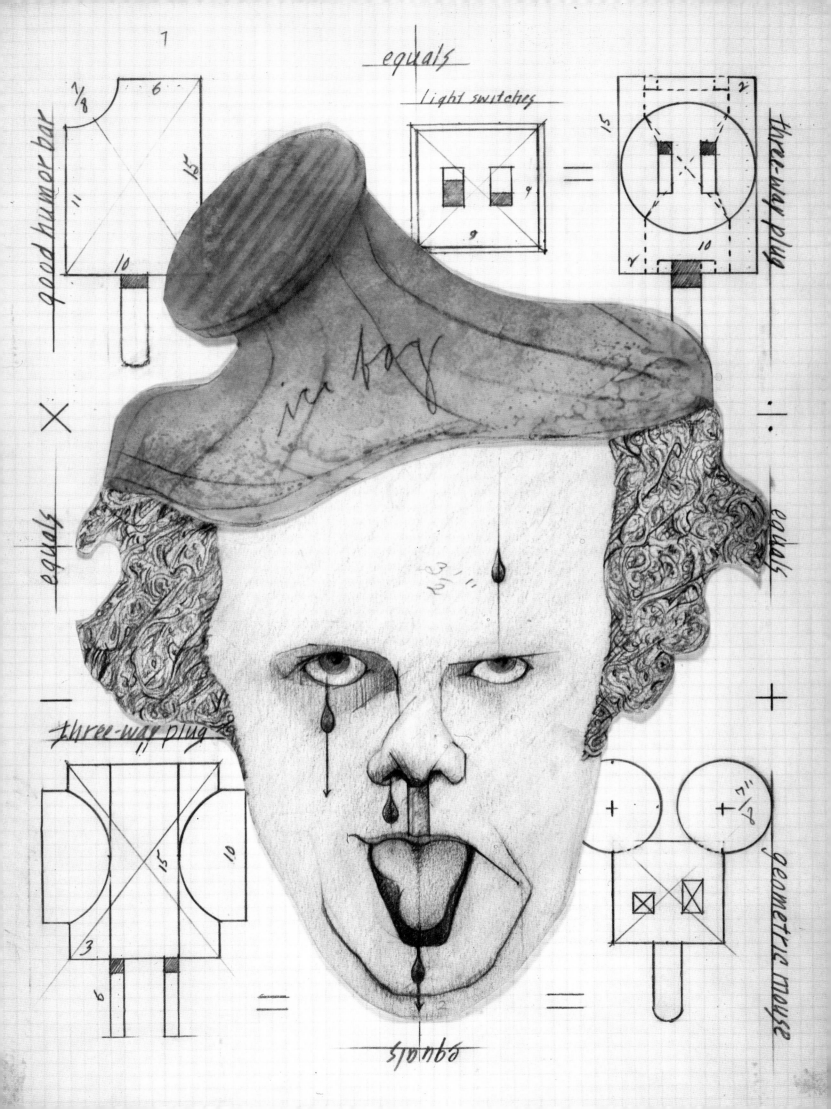

188. Giant Ice Bag – Cross Section
View I, W.E.D., *1969. Pencil, graphite,
and colored pencil on paper, 11 x 13¼
inches (27.9 x 34.9 cm). National Gallery
of Canada, Ottawa.*

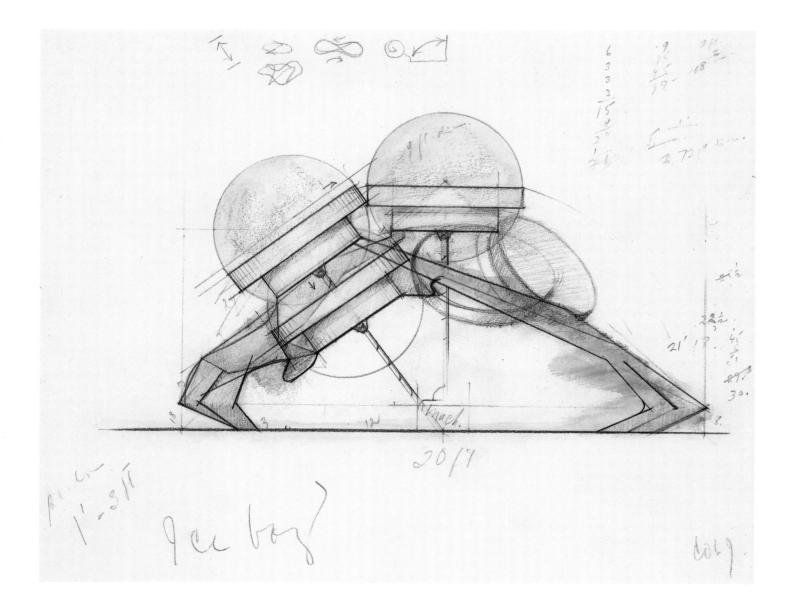

I think perhaps my approach to technology
is to remove the difficulty of technology,
as to take something which is formidable in
its complexity, and make it do some very
foolish thing--and I sort of like the idea
that all this time and effort was spent on
the Icebag. I'm creating something which
really doesn't do very much. It just does
something very simple; and it doesn't do
anything more really than a leaf does in
the wind.

(1971)

pages 324–25:
189. Giant Ice Bag, *1969–70, included in*
Gemini G.E.L.: Art and Collaboration,
National Gallery of Art, Washington,
D.C., November 18, 1984–February 24,
1985.

190. System of Iconography: Plug,
Mouse, Good Humor Bar, Switches and
Lipstick – Version I, *1970. Pencil and
crayon on paper, 22 x 15 inches (55.9 x
38.1 cm). Stedelijk Museum, Amsterdam.*

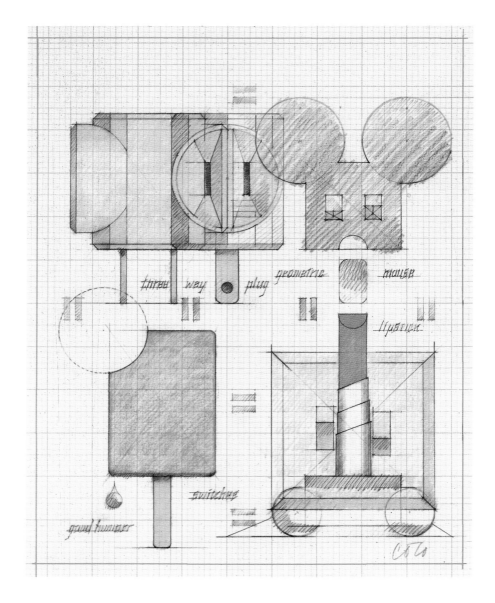

191. Study for Feasible Monument:
Lipstick, Yale, *1969. Pencil and spray
enamel on paper, 16¼ x 10¼ inches (41.3 x
27.3 cm). Private collection.*

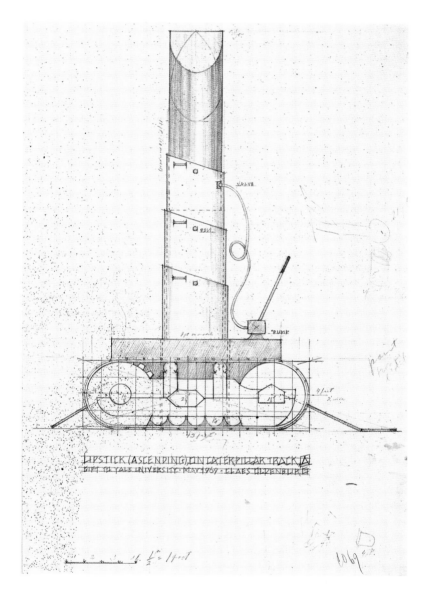

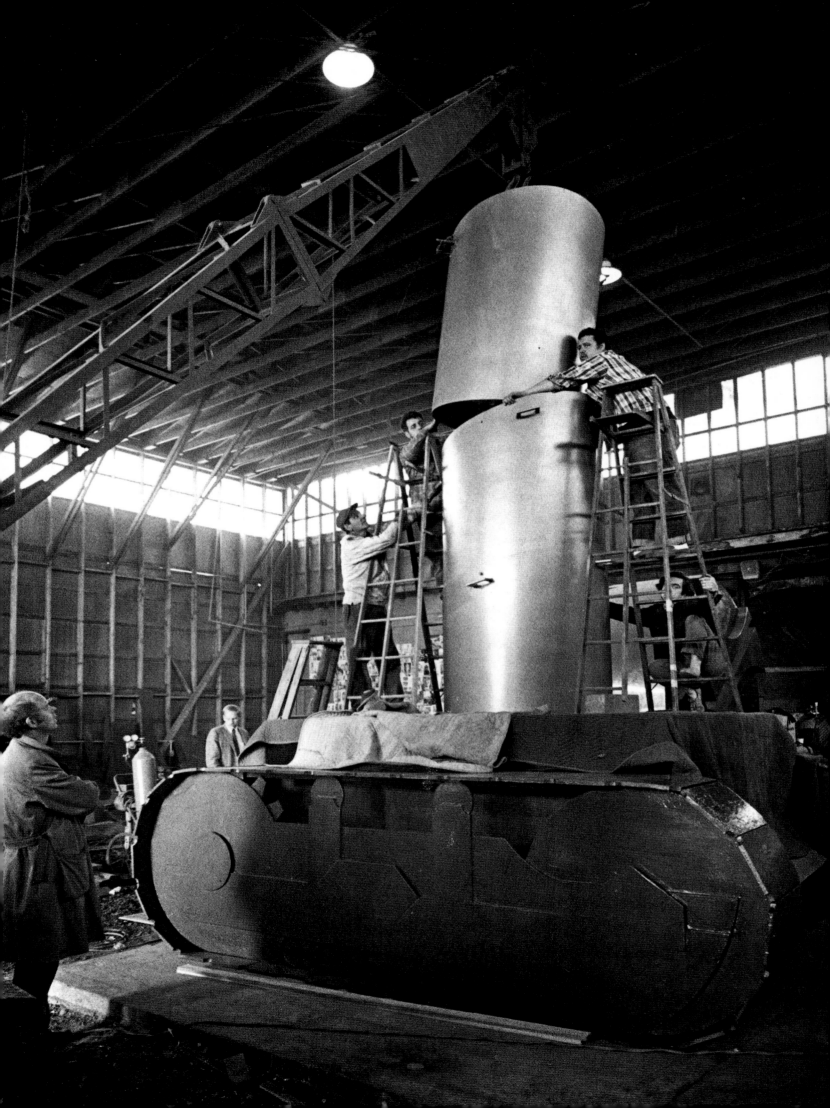

194. Lipstick (Ascending) on Caterpillar Tracks, 1969, installed at Beinecke Plaza, Yale University, New Haven, Connecticut, May 15, 1969–March 1970. Steel, aluminum, and wood, painted with enamel, 23 feet 6 inches x 24 feet 10½ inches x 10 feet 11 inches (7.16 x 7.58 x 3.33 m). Yale University Art Gallery, Gift of Colossal Keepsake Corporation.

195. Giant Three-Way Plug,
Scale A – 2/3, 1970–71. *Cor-Ten steel and*
bronze, 9 feet 8 inches x 6 feet 6 inches x
4 feet 9 inches (2.95 x 1.98 x 1.45 m).
The Saint Louis Art Museum, Gift of
The Shoenberg Foundation, Inc.

196. Three-Way Plug, Scale A,
Soft, Brown, 1975. *Vinyl filled with*
soft polyurethane foam; Masonite; wood;
wire mesh; metal; and rope; 144 x 77 x
59 inches (365.8 x 195.6 x 149.9 cm).
Walker Art Center, Minneapolis,
Gift of the artist.

197. Standing Mitt with Ball (Model), 1973. Steel, lead, and wood, 42 x 26 x 16½ inches (106.7 x 66 x 41.9 cm). The Edward R. Broida Trust.

198. Standing Mitt with Ball, 1973. Steel, lead, and wood, 12 feet (3.66 m) high. Collection of Agnes Gund, New York, On long-term loan to the Storm King Art Center, Mountainville, New York.

199. Inverted Q, Black – 1/2, 1976–78.
Cast resin, painted with urethane enamel,
72 x 70 x 63 inches (182.9 x 177.8 x
160 cm). Collection of Barbara and
Richard S. Lane.

200. Typewriter Eraser, 1976. Stainless steel, ferrocement, and aluminum, on steel base, 89 x 90 x 63 inches (226.1 x 228.6 x 160 cm). The Patsy R. and Raymond D. Nasher Collection, Dallas.

201. Alphabet as Good Humor Bar,
*1970. Colored pencil and crayon on paper,
28½ x 22½ inches (72.4 x 57.2 cm).
Courtesy of Leo Castelli Gallery.*

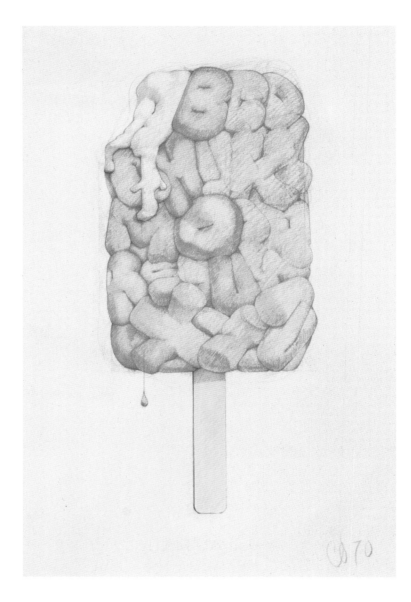

202. Project for a Beachhouse in the Form of the Letter Q, *1972. Pencil, colored pencil, and pastel on paper, 29 x 23 inches (73.7 x 58.4 cm). The Museum of Contemporary Art, Los Angeles, Gift of The Melville J. Kolliner Family Trust in memory of Beatrice S. Kolliner.*

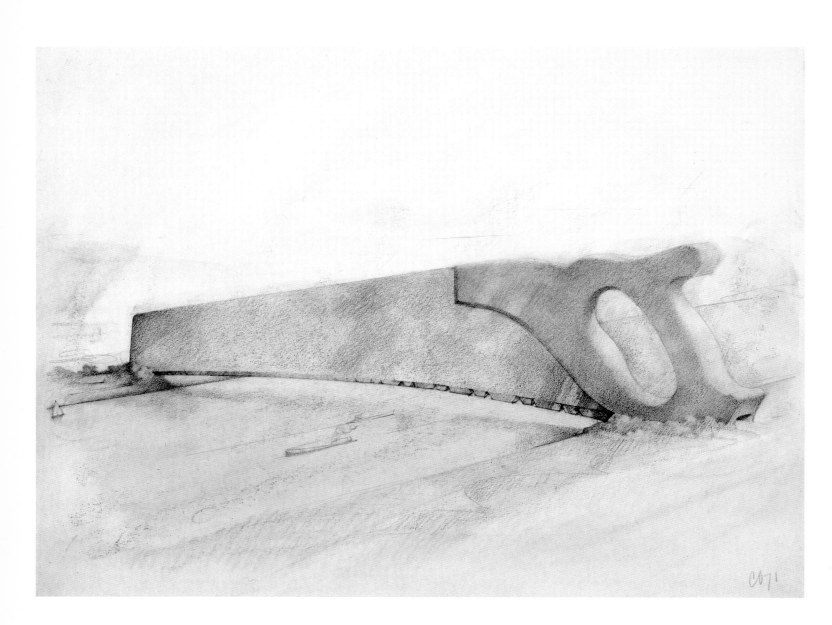

204. Cemetery in the Shape of a Screw:
Skyscraper for São Paulo, Brazil, *1971.*
Pencil and colored pencil on paper, 14 ⁷⁄₁₆ x
11 ½ inches (36. 7 x 29. 2 cm). Collection of
Claes Oldenburg and Coosje van Bruggen,
New York.

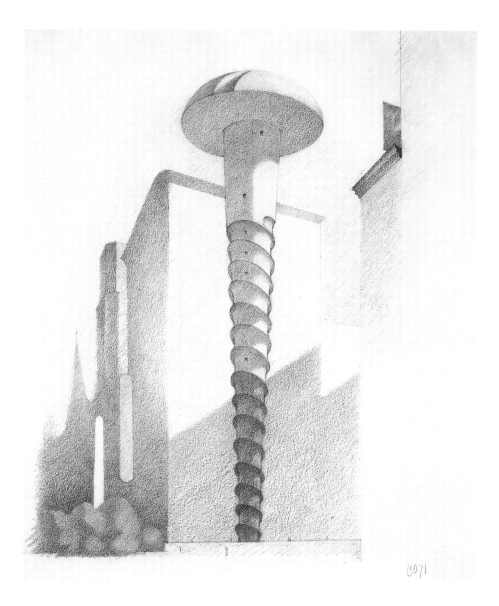

205. Proposal for a Cathedral in the
Form of a Colossal Faucet, Lake Union,
Seattle, *1972. Watercolor, graphite, and
colored pencil; image: 25⁷/₈ x 20 inches
(65.7 x 50.8 cm); sheet: 29 x 22⁷/₈ inches
(73.7 x 58.1 cm). Whitney Museum of
American Art, New York, Purchase, with
funds from Knoll International, Inc.*

206. Proposal for a Building in the
Form of a Colossal Flashlight in Place
of the Hoover Dam, Nevada, *1982.*
Pencil, colored pencil, and watercolor on
paper, 40 x 30 inches (101.6 x 76.2 cm).
Collection of Cheryl and Henry Welt.

Railroad Station in the Form of a
Wristwatch, for Florence, Italy (Two
Views), 1984. Pencil, colored pencil, and
watercolor on paper, 30 x 40 inches (76.2 x
101.6 cm). Collection of Robin Quist Gates.

208. Tongue Cloud, over St. Louis (with
Arch and Colossal Raisin Bread), *1975.*
Pencil, colored pencil, crayon, pastel, chalk,
and watercolor on paper, 40 x 30 inches
(101.6 x 76.2 cm). The Helman Collection.

NOTES ON THE GEOMETRIC MOUSE SUBJECT

The GM has been around in my work since 1963, and has been put to many uses.

The subject is not a whole mouse, just the head. The GM is a mechanical or conceptual version of an organic subject--therefore a "head" subject.

The GM is hieratic as well as mathematical. It has been used as a Mask--in a performance of Moveyhouse, a "happening" in 1965.

The GM is a sign and a typographical presence. Two prominent characters in the GM are "H" and "M". My typewriter is a Geometric Mouse.

For the animator, the mouse is a symbol of pen or pencil in motion and therefore a natural subject. On of the images contained in the GM sign is the early film camera, in silhouette, flat like film.

The precise mechanism of the GM C suggests a camera. The surface feels and looks like the inside of an old box Kodak.

The GM is a face and also a facade--a housefront, a scenery flat. The GM can be imagined to be any size.

As a good luck charm and as an autoportrait, the GM was used as an announcement, a letterhead and a banner.

Mouse--Mouseum--Mouseoleum.

GM--GeMini (Minnie).

The GM is a monument to the senses in the head: the eyes, the ears, the nose. The sense of touch is supplied in setting up the monument.

The GM is nocturnal, and therefore is the reverse of Ignatz (in Krazy Kat), who is a white mouse in a night world. The GM is a night mouse in a white world, a slice, a leftover of darkness.

The GM is its own shadow.

The hatches/windows/shades/shutters/lids indicate stages of somnolence or wakefulness. The GM arrives asleep, flat like a drawing. It rises from bed, to start its daily exercises (with your help).

The shapes are extremely general-- rectangles, circles. Only the "nose" is somewhat subjective and particular, like a spill of oil, though it is defined by structural requirements. The GM is a device for detecting certain conditions of nature, especially gravity and the changing appearances of planes in space. The "tears" (shade pulls) are like pods, finding the level of the surface on which the GM rests. Anchors to the bottom, double stethoscopes and monocles. The settling down on several points of contact suggests lunar landings.

The GM became three-dimensional in response to the technique of steel planes welded together at Lippincott Inc. I wanted to set several planes of steel into the air--space cleavers--and the GM subject fit the intention. The GM has been done in four scales, from the X--having an "ear" diameter of nine feet--to the C, whose "ear" diameter is nine inches. An Easter Island head which happened to be on the Lippincott Inc. premises for copying influenced the scale of GMA--a six foot "ear". Scale B has an "ear" diameter of eighteen inches.

GM C is a tabletop sculpture, a portrait, a skull, and recalls the Sleeping Muse (Mouse) of Brancusi, when set in the so called basic position (Position 1). In the larger scales X and A, this position is fixed--the parts cannot be moved.

Being totally black, the GM tends to cancel a depth sensation and produces a variety of "flat" images, returning again to the drawing inkblot stage--though its wings are spread in space.

These changes are changes of "Expression" too, which is interesting because the GM at rest is very little more than a grouping of similar geometric figures, with no expression whatsoever.

(1971)

209. Scales of the Geometric Mouse,
1971. Pencil and colored pencil on paper,
23⅛ x 29 inches (58.8 x 73.7 cm).
Walker Art Center, Minneapolis, Gift of
the artist, 1974.

210. Geometric Mouse, Scale C, 1971.
Anodized aluminum, 24½ x 20 x 18 inches
(62.2 x 50.8 x 45.7 cm), variable.
Collection of Claes Oldenburg and Coosje
van Bruggen, New York.

211. Geometric Mouse, Scale X, Red, *1971, included in* Monumenta: Sculpture in Environment, *Newport, Rhode Island, August 17–October 13, 1974.*

212. Geometric Mouse Banners, *1969,* installed outside the Museum of Modern Art, New York, September 25–November 23, *1969.*

213. *Poster for* Mouse Museum *at* Documenta 5, Kassel, 1972. *Four-color offset lithograph, 33⅛ x 23⅛ inches (83.8 x 58.7 cm). Collection of Claes Oldenburg and Coosje van Bruggen, New York.*

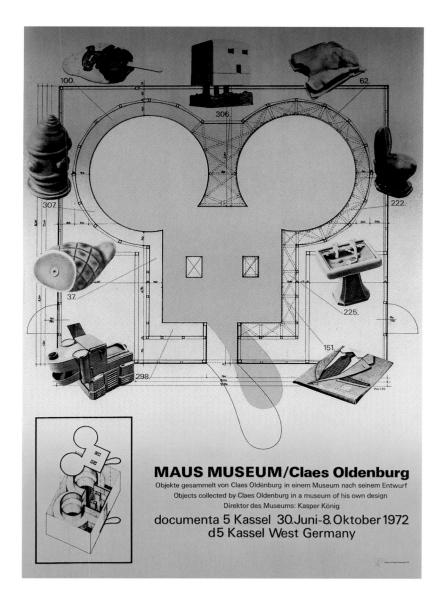

MAUS MUSEUM/Claes Oldenburg
Objekte gesammelt von Claes Oldenburg in einem Museum nach seinem Entwurf
Objects collected by Claes Oldenburg in a museum of his own design
Direktor des Museums: Kasper König
**documenta 5 Kassel 30.Juni–8.Oktober 1972
d5 Kassel West Germany**

214. Mouse Museum, *1977, installed at the Rijksmuseum Kröller-Müller, Otterlo, the Netherlands, June 16 — July 29, 1979.*

pages 356—57:
215. Mouse Museum, *1977, interior view, installed at the Whitney Museum of American Art, New York, September 28 — November 26, 1978.*

pages 358—59:
216. *Collection of objects at Oldenburg's Broome Street studio, New York, 1994.*

1977-1994

New York City
North Haven, Connecticut
Deventer, The Netherlands
Venice, Italy

Large Scale Projects with
Coosje van Bruggen:

Trowel; Batcolumn; Pool
Balls; Crusoe Umbrella;
Flashlight; Split Button;
Hat in Three Stages of
Landing; Spitzhacke; Gar-
tenschlauch; Screwarch;
Cross Section of a Tooth-
brush; Stake Hitch; Balan-
cing Tools;

(cont'd)

(cont'd)

Toppling Ladder; Spoon-
bridge and Cherry; Drop-
ped Bowl with Scattered
Slices and Peels; Bicyc-
lette Ensevelie; Monu-
ment to the Last Horse;
Binoculars (with Frank
O. Gehry); Free Stamp;
Mistos; Bottle of Notes;
Inverted Collar and Tie;
Shuttlecocks

Tools of the Trade; Tube
Supported by Its Contents

Il Corso del Coltello,
with Coosje van Bruggen
and Frank O. Gehry

Haunted House; Piano/
Hammock; Extinguished
Match; Clarinet, Harps,
Saxophones; Apple Cores;
Leaf Boat

Exhibitions with Coosje
van Bruggen:

From the Entropic Library;
The European Desk Top

The Sculptor versus the Architect

Germano Celant

The Ideal versus the Real

Formulating criteria for defining the city is a laborious task; despite centuries of exuberant social, historical, and philosophical efforts, no one has yet managed to arrive at a final definition. The city has remained an idea and a perception, a recognizable entity, but with vast and diverse features that keep it from being pinpointed. Writers have discussed the city's design and depictability,[1] its form and aesthetics.[2] But every theoretical or practical construction has met with a series of dialectics: between the configuration of the present and the articulation of future goals; between the re-elaboration or preservation of the status quo and the planning or discovery of enlightened and forward-looking transformations; between ancient and modern; between praxis and fancy—or, in terms cherished by the Renaissance, the encounter or confrontation between the *real* city and the *ideal* city.

A twofold approach to the dichotomy between and the coexistence of the concrete city and the fantastic city has always existed. One side is characterized by rigidity, paralysis—the halting of motion in which the city expresses its architectural and urban riches. The other side is marked by the threat of imminent explosion due to a precarious creativity that seeks spaces and territories for its expression, thereby producing images and edifices, routes and figurations that reveal the impassioned results of a life lived in art and architecture.

The concrete city vampirizes every idea of changing or overthrowing the status quo so that the fantastic participation is dispossessed. It imposes itself as petrification and congealment, draining the vital energies that build and mold the city as a flow. The real city offers an experience of aridity: it is a clot of empty spaces and conglomerations of glass that generate a menacing and asphyxiating tension, an imperturbable and antagonistic lack of being. The consequence of a process of historical and existential refinement, the product of stockpiling and stultification, the real city is a labyrinth with a shapeless, shadowy geography, a vortex that inflicts aimlessness and alienation. The informational criteria of the real city, based on a nuclear and hierarchical vision, are meant to lead back to a pragmatic meaning tied to the practical and functional dimension of living.

The ideal, ephemeral city, in contrast, betrays a latent desire for a dream with an urgent drive to reveal and disseminate itself through reality. It can be thought of as a wedge that passes through the meshes of practice, function, and existence. It can also be compared with the planned fantastic city of the Renaissance[3] and its demand for a visual magic to delineate the obscure, intense space of the Medieval urban scene.

The urban magic that connotes the ideal city derives from a new vision. Humanist hero worship compelled a pope, a king, or a grand duke to perform ritual gestures over the city— gestures translated into representations of his existence as a cultural and economic power. Thus were born the New City and the Ephemeral City, which triggered a mechanism and ceremony of energies that changed the urban physiognomy in an imaginary sense by opening up large avenues and vast, spectacular thoroughfares arranged in an unusual luminous layout. The urban metamorphoses favored by pontiffs and monarchs—from Pope Picolomini (Pius II) to Charles V, from Frederick II to Cosimo de' Medici—for such towns as Pienza and Cosenza, Capua and Florence show how deeply the architectural construction, in surges of pure volatility and fleeting intensity, marked the history of urbanism.

The necessity of creating a glittering pageant closely tied to happy and dismal events—such as birth and death, journeys and pilgrimages—inspired the imagery of artists and architects from Antonio Rossellino to Giambologna, from Donato Bramante to Sebastiano Serlio, from Gianlorenzo Bernini to Francesco Borromini: they produced an ardent figuration that could ignite the cities of the Renaissance and the Baroque.[4]

The result was a beautiful weave of buildings and bridges, squares and houses, passages and gardens, fountains and canopies, gates and arches of triumph, monuments and festive adornments. In using these structures (often adorned with allegorical motifs) to support the apotheosis of a pope or king, the artists and architects worked a fantastic and imaginary transformation of the city, splitting its identity into sleep and dream. With all their might, they attempted to give the urban texture a heroic status that legitimized the social and ritual importance of the design—no less intense in helping to form the contours of the real and the functional—while attending to the pleasures of life and social existence. In the joyful metamorphosis that took place through the sparkling of symbolic and figurative landscapes, the city underwent a process of purification, the index of a new mindset that was ideal and utopian.

The same impulse was felt in the eighteenth century when an architect/artist such as Etienne-Louis Boullée began to establish a system of architectural principles based on an artistic vision.[5] His projects, together with those of Claude Nicolas Ledoux and Jean-Jacques Lequeu, constituted a visionary architecture that looked to the paintings of Raphael and Jacques-Louis David in order to achieve an extreme rationalism that excluded fortuitous expression while promoting a rational control of pure visual and volumetric forms. Their ideal city, fusing the classical and the intelligible, the intellectual and the passionate, the metaphorical and the emotional, incarnated a new vision of architecture and the city that eliminated the obstacle of concreteness and functionalism.

This ceremonial approach[6] was repeated in post-1917 Russia: artists such as Ivan Leonidov, Kazimir Malevich, Aleksandr Rodchenko, Vladimir Tatlin, and the brothers Aleksandr, Leonid, and Viktor Vesnin reappropriated the city and its means of communication in order to transmit the renewal of life, the advent of a cultural and visual revolution. The anniversary of the Russian Revolution was the occasion for an immense sculptural and chromatic beautification of Moscow's streets and squares—the Constructivist reflection of a Renaissance and Baroque vision drawn from *Civitas Solis* by Tommaso Campanella. Here, too, the portals and gardens, the streets and edifices, the monuments and festivals, the arches and settings make up a utopian dream that contrasts with reality.

Starved and impoverished by centuries of exploitation and decades of war, by an eclipse of life and imagination, a degraded and devitalized Soviet society was magically transmuted as it became the stage for a construction emancipated from any formal or iconic yoke. The power that was celebrated was the energetic freedom of existence without limits or parameters, and images were now objects of pleasure and delight.

The agitprop trains and cinema buses, the mass performances about the end of tsarist rule or about the

Gianlorenzo Bernini, Ecstasy of Saint Theresa, *1645–52. S. Maria della Vittoria, Rome.*

Francesco Borromini, S. Carlo alle Quattro Fontane, 1665–67. Rome.

Liubov Popova, Production Clothing for Actor No. 7, *1922. Ink, gouache, varnish, and collage on paper, 12⅞ x 9⅛ inches (32.8 x 23.3 cm). Collection of Merrill C. Berman.*

1983 reconstruction of Vladimir Tatlin, Model of the Monument to the Third International, *1920. Hirshhorn Museum and Sculpture Garden, Smithsonian Institution, Washington, D.C.*

International Commune, together with projects for buildings and monuments, carnivals and pageants, were designed by El Lissitzky and Vsevolod Meierkhold, Gustav Klutsis and Liubov Popova, members of Lef and of Vkhutemas. This renewal was a return to pure and ideal scenography, to spectacle that strives toward permanency.

The result was a system of signs and forms that served as the foundation for a social and architectural project borrowed from a method of very precise control. The goal was to formalize a disciplinary experience with typological and morphological variants that would manage to make the planning process scientific, or at least program it. Techniques of rationalization that were meant to help clarify the problem of mass communication were targeted at an uneducated society that was trying to become democratic.

The aim of employing the instruments of creation and planning to help urban operations was anchored to a vision of aesthetic totalization typical of historical vanguards, from Expressionism to Constructivism and from Futurism to Neo-Plasticism. Among the key figures to mention are Bruno Taut and Hermann Finsterlin, Hans Scharoun and Frederick Kiesler, Georgii and Vladimir Stenberg, Iakov Chernikhov, Fortunato Depero and Virgilio Marchi, Gerrit Rietveld and J. J. P. Oud, Georges Vantongerloo and Jean Gorin, whose *metropolis* projects, situated beyond reality, were offered as the only possible reality for a new society.

However, the designs for their cities, or at least an ideal or utopian architecture of universal value, never progressed beyond the blueprint stage. The proposed society was unattainable in that it suspended the real city in a universe without history. In each case it indicated a direction that rejected the vortex of the concrete and the functional, the useful and the practical. Nevertheless, this trend was an effort to open an "inner gaze" in which singularity, rather than diminishing and disappearing altogether, attempted to synchronize with history and its absorbing burden.

Throughout the ages, the ideal city has operated as a font of meanings on the level of transformation and fruition. It has been a site of absolute availability, a territory of condensation, and its formulations, in the course of time, have proved to be magical and magnetic. From the fifteenth through the twentieth century, the ideal city has been the emblem of a creative force turned outward, redirecting the functional toward rarified and cerebral forms and figures that might vanquish the suffocating and reassuring sublimation of a blocked and crystallized society.

If the ideal city's function has been to challenge continually the traditional criteria of building and visualization, that function is capable of being distorted. In the 1930s and 1940s, during totalitarian periods in Rome, Berlin, and Moscow, the ideal city risked being informed by strong ideological models, producing visions of absolutism.[7] These visions focused on co-opting the assent of the masses, thereby transforming the concepts of planning and organization into trickery, which was often imposed by force.

Oscillating between critical approval of the political status quo and survival of the very notion of the artistic ideal, the concept of the ideal city or the arts has kept circulating, though increasingly reduced to ornamentation, which excludes urban and architectural planning. This development can be traced from the designs for the Milan *Triennale* to those for EUR, from the Bauhaus to the WPA.

During the 1950s, a period defined by the antithetical ideologies of communism and capitalism, the design of the ideal city became detached from its vital primordial roots. Aside from a few examples by Paolo Soleri and Nicholas Schoffer, the proliferation of urban images and architectural and sculptural models no longer reflected great creativity. Instead, it heeded the imperative to depict the acceptance of a world that believed in opposing categories of economy and existence. The ideal city was thus manipulated via propaganda as a place symbolizing the future rationality of society. During the 1960s, the memory of that manipulation altered the very idea of the monument as a public sculpture or building, and the ensuing re-analyses tended to steer clear of any political or ideological associations. Such structures began to avoid any metaphysical or propagandistic meaning, since the latter was considered apologetic and rhetorical and consequently characteristic of a closed, totalitarian system.

What was needed was a non-symbolic alternative fully devoted to the imaginary and bearing existential needs beyond all representational or political legitimacy. Efforts concentrated on finding a mode of coexistence for personal identity and public intervention—a collaboration that established an accord between political power and artistic communication. These efforts at legitimizing the image were not expected to serve ideology or incorporate any political or social theory; the goal was a fantastic architecture based on the primacy of intellect and imagination.

What is defined as "public art" is the residue of a creative exuberance that imbued both the theory and the planning of the ideal city. Such art has been the government's compensation for a utopian double that, unable to penetrate reality, was isolated and abandoned in the squares and silent territories of the city—an ancient equestrian monument, a fountain—to maintain the presence/absence of an alternative dream and desire, whose realization was increasingly deferred.

The compensatory character of sculptural monuments, placed at the midpoints of urban centers or strongly connoted on the level of traffic and street circulation, is an utter betrayal of the logic of the revolutionary project, or at least the alternative project of the city. Rather than cultivating figural or formal invention, it isolates and devitalizes it. Monumental art and architecture are no longer champions of society; they no longer open toward new horizons of rationality or imagination. Slowly losing the measure of a relationship to the townscape, they become unbearable vestiges of shapeless materials and banal abstract forms.

Compared with the great contributions of the Renaissance and the Baroque eras or the mass representations of historical vanguards, the figural weight of public monuments has been reduced: no effective relationship of scale or dimension, image or architectural complexity, is established within historical and territorial reality.

Liaisons Dangereuses

During the 1960s, the effort to restore an ideal urban impact that could compete with the existing cityscape was taken up by Claes Oldenburg, whose proposals for monuments and buildings from 1965 to 1969 transformed sculpture into geographic invention. Most important, Oldenburg, before many architects, seemed to confront the importance of the city's visual value, not as urban design, but in a figurative direction involving iconographic, if not functional, shifts.

Transferring urbanism from one language, architecture, to another, art, he restructured the cityscape by presenting it in the guise of a childlike, daily memory composed of toys, objects, and writings.

Oldenburg seeks an iconic acceleration that entrusts the modification of the cityscape not to a formal, illuminist discipline but to an irrationality that includes an avalanche of heteroclite objects. His discourse always concerns the urban *ratio*; however, the icon's provocative violence alters and deforms the functional and utopian layouts, the flat and orderly values. He negates them in order to construct an imaginary city scenery in which the functional model is replaced by the fantastic design. Oldenburg is therefore intent on multiplying the element of surprise that distorts the laws of construction by imposing a phantasmagorical scene that explores a language of figural excess—a language open to the flow of artistic and other surprises.

To achieve this urbanist result, Oldenburg necessarily began with architecture, and his homage shows an awareness of the illuminist designs of Boullée, Ledoux, and Lequeu.[8] However, he also sees the flaw in their approach: an exclusive knowledge tied to the extreme frailty of an absolute logic inevitably leads to the totalitarian monument, as can be found in works from Albert Speer's Great Assembly Hall of 1939 to Marcello Piacentini's EUR of 1942.

Oldenburg knows quite well that public intervention involves a bond between form and effectiveness, appearance and ritual, ceremony and rhetoric. But in its morphological matrix, urban decoration (from the impersonal Latin verb *decet*) means "to pay tribute, honor, and remember." It refers to a "festive" rationality that implies veneration and memory.

In approaching a "colossal" monument, Oldenburg realizes he might encounter a historical experience that, both metaphysical and symbolic, is highly compromised because it is meant to convince, delight, and move. Hence, his first few subjects, as summed up in their titles, included *Monument to Immigration* (1961) and *Proposed Monument for the Intersection of Canal Street and Broadway, New York: Block of Concrete Inscribed with the Names of War Heroes* (1965, fig. 145)—except that it was iconology and not ideology that triumphed in these projects. The cause and foundation of Oldenburg's monuments or memorials were, in fact, the figural relationship between an object or building and the sphere of everyday life. The goal was to furnish the image of a culture, not its belief or transcendence.

A number of the utopian and rhetorical visions involved ideological failure. In works depicting an oversize teddy bear, a lipstick, an extension plug, or a vacuum cleaner, Oldenburg adhered to the beauty of the iconic circumstance—that inescapable causal nexus (in Walter Benjamin's terms) between *found* image and *found* city. Through the image, Oldenburg comes and goes from inspiration to planning, from art to architecture—a dialectics of knowing and seeing. As a result, he moves between these two poles, eliminating any persuasive and propagandistic connotation linked to the categories of tradition. Instead, he refers to a present that can only be its own tautology: the quotidian.

Oldenburg is from Chicago, a city closely identified with Louis Sullivan and Mies van der Rohe. Due in part to his roots in the city, Oldenburg is aware of the potential urbanistic value of the everyday object, which, coming from "elsewhere," creates an effect of displacement and disorder within the

Fortunato Depero, Book Pavilion,
*1927. Pencil and china ink on paper,
16 ¼ x 20 ⅛ inches (42.5 x 51.1 cm).
Galleria Museo Depero, Rovereto, Italy.*

Frederick Kiesler, Model for the
Endless House, *1959. Cement and wire
mesh with Plexiglas, 39 x 97 ¼ x 42 inches
(96.5 x 247 x 106.7 cm). Whitney
Museum of American Art, Gift of
Mrs. Lillian Kiesler.*

townscape. This effect is capable of producing an aesthetic upheaval.

My work is architecture. . . . Nothing is as important as the scale and the relation of different volumes . . . planes, lines . . . my personal architecture.[9]

In his quest for an alternative form to the monument (always at risk of relapsing into praise and honor for the ruling social system), Oldenburg looked to a liberation of the symbol and to solutions based on freedom of expression. If, at the end of this century, an ideal city could be built, its possibilities would have to be sought in creative play, and the liberation from the symbolic would necessitate widening the distance between the existential and the symbolic. Oldenburg's similar perspective in 1965 translated into an expressive formulation deriving from his artistic activity, which was already mature and affirmed. Instead of being restricted to a simple intellectual level, it was "twisted" and used toward architectural and urban ends. The convergence of these contradictory factors became a mirage, a set of proposals for monuments and buildings, a solution for transcending the incompatibility between existence and symbolism, individual and society, sculpture and architecture or urbanism. It was only by accepting a contradiction and its implication that Oldenburg could employ an alternative leading to a transcendence of the urban monument as testimony to totalizing ideologies.

Drawing his proposals on paper and explaining them in words,[10] Oldenburg never conceals the insecurity and irreconcilability of artistic existence in the face of social responsibility—namely, the job of producing symbolic objects such as buildings and monuments for urban geography. Nonetheless, he does not seek mutual approval or a mutually complementary situation; hence the ideal city becomes a place for recognizing the existence of not only the exceptional but also the quotidian. The quotidian is the present in which we live: it is neither tradition nor innovation, country nor utopia, antiquity nor future. It is something that is determined because it exists, in and of itself. Hence, accepting the quotidian means assuming one's own historicity. It means giving due consideration to existing in the moment, in the present.

Since 1959, the center of Oldenburg's work has been the quotidian: the street and the store, the object and the situation. He demonstrates an ability to experience the meaning of existence in the reality of its present and its repetition.

In adhering to the everyday life of things and events, he excludes the Celestial City or the advent of a perfect society. He recognizes these aspirations, but he does not propel them to the future; what attracts him is the utter nakedness of reality, which never aims, by means of symbolic and ritual operations, to a superreality.

Sinking into everyday life thus becomes an ever-new adventure. The artist submerges himself in his geography, discovering and examining its sediment. Like Jonathan Swift, he appropriates and implements his discoveries. The geographic exploration turns into an archeology of the banal, a recovery of the terrain of objects and things, whose universal and organic significance eludes our gaze and interrogation. It culls the mythic substance of objects and offers a specific way of viewing them. It reveals their enigma, which is ironic and alienating. It turns them into a theater of surprise.

Oldenburg actually uses the object in his provocative relationship with the landscape, the city, and the environment, as a distortion or twisting of meaning. The loss of proportionality drives the image and the object beyond symmetry, imposing a dynamic principle that transforms them into a Baroque wit,[11] an excess of inventive energy. Such works as the abovementioned *Proposed Monument for the Intersection of Canal Street and Broadway, New York* and *Proposed Colossal Monument for Park Avenue, New York: Good Humor Bar* (1965, fig. 144) attempt to define a figure that cannot be reduced to a representative urban harmony, to pinpoint something perverse in that harmony. This perversion of the architectural equilibrium is meant as a reality that has to be discovered. The term "perversion" is used here in its original sense: "contortion, transgression, upheaval"; but it also implies eros as a desired intermediary passage between two realities. Oldenburg seems to realize that he is straddling those poles—transgression and eros—so that the skewing of the landscape is accompanied by the flouting of the sexual taboo, as in *Proposed Monument for Oslo: Frozen Ejaculation (Ski Jump)* (1966).

An object foreign to the urban panorama is introduced into it, and by conjoining both identities it turns two mutually negating realities into partners. A relationship and a dialogue are worked out between two mutually indifferent things, producing networks of images, whose analysis requires adopting a code of both the private and the social unconscious. This twofold perspective makes us hear the call to existence and to the repression that tends to conceal existence as well as the desire to find a new horizon in society.

The monumental *Lipstick (Ascending) on Caterpillar Tracks* (1969–70, fig. 194; reconstructed 1974) moves in a conceptual space between militancy and corporality. By reflecting on the body, the erotic investment in the inflatable lipstick, Oldenburg succeeds in constructing a work that elicits an *esprit de corps*—that is, solidarity, the awareness of belonging to a *societas*.

When students at Yale University formed the Colossal Keepsake Corporation to commission a piece by Oldenburg, they were impelled not so much by fanatical enthusiasm or aggressive fury as by the sheer pleasure of a concerted action. With its tractor-like base, *Lipstick (Ascending) on Caterpillar Tracks* recalls the militancy and camaraderie of the campus; it also replaces the "armed" arm with a lipstick in gradual erection. The combination follows the conceptual model of a belief in the political idea, reminding us that citizenship in a *societas* does not mean forgetting about one's own pleasure. Hence, militancy is not set up as an abstract and transcendent entity; rather, it is as real as the symbol of (sexual) love.

Inspired by Tatlin's *Monument to the Third International* (1920),[12] *Lipstick* represents an osmosis between the subjectivity of pleasure and the collectivity of a common idea. As such, it celebrates neither erotic nudity nor an ideological party; instead, it represents a body-machine in which sex and mechanism are interchangeable.

With this *contaminatio* Oldenburg tries to establish a collective rite that pays heed to the dialogue between absolute knowledge and natural knowledge, between supreme values and ephemeral values. His piece mediates between everything and everyone. By establishing a complicity between different entities, sex and work, it proves that the true meaning of their existence is the subject.

Oldenburg brings opposites together, so that they belong to

and speak to each other, permitting a dialogue between *pars destruens* and *pars construens*. On the level of its historical milieu, *Lipstick* shares the climate of the new student contestations and the theories of Herbert Marcuse. In order to enable the student rebellion to enter into a dialogue with the provocativeness of historical and contemporary vanguards, *Lipstick* interweaves two complementary aspects of cultural massification. The result is a mass avant-garde.

Harking back to Tatlin, Oldenburg underscores his wish to be inspired by a "protest" creativity that does not isolate itself in the artistic absolute, which is characterized by social parasitism. Rather, he wants to use his "extravagance" by connecting it to the system of production and the overall social system. His approach is a symbol of contradiction between work and desire, task and expressivity, consumption and protest; the goal is to dispossess and surpass "elite art," thereby moving it to the territory of the masses.

In 1968, the urgency of this passage was tied to the crisis generally suffered by artists, who found they no longer had a function. They had to cope with a civilization uninterested in the *métier* of the imagination, which was opposed by the structuralism of the sciences and by the triumph of technologies. In addition, they witnessed an explosion of the mass media, which rejected any individual form of protest. Like the students, artists wanted to achieve a synthesis that would integrate the vehemence of contestation or revolutionary potential with the ruling imagination. Thus the only possible solution remained a mass avant-garde.[13]

The years 1968–69 were dominated by a maturing of radical thought, which fused individual and collective pleasure. *Lipstick* confronted the separation between elite art and the student masses. It tried to bridge the gap by mingling transgressive thought and monument, thereby making the work a symbol of or an homage to the idea of the "desire for power."

I have always felt the need of correspondence between one's art and one's life. I feel my purpose is to say something about the times . . . for me this involves a recreation of my vision of the times. . . . I am making symbols of my time through my experience.[14]

The relationship between the lipstick and the Caterpillar tractor changes the sculpture into an object with an "incestuous" relationship between eros and machine, between anthropomorphic monument and urban site. The university campus thus becomes a city plaza in which work coincides with sensuality. Yale is transformed into a space in which to lose oneself, a territory where desire can grow, becoming a game between law and prohibition.

In terms of the ideal city, Yale, like all great urban universities, is a "utopia"—that is, both *ou-topos*, a non-place, and *eu-topos*, a happy place. And Oldenburg responds with a fable, a consoling order (as Michel Foucault puts it) describing an "elsewhere" that envelopes extremes: *ou-topos* is the virtual territory in which tensions are resolved and conflicts settled.

The Found Totem

By 1970, the utopian visions of 1968 had become a vague prescription for an alternative order that would never manage to capture or solidify a final and total form. The great radical dream revealed merely a loss of center, producing confusion and a fluctuation of security and limits. Although the points of

"Capric" – Adapted to a Monument for a Park, *1966. Crayon and watercolor on paper, 22 x 30 inches (55.9 x 76.2 cm). Collection of Kimiko and John Powers.*

contact and the significant connections between things and places had multiplied, the politics had become bankrupt. The 1960s dream of the Happy City never came true; instead, the ultimate weakness of its logic and destiny were revealed.

Similarly, in 1970, when Oldenburg abandoned the hypothesis of an ideal identification for his colossal monuments, he began to seek objects and locations that could maximize the potential for surprise. He did not invert or confuse objects to promote a metaphor that risked becoming an illusion, nor did he create utopian blueprints for the dialectics of positive and negative, of Civitas Dei and Civitas Diaboli, of eros and technology, which negate the thing, transforming it into "something else." Instead, Oldenburg relied on the thing-object for its "primitive" and tribal power. The gradual moving toward large scale and away from enigmatic grafting (exemplified by the lipstick onto the tractor) enabled Oldenburg to avoid the strange conjunctions or dreamlike Surrealist "incestuousness" between objects and enter directly into the display. The latter reduces the subjective component in favor of generalized objecthood, in which the thing falls and rises within a context such as a building— except that the object replaces the building.

In subject matter it is a question of how specific or how powerful the subject is. One reason I use objects is to keep the reference general and to deemphasize the subject matter, keep it in its place. The use of subject matter for effect is too easy, and I tend to avoid it. I use things but not subjects, which is the whole distinction. . . . Things are merely structures, available in the space around me.[15]

This new strategy can derail traditional systems of art and architecture. Not only can it "select" an object (as in the proposals for colossal monuments) and "design" it as a fantasy in the landscape; it can also construct it in a real landscape. To go beyond the dead end reached by Marcel Duchamp, Dada, and Neo-Dada, which kept all things ambiguous (to act or not to act? to urinate or to comment? to use or to contemplate?), the artist must return the object to the urban universe, to its architecture. Museums and galleries and the world of fantasy are poeticized by painting, drawing, and sculpture, but the cityscape is poeticized by a building in the shape of an object and an object the size of a building.

Why should buildings always be boxes? I suggest the use of objects as "found" design, to construct colossal things as seriously as buildings are built. The sculptor vs. the architect.[16]

Nevertheless, the movement between art and architecture is not a swift one; it requires instruments that can implement planning from a small sketch to a large construction. If a goal is to achieve a sculpture on an urban scale, the methodology changes; forced to take heed of pragmatic and procedural implications, the artist's thoughts become "productive." Unlike the passive, contemplative dimension of traditional art, a building is active: it involves a perfected intervention that takes into account the intricate conceptual and organizational instrumentation required by the surrounding conditions. Art enters a system of thinking and planning, forgoing the use of simple "expedients" to solve problems of the "formation" of reality, a formation defined by praxis. The planning method assumes other forms of control; it takes off from an idea that functions as a model to ultimately challenge technology with its wide margin of error. In contrast to the use of uncertainty as the creative method, the artist/architect must employ the certainty of the technological sciences, confront the problems of prediction and optimization, and make possible an intuition and an impression.

Since Oldenburg has always worked on a large scale, the method for him is a principle:

After a subject has been realized by an impressionistic drawing, it is necessary to make a technical study of it, leading to the construction of a model.[17]

Architects and planners produce a model that generates structural solutions and their often too literal adaptations to a context. As an artist, Oldenburg realizes that in order to reach an architectural and urban scale, he must cope with the logistical difficulties of a project. Nevertheless he reserves the right to discuss or at least compare them, because in this "science/fiction" relationship, "I am a technological liar."[18]

Oldenburg addresses this dichotomy in his *Symbolic Self-Portrait with Equals* (1969, fig. 187), depicting the double identity of the clown/magician in a technical drawing. During the period 1969–70, the solution to the dichotomy was concretized as Oldenburg turned to "abstract" and "technological" work that annuls any single solution in order to achieve a monument or sculpture that originates in a totality of creative processes, from art to design, from industry to technology.

In 1970, the artist revealed the abstraction or crystallization of the object by employing rigid materials (such as metal, cardboard, and plywood) or a geometric definition of contours, which then become linear and elementary. It was as if the imagined and desired world of a tactile and sensual object were to assume a different identity, take on a different aspect, in its move from soft to hard. With this twofold internal movement, from sensual to ideal, from pliant to rigid, several pieces, from 1970 to 1976, were "regenerated" in a visual and productive sense, including *Giant Three-Way Plug* (1970–71, fig. 195), the *Geometric Mouse* in its various scales (1971, figs. 210–11, for example), *Clothespin* (1976, fig. 220) and *Typewriter Eraser* (1976, fig. 200).

After a period of recovering a sensuality that the 1968 student movements had ultimately made their own, the mutation brought Oldenburg to a new sculptural analysis, requiring a hardening and compactness that sharpened sensitivity. Tough and dense, refined and absolute, this acute sensitivity transported the sculptures, metaphorically, into a new territory of feeling; no longer personal, they were now public and collective. Accompanying the change in consistency was an assertion of fullness and unity. The work lost the sense of flaccid and tender, thick and dense, soft and fluid that was typical of the earlier soft sculptures; instead it moved toward the solidity of planning and material found in his *Bedroom Ensemble* (1963, see fig. 112), which "might have been called composition for (rhomboids), columns and disks. Using names for things may underline the 'abstract' nature of the subject or all the emphasis can do this. Subject matter is not necessar[ily] an obstacle to seeing 'pure' form and color."[19]

The pure and abstract forms stripped by time acquire a "functional" physiology that reenters the system of life, from the bedroom to the city. Simultaneously the torn and sewn, soft and tender materials, charged with tactile sensuality, leave

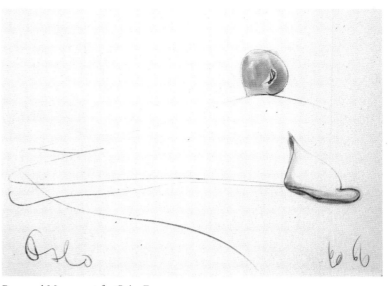

Proposed Monument for Oslo: Frozen Ejaculation (Ski Jump), *1966. Crayon and watercolor on paper, 22 x 30 inches (55.9 x 76.2 cm). Private collection.*

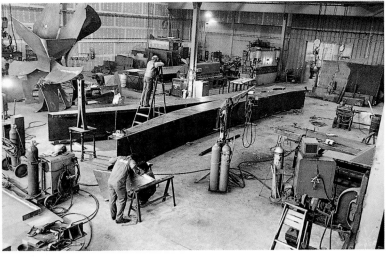

Clothespin *under consturction at Lippincott, Inc., North Haven, Connecticut, 1976.*

room for hard, dry surfaces (such as plywood or cardboard) that seem to correspond more to a "spirituality" or, more precisely, an ideal; they exclude the fragment and the individual in favor of unity and the collective.

In exalting a modeled and planned substantiality (this series of sculptures was realized with the assistance of Lippincott Inc. in North Haven, Connecticut and of other factories), Oldenburg introduced into his work the concept of functionality. In the soft sculptures, the chosen object had been "anarchic" in that it refused to supply unique responses as to its disposition and meaning, its completeness and arrangement, its form and volumetry—all of which were open and uncontrollable features. But with the advent of the huge stable and rigid sculptures, the object regained a "utilitarian" preoccupation that, on the social level, became, in effect, social authority. In 1970, Oldenburg seemed to criticize the autonomous and romantic standpoint of the artist whose sole attitude is "anti-objective" or "anti-aesthetic"—a position tied to Dadaist and Surrealist nonsense. Instead, he returned to treating art as teleological, that is, as having rigorous social ends. He shifted toward the rationalist, socialist axis that fused the Renaissance with Russian Constructivism, Leonardo da Vinci with Tatlin. Rediscovering the fetish and the everyday totem—as in *Giant Three-Way Plug* or *Clothespin*—Oldenburg gave them a different function. He saw these not as anti-objects, but as monuments and buildings in the city.

The main reason for the colossal objects is the obvious one—to expand and intensify the presence of the vessel—the object. Perhaps I am more a still life painter—using the city as a tablecloth.[20]

Coagulation and planning eliminate discontinuity and randomness. The work is inserted into a constellation that aspires to a "total" fusion of object and environment—analogous to Leonardo's landscapes: without a hierarchy of close and distant realities, it can focus on both minute details and wide-ranging problems.

If I am a landscape painter (and my "monuments" are an excuse for doing landscapes), then I am a painter of the complete landscape, not only the look of the weather and the lay of the land, etc., but also the emotions of the place (mine and others'), the history of the place (some of which I imagine), and whatever else I am aware of in a place.[21]

That statement dovetails with one of Leonardo's:

The painter is the master of all the things that can occur to the human mind, so that if he desires to see beautiful things that he falls in love with, he is the master of generating them; if he wants to see monstrous things that are terrifying or ludicrous and laughable or truly pitiful, then he is their lord and creator.[22]

The demand for structurally coordinating the universe of streets, objects, houses, passersby, advertisements, clothes, and overall urban life was introverted early on in Oldenburg's work, as in the installation *The Street* (1960, pages 44–59). But in 1969–70, this demand became extroverted as the artist began to regulate his work as an outward reflection. Taking the habitat of his sculpture as a determining factor for a structured complex of stimuli that were associatively mirrored in his work, he made a leap of aesthetic "ecologism," planned "sculptures in situations"—in direct interdependence with the given context. In this development, he created his own imaginary situation, constructing an iconography through a process of refraction tied to the environmental input.

Lipstick (Ascending) on Caterpillar Tracks and *Giant Ice Bag* (1969–70, fig. 189) are objects that slide or fluctuate on land and water—that is, they use each context as a "base," from which, however, they are detached. By contrast, subsequent pieces, from *Trowel I* (1971, see fig. 217) to *Clothespin*, from *Batcolumn* (1977, fig. 221) to *Flashlight* (1981, fig. 225), are founded on and wed to their surroundings. Such rooting, both physical and symbolic, betokens a withdrawal from abstraction. It submits to a sociocultural connection that defines its setting and content, becoming their synthesis. The object in these cases gives itself to its surroundings, declaring its immovability and dovetailing with the landscape. It loses its ability to move quickly from one situation to another, an ability found in Oldenburg's sculptures made between 1959 and 1969.

Oldenburg's new phase was the beginning of a challenge, for although the essence of art was fixed in both the artist and time, it was no longer located in fluctuating data—designs or models, writings or sculptures. Instead, we see a praxis based on a concrete and structural foundation whose operative definitions are, as for any building, related to the history and the past and present events of the site and the environment. Finally, the creative adventure passed from an intuitive system (which could be that of the proposals for colossal monuments) to a practical system of solutions based substantially on the growing complexity that accompanied the ever-increasing number of variables and participants (such as engineers) needed.

The planning[23] for these projects begins with an invitation or commission for a work and the necessity for a definition of the problem: this is made up of two elements—the form or image and the given context. The context is the sum of the historical and cultural connotations, its demands and obligations, for which a correspondence with the chosen form or image is sought. This procedure is based on a continuous self-questioning as to the environmental, historical, and iconographic variables of the site on which the monument or structure will stand or establish its foundation, its roots.

Until 1969–70, Oldenburg developed a planning consistent with America's industrial vision—which depends on the movement of goods—creating objects and sculptures that could be transported to various exhibition venues. Thus in 1969, when Oldenburg was asked to furnish a piece for *Sonsbeek 71*, an outdoor exhibition held in the Netherlands, he first suggested a vehicle, "a tractor towing two huge inflated bags." But the project was debated in terms of the European vision, which was preoccupied with the ephemeral and mobile status of the work as well with as its technological aggressiveness.[24]

So the artist decided to propose *Trowel*, which corresponds to the linguistic norms and criteria that for him are diverse and unusual. First, he worked out the adherence to the landscape—a method that subsequently would induce him to always seek a reference to both the inner and outer context. He decided to exclude the artwork's performance value, which not only involves exhibition and spectacle but also defines the work as a solemn and stable operation adequate to a culture, European, that is alive with permanence and history.

The territorial rooting promotes close connections between art and landscape, personal fantasy and public dimension,

Batcolumn *en route to its Chicago installation site, 1977.*

while introducing a democratic participation. It conforms to a society and cuts off, or at least cools, any metaphysical tendency.

A "cool" hard romanticism: romanticism of the objective. I wish to reflect things as they are now and always without sentimentality. To face the facts and learn their beauty. Actual volume of the sculpture. . . . The relief planes move in space as spectator moves and the effect is this too like changing collage which is how landscape is seen as, for example, from a moving car.[25]

In addition, the intuitive occasion turns into permanence, rather than circumstance. Instead of introducing a surprising object, destined for a private collection or a museum, the artist decides to construct an enchantment that can be owned by anyone, any time, any place, because it can be "seen from a moving car" of the collective and is perhaps permanent. Thus we have the choice of site (Sonsbeek Park) and material (metal). Both are metaphors for a political consciousness ("political" derives from *polis*, or "city") of the artistic process as an exercise in relation to community as well as the past, the present, and the future.

Oldenburg's focus on these historical and environmental questions of aesthetics coincided with the opening of a dialogue with the European mind. The artist discussed the iconographic and historical reasons for *Trowel* with Coosje van Bruggen, the co-editor of the *Sonsbeek 71* catalogue. The discussion involved a conceptual analysis of the work, thereby defining the logic of what was intuited. Van Bruggen is a writer and art historian who explored the work's existence as a linguistic transgression. This launched a collaboration in which the image became the common subject. The two based their approach on the intuitive and fantastic vision of two- and three-dimensional figurations, while the logic of the method rotated around values from other disciplines, considering images that are literary and historical, philosophical and psychological, social and political.

The two perspectives compensate for one another. Both are creative because they share the goal of producing images that can be appreciated in terms of aesthetic transgression and social and historical effectiveness.

Large-Scale Projects

A construction, sculpture, event, monument, or building that enters a context and transforms it is inseparably joined to the history of the place and its surroundings. The planning for a large-scale project is not based on a simple figural intuition; rather, it goes through the complex process of defining a problem, studying the variables and standards, working out the main idea, analyzing past and present, considering the optimal methods of construction, examining the details, making the models and prototypes, drafting the technical designs, estimating the developments, and carrying out the construction. All these stages require teamwork on the part of Oldenburg and van Bruggen in regard to the creative method, and to the possible solutions to the problem at hand.

Oldenburg and van Bruggen work together on the originality of the artistic message, checking all unforeseeable elements in the grouping of signs and symbols—designed or hypothesized, iconic or philosophical—that make up that message. Eliminating the foreseeable and therefore unoriginal elements, they measure the communication of the work through all its media—from design to model, from technical prototype to small scale—until construction is completed. Similarly, they reduce any redundant information, trying to build or rebuild, through a "case history," the fragments of the deciphering of the work, at the same time making it more legible and perceptible. And yet its intelligibility depends on the perception and interpretation of forms and colors, of the articulation of signs. We can thus understand why initially, from 1975 through 1979, van Bruggen's role was to verify and critically read semantic and informational quantities of Oldenburg's work through his notes, texts, and theoretical analyses, which immediately transformed the activity of the imagination. This theoretical and critical practice was hitched to a creative collaboration that led to the invention and definition of the images—an exchange and dialogue that have continued on both fronts.

In *Trowel*, the chromatic definition was changed when the first version was reconstructed in 1976:

Coosje felt that the silvery finish of the first version, together with its elegant outline, had turned the sculpture into an artifact or table utensil. Instead she proposed a shade of blue associated with labor— the blue of Dutch workmen's overalls and of the tarpaulins used by truckers and sailors—in order to reassert the subject's function as a tool.[26]

Within Oldenburg's artistic development, the dialogue with van Bruggen offers a permanent possibility of testing, through close analysis, the relationship between occasion and inspiration, between context and project. Furthermore, by means of a historical and critical position and an imaginary "outside," this dialogue parenthesizes the subjective peculiarity of their efforts, so that it adapts to the situation. Van Bruggen's task is to bring out the iconic efficiency of thought and theory, of storytelling and aesthetic invention, through words and writing—which can emerge from associative images evoked by both members of the artistic team. This osmosis is typical of the modernity that Charles Baudelaire describes in his 1863 essay *Le peintre de la vie moderne*, in which he defines the artist as a poet who is not merely a specialist of words or colors, but above all a man of the world, capable of sharing his own time with others, from the individual to the masses of the metropolis.

When Oldenburg and van Bruggen receive a commission or invitation, the occasion turns into a meeting place between art, poetry, and history, which are seen as reciprocal. However, the meeting is no longer based exclusively on the temporary and unsuspected character of inspiration; instead, it now covers the entire planning process, which is linked to the problems of context and iconographic subject selected as a mirrorlike response. It stems from the instantaneous circumstance, which is translated into notes and sketches, through a permanent response. The methodological leap is important because it definitively excludes the typical automatism of Action Painting. Instead, it combines an exactness and theoretical planning with a Minimalist and Conceptual contemporaneity, according to which the image results from a relationship to the concrete and logical circumstances of the occasion.

The working method, the processes, and the artistic components of the large-scale projects in general can be exemplified by the case history of *Flashlight*, the first piece to be signed by both of them. In 1978, after the realization of

Clothespin in Philadelphia and *Batcolumn* in Chicago, Oldenburg was invited to make a public sculpture between two auditoriums—a concert hall and a theater—at the University of Nevada at Las Vegas .

The occasion of the project was closely tied to the magic of the lights of Las Vegas, whose existence is based not on the beauty and antiquity of the permanent, but on the effectiveness of the present, of decoration and transience—all conveyed through the luminous splendor of huge neon signs. When Oldenburg first saw the nocturnal city from an airplane, it looked to him like a patch of light.[27] The urban splendor of the city and its form impelled him to consider a flashlight:

Light had been my first association with Las Vegas. After having tried the concept of a "diamond ring" of stainless steel, whose stone would sparkle with reflected daylight, the idea had occurred of making some sort of beacon of self-generated light shining in the sky based on my recollections of passing over Las Vegas on nighttime flights to Los Angeles. Looking for an equivalent in human scale, I came up with a flashlight, which also seemed to suit the mood of anticipation of audiences gathered in the plaza, about to be ushered to their seats.[28]

Once the concept and form of the flashlight had been settled on intuitively, the two collaborators began implementing a thought and a planning process and to define the designs and models. They also looked for the historical and semiotic references of the object, both in Oldenburg's iconic background and in the urban iconography of New York and Las Vegas—a rich humus for the project's ideas and images.

The first reference to the flashlight occurs in Oldenburg's notes of 1968, in which the object is imagined

as a modest dam for a reservoir in the Hollywood Hills. . . . The flashlight is specifically a black one and . . . "the escaping water is colored a hot yellow and is lighted at night. . . . It gives all Hollywood the persistent sunset of far northern cities in summertime."[29]

Next, the artists began to seek an object prototype, so that the design started to interact with a concrete image. "The particular flashlight chosen as a starting point was a waterproof type, covered with rubberlike plastic, a feature that softens its contours."[30] The flashlight as icon had been introduced into Modern art by Jasper Johns, who "had chosen a similar version in which to cast his flashlight sculptures, I and II, from 1958."[31] After identifying the object, Oldenburg and van Bruggen tried to pinpoint the technical solutions: "Purchased on Canal Street in New York, the flashlight was given to J. Robert Jennings so that he could render an elevation, which was then modified, leading to the final form of the sculpture."[32]

Next came the systematic designs, which analyzed the specific factors and the logic of the overall approach: weight, wind resistance, weather resistance, safety, feasibility of the monument within its context, points of departure, and so forth. At the same time, the technical and physical features were examined in terms of sociology and semantics—their impact on the campus and their functions as signs. In response to the university's request for an attention-getting signal, Oldenburg and van Bruggen considered the work's scale in relation to a lighthouse at the northern end of Roosevelt Island, in New York's East River.[33] Nor did they neglect specifying the details in the process of making the object glow in harmony with the bright backdrop of Las Vegas. They also recognized a certain erotic symbolism in the flashlight:

The monolithic sculpture had an affinity with the sign advertising the Dunes Hotel on the Strip, whose designer, Lee Klay, recalled that the hotel owners had specified "a big phallic symbol going up in the sky as far as you can make it."[34]

In its phallus/beacon version, *Flashlight* did not appeal to van Bruggen, who saw it as violence ritualized by both technology and sexual symbolism. The image, she felt, was too charged with the consumerist energy of Las Vegas—a city defined by the casino and the brothel. Van Bruggen was interested in a different appeal, that of intimacy and contextual history—the internal and prickly force that comes from a hidden, introverted, withdrawing energy, like that of a cactus in the desert. This meant changing the dramatic sign to define a different energy and to communicate a different image.

To her, especially as seen from the site, the Strip was just a smudge under the silhouettes of vast desert mountains, particularly at dusk, when preparations for theater goers commence. The Flashlight *was too mechanical, lacking in mystery, and did not reflect the overwhelming presence of the desert. Making an analogy to the monumentalization of tiny plant forms in Karl Blossfeldt's* Urformen der Kunst, *Coosje compared the sculpture to a cactus, which led to a new formulation of its appearance. As a substitute for the grandiose concept of the tower, she also suggested turning the flashlight over to create a subdued ring of light, whose intimate glow would contrast with the garish illumination of the Strip, and harmonize with the stagelike illumination of the plaza.[35]*

Once van Bruggen's suggestion was accepted for the definitive version, the final step, construction, was taken in 1980. The piece was constructed at Lippincott following Jennings's technical designs, transported, and installed during the subsequent year:

The sculpture is 38 feet 6 inches tall; its widest diameter is 10 feet 6 inches, the narrowest 7 feet 10 ¹/₂ inches. The support cylinder is welded to a base plate bolted to a foundation 18 inches below the floor of the plaza. The piece weighs 74,000 pounds. Twenty-four fluorescent lights are contained in a well surrounding the bottom of the sculpture and covered with curved sections of frosted plastic.[36]

In contrast to the sculptures from 1959 to 1979, the large-scale projects, with their rootedness but also their aura of disorientation, became a mixture of the remote and the familiar, the individual and the collective, the personal and the foreign. They preserve all these contradictions as if to create a dialectics between private experience and collective and popular vision. This broadening was induced by the urgent need for an "effective" city dimension. In this sense, the blending of monument and building is fundamental. The artists aspired to a fusion that was a split between the two in order to debate the status of each. They dealt with this nexus and interweaving when they began to work with architects. Their dialogue with Philip Johnson and John Burgee resulted in *Paint Splats (for a Wall by P.J.)* (1978), proposed for the façade of the Marshall Field and Company department store in Houston; while their collaboration with Frank O. Gehry led to the performance *Il Corso del Coltello* in Venice (1985, pages 419–39) and to the Chiat/Day Building in Santa Monica, California (1991, fig. 284).

Iconophilia and Iconoclasm

Contrary to the shift of the imagination in Surrealism and Pop art, Oldenburg and van Bruggen adopted neo-Baroque "scenography," a generalized *mise-en-scène* of an eroticization of the personal and the collective, reconciled in the impersonal object: an amorous rapport that creates a harmony between beauty and ugliness, knowledge and ignorance, kitsch and design, art and decoration, monument and building, the individual and society. In terms of iconography, the large-scale projects bridge a gap between linked but antithetical universes. Magnified to a large scale, they extend through a cityscape, their foreign character cutting into its profile. Above all, the large-scale projects forming an iconographic itinerary in the cityscapes are a return to the figuration of architecture: their iconic theme counteracts the "abstract" volumetry and geometry of modern architecture. An Oldenburg/van Bruggen proposal is figurative and literary, moving toward the iconophilia of construction. It relies on the relationship that art and architecture have with memory and myth, in which the figuration is social, making references to the imaginary metaphysics of culture and society. It has an ethnocentric aspect that continues the tradition of the zoomorphic architecture of "primitives," [37] except that the figurative images of the world—such as the familiar bird, snail, or turtle of "primitive" art—are replaced by depictions of banal, everyday objects: a button or a needle, a hat or a screw, a pickaxe or an umbrella.

The passage from animal to mundane symbolism tied to industrial products seems to indicate, in architecture, a social and cultural transformation in which all the deep, primary, and organic forces in the unconscious and in instinct are supplanted by an artificial and repetitive consciousness regulated by the system of mass-produced objects in consumer society. Their insertion into the urban context is a response to a historical need. Just as "primitive" tribes remember a vanishing animality, artists bear witness to the present state of an environment whose "animality"—likewise dying out through the immateriality of future existence—is signified by functional objects. The objects chosen by Oldenburg and van Bruggen are often linked to labor, male and female, from *Spitzhacke* (Pickaxe, 1982, fig. 231) to *Balancing Tools* (1984, fig. 242); from *Clothespin* to *Split Button* (1981, fig. 230). Instead of challenging affective and personal bonds, they show that people belong to a group through their use of a common object. Furthermore, their scale and monumentality, their siting in urban and public locations, reinforce this social allegory. In the personalized and oneiric world of Surrealism and Dada, the goals of Salvador Dalí and André Breton were perverse and erotic, paranoid and automatic in their use of objects. In contrast, Oldenburg and van Bruggen focus on a machinery that, starting with the personal, reaches an ironic and critical reflection on society—or at least on the city. In this sense, the objects constructed by Oldenburg on the basis of his dialogue with van Bruggen lost the earlier work's surreal connotation tied to food and sex, softness and tactility—a connotation terminated by *Lipstick (Ascending) on Caterpillar Tracks*. Instead, they ventured into the territory of the conceptual and philosophical; they became ideological and

political constructions marked by linearity and programming, rigidity and wisdom.

Beyond their relationship to the individual's erotic and sensual, gastronomic and digestive aspects, the chosen objects are connected to dream and desire, memory and community history. This is a kind of social psychology in which the figure of the object sums up the identity of the site and its events. *Batcolumn* resulted from manifold visual associations ranging from Chicago's fireplugs Adolf Loos's famed proposal for a building based on a Doric column (his entry in the 1922 competition for the Chicago Tribune competition). And naturally it is tied to the architectural impact of the city.

The real art here is architecture, or anything really that stands up, making a perpendicular to the magnificent horizontal. Any chimney, any tree, any object (any fire plug). [38]

But more important, *Batcolumn* fuses a neoclassical symbol with a local object steeped in civic nostalgia.

In Salinas, California, *Hat in Three Stages of Landing* (1982, fig. 232) achieves a different kind of spectacle, close to the myth of the West, with its rodeos and attendant costumes. For this large-scale project, Oldenburg and van Bruggen formulated the idea of "a hat tossed out of the rodeo stands, rolling or 'exercising' across the field of the park along a single line or several parallel ones." [39]

If the iconography of *Batcolumn* is raised completely to a large scale, the figure of the cowboy hat in *Hat in Three Stages of Landing* undergoes but a modification: "The curve of the brim was reversed." [40] Aside from displaying the conical formulation of the crown, which now can be likened to a table lamp, the reversion illuminates the "volatile" meaning of the object, transmuting the brim into bird wings. On a symbolic level, the reversal interferes with the aggressive erection of the creases, replacing ascent with descent—a sexual turnabout that runs counter to the symbolism found in the world of the cowboy.

Since a slight iconographic modification can broaden the associative network of meanings, Oldenburg and van Bruggen often employ such changes to produce an effect of "surplus," which surprises and bewilders the average observer. *Spitzhacke* and *Free Stamp* (1991, fig. 283) are eloquent renderings of the slight linguistic shift caused by leaning or falling, which convey the idea and perception of an object randomly tossed from one part of a city to another. Aside from recalling the passion for gardening and the stories of the Brothers Grimm, who were natives of Kassel, *Spitzhacke*, sited in that German city, looks almost as if it had been hurled by Hercules, a twenty-six-foot statue of whom looms atop Kassel's Karlsberg Castle. In *Free Stamp*, the Herculean gesture of a giant object flung or thrown back has fewer mythological overtones. It hints at the rejection of the project by Standard Oil of Ohio, which originally commissioned the Cleveland piece.

By including visual instability, these works make us aware of the artists' use of the original objects. Instead of producing a "servile" imitation and reproduction of the subject, they continually alter the mimicry—a process that, in altering the vision, is iconoclastic. This iconoclastic dimension spurns reality. Refusing subordination, it strives for chaos and throws a monkey wrench into all truths and all fictions. This dialectic between iconophilia and iconoclasm involves the unwonted charge of the work of Oldenburg and van Bruggen, who, rather than pitting those two forces against one another, integrate them. The artists become apologists for the everyday object, but turn it into a hallucinatory entity. By exaggeratedly affirming its presence, they caricature it but also deify it. They declare themselves to be destroyers and worshippers, honoring and demolishing the cult of images and things.

The themes of explosion and annihilation of objects, of their fragmentation and the stripping to the bone provide the underpinnings for several further projects, including *Dropped Bowl with Scattered Slices and Peels* (1990, fig. 280) and *Haunted House* (1987, pages 460–63); *Mistos (Match Cover*, 1992, fig. 287) and *Piano/Hammock* (1987, fig. 267); *The European Desktop* (1990, pages 491–501), and *Shuttlecocks* (1994, fig. 305). The shattering of the object is accompanied by a freeing from the constriction of outlines and limits. This freedom helps to expose and liberate a constant uprooting of the object, and ultimately its disclosure into death. Modern society, based on the endless distribution and consumption of things, prohibits the death of an object. The revocation of the mortality of things and products is connected to the desire to accumulate—a stimulus typical of capitalism and consumerism. This economic system is pushed down into the unconscious, where it is transformed and hidden from view. The cemetery of objects is absent, and if it does exist, the objects are changed into antiques and modern collectibles. The goal is to tranquilize the consumer of everyday objects: he or she must never grieve for an object that dies upon being born. The smooth and lucid object, however, is a sign of the functional life of human beings; the broken and open object, with its entrails exposed, is dead. Showing these two aspects means talking about life and death, anticipating a fate that is immanent but not immediately heralded: "The factor of distance in time; of choosing a subject far enough away to be on the verge of disappearing from function to archetype."[41]

To exist for the end and for death is the destiny of the object and of the human being.

Man-made things do look like human beings, symmetrical, visage-like, body-like. Man wants his own image or simply doesn't know any other way.[42]

Death is a possibility of existing—a certain and insuperable possibility. A consciousness that creates angst and frees us from illusions. The existential nullity that accompanies the breaking and fragmenting of the object began to appear in the Oldenburg/van Bruggen oeuvre with *Split Button*. It then developed after *Il Corso del Coltello* through a number of works, including *From the Entropic Library* (1989, fig. 271). The image of death was established as a point of departure for the vitality of the object[43] through Oldenburg's collaboration with van Bruggen and the experience of a European culture that uses death, or rather ruin and history, memory and archeology, as the foundation of a present and contemporary reality.

The European arts, from architecture to sculpture, from design to painting, from music to dance, continually attempt to atone for the crime of the new. Trying to obliterate the new, they claim an identity in the past.[44]

There is a similar tendency to consider the simulation of death as the initiation into life: this attitude, according to Jean Baudrillard, marks both "primitive" society and the Baroque tradition, in which death is the prerequisite for entering the grand theater of life.[45] Hence death is a historical memory as well as the threshold of life.

The discovery of the ruins of a divided Germany must have inspired *Haunted House*, just as the dichotomy between Francoist and socialist Spain must have stimulated *Mistos*. In opening and shattering the limits of cultural and ethnic definitions, the Paris exhibition *Magiciens de la terre* implied a history of ruin and abandonment, an awareness of the intellectual dimension of colonialism and anti-colonialism. That awareness was concretized in the "ruins" of *From the Entropic Library*, Oldenburg and van Bruggen's entry in the show.

The same meditation on ruins and fragments recurs in *Dropped Bowl with Scattered Slices and Peels*. The depiction of a plate and orange broken into dozens of pieces was an attempt to portray Florida's largest city as a different kind of culture: endless and labyrinthine, ramified and disjointed. Oldenburg and van Bruggen were faced with an urban jumble of ethnic groups and styles—Anglo, Cuban, Ecuadoran, Jewish, Haitian, Mexican, and Vietnamese, retirees and exiles. The existential dimension of death and ruin is joined by the dimension of time, a different explanation of historical continuity. This explanation, operating at the center of mobility and persistence, is accompanied by tales and legends, historiography and destiny. The fragmentation can be taken as a series of instants constantly present in the events of a culture, and it can also be replaced by a linearity that demonstrates an abstractly infinite flow.

In *Bottle of Notes* (1993, fig. 293), the complex articulation of the sculptural envelope arises from the use of handwriting as a motif. What is important is the transit, which is not a transcendence, but a movement from same to same. Yet the coincidence between script and object (the bottle) underscores a perfect equivalence of languages: that of tale and theory, of vision and image. In fact, this language mingles the adventures of Captain Cook with those of Gulliver and the prose and poetry of Edgar Allan Poe, while van Bruggen's poetic skill blends with Oldenburg's sculptural ability. The language that speaks and the language that shows are identified with one another, becoming indistinguishable peers. This colloquy adds to the presence of the things that appear here. In their dialectical and nihilistic relationship, poetry and logic overwhelm both figure and representation, but the latter feeds on the former and vice versa. The dialogue is subjective, but it is then concealed in forms that reflect a history and a city, for which the subject or subjects move through the language of art and poetry; they set the opposites aright and achieve a different kind of knowledge. *Bottle of Notes* is the metaphor for a collaboration, a togetherness in the presence of a thing that includes both, conveying them to a different place.

In *Shuttlecocks*, the most recent of their large-scale projects to be realized, various elements are combined: bird feathers and a ball, a cone and a sphere. The piece is a grafting of nature and thought, a blend of different cultures. In it, the profound significance of pure volumetry fuses with the symbolism of leap and fall, angel and demon, emblematized by the winged creature. Arising from the encounter between reason and delirium, balance and irrationality, self-control and fall, nature and sports, the *thing* chosen by Oldenburg and van Bruggen is an enigma par excellence, questioning the object as an entity of salvation and perdition.

Like any other enigma, *Shuttlecocks* supplies no response. It neither reveals nor conceals: rather, it alludes to the infinite plurality of questions and answers. Above all, this work is the result of a descent to earth, and its parts are set up at different places in the garden, in various forms and positions typical of alighting birds. The site of the project is the Nelson-Atkins Museum of Art in Kansas City, Missouri. *Shuttlecocks* transforms the grassy lawns around the museum into a playing field, while the institution itself becomes a net that fishes for—even as it contains—that still unsolved mystery: art.

Translated, from the Italian, by Joachim Neugroschel.

1. Kevin Lynch, *The Image of the City* (Cambridge, Mass., 1960).
2. Vittorio Gregotti, *Il territorio dell'architettura* (Milan, 1966); Marco Romano, *L'estetica della città europea* (Turin, 1993).
3. Marcello Fagioli, ed., *La città effimera e l'universo artificiale del giardino* (Rome, 1980).
4. Maurizio Fagiolo dell'Arco and Silvia Corradini, *L'effimero barocco* (Rome, 1977).
5. Etienne-Louis Boullée, *Architecture, Essai sur l'art*.
6. Vladimir Tolstoy, Irina Bibikova, Catherine Cooke, *Street Art of the Revolution, Festivals and Celebrations in Russia, 1918–33* (Moscow, 1984).
7. Umberto Silva, *Ideologia e arte del fascismo* (Milan, 1973); Bertold Hinz, *Die Malerei im deutschen Fascismus. Kunst und Konterrevolution* (Munich, 1974); Igor Golomstock, *Totalitarian Art* (London, 1990).
8. Claes Oldenburg, *Proposals for Monuments and Buildings, 1965–1969* (Chicago: Big Table, 1969), p. 14. Presumably, the book that Oldenburg had read was Emil Kaufman's *Three Revolutionary Architects: Boullée, Ledoux and Lequeu* (Philadelphia, 1952).
9. Oldenburg, *Notes*, Los Angeles, 1963.
10. "The Poetry of Scale," interview with Paul Carroll, in Oldenburg, *Proposals for Monuments and Buildings, 1965–1969*, pp. 11–36.
11. Severo Sarduy, *Barocco* (Paris, 1975).
12. Conversation with the artist.
13. Maurizio Calvesi, *Avanguardia di massa* (Milan, 1978), pp. 82–83.
14. Oldenburg, *Notes*, New York, 6, 1960.
15. Oldenburg, *Notes*, New York. 1967.
16. Oldenburg, *Notes*, Gemini G. E. L., Los Angeles, 1968.
17. Oldenburg, *Notes*, 1963.
18. Oldenburg, quoted in *Claes Oldenburg, Skulpturer och teckningar* (Stockholm: Moderna Museet, 1966).
19. Claes Oldenburg, "Statement," in catalogue for the ninthe São Paulo *Bienal*, 1967.
20. Oldenburg, *Notes*, 1963.
21. Oldenburg, *Notes*, 1969.
22. Leonardo da Vinci, *Trattato della pittura*, 9, 14.
23. Gui Bonsiepe, "Arabesken der Rationalität," in *Bauen + Wohnen*, no. 6, 1967.
24. Claes Oldenburg and Coosje van Bruggen, *Claes Oldenburg and Coosje van Bruggen, Large-Scale Projects* (New York: The Monacelli Press, 1994), p. 222. R. W. Oxenaar, acting as "chairman of the work group *Sonsbeek 71*, had serious doubts about the piece. On December 29, 1969, he wrote to Oldenburg: 'If it goes around on the grass, nothing will be left of the grounds after four months. '" Ibid.
25. Oldenburg, *Notes*, 1961.
26. Oldenburg and van Bruggen, pp. 228–29.
27. Ibid., p. 292. The iconographic data on the project as a whole are drawn from the case history of *Flashlight*, pp. 292–309.
28. Ibid., p. 292.
29. Ibid., p. 294.
30. Ibid., p. 292.
31. Ibid.
32. Ibid.
33. Ibid., p. 297.
34. Ibid.
35. Ibid., p. 298.
36. Ibid., p. 308.
37. Enrico Giudoni, *Architettura primitiva* (Milan, 1975).
38. Oldenburg, *Notes*, 1968.
39. Oldenburg and van Bruggen, p. 323.
40. Ibid., p. 327.
41. Oldenburg, *Notes*, New York, 1965–66.
42. Oldenburg, *Notes*, New York, 1966.
43. Oldenburg and van Bruggen, p. 313. *Split Button* came to life with the cut, the solution to the problem of how to assert the button as a form. "Split across but not totally disconnected, the button could rise, presenting itself as a sculpture."
44. Mario Perniola, *La società dei simulacri* (Bologna, 1980).
45. Jean Baudrillard, *L'Echange symbolique et la mort* (Paris, 1976).

pages 382–83:
*217. Trowel I, 1976 reconstruction of a
1971 original. Steel, painted with
polyurethane enamel, 41 feet 9 inches x
11 feet 3 ⅛ inches x 14 feet 6 ¼ inches
(12.73 x 3.43 x 4.44 m); sited:
38 feet 4 ½ inches x 11 feet 3 ⅛ inches x
7 feet 4 ½ inches (11.7 x 3.43 x 2.25 m).
Rijksmuseum Kröller-Müller, Otterlo,
the Netherlands.*

218. Study for a Large Outdoor Sculpture in the Form of a Clothespin, 1972–73. Painted cardboard, 48½ x 16½ x 6¾ inches (123.2 x 41.9 x 17.2 cm). Gift of Mrs. E. T. Meredith, Jr., Des Moines Art Center Permanent Collection, 1980.31.

219. Clothespin – 45 Foot Version (Model), 1976–79. Cor-Ten and stainless steel, 60 x 24 x 19⅝ inches (152.4 x 61 x 49.9 cm). Collection of Michael and Judy Ovitz.

220. Clothespin, 1976. Cor-Ten and stainless steel, 45 feet x 12 feet 3¼ inches x 4 feet 6 inches (13.72 x 3.74 x 1.37 m). Centre Square Plaza, Fifteenth and Market streets, Philadelphia.

221. Batcolumn, *1977. Steel and aluminum, painted with polyurethane enamel, bat: 96 feet 8 inches (29.46 m) high, 9 feet 9 inches (2.97 m) in diameter; base: 4 feet (1.22 m) high, 10 feet (3.05 m) in diameter. Harold Washington Social Security Center, 600 West Madison Street, Chicago.*

222. Study Defining the Outline of the Batcolumn, *1976. Pencil, watercolor, and tape on paper, 37⅞ x 9⅛ inches (96.2 x 28.3 cm). Collection of Claes Oldenburg and Coosje van Bruggen, New York.*

223. Batcolumn (Model), *1980. Painted steel, 115 x 20 x 20 inches (292 x 50.8 x 50.8 cm). The Edward R. Broida Trust.*

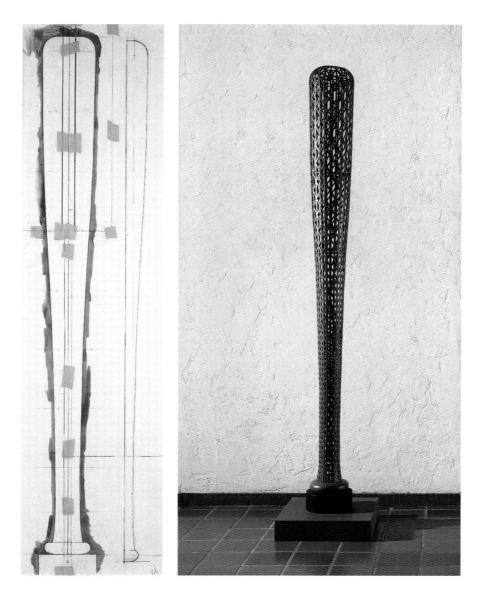

224. Flashlight (Final Model), *1980. Steel,
painted with polyurethane enamel, on
plastic-and-aluminum base, flashlight:
37 inches (94 cm) high, 10½ inches
(26.7 cm) in diameter; base: ½ x 20½ x
20½ inches (1.3 x 52.1 x 52.1 cm). Collection
of Dr. and Mrs. Phillip T. George, Miami.*

facing page:
225. Flashlight, *1981. Steel, painted with
polyurethane enamel; and fluorescent lights;
38 feet 6 inches (11.73 m) high,
10 feet 6 inches (3.2 m) in diameter.
University of Nevada, Las Vegas.*

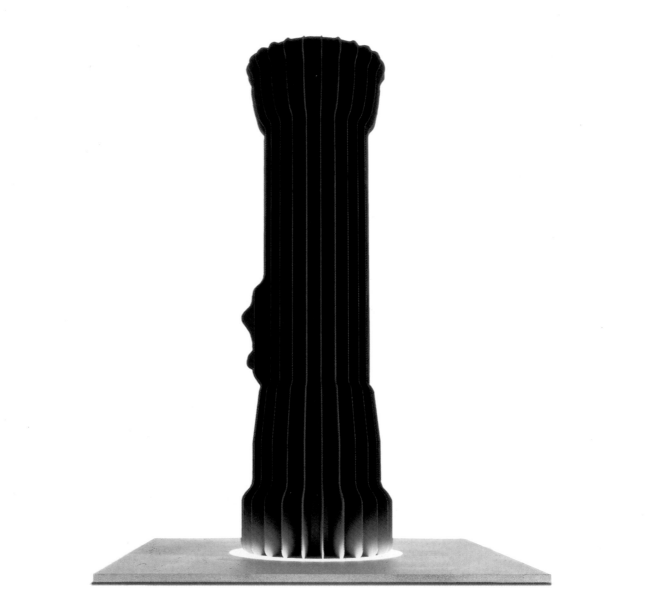

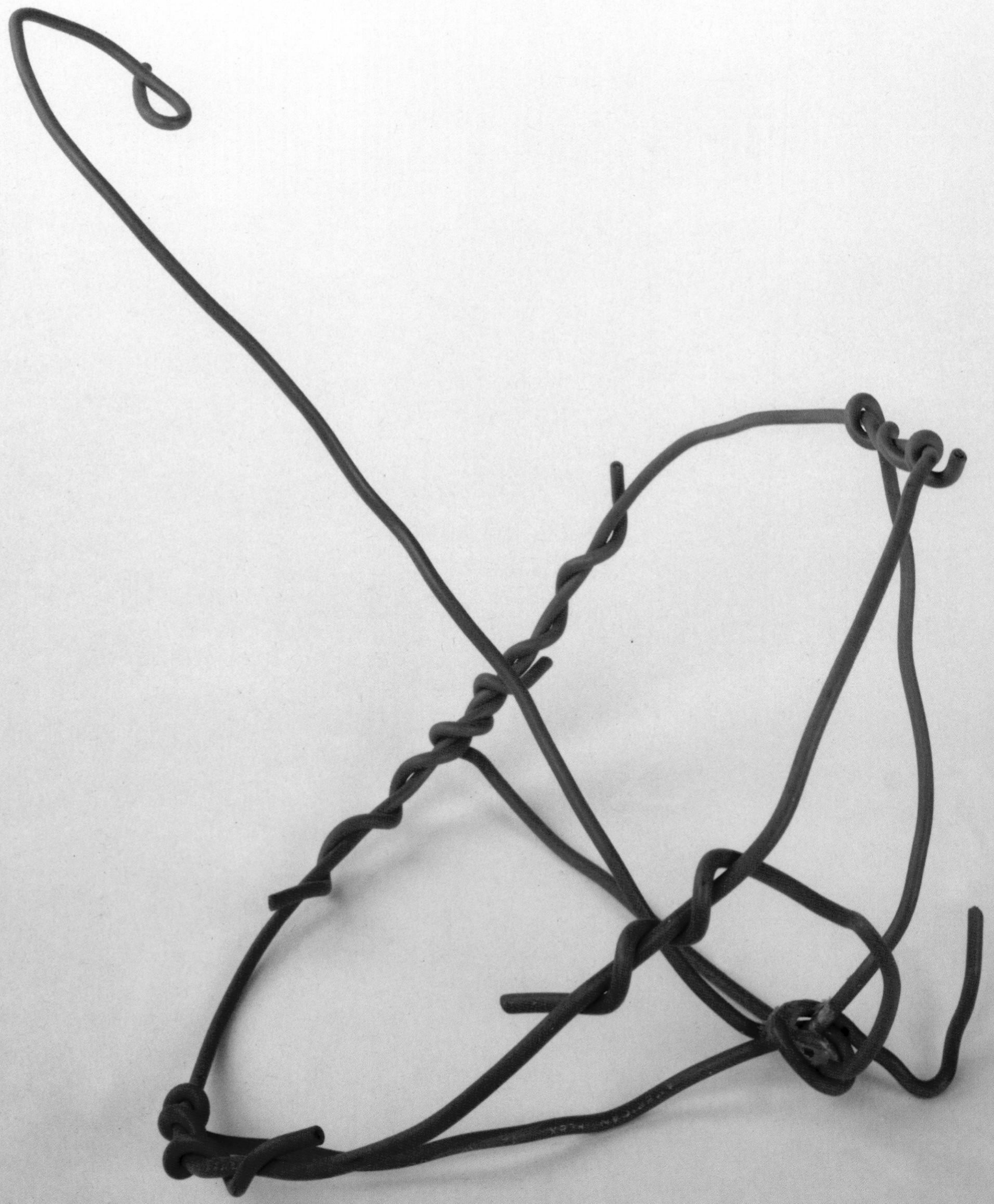

226. Preliminary Model for the Crusoe Umbrella, *1978. Wire, coated with plastic, 9$^{13}/_{16}$ x 14½ x 14½ inches (24.9 x 36.8 x 36.8 cm). Collection of Claes Oldenburg and Coosje van Bruggen, New York.*

227. Preliminary Model for the Crusoe
Umbrella, *1979. Wood, rope, and glue,
20½ x 30¾ x 14⅛ inches (52.1 x 78.1 x
35.9 cm). Collection of Claes Oldenburg
and Coosje van Bruggen, New York.*

228. Final Model for the Crusoe
Umbrella, *1979. Aluminum, painted with
enamel, 16½ x 16½ x 28½ inches (41.9 x
41.9 x 72.4 cm). Collection of Claes
Oldenburg and Coosje van Bruggen,
New York.*

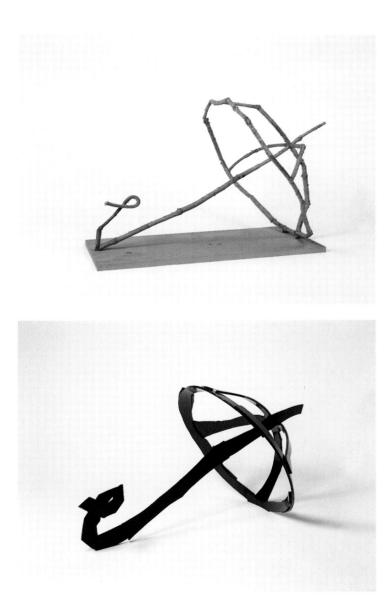

233. Gartenschlauch (Garden Hose),
1983. Steel, painted with polyurethane
enamel, faucet: 35 feet 5 inches x
8 feet 11½ inches x 7 feet ⅛ inches (10.8 x
2.73 x 2.15 m); hose: 410 feet (124.97 m)
long, 19 ⁹⁄₁₆ inches (50 cm) in diameter.
Stühlinger Park, Freiburg im Breisgau,
Germany.

234. Screwarch Bridge (Model), *1980–81.*
Bronze, aluminum, and plastic, painted,
on steel table, model: 19⅞ x 99⅝ x
44⅞ inches (50.5 x 253 x 114 cm); table:
33⅛₆ x 85⅝₆ x 31⅛ inches (84 x 218 x
79 cm). Museum Boymans-van Beuningen,
Rotterdam.

235. Screwarch, *1983. Aluminum,*
painted with polyurethane enamel,
12 feet 8 inches x 21 feet 6 inches x
7 feet 10 inches (3.86 x 6.55 x 2.39 m).
Museum Boymans-van Beuningen,
Rotterdam.

236. Cross Section of a Toothbrush with Paste, in a Cup, on a Sink: Portrait of Coosje's Thinking (Model), *1981. Cardboard, wood, and sand, painted, 19 x 11¼ x 6⅝ inches (48.3 x 28.6 x 16.8 cm). Collection of Claes Oldenburg and Coosje van Bruggen, New York.*

237. Cross Section (Slice Through) of a Toothbrush with Paste, in a Cup, on a Sink: Portrait of Coosje's Thinking (Model), *1982. Aluminum, painted, 132¼ x 54¼ x 15⅛ inches (335.9 x 137.8 x 38.4 cm). The Edward R. Broida Trust.*

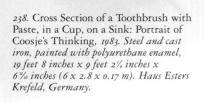

238. Cross Section of a Toothbrush with Paste, in a Cup, on a Sink: Portrait of Coosje's Thinking, *1983. Steel and cast iron, painted with polyurethane enamel, 19 feet 8 inches x 9 feet 2¼ inches x 6⁹⁄₁₀ inches (6 x 2.8 x 0.17 m). Haus Esters Krefeld, Germany.*

below and facing page:
239. Stake Hitch, *1984. Three views.*
Aluminum, steel, and epoxy, painted with
polyurethane enamel; and polyurethane
foam, plastic, and fiberglass-reinforced
plastic, painted with latex; stake, upper
floor: 13 feet 6 inches x 18 feet 2 inches x
14 feet 7 inches (4.11 x 5.54 x 4.45 m);
stake, lower floor: 12 feet 9½ inches x
5 feet x 3 feet (3.9 x 1.52 x 0.91 m);
rope: 20 inches (51 cm) in diameter;
53 feet 6 inches (16.31 m) high overall.
Dallas Museum of Art.

240. Balancing Tools (Model), *1983.*
Cardboard, wood, and metal, painted,
11⁷⁄₁₆ x 9⁷⁄₁₆ x 14½ inches (29.1 x 24 x
36.8 cm). Collection of Claes Oldenburg
and Coosje van Bruggen, New York.

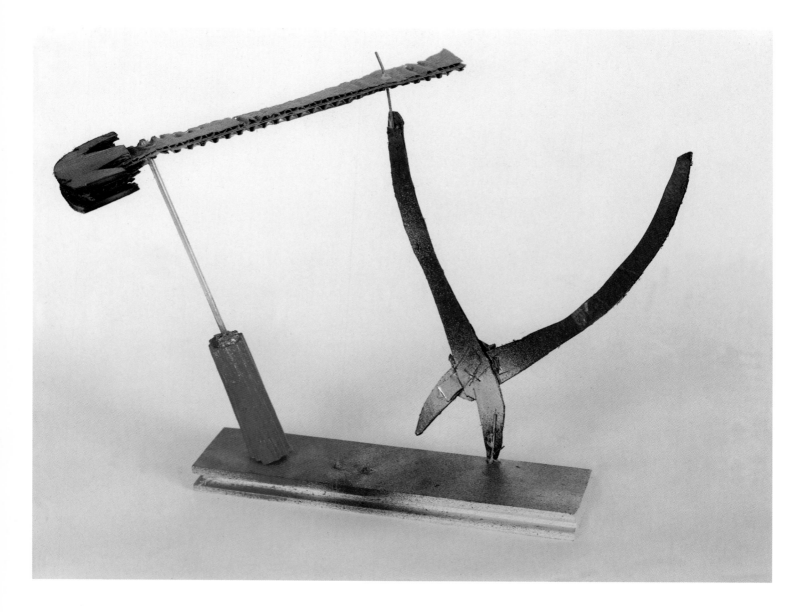

241. Balancing Tools (Model), *1985. Steel,*
painted with enamel, 46 x 54 x 42 inches
(116.8 x 137.2 x 106.7 cm). Collection of
John and Mary Pappajohn.

242. Balancing Tools, 1984. Steel,
painted with polyurethane enamel,
26 feet 3 inches x 29 feet 6 inches x
19 feet 10 inches (8 x 9 x 6.05 m). Vitra
International AG, Weil am Rhein,
Germany.

412

FIRST THOUGHTS

Il Coltello (The Knife)
thoughts on waking
The ray-gun angle more acute: the elbow.
The elbow I sleep with mine and Cos'
A stage set up over and over in different
parts of the city, each time differently
and with difficulty as if one had forgot the
plans somehow (loss of historical memory).
After each performance something is left
permanently attached at the site, maybe a
coltello in one scale or another, in one
situation or another.
Souvenirs given out, pocket coltellos
reconstructable, variable construction
suitable for a sort of stage
A. Bott & Coltello
Frank Coltello A mobster (who) assassinated
in his barber's chair in NYC
The More's tragedy. more strategy
Commedia dell' Arte--conehead
some incidents enacted, other described or
represented in reduced scale
Dr. Coltello is a tour guide, harassed,
with no expectations, not at all honest or
attractive, a man just getting on & waiting
for his transformation, his
"awakening".....
He is our hero, a likely sort, whom we now
see wake and leave his miserable chamber in
a forgotten part of town....... He cuts his
way out, just as the night before, wanting
a bit of air, he cut himself a window. You
can be direct with architecture, being a
knife as he is.

(1986)

Setting
The Piazzetta of San Marco as depicted by
Canaletto, Superimposed upon the Campo
dell'Arsenale.

Time
Any time since 1730.

Argument
The foreshadowing in many disguises of a
contemporary symbol of Venice, in the form
of a Coltello Ship, set in a Canaletto-like
panorama, the Campo dell' Arsenale. Within
this panorama swirl the contending forces
of Venice: tourism versus culture, machoism
versus feminism, imagination versus
reality, life versus death / These forces
are reflected in the characters and the
objects gathered there. Sometimes the
people seem in control, sometimes the
objects take over, in an ongoing tug-of-
war.
   This complex Venetian environment is
concentrated in one summarizing image, the
Coltello Ship, which is launched from the
ancient naval yard of the Arsenale. It
flexes its blades and screw, picks up the
central characters, and slices into the
future!

The Café--Prologue
An audience gathers in a café on Campo
dell'Arsenale to hear a lecture by Frankie
P. Toronto.

The Lecture
Interest in the lecture is diverted by Dr.
Coltello presenting his wares, the arrival
of Georgia Sandbag on a mule and large
objects in movement.

The Bridge
Sandbag leads her cavalcade across the
Ponte del Paradiso, which becomes the
setting for a tug of war involving a sliced
column.

The Ship--Finale
As predicted by Basta Carambola, the
objects take over. The Coltello Ship
arrives; Dr. Coltello, Georgia Sandbag and
Frankie P. Toronto board and sail into the
Arsenale.

(Claes Oldenburg and Coosje van Bruggen,
1986)

DR. COLTELLO

246. *Dr. Coltello in* Il Corso del Coltello, *Campo dell'Arsenale, Venice, September 6–8, 1985.*

Dr. Coltello, also called the Kitsch-Dragon or Murky Apollo, is an importer of souvenirs from Switzerland who tries to sell his wares without a license while posing as a tourist. He is a master of disguises. Obsessed with expansion, exploration, and invention, he turns imagination into reality under his motto, "I made it up when I was a little kid." As a boy Dr. Coltello used to wander along the shores of Lake Michigan pretending that he was flying over the Sahara desert. Inspired by the travels of Marco Polo, he studied the maps of exotic places and discovered a country of his own, which he called Neubern. A palmist advised him once to buy an airplane company in order to visit the many little pieces of him she saw scattered all over the world; moreover, the form of his thumb indicated that he would always survive a building collapse. Estimating the scale of things by using the same unique thumb, Dr. Coltello is on his way to becoming a notorious Sunday painter, in the style of Francesco Guardi.

A connoisseur of hedonistic flotsam, aware of his weakness for accumulating collectibles, Coltello confines himself to no more luggage than the number of letters of his own name, but the bags and crates have become enormous due to his lack of restraint. Among his treasures, the most popular items are three souvenirs of Venice: the Leopard Woman, D'Artagnan, and the Knife Dancer. To keep him company, to watch over his goods, and to provide himself with an uncritical audience, Dr. Coltello has created the Knife Dogs, a special breed, in his likeness.

(Character descriptions for Il Corso del Coltello by Coosje van Bruggen, 1986)

Georgia Sandbag was formerly a travel agent who developed a taste for adventure while sitting behind a desk all day helping others journey to exotic places. Her job reminded her of an incident that took place in her youth: her cousin had just become a Boy Scout and had gotten his first pocketknife, with two folding blades, a corkscrew, and tweezers. She still treasures the moment she first held the knife, feeling the cold steel blades, their razor sharpness. But just before putting the knife back in the safe darkness of his pocket, the cousin had screamed with joy: "Let's play horse. I have the knife, so I am the driver. You are the horse!"

   The maverick Sandbag is now exploring the "sweet life" on her own. She is a self-made writer in the tradition of Calamity Jane, and keeps her own "intimate journals." To her, at all times, experiencing life and nature surpasses the pleasures of man-made wonders of art and architecture.

   Dressed in a cornflower-blue Western overcoat patched with travel stickers, Georgia crosses the Alps by mule, along untrodden paths. Dreaming of Constantinople and the Orient, she makes her appearance in Venice, where she initiates a movable "Salon des Refusés" which includes the Isadora Duncan scholar Sleazy Dora; Lord Styrofoam, a troubadour following in Byronic footsteps; and Chateaubriand, a lion aspiring to be Othello.

(Coosje van Bruggen, 1986)

FRANKIE P. TORONTO

Frankie P. Toronto is a barber from Venice,
California, on a perpetual lecture tour
presenting his theory of "disorganized
order" in architecture derived from the
cutting and slicing effects of a Swiss Army
knife. In pursuit of his childhood
fantasies, he especially likes to elaborate
on the metamorphoses of the knife into the
biomorphic structures of fish and snake.

  When he was a boy, living in Toronto, his
grandmother would take him on Thursdays to
the market where they would buy live carp.
He recalls the fish swimming in the bathtub
until it would be cut up and turned into
gefilte fish. After dinner his grandmother
would sit next to him on the floor and
together they would build large cities out
of blocks which, while playing earthquake,
he loved to kick over.

  Though he is a successful barber, Toronto
dreams of using the connections of his
mobster clientele to further his ambition
of becoming a contemporary Palladio. He has
taken up residence in Venice, Italy, where
in anticipation of his breakthrough he has
built his own Temple Shack, classical in
form but covered with modern tar paper on
which graffiti is scrawled. During the
evenings Toronto, dressed up in a camel-
colored suit of protruding architectural
fragments, lectures to tourists in the
local café next door. There he becomes
acquainted with Dr. Coltello and Georgia
Sandbag, who, as a token of her friendship
and at the request of the oldest Knife Dog,
shaves off Toronto's moustache to help him
reveal his true self.

(Coosje van Bruggen, 1986)

BASTA CARAMBOLA

Basta Carambola is an itinerant poolroom
"hustler" and translator from Trieste who
organizes lectures by foreigners wherever
his Hungarian gypsy blood leads him....
  A bird-watcher in his rare leisure time,
Carambola takes great pleasure in
transforming thought processes into bird
language; chattering with the birds reveals
his more philosophical side. A fierce
opponent of the Aristotelian theory of the
Unmoved Mover, he advocates a movement
spontaneously generated. As a result he
pops up in such highly crowded places as
the Piazza San Marco, where strange birds
of multicolored plumage mingle. Carambola
dreams of applying Giordano Bruno's
theories of "pantheistic immanentism" to
the birds. Like this sixteenth century
unorthodox philosopher, Carambola would
love to be martyred for his beliefs, and
has already built up a reputation for
uttering provocative proverbs. But his
predictions of catastrophes, in particular
--for example, his warning that a huge ball
of household possessions, rolled over the
Bridge of Paradise, will run amok crashing
everything in its path--may bring him
eventually to the stake.

PRIMO SPORTYCUSS

Primo Sportycuss is a touring boxer from
Novaya Zemlya who proudly wears upon his
robe all the medals he received over the
years during his championships. Sportycuss
is a connoisseur of patriotic bric-a-brac,
which makes his stay in Venice a delight.
He visits historical monuments and becomes
involved with the souvenir salesman, Dr.
Coltello, who recommends that he buy an
ancient costume which combines St. Theodore
and a crocodile. Inquiring into the source
of his purchase, the boxer discovers the
uncertain origins of St. Theodore. He might
have been a warrior saint, a monk, or just
a commander-in-chief. Primo thinks he may
even be related to Siegfried. When
Sportycuss, who sympathizes with the
outcasts of the world, finds out that St.
Theodore was the original patron saint of
Venice--pushed aside by a usurper, the
Chinese "chimera" of St. Mark--he decides
to fight for St. Theodore's cause. Dressed
in Coltello's St. Theodore-and-crocodile-
in-one costume he competes with
Chateaubriand, a local lion trophy, for the
honor of receiving wings and the book, the
attributes that elevate Primo/St. Theodore,
the prizefighter, to the position of
legitimate patron saint of Venice.

(Coosje van Bruggen, 1986)

SLEAZY DORA

Sleazy Dora is a graduate of the last
Bauhaus extension in Boise, Idaho, where
she majored in Oskar Schlemmer. Dora's
childhood fantasies caused her to live in a
world of her own, roller-skating patterns
or playing "haunted mansion" all day in
deserted garages. A member of the lost
generation ten times removed, she is on her
first visit to Europe....As performance
sites she prefers street corners and
piazzas to the stage. On her way to Capri,
Sleazy Dora debarks in Venice at the
entrance to the Arsenale, where she finds
not only the perfect site for trampoline
jumps in the midst of classical statues,
but also kindred spirits in Georgia
Sandbag, Lord Styrofoam, and Chateaubriand,
a lion.

LORD STYROFOAM

Lord Styrofoam turned troubadour when he
was rejected by the Coast Guard for flat
feet, and now sings and swims himself
around the world. A great admirer of Lord
Byron, he has come to Venice to retrace the
poet's footsteps. In vain he seeks
inspiration on the Bridge of Fists, the
Bridge of Courtesy, the Bridge of Straw,
the Bridge of the Honest Woman, and the
Bridge of Humility....

CHATEAUBRIAND

Chateaubriand is the front-end fragment of
a marble lion of uncertain origin. Is he
part of the lion with runic inscriptions on
its flank, brought back as a trophy from
Piraeus, or of an Assyrian "chimera," or
just of a large Venice alley cat? His lack
of a rear end may account for his inability
to decide among his ambitions: should he
become a fountain placed against a wall
spitting water, or should he perhaps
audition for the city opera? -- the stage,
with its frontal emphasis, would be well
suited to half a lion.
  As a slice he could perform Coltello or
rather Otello. Then on the other hand, why
not replace the lion of St. Mark, if only
he were whole, could hold a book, had
wings, and weren't afraid of heights.

In addition, a number of other characters
activate the situation, including: Waiters;
Busboys and Busgirls; Porters; Washers--who
are also Students of Architecture; a Rower;
a Violinist; a Projectionist; Longshoremen;
and the Crew of the Coltello Ship. Because
the performance space must be open to
pasage by residents of the area, some of
these may turn into "performers" as well.

(Coosje van Bruggen, 1986)

250. Chateaubriand *in* Il Corso del
Coltello.

pages 428–39:
251. *Scenes from* Il Corso del Coltello.

pages 440–41:
252. Knife Ship I, *1985. Prop from
performance of* Il Corso del Coltello.
*Wood covered with vinyl; steel;
aluminum; and motors; blades vertical:
31 feet 8 inches x 31 feet 6 inches x
40 feet 5 inches (9.66 x 9.60 x 12.32 m),
including oars. GFT (USA) Corp.,
New York. Installed at Palacio de Cristal,
Madrid, June 18–September 9, 1986.*

pages 442–43:
253. Knife Ship II, *1986, installed at
the Solomon R. Guggenheim Museum,
New York, December 16, 1986–
February 16, 1987.*

pages 444–45:
254. Knife Ship II, *1986, installed at the
Museum of Contemporary Art, Los
Angeles, October 12, 1987–March 1988.*

256. Dr. Coltello Costume – Enlarged
Version, *1986. Canvas filled with soft
polyurethane foam, painted with latex,
104 x 60 x 20 inches (264.2 x 152.4 x
50.8 cm). Collection of Claes Oldenburg
and Coosje van Bruggen, New York.*

below and facing page:
257. Frankie P. Toronto Costume –
Enlarged Version, *1986. Canvas filled*
with soft polyurethane foam, painted with
latex; pants: 75 x 13 inches (190 x 33 cm);
jacket with hat: 79 x 84 x 32 inches
(200 x 213 x 81 cm). Collection of
Claes Oldenburg and Coosje van Bruggen,
Courtesy of PaceWildenstein.

258. Georgia Sandbag Costume –
Enlarged Version, *1986. Canvas filled
with soft polyurethane foam, painted with
latex; bag: 13 x 39 x 12 inches (33 x 99.1 x
30.5 cm); "O": 75 x 144 x 8 inches
(190.5 x 365.8 x 20.3 cm). Collection of
Claes Oldenburg and Coosje van Bruggen,
New York.*

259. Soft Easel with Stretcher and
Paintings, *1986. Muslin stiffened with
glue, filled with polyurethane foam,
painted with latex; five parts, easel:
68 x 30 x 5 inches (172.7 x 76.2 x 12.7 cm);
stretcher: 23 x 17 x 2 inches (58.4 x 43.2 x
5.1 cm); paintings: 19 x 24 x 2 inches
(48.3 x 61 x 5.1 cm) each. Private
collection, New York.*

In August 1983, Claes and I spent two weeks in Frank Gehry's office in Venice, California, where we sharpened our understanding of his architecture by following his daily routine. We made a tour of his current projects in the area, which were in various stages of completion--from a newly excavated site at Exposition Park, where the skeleton of the California Aerospace Museum was under construction, to the nearly finished campus of the Loyola Law School in downtown Los Angeles.

Our concern in the large-scale projects is with the balance between "thing-ness" and abstraction. A thing in the form of a building also adds to the tension, especially if the building has a specific function. Considering subjects that would take an architectural approach into account, we thought of, for example, a row of jars and boxes on a shelf (of the kind we had seen in Frank's carpentry shop), a situation that would have a diffused organization and that could also interrelate abstractions and representational objects.

Frank Gehry's method is focused on process and is more open that that of most architects, allowing for continuous change. As not everything is built at once, there is always the opportunity for adjustments. The fact that he is able to set one plastic form next to another disparate one seemed to open up a way in which we could all work together on an equal basis. We became more and more aware of the potential of collaborating on a project, and all three of us were willing, as Frank put it, "to leap into the unknown."

A concrete result of that visit was a tiny model of a toppling ladder on which a can of paint was perched, which Claes conceived in response to a remark Frank had made during our visit to the Loyola Law School campus. In pointing out the sturdy row of four, rather fat, concrete columns in front of Merrifield Hall, he said that he would have liked to see one in a horizontal position to upset the scheme but that the university had not allowed him to execute this idea. A model of the ladder was placed on the maquette as a stand-in for the fifth column.

Frank felt that a program of contemporary art was needed to complete the campus. He had already proposed having a mural by Ed Ruscha on the subject of the law along one side of Merrifield Hall, and stained-glass windows by Jeremy Gilbert-Rolfe in the chapel. To these he now added the ladder and paint can idea, which, three years later, would be the only one of the projects to be realized.

(Coosje van Bruggen, 1994)

261. *Gehry, van Bruggen, and Oldenburg in Gehry's Santa Monica office, 1988.*

pages 456–57:
262. Toppling Ladder with Spilling Paint, 1986. *Steel and aluminum, painted with polyurethane enamel, 14 feet 2 inches x 10 feet 8 inches x 7 feet 7 inches (4.32 x 3.25 x 2.31 m). Loyola Law School, Los Angeles.*

The Haunted House, made for the Museum Haus Esters in Krefeld in 1987, was a metaphor for the return to the gallery in the form of throwing the objects into the museum through the window. And these objects that were thrown through the window were, of course, objects that might offend a museum. They were things found in the average suburban backyard: an apple core, a broken muffler, half of an automobile tire, totally rejected objects such as an old stuffed rabbit that nobody wanted anymore.

This time around the objects had a theatrical character, either because of the Coltello influence or because history had made the process self-conscious. The museum, transformed into the Haunted House, with the famous Mies van der Rohe windows made to seem broken by the forced entry of rude objects, was a kind of set. But there was also a new thematic content: Europe, influenced by Coosje's vision also. The important manifestations of this period took place in European museums and galleries.

In these works, the canvas became stiffened, the soft effects became frozen by the use of resins, creating a look that was soft but hard to the touch. And water-based latex was used rather than oil enamels. It was still store-bought. The approach was a bit like the house-painter's, but the palette had more white in the colors and varied from matte to gloss.

That sort of material and approach to the subject continued through From the Entropic Library, for the Magiciens de la Terre show in Paris and the European Desk Top in Milan, which was a kind of reflection on the decomposition of Europe.

(1990)

263. Haunted House (Original for Poster), 1987. Charcoal, chalk, and pastel on paper, 40 x 30 inches (101.6 x 76.2 cm). Kaiser Wilhelm Museum, Krefeld, On long-term loan from the Support Circle.

pages 460–61:
264. Cross Section of a Toothbrush with Paste, in a Cup, on a Sink; Portrait of Coosje's Thinking, Soft and Uprooted Version, with Foundation, 1987, installed at Museum Haus Esters Krefeld, May 31–June 26, 1987.

pages 462–63:
265. The Haunted House, Museum Haus Esters Krefeld, May 31–June 26, 1987.

266. Extinguished Match, *1987. Steel and rigid polyurethane foam, painted with latex, 94 x 270 x 29 inches (238.8 x 685.8 x 73.7 cm). Private collection.*

pages 466–67:
267. Piano/Hammock, *1987. Steel, stainless steel, and cast aluminum, 63 x 192 x 77 inches (160 x 487.7 x 195.6 cm). Stedelijk Museum, Amsterdam. Installed at the Mälmo Konsthall, Sweden, April 29–August 6, 1989.*

268. View of Spoonbridge and Cherry,
with Sailboat and Running Man, *1988.
Pastel on paper, 33½ x 20 inches (85.1 x
50.8 cm). Walker Art Center, Minneapolis,
Acquired in conjunction with the
commissioning of* Spoonbridge and
Cherry *for the Minneapolis Sculpture
Garden, 1991.*

269. Spoonbridge and Cherry (Model),
1987. Painted wood and Plexiglas, 22½ x
22½ x 49½ inches (57.2 x 57.2 x 125.7 cm).
Walker Art Center, Minneapolis,
Acquired in connection with construction
of the Sculpture Garden, 1986.

pages 470–71:
270. Spoonbridge and Cherry, 1988.
Aluminum, painted with polyurethane
enamel, and stainless steel,
29 feet 6 inches x 51 feet 6 inches x
13 feet 6 inches (9 x 15.7 x 4.1 m).
Minneapolis Sculpture Garden, Walker
Art Center, Minneapolis.

From the Entropic Library

Dieter Koepplin

In thematic terms, still-life painting began during the fourteenth and fifteenth centuries, when depictions of holy or otherwise venerable books (as well as such objects as pitchers, wash basins, and liturgical items) were made to look deceptively genuine. These objects were virtually inserted into illusionistically represented niches, with the pictorial surface likewise opening up as a niche. The depicted books belonged to holy men: prophets, Church fathers, priests, pious scholars in their studios. In striving to make their still lifes seem authentic but also compositionally appealing, the painters would attempt to bring a little disorder into the bookshelves. They could claim the fiction that the books, lying around, were the leftovers of a user's spiritual and intellectual labor; they were more or less abandoned, and the real issue was the mental work itself. Examples of such arrangements of books were found chiefly in Netherlandish painting—from the fifteenth-century Master of the Annunciation of Aix, who was trained in Netherlandish art, to seventeenth-century Dutch artists, through to Vincent van Gogh.[1]

From pictures of abandoned books in disorderly piles it was only a small step to the *vanitas* still lifes of the Baroque period featuring tattered—one might say "entropic"—books, accompanied by perhaps a skull, an hourglass, a guttering candle, and similarly meaningful objects. The viewer was meant to understand, and literally see, that even written texts, including the spiritual treasures pressed between two book covers, could not escape decay. "Entropy" does not spare the symbols of literary fame, or the Holy Scriptures, or even writings about transience and futility.[2] A death's head cannot read. The unread books are dead, futile—though not for the visual artist.

From the Entropic Library (fig. 271), a work created jointly by Claes Oldenburg and Coosje van Bruggen, does not quote art history. But it looks toward Europe and from there toward Africa, mulling over the colonizing past of the West. Not a painting, it is more like a painterly sculpture, a sculptural picture. Given its size, it could almost be called a monument—a monument to a disintegrating, somehow displaced European written culture. But why disintegrated, and how displaced?

This gigantic work is not, like the artists' large-scale projects, situated outside in an urban environment, but rather in a museum, surrounded by paintings and smaller sculptures. The base barely raises the work; the viewer stands practically on the same ground as the sculpture. What the base does is stake off the terrain of the piece, in effect saying, "Come closer, but do not enter; this is where the 'tableau' begins, the work is 'enacted' on this stage." Its restrained theatricality is not insignificant. *From the Entropic Library* postdates their 1985 Venice performance *Il Corso del Coltello* (pages 419–39), and, as Oldenburg has noted, a peculiar "theatrical dimension" characterizes the post-*Coltello* work. "Venice has an aftereffect with completely new colors," noted the artist.[3] In this case the colors are cool, broken by white and gray and strongly articulated in connection with the "architecture" of the multipart work and its white base. The delimitation of this four-inch-high rectangular base, which is more a surface than a three-dimensional object, prevents the virtually disintegrating, yet dynamic, sculpture from overflowing.

The "entropic" dynamic of the sculpture allows the viewer to make associations, both concrete and general. Two types of processes constitute the foundation of the internal motion, the richness, and the strange integrity of the work: pushing, pressing, urging, condensing on the one hand, and crumbling, tumbling, toppling, falling, collapsing, dissolving on the other. The work is composed of familiar object forms: books between bookends and a shattered lamp above them. These, by association, suggest other things and processes, and they evidence their own rhythmic interplay beyond the seemingly dominant effect of concreteness.

The principles of composition here are related to some of Oldenburg's earlier works and experiences. In terms of the piece's motifs, this is true especially of the elephant heads that figure in the bookends and the use of handwriting strokes as forms. It also applies generally to the polarity of concentrated absorption and ghostly decay, extending from *The Street* (1960, pages 44–59) to *The Haunted House* (1987, pages 459–63). In viewing *From the Entropic Library*, one witnesses not only the results but also the development of the sculpture as motion. By 1961, Oldenburg had realized that "my work is always on the way from one point to another."[4] That statement is pertinent both for the interrelatedness of his oeuvre and for the genesis of each individual piece—indeed, it holds true for the various forms and motifs in all his works, each of which is fundamentally in motion and affected by time.

The movement in *From the Entropic Library* ranges from the basic forces of pushing and pressing, toppling and disintegrating to the interweaving of motifs in the bookends (elephant head, outboard motor, L-support), and the coating of the surfaces with gestural, quasi–Abstract Expressionist brushstrokes and ubiquitously sprayed colors. In a recent interview, Oldenburg said:

I like to treat paint as material—to daub it, drop it, let it slide. There was Action Painting, but I also compare it to paint effects found on the streets. This approach is superimposed on a sculptural surface that is also "painterly."[5]

The paint hurled and splashed on the surface adds something light, even sketchy to the sculpture. The Italian word for "splash" is *schizzare*, which leads to the English *sketch*, the French *esquisser*, and the German *skizzieren*. And indeed the treatment of the surface of this huge sculpture, whose execution required a disciplined planning process that included drawings and models, thoroughly underscores the sketchiness of the overall character of the piece (almost in spite of its architectural definiteness).

The sculpture lays claim to function flawlessly and to endure, much as an automobile should function and a building should endure. At times, Oldenburg has appeared to be a constructor, constructing, among other things, a *Soft Pay-Telephone* (1963, fig. 100) and more than one drainpipe (1967, figs. 162–63). Indeed, he once meticulously designed a huge bridge across the Rhine River near Rotterdam—though in ultimately liberating terms, as a "technological liar,"[6] an artist playing the role of a constructor. Oldenburg has gone so far in role-playing to assume that of one Dr. Coltello (also known as the Kitsch Dragon or Murky Apollo), the unlicensed souvenir peddler in *Il Corso del Coltello*.[7]

Oldenburg's objects and commissioned pieces (such as the monumental public sculptures), *appear* to point in an entirely different direction: toward freedom, toward an art that is free. But that is only partly so. Oldenburg has always systematically sought complicated, ambivalent, multivalent situations in

Vincent van Gogh, Parisian Novels, *1888. Oil on canvas, 20⅞ x 28½ inches (53 x 72.5 cm). Vincent van Gogh Foundation, Amsterdam.*

which he could remain in immediate contact with the realities of life. Nevertheless, standing *in medias res*, he needed a way to maintain the possibilities of transformatively shaping that which he wanted to shape anyway, "lying" in a meaningful way, playing seriously, creating a new and convincing artistic reality, and finding a clear and lively form for a fictive reality. Oldenburg likes getting involved in complex situations. These include, especially, the large-scale projects (since 1976 created with van Bruggen), huge commissioned pieces in public spaces to which the artists, as few in our time, have given stimulating, demanding, and universally interesting forms.[8]

Although not commissioned, *From the Entropic Library* was created with a view to a specific project. As part of Jean-Hubert Martin's 1989 Paris exhibition *Magiciens de la Terre*, the sculpture was to occupy a prominent place. This dictated its size and, as will be seen, influenced its content. The show was billed as a "truly international exhibition," bringing together works by one hundred "Third World" and contemporary Western artists who view contemporary "Third World" artworks as art, not merely as anthropological items, yet do not themselves use a "primitive" formal language. The works from both areas were united, according to the organizers of this unusual presentation, by their "magical" effulgence—their aura.[9] Each artist was asked to reply to the question "What is art?" for the exhibition catalogue. The idea of posing this question was suggested by one of the participants, Lawrence Weiner (who provided a terse answer), while many others, particularly Westerners, did not care to respond (surely, a Sigmar Polke, Christian Boltanski, or Daniel Buren could not be expected to do so). Several "Third World" participants emphasized that making art made them happy even if they were not happy otherwise, and that art was simply their life. A Pakistani artist, Rasheed Araeen, penned a memorable statement: "Art is not magic, and magic is not art. Indeed when art and magic meet, they destroy one another."

For *From the Entropic Library*, the catalogue included a color drawing of the piece by Oldenburg; naturally the sculpture itself could not yet be reproduced on its designated site. Under the rubric "Qu'est-ce que l'art?" were printed thirteen text fragments chosen by van Bruggen from initially unidentified statements and writings by, respectively, Henry David Thoreau, William Carlos Williams, Oldenburg, van Bruggen herself, H. D. quoting Sigmund Freud, Jorge Luis Borges, Samuel Beckett, and Marcel Proust. From these anonymous, almost random fragments, overheard, barely registered, and almost inaudible, a few isolated words were plucked out. Falling, as it were, from the realm of writings and books, three of these words—"futility," "smashingly," and "beautiful"—whose importance and aleatory appearance remain open, are scattered over the base, like objects, almost like autumn leaves or, according to Oldenburg and van Bruggen, like dead insects. The last two words do, indeed, belong together; but on the pictorial plane of the sculpture's base, they too are doomed to be fragments. Other words, sheering out of their contexts—and all of them "written" in Oldenburg's hand—are like reliefs covering three loose "pages" that are inserted into the books of this highly personal reference library.[10] The handwriting peeps out only partially. It is legible in theory, but scarcely in practice: actual words are enclosed in the forms, which seem to move freely as gestures and which, it turns out, are more than pseudo-writing (like that made by children or by Jean Dubuffet in his late work).[11] Nevertheless, the penmanship and

the "pages" containing it appear to approach illegibility, a visual-linguistic white noise. One can regard this writing as clues to a secret—clues left by the unknown author who at some point wrote the words within longer texts. However, that author has long since disappeared. (Elias Canetti's aphorism is appropriate here: "No writing is secret enough for a person to truly express himself in it.") Parts of the words are covered by the books. Today, fragmentation characterizes all of one's thinking and perception.

The text fragments and the words taken from them certainly do not provide *the* key to understanding Oldenburg's and van Bruggen's sculpture. But one does establish that the written words, this hard evidence of writing, belong to the sculpture, a work that does anything but reject a connection with thinking, speaking, writing, and literature. The sculpture reveals that the world of pictures and the world of words—both of them specifically human worlds—cannot simply overlap, not even in the ideal motif of the *Library*, in which hand-written notes, a closed packet of letters (in the center of the piece), and other bits of paper were slipped in between the books. The bundled letters are silent about their contents. Were they factual, poetic, amorous, or familial? Who knows, who wants to know?

The flat, scattered text-objects do not deny that they are somewhat bizarre; the word "crazy" (from "Crazy Horse Road")[12] is among the word fragments. The handwriting in Oldenburg's "autumn-leaf words" is his own. By contrast, *The European Desktop* (1990, pages 491–501) employs, mirrorlike, van Bruggen's handwriting (she is left-handed, like Leonardo da Vinci, whose text mixes with van Bruggen's letter "to Frédéric [Chopin]" (page 498).[13] The 1993 large-scale project *Bottle of Notes* (fig. 293)[14] includes both handwritings: his on the outside, hers on the inside. In discussing the sculpture after its concept and shape were worked out, Oldenburg recalled that his use of penmanship dates back to *The Street*:

When I first came to New York City in late 1956, what struck me most was the agitated writing on the surface of the city: the walls, the streets, every place that could be marked. Graffiti had not yet become self-conscious or stylized; these were anonymous messages of experience and survival.

I began to copy them and make monoprints which I put up in the city. After a while I made constructions out of the writing/drawing, using the patterns of newspapers and buildings. In a third stage, I began to see the spatial possibilities of the relation between writing and its ground.[15]

Should one then assume that the handwriting elements in *From the Entropic Library*—which, despite their specific origins are once again "anonymous"—are likewise ultimately "messages of survival," not in a social, but in a more general sense?

The three delicate handwriting "objects" surrounding the books on the surface of the base are loosely connected to a few other scattered oddities. Two multifingered "ink splotches" are colored gray like the handwriting and burst out in all directions. They are vaguely related to the outlines of the fluttering elephant ears that energize the angular bookends. Since the 1960s, Oldenburg has repeatedly depicted explosive formations of liquids that ejaculate suddenly, unavoidably, and uncontrollably. Their shapes, colors, and materialities provide one (in everyday life) with something that is viewed, depending on one's attitude, either as an irksome annoyance, a catastrophe or a violent invasion, or as something comically

alive, magical, ghostly, merry. Can these simple splotches—
that elude the biological forms of similar phenomena in the
work of Jean Arp or Henri Matisse[16]—be regarded as artistic
products? For many years, Oldenburg pursued such sculptural
action forms in various guises: drawings of coffee pouring out
of knocked-over cups, paint hurled against a wall (as in the
unrealized large-scale project *Paint Splats (On a Wall by P. J.)*,
drops of nail polish, melted chocolate overflowing onto a
profiterole, tea oozing from a teabag, ink splashing out of a
shattering inkwell (inspired by a legend involving Martin
Luther), or just splotches.[17]

In *From the Entropic Library,* near one of the ink splotches, a
piece of handwriting spelling out the word "futility" lies on a
scrap of notebook paper. The perforated scrap, showing a hasty,
undecipherable, figurative red sketch is disintegrating. Next to
it, sculpturally formed bits of a burst lightbulb have landed,
with the remnant hanging from the "torn" wire suspended over
the books. All this hints at narrative and figuration but is not
naturalistic. The motifs are translated into an artistic reality
that has its own formal laws, its own internal architecture,[18] its
own continuous color quality. However, none of this
overwhelms the objects themselves.

The shattered lamp, although "dead," casts a light on the
fiction that has been elaborated into a concrete pinpointing of
the still life of books. Comparable to the snuffed-out candle in
the Dutch *vanitas* still lifes of the seventeenth century, the
electric bulb, we may assume, once had the function of
allowing the books to be used at night, when they were as yet
undevoured: light for the imaginary person who, both writing
and reading, used the books, pads, letters, and maps, which
were at one time tidily held together by two "tranquil"
bookends. But time has marched across them, and its passage
has not been merely passive: despite the title of the work, the
library has not been only entropic, in terms of decay and
growing disorder. Clearly a new and different liveliness has
been created by the imagination. (Joseph Beuys felt that every
artist, indeed every human being, constantly "proves the reality
of the idea and the invalidity of the theory of entropy."[19])
During the period of decay, much has happened, and a great
deal is still happening in the pictorial dynamics of the
sculpture, which has been seized by new minds. The *nature
morte* has gained a life of its own. Does one miss the writer and
the reader, without whom the books are dead and have no
intellectual reality? In one sense he is in them in an imaginary
way and partly he has truly evaporated (he would have to be a
giant), leaving the terrain to other forces. Oldenburg has said:
"A life cycle can be imposed on an object. An object can be
very energetic and active, and then it has a dying phase and a
phase of decomposition."[20] Decomposition, however, involves
not only loss but also gain: a transformation occurs. A very
baroque chalk drawing by Oldenburg from late 1990, *The
Entropic Library in a Later Stage, No. 2*, provides an image of
the subsequent metamorphosis. The two bookends are keeling
over, and the library as a whole looks like a rock formation that
has been eroding since time immemorial—a sculptural,
objectual, human landscape with the elephant—and that, in
its combination of forms, is almost a self-portrait.

The effects that physical forces have on things have always
constituted a cherished theme in Oldenburg's sculpture.
Indeed, he describes gravity as "my favorite form creator."[21]
This force plays a part in decay. Forces and activities—for

Outline, Page of Words for the Entropic
Library – "Smile," *1989. Pencil on paper,
12 x 9 inches (30.5 x 22.9 cm). Collection of
Claes Oldenburg and Coosje van Bruggen,
New York.*

Paint Splats (On a Wall by P. J.)
(Model), *1978–79. Painted aluminum,
27 x 89½ x 21 inches (68.5 x 227.5 x
53.2 cm). Collection of Claes Oldenburg
and Coosje van Bruggen, New York.*

Elephant Mask, *1959. Newspaper soaked in wheat paste over wire frame, painted with latex, 37 x 27 x 24 inches (76.2 x 68.6 x 61 cm). Collection of Claes Oldenburg and Coosje van Bruggen, New York.*

Row of Buildings in the Form of Bitten Knäckebröd, Stockholm, *1966–71. Knäckebröd, cardboard, wood, and pencil, painted with watercolor, 21 x 17 inches (53.3 x 43.2 cm). Destroyed.*

instance, construction and decomposition—operate in time whereby the latter can be livelier than the former. It is precisely death that breathes new life into the library. Its new lease on life becomes possible only with the departure of the imaginary and unknown book user, when the books are left to their ultimate fate. In 1966, Oldenburg commented on his earlier use of things as subjects:

I am unable to leave out, so I compress and superimpose to get a subject I can handle. The thing as subject is a device for externalizing. Things have presence only when they are alone— without visible agents or users.[22]

In *From the Entropic Library* one experiences a twofold solitude of the thing, or a shift in its solitude: initially, the books were possessed by the absent agent, who was succeeded by other forces, those of nature, which were still in the minds of the artists who had previously dispatched the owner of the books. Why do away with these? There were probably two reasons. First, at a glance it appears realistic in terms of present-day culture. Second, only then can one imagine what might happen to the abandoned thing, what metamorphosis under the impact of what forces could compress the thing on a new level: the possibilities for formation out of entropy spring not only from artistic whim. Despite all the conceits, one remains on the terrain of realities. Decay and oblivion are very real and can be terrifying in a real way.

The realistic conceit of abandonment and the ghostly reanimation of things especially marked those works by Oldenburg that directly preceded *From the Entropic Library* and which, incidentally, are all (and this applies to the *Library* as well) thematically grounded in Europe (and Africa, seen from a European vantage point). These include *The European Desktop*[23]; *Piano/Hammock* (1987, fig. 267), with its disintegrating keyboard[24]; and the environmental work *The Haunted House*, which van Bruggen called a "still-life drama" in which "entropy sets in."[25]

Physical forces that become operative in the processes of decay and construction join drives and emotions in the human and animal worlds. The instinct for food, whether human or animal, can create sculptural forms. The books in the library appear to have been neatly nibbled by mice. It is no coincidence that an Oldenburg work of 1966–71—*Proposed Colossal Monument in the Form of Bitten Knäckebröd, Stockholm* and its model, *Row of Buildings in the Form of Bitten Knäckebröd, Stockholm*—which bears some similarity to *From the Entropic Library*, was inspired by food and by biting. Oldenburg, who was born in Stockholm, grew up in the United States, and returned to Stockholm for a 1966 retrospective of his work, commented, "I eat Knäckebröd all the time. They come in stacks and packages. I took a stack and made one of my disappearing food images by biting."[26]

One feels physical human closeness in this instance even more directly than in a library that is tastier to mice than to people (indeed, it would not be far-fetched to recall that one of Oldenburg's guises is that of the geometric mouse). In contrast to *From the Entropic Library*, the dissolution of the Knäckebröd monument seems less like the crumbling of decay and more like an emphatically orderly, gradual decline and sinking of elements, which remain upright to the very end. (In a 1972 drawing they solemnly descend a hill and sink into the sea). The books in the *Library*, on the other hand, are in the process of tipping over, each book pressing upon the next.[27] One of the elephant bookends offers some resistance; the other, with its own strange dynamics, triggers the chain reaction of tipping over and pressing (features intrinsic to books). The realm of the books and bookends as active agents is easily comprehended. As in all works by Oldenburg and by Oldenburg and van Bruggen, the character of the model is neatly preserved. This art is not afraid of calm self-awareness. Obsession and self-distancing are not antithetical.

From the Entropic Library achieved its shape not only by being nibbled, by toppling, by decomposing, and so forth, but also, in terms of its motifs, as the result of a constructive action by the person who has set up the library and installed a reading light above it. In the genesis of the sculpture, an imaginary history assumed by the two artists played an animating role. This novel-like as well as pictorial, object-oriented kind of imagination fostered the preliminary sketches for the project.

The basic fiction, conceived by van Bruggen in the fall of 1988, went as follows: Somewhere in Africa, in a makeshift shelter, an explorer set up his library along with a few notebooks, slips of paper, bundled-up letters, and maps, and installed a lightbulb overhead—still and all, powered by electricity: European light over European books. (Perhaps European banknotes or dollar bills were hidden among the books.) The word "money" appears at the top center of a detailed sketch of early 1989. At some point, the explorer suddenly abandoned his place of activity in Africa and never returned. The books and several items inserted into and between them were left behind. These gradually decomposed; the lightbulb broke. The intensive forces of tropical nature took over, working in their own way on the library. The library was "eaten by time," according to van Bruggen. The now useless library "died"—that is, it gained a different kind of life, shape, madness, meaning, precision, and movement.

From the outset, the fictive library moved within the realm of the pictorial. The drawings help to trace this development. In the context of the exhibition *Magiciens de la Terre*, in which several pieces by African artists were expected to be shown, Oldenburg suggested a subject he had experimented with in earlier work before settling on the idea of the library: the head of an elephant, specifically African because of its big ears. Since *Elephant Mask* (1959), he has enjoyed being accompanied by this animal—as much as by a mouse—more precisely, by the *head* of an elephant, which struck him as suitable even for a bridge project in 1975.[28]

The first sketches that Oldenburg made in the fall of 1988[29] were linked to a 1966 drawing, *Elephant Head Combined with Outboard Motor, Etc., No. 2.*[30] This drawing, which was never turned into a sculpture, involved a fusion so extreme—the combination of an elephant's head with an outboard motor and a drainpipe—as to raise doubts about the importance of the contents.[31] The drainpipe is shaped like an elephant's trunk (at issue were the *forms* of the trunk and the drainpipe, but they retained their identities as objects nonetheless). As an *object*, however, the drainpipe was out of place in Africa, and so it was finally eliminated. Oldenburg and van Bruggen view the 1988 sketches as a first attempt at finding a kind of sculptural emblem for the Paris show, which they interpreted as a "site-specific situation" (like those of the sculptures in public spaces). In one, the elephant was shown with a pistol stuck into its head, and here, linked with the outboard motor, it

From the Entropic Library... in a Later Stage, No. 2, 1990. *Charcoal and pastel on paper, 29¼ x 39⅜ inches (99.7 x 100 cm). Collection of Claes Oldenburg and Coosje van Bruggen, New York.*

Elephant Head Combined with Outboard Motor, Etc., No. 2, 1966. *Crayon and watercolor on paper, 18¼ x 15 inches (46.4 x 38.1 cm). Collection of Claes Oldenburg and Coosje van Bruggen, New York.*

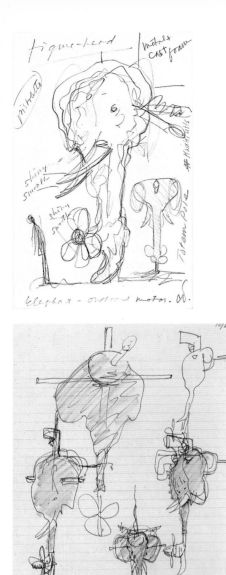

Notebook Page: Study for a Sculpture Combining an Elephant and an Outboard Motor, *1988 (detail). Pencil on paper, 11 x 8½ inches (27.9 x 21.6 cm). Kunstmuseum, Basel.*

Notebook Page: Studies for Elephant Outboard Motor, with Pistol, *1988. Pencil and ballpoint pen on paper, 11 x 8½ inches (27.9 x 21.6 cm). Collection of Claes Oldenburg and Coosje van Bruggen.*

embodied an endangered Africa. The motor in the trunk could have betokened colonial technology together with environmental exploitation and pollution, that is, the threat posed to Africa by European technology and industrialization. The executed piece could have functioned as a hanging soft sculpture. The trunk, equipped with a ship's propeller, could have piled up on the ground. However, such combinations of motifs are ultimately grounded not in the world of naturalistic objects but in the inventive imagination of forms—an imagination that, to be sure, does not resist comparison with familiar objects; indeed, it plays with them.

In one sketch Oldenburg made in November 1988, which indicated the differences in scale between *Elephant – Outboard Motor* and a viewer standing in front of it, one can see an alternative, a secondary pictorial thought, on the right side of the drawing. Fitting in with the exhibition theme—this time from an American viewpoint—a rigid and extremely stylized elephant/outboard motor is planted in the ground, with the words "Totem Pole" and "Kwakiutls" written next to it. Such a sculpture would have recalled the tremendous Amerindian totem poles of this tribe.

Almost simultaneously, during the artists' stay in Paris in the fall of 1988, van Bruggen suggested the motif theme of the decaying library abandoned by a European explorer in Africa. At first, Oldenburg did not feel that the subject would lend itself to a large sculpture, fearing it would be too static. Nevertheless, he produced a few sketches using the idea. In one version he transferred the *Elephant – Outboard Motor* to the context of a library. He drew the first formation of van Bruggen's idea ("content," as is noted in the upper right-hand margin of the sheet) in a two-part sketch. The right side of the first of the drawings features the books, looking roughly like a cluster of houses; the left side shows the elephant, theoretically supported by thé strange propeller and thrusting its tusks and forehead into an L-shaped bookend. In this version the propeller sits not on the elephant's trunk, but rather on its own shaft, facing outward and backward. Oldenburg gave his own initials to this attractive crossbreed (gray above, incarnadine below—not unerotic), while he wrote "Cos" (Coosje) for the books. The word "souvenir" recalls the unlicensed souvenir vendor, played by Oldenburg, in *Il Corso del Coltello*, and it is also reminiscent of actual bookends with similar motifs that are sold in souvenir shops.

The *Elephant – Outboard Motor* had found its niche in the project—until the final execution of the sculpture. The elephant's presence made sense also because in 1989 Paris was celebrating the bicentennial of the French Revolution. An "elephant's memory" is notorious, while human memory—at least, historical memory—is best preserved in books and files. Thus under the rubric of its recollection, the elephant dovetailed with the books, in excellent cooperation.

The comparability of books and houses likewise remained until the finished piece. Originally, the sculpture was intended for the segment of the exhibition slated for the Centre Georges Pompidou. Van Bruggen felt that the houses around the Pompidou recalled the books in a library, especially when viewed from the upper floors of the complex. Later on, however, the artists decided to move the sculpture to another site hosting the exhibition, La Grande Halle–La Villette, on the outskirts of Paris. The spines of the books in the sculpture formally constitute something like a façade—according to Oldenburg and van Bruggen—a streetfront in a slum in which the exterior is partially maintained, but everything behind it is deteriorating. For Oldenburg,

The problem in drawing was that the books somehow had to be interesting: something had to happen to them. In making the comparison to a street in the slums, we distinguished between the façades and the decaying backs of the houses. The words "keep this wall" and "devoured rectangles" are noted in the drawing. The word "money" is a reminder that some people stick paper money into books.[32]

The contrast between the façadelike spines of the books and the fraying beyond proved to be the best solution. The artists rejected a more painterly variant—more like a still life—for the arrangement of the books between L-shaped supports represented as elephant heads rolled up into balls. This sketch from early 1989 also included the lamp motif suggested by van Bruggen. Oldenburg made it (like everything else) extremely sculptural—a nibbled bulb falling to pieces. The incandescent filament appears as a small analogue to the detached spiral binding from a notebook found in the midst of the books. The lamp, imagined as turned on, subsequently reminded the artists of the memorable lamp in Pablo Picasso's *Guernica* shedding a harsh light on history, as oblivion takes over the *Library*. A similar dimension of experience is also offered within the framework of an exhibition that revealed the historical consequences of colonialism, activated in the bicentennial year of the French Revolution and also valid given the overall malaise that today's consumer society feels toward history.

An especially delirious version, drawn in late November 1988, remained a detour—albeit an attractive one—leading to the idea of the library. Concocted by the two artists during a train trip from Brussels to Paris, it features a single, open book with tattered pages lying on its spine on the ground, "giving up its ghost" in an almost heroic pose—a final waning, a final flaunting in mad excitement. The picture remotely conjures up a book burning (with the corresponding historical memories). This would have been the explorer's well-worn book: the Dutch word *ezelsoor* (dog ear) appears next to it. One could have, as van Bruggen imagined, literally "walked through" and "under" the spine of this catafalque book. She added the title to the drawing, which was subsequently retained: *de la bibliothèque entropique.*

The fluttering book pages lie somewhat further in the dynamic ears of the elephant heads as realized in the sculpture. Somewhat later, Oldenburg created airy, actionistic, but now virtually private, nonmonumental notebook constructions in sculptures entitled *Torn Notebooks* (1992, figs. 288–90): tossed-away (personal) sketchbooks or pocket calenders, their torn-apart halves barely held together by spiral bindings. On the randomly exposed pages, one catches fragments of handwriting and calendar dates.[33]

The curving form of the detached spiral notebook spine claimed a prominent position in the center of *From the Entropic Library*. Initially, the spiral stood upright—as in two sketches from December 1988 and from 1989. The first was almost a blueprint for a model; the other was a large-format pencil drawing, *From the Entropic Library (Fourth Version)*, in which both bookends remain vertical. In the final version, the nibbled notebook was turned ninety degrees, so that the spiral, now useless because of the decayed state of the notebook, loomed

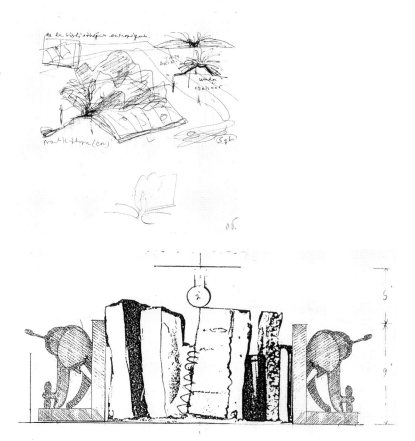

Study for the Entropic Library – "Walk Thru" Book with Torn Pages, *1988. Ink on paper, 4⅝ x 7¾ inches (11.9 x 19.7 cm). Öffentliche Kunstsammlung Basel, Kupferstichkabinett.*

Notebook Page: Study for the Entropic Library, *1988 (detail). Pencil, ballpoint pen, and photoprint on paper, 11 x 8½ inches (27.9 x 21.6 cm) Collection of Claes Oldenburg and Coosje van Bruggen, New York.*

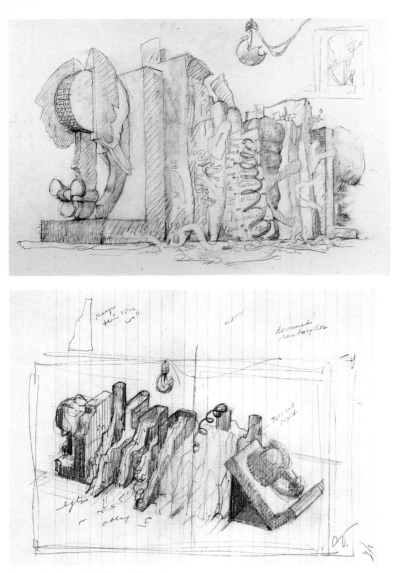

From the Entropic Library (Fourth Version), *1989. Pencil on paper, 28½ x 40 inches (72.4 x 101.6 cm). Collection of Claes Oldenburg and Coosje van Bruggen, New York.*

Notebook Page: Study for the Entropic Library, Overhead View, *1989. Pencil on paper, 8½ x 11 inches (21.6 x 27.9 cm). Kunstmuseum Basel.*

and whipped in the air. The spiral lends an effective accent not only through its material (flexible metal) but also as a pure line turning freely in the air. This linear object asserts itself boldly and a bit eerily over the sculptural mass. After earthquakes and bombings such remnants sometimes survive in ghostly form. "Bookmarks" extend out of a few of the books, like antennae stretching upward.

After the decision was reached to hold the group of books together by means of two flanking L-supports, in *Elephant – Outboard Motor*, the artists tried to achieve the desired dynamics and the "entropy" of the library by pushing the bookends very far apart. As a result, some of the books leaned toward one side, the rest toward the other, thereby creating a wedge-shaped opening in the middle; above it hovered the electric lightbulb. The central opening revealed—as Oldenburg noted on a sketch—"lassitude in center = entropy."

Soon afterward, however, van Bruggen suggested tilting one bookend and having all the books lean in the same direction. This produced a stronger pressure and an urgent movement toward the other bookend. In early 1989, Oldenburg, using this approach, made a crayon drawing of a top view of the projected sculpture at a slight angle, enabling one to look into the "interiors" of the disintegrating books. In the process of decay they reveal their insides. This fairly detailed work was the basis for a large drawing (the one in the *Magiciens de la Terre* catalogue) executed with colored cross-hatching and constructive precision. Two flattened bunches of green leaves peep out from between the books: the imaginary explorer was also interested in botany—he pressed leaves between the book pages.

On the basis of this drawing, Oldenburg conducted himself like an architect in executing his sculptural model. The outlines of the books and other elements were each captured individually in precise designs. Next, he began on the sculpture itself, layer by layer. First, he produced a medium-size format of the model (fig. 272), planning it as an intermediary stage, but also as a self-contained work. He then made the final sculpture, which now stands in the Museum of St. Etienne, southwest of Lyons. The sculpture is roughly two-thirds higher than a standing person: mighty, yet not oppressive, it is a painterly interior monument that resembles an architectural model.

The three-dimensional "geological" plates of the books, the cluster of invisible letters, the handwritten notes, and the other elements were piled side by side, at increasingly sharper slants, held up by a single elephant-head bookend. The result was a work that was both disparate and integrated, whereby the totality lends an intrinsic value to every element, indeed every detail. Aside from the rough, splashed layer of weathered gaudy paint, the element that contributes most to the integrity is the increasing tilt of the books, that is, the consistently growing pressure; or, to put it in general terms, the progressive dynamic of the compressed sculpture, which is decaying in the imagination—the imaginary metamorphosis.

In terms of the material from which they are formed, the individual elements are fairly elastic. Resisting pressure, yielding a bit, bending slightly, displaying the barely tamed energy of the shove and the counter pressure—these features are characteristics potentially inherent in the resin-coated polystyrene used. Above all, they are in line with the artistic intentions of the work.

The toppling of one bookend, with its consequently

upwardly fluttering elephant ears, cannot be regarded as the *cause* of the leaning of the books. The position of this support almost transcends functional rules and naturalistic viewpoints. The rebellious, exuberant, somewhat sinister-looking gray elephant-head bookend, which both lunges and dances (while the other bookend holds its position) is "permitted" to move all the more because it is a thoroughly artificial figure—though justifiable, as it were, and not exclusively fantastic.

Ultimately, despite its meticulously thought-out iconography, *From the Entropic Library* eludes mere narration, depiction, illustration, and indeed, to some extent, meaning. It is true that much has changed since 1963, when Oldenburg jotted down the following statements, and his collaboration with van Bruggen has strengthened the ideal connections (which go beyond the object, yet are linked to it). Nevertheless, his words are still fundamentally valid:

Although my art gives the (deliberate) impression of being concerned with the outside world, in fact it is simply the personal elaboration of imaginary forms of a limited number, in the guise of occasional appearances. . . . Its use of the elimination of appearances, frankly and directly, is offered as an alternative to saying more effectively that appearances are not what count. It is the forms that count. It is the same to me whether my material image is a cathedral or a girdle . . . a telephone dial or a stained glass window . . . the resemblance, while amusing, means nothing. You could say that I have aimed at neutralizing meaning. . . . To eliminate appearances seems to be impossible, and therefore artificial. Simply grasp them and show how little they mean—this is what Cézanne did.[34]

Oldenburg would like to eliminate as far as possible the apparent antitheses between the many interesting details (found or invented and in which he likes to "lose" himself), the many potential meanings, and the general structures of his work. Van Bruggen has tied this to the reality of Platonic ideas or at least to Platonic mathematics and geometry.[35] Ultimately, Oldenburg relies on the strength of form, on the "underlying architecture."[36] Artists—and indeed all people who create in full awareness of their freedom—operate by inventing forms. They operate creatively, like God, so to speak, or like a "magician of the earth."

The inventing is no less "magical" if the artist uses "guise" or "amusing resemblance." He is thereby operating in terms of an initial communication between the human being, the world of things, and the artwork—an *initial* communication, whose semblance is soon made obvious—that is, unmasked, ultimately frustrating the bewildered viewer.[37] No regained artwork-thing-magic could, as Oldenburg once announced, bring that about:

This elevation of simplicity above bourgeois values, which is also a simplicity of return to truth and first values, will (hopefully) destroy the notion of art and give the object back its power. Then the magic inherent in the universe will be restored and people will live in sympathetic religious exchange with the materials and objects surrounding them. They will not feel so different from these objects, and the animate/inanimate schism {will be} mended. What is now called an art object is a debased understanding of a magic object.[38]

In later years, when Oldenburg began to focus on possible monumental sculptures in the form of everyday objects, he

From the Entropic Library (Final Study), *1989. Pencil and colored pencil on paper, 30 x 40 inches (76 x 101.5 cm). Private collection.*

realized his interest had shifted:

The idea of an object as a magic thing no longer obsesses me as it once did. . . . I became far more interested in the architectural form.[39]

This tendency has been strengthened by his collaboration with van Bruggen. At the same time, their work has evinced a denser network of possible revealed meanings and the concomitant ideas—so much denser that the question of "what counts" seems almost meaningless. In this non-reductive, at once serious and cheerful art, which transcends boundaries, many things count. Contradictions count, as does a polar *totality* in a specific form that is experienced as an *event*.

Translated, from the German, by Joachim Neugroschel.

1. Oldenburg and van Bruggen knew of several such examples without directly referring to them.

2. See Sabine Schwarz, *Das Bücherstilleben in der Malerei des 17. Jahrhunderts* (Wiesbaden: O. Harrassowitz, 1987); and Barbara John, *Stilleben in Italien. Die Anfänge der Bildgattung im 14. und 15. Jahrhundert* (Frankfurt: P. Lang, 1991).

3. Felix Schmidt, "Neue Welt nach Regeln der Phantasie," *Art* (Hamburg) 12 (Dec. 1991), p. 44.

4. Barbara Rose, *Claes Oldenburg* (exh. cat.; New York: The Museum of Modern Art, 1970), p. 189.

5. Quoted (not in regard to *From the Entropic Library*) in an interview with Arne Glimcher, in *Claes Oldenburg* (exh. cat.; New York: The Pace Gallery, 1992), p. 12.

6. *Claes Oldenburg: Skulpturer och teckningar* (exh. cat.; Stockholm: Moderna Museet, 1966), unpaginated.

7. Germano Celant, *The Course of the Knife* (Milan: Electa, 1986), p. 94. In Bernhard Kerber, *Claes Oldenburg: Schreibmaschine* (Stuttgart: Philipp Reclam, 1971), p. 15, Oldenburg says, "By dealing with the imaginary, I am once again superfluous in an industrial society. So I act as if I'm playing a part. By imitating the baker or the butcher, I play the worker."

8. *Claes Oldenburg: Large-Scale Projects, 1977–1980* (New York: Rizzoli, 1980). *A Bottle of Notes and Some Voyages* (exch. cat.; Sunderland: Northern Centre for Contemporary Art; Leeds: The Henry Moore Centre for the Study of Sculpture, Leeds City Art Galleries, 1988).

9. Jean-Hubert Martin, preface, in *Magiciens de la Terre* (Paris: Réunion des Musées Nationaux, 1989).

10. The following text fragments, reframented and semi-concealed, are included in the sculpture: "it is a great art to *saunter*" (Henry David Thoreau); "no ideas but in *things*" (William Carlos Williams); "barges and *tugboats* and freighters going in all directions" (Oldenburg); "the *futility* of *yearning* for perfection (van Bruggen); "*Crazy* Horse Road" (van Bruggen); "not mere repetition but re-creation" (van Bruggen); "in Rome, even I could afford to wear a *gardenia*" (H[ilde] D[oolitle], quoting Sigmund Freud); "you may have to get it done on your own terms" (van Bruggen); "crossing things out so *smashingly beautiful*" (van Bruggen); "the *danger* is in the neatness of identification" (Samuel Beckett); "OK, I found a *fish-joint*, and if that doesn't do it. . . ." (Oldenburg); "the *faint trace* of a *smile* or of a *word* (Jorge Luis Borges); "houses, *avenues*, roads are, *alas* as fugitive as the *years*" (Marcel Proust). Italics indicate words that Oldenburg either isolated completely and placed on the pedestal ("futility," "smashingly," "beautiful") or assigned to the three loose "pages" inserted among the books. On the first "page" one can read (in Oldenburg's handwriting) the following words, which jut out halfway: crazy, gardenia, word, years, faint; on the second "page": smile, alas, danger, fish-joint, trace; and on the third "page": saunter, avenues, things, tugboats, yearning.

11. Regarding Dubuffet, see Rose, p. 37; Coosje van Bruggen, *Claes Oldenburg: Nur ein anderer Raum/Just Another Room* (Frankfurt: Museum für Moderne Kunst, 1991), pp. 14ff.

12. When interviewed by Alfons Schilling about his early "proposed colossal monuments," Oldenburg recalled "another guy out there [Korczak Ziolkowski] who wants to make an enormous statue of an Indian, Crazy Horse, he bought a whole mountain [in Custer, South Dakota]. He started a long time ago. I am afraid that this kind of scale would not let me do all the other things I want to do. One of the beautiful things about just drawing these things is that you don't have to build it. . . . It's just difficult to imagine what the effect of it would be. I think we should try one of them anyway, to see." In Alfons Schilling, *Bau: Zeitschrift für Architektur und Städtebau* (Vienna) 4 (1966), p. 87b.

13. Claes Oldenburg and Coosje van Bruggen, *Claes Oldenburg: Sketches and Blottings toward the European Desk Top* (Milan and Turin: Galleria Christian Stein; Florence: Hopeful Monster, 1990). In this work Oldenburg likewise used texts chosen or authored by van Bruggen.

14. *A Bottle of Notes and Some Voyages*, pp. 220ff.

15. Ibid., p. 224. An early jotting by Oldenburg, quoted in van Bruggen (p. 14), reads, "All is read on the walls of the city."

16. When planning *Paint Splats (On a Wall by P. J.)* for the entrance façade of Marshall Field & Company department store in Houston (1978–79, a large-scale project that was never executed) van Bruggen and Oldenburg returned to a sketch in a 1965 notebook: *Stains of Nail Polish, "Jamaica Bay," New York*. Oldenburg commented in regard to the wall project of 1978–79: "But in any case the shapes, we agreed, had to remain paint specks and not become a composition with biomorphic shapes in the manner of Arp or arabesques in the manner of Matisse or even drips in the manner of Pollock, but real paint traces. The huge blobs could be manufactured out of plastic or painted aluminum" (*Claes Oldenburg: Large-Scale Projects, 1977–1980*, p. 72). Stated Oldenburg in 1966, "So if I see an Arp and I put that Arp into the form of some ketchup, does that reduce the Arp or does it enlarge the ketchup . . . ?" (Bruce Glaser, "Oldenburg, Lichtenstein, Warhol: A Discussion," *Artforum* [Los Angeles] 4, no. 6 [Feb. 1966], p. 23).

17. Specific examples: *Dropped Cup of Coffee – Study for "Image of the Buddha Preaching" by Frank O'Hara* (1967); *Stains of Nail Polish, "Jamaica Bay," New York* (1965).

18. In Glimcher (p. 14) Oldenburg states, "Movement and texture are most important to me, but there is always an underlying architecture."

19. Christos M. Joachimides and Norman Rosenthal, *Zeitgeist* (Berlin: Martin-Gropius-Bau, 1982), p. 82. Beuys had unique ideas about the quality and genesis of heat. "Entropic," vis-à-vis *From the Entropic Library*, probably refers to a kind of disorder and mingling in which all written things become so chaotic in their decay that no one text maintains its own clarity and energy.

20. Glimcher, p. 9.

21. Rose, p. 135.

22. *Claes Oldenburg: Constructions, Models, and Drawings* (exh. cat.; Chicago: Richard Feigen Gallery, 1969), p. 3.

23. Schilling, p. 87b.

24. *A Bottle of Notes and Some Voyages*, pp. 211ff.

25. Ibid., pp. 201 and 196 ("entropy sets in").

26. Barbara Haskell, *Claes Oldenburg: Object into Monument* (exh. cat.; Pasadena, Calif.: Pasadena Art Museum; Los Angeles: The Ward Ritchie Press, 1971), p. 31.

27. Van Bruggen later found the following passage in the writings of Leonardo: "One pushes the other. By these square-blocks {which Leonardo drew while tipping and pressing them] are meant the life and the studies of men" (*The Notebooks of Leonardo da Vinci*, Vol. II, *Morals*).

28. In 1975, Oldenburg drew *Bridge for Duisburg, Derived from an Inverted Elephant Head*.

29. See Dieter Koepplin, *Zeichnungen von Beuys, Clemente, Disler, Judd, Nauman, Oldenburg, Penck und Stella aus dem Kupferstichkabinett Basel* (Nuremberg: Kunsthalle Nürnberg, 1990), pp. 11–13.

30. *Claes Oldenburg: Dibujos/Drawings 1959–1989* (Valencia: IVAM Centre Julio González, 1989), p. 30.

31. Around the same time, Oldenburg produced separate drawings of the outboard motor and the drainpipe.

32. From a conversation with the artist, New York, 1990.

33. Glimcher, pp. 7, 17, and 48ff.

34. Quoted in Rose, p. 192. In London in 1966, Oldenburg noted: "Only when someone looks at nature does it mean something. Because my work is naturally non-meaningful, the meaning found in it will remain doubtful and inconsistent—which is the way it should be. All that I care about is that, like any *startling* piece of nature, it should be capable of stimulating meaning" (Rose, p. 198).

35. *Claes Oldenburg: Dibujos/Drawings 1959–1989*, p. 14.

36. Glimcher, p. 14.

37. In 1966, Oldenburg also commented, "The pieces depend not only on the participation of the spectator but his frustration—which is really a technique of definition: this is not a *real* object" (Rose, p. 194).

38. Claes Oldenburg, *Store Days: Documents from The Store (1961) and Ray Gun Theater (1962)* (New York: Something Else Press, 1967), p. 60.

39. *Claes Oldenburg: Proposals for Monuments and Buildings, 1965–1969* (Chicago: Big Table, 1969), p. 33.

FROM THE ENTROPIC LIBRARY

pages 485–87:
271. From the Entropic Library, *1989,*
included in Magiciens de la Terre,
La Grande Halle – La Villette, Paris,
May 18 – August 14, 1989.

"it is a great art to saunter"
"no ideas but in things"
"barges and tugboats and freighters going
in all directions"
"the futility of yearning for perfection"
"Crazy Horse Road"
"not mere repetition, but re-creation"
"in Rome, even I could afford to wear a
gardenia"
"you may have to get it done on your own
terms"
"crossing things out so smashingly
beautiful"
"the danger is in the neatness of
identification"
"OK, I found a fish-joint, and if that
doesn't do it..."
"the faint trace of a smile or of a word"
"houses, avenues, roads are, alas, as
fugitive as the years"

(Coosje van Bruggen, 1989)

February 5 1990

Undoing Yalta, 45 Years Later,
a New Europe. (Herald Tribune)

Crashing surfaces
of shredded treaties
Colors sliding
off the map
Dissolve boundaries
beyond recall.

Coosje van Bruggen, in response to
"Undoing Yalta, 45 Years Later,
a New Europe," International Herald-
Tribune, *February 5, 1990.*

273. Stamp Blotter on Fragment of
Desk Pad (Study for Rolling Blotter),
1990. Charcoal and watercolor on paper,
38⅛ x 50 inches (96.8 x 127 cm).
Collection of Claes Oldenburg and Coosje
van Bruggen, New York.

274. Stamp Blotters on Shattered
Desk Pad, *1990. Charcoal, pencil, and
pastel on paper, 38 ⅛ x 50 ⅛ inches
(97 x 127.3 cm). Collection of Claes
Oldenburg and Coosje van Bruggen,
New York.*

275. Shattered Desk Pad, with Stamp Blotters, *1990. Expanded polystyrene, wood, cardboard, and resin, painted with latex, 13 x 72 x 48 inches (33 x 182.9 x 121.9 cm). Collection of Claes Oldenburg and Coosje van Bruggen, New York.*

276. Sculpture in the Form of a Stamp
Blotter, Rearing, on a Fragment of Desk
Pad, 1990. Expanded polystyrene, steel,
wood, cardboard, and resin, painted
with latex, 6 feet 8⁹⁄₁₆ inches x
12 feet 7½ inches x 10 feet 9⁹⁄₁₆ inches
(2.05 x 3.85 x 3.30 m). Collection of
Claes Oldenburg and Coosje van Bruggen,
New York.

to Frédéric

Sitting at my desk in solitary
pursuit of fleeting thoughts shards
of your nocturnes sing in my head.
Suddenly the ear splitting siren of
a passing ambulance dissipates
the theme, thin as air, you had
awakened in me, never to be
recaptured.
Once amnesia has set in, I am left
with an unshakable sadness and
rising melancholia. Pens broken and
keyboard untouched, your phantoms,
Pole, now overshadow my lines, and
my cold tears turn into the very
raindrops against your window,
that nightmarish afternoon in Majorca,
that made you see yourself floating
on a lake, foreboding death.

Coosje van Bruggen, letter "to Fréderic,"
1990.

277. Writing Quill and Exploding Ink
Bottle, *1989. Charcoal on paper, 30 x
40 inches (76.2 x 101.6 cm). Collection of
Claes Oldenburg and Coosje van Bruggen,
New York.*

278. Sculpture in the Form of a Writing
Quill and an Exploding Ink Bottle, on a
Fragment of Desk Pad, *1990. Expanded
polystyrene, steel, wood, cloth, and resin,
painted with latex, 7 feet 8 inches x
22 feet 11 inches x 11 feet 9 inches (2.34 x
7 x 3.58 m). Collection of Claes Oldenburg
and Coosje van Bruggen, New York.*

pages 500—01:
279. Sculpture in the Form of a
Collapsed European Postal Scale, *1990.
Expanded polystyrene, aluminum,
cloth, and resin, painted with latex,
5 feet 1 inch x 21 feet x 19 feet ⅛ inches
(1.55 x 6.4 x 5.80 m). Collection of
Claes Oldenburg and Coosje van Bruggen,
New York.*

pages 502–03:

280. Dropped Bowl with Scattered Slices and Peels, 1990. Reinforced concrete, steel, and fiberglass-reinforced plastic, painted with polyurethane enamel; and stainless steel; 17 parts, 16 feet 9 inches x 91 feet x 105 feet (5.11 x 27.7 x 32 m) overall. Metro-Dade Open Space Park, Miami.

281. Bicyclette Ensevelie (Buried Bicycle), 1990. Steel, aluminum, and fiberglass, painted with polyurethane enamel; four parts, wheel: 9 feet 2¼ inches x 53 feet 4⅜ inches x 10 feet 4 inches (2.8 x 16.26 x 3.15 m); handlebar and bell: 23 feet 8¼ inches x 20 feet 4⅞ inches x 15 feet 6⅛ inches (7.22 x 6.22 x 4.74 m); seat: 11 feet 3⁹⁄₁₆ inches x 23 feet 9 inches x 13 feet 7 inches (3.45 x 7.24 x 4.14 m); pedal: 16 feet 3¹⁵⁄₁₆ inches x 20 feet 1¹⁄₁₆ inches x 6 feet 10¹³⁄₁₆ inches (4.97 x 6.13 x 2.1 m). Parc de La Villette, Paris.

ANIMO ET FIDE

pages 506–07:
282. Monument to the Last Horse, *1991.*
Aluminum and polyurethane foam,
painted with polyurethane enamel,
19 feet 8 inches x 17 feet x 12 feet 4 inches
(6 x 5.18 x 3.76 m). The Chinati
Foundation, Marfa, Texas.

283. Free Stamp, *1991. Steel and*
aluminum, painted with polyurethane
enamel, 28 feet 9⅛ inches x 26 feet x 49 feet
(8.78 x 7.92 x 14.94 m). Willard Park,
Cleveland.

pages 510–11:
284. Binoculars, Chiat/Day Building,
1991. Concrete and cement plaster, painted
with elastomeric paint, over steel frame,
45 x 44 x 18 feet (13.72 x 13.41 x 5.49 m).
Chiat/Day, Inc., 340 Main Street, Venice,
California.

285. Stirring Up Spanish Themes, *1987.*
Pencil, watercolor, and felt pen on paper,
30⅛ x 23¼ inches (76.5 x 59.1 cm).
Collection of Claes Oldenburg and
Coosje van Bruggen, New York.

286. Sculpture in the Form of a Match
Cover with Loose Matches, *1987. Steel*
and expanded polyurethane epoxy, painted
with latex, 40 x 78¾ x 78¾ inches (101.6 x
200 x 200 cm), including base. Collection of
Claes Oldenburg and Coosje van Bruggen,
Courtesy of PaceWildenstein.

287. Mistos (Match Cover), 1992. Steel, aluminum, and fiberglass-reinforced plastic, painted with polyurethane enamel, 68 feet x 33 feet x 43 feet 4 inches (20.73 x 10.06 x 13.21 m) overall. La Vall d'Hebron, Barcelona.

288. Torn Notebook Studies A, B, C, 1992. Notebooks and resin, painted with latex, mounted on steel bases, study A: 8 x 5¼ x 4¼ inches (20.3 x 13.3 x 10.8 cm); study B: 6¾ x 6½ x 6⅜ inches (17.2 x 16.5 x 16.2 cm); study C: 7⅛ x 7½ x 4¾ inches (18.1 x 19.1 x 12.1 cm). Collection of Aaron Fleischman.

289. Torn Notebook, One, *1992. Muslin, chicken wire, clothesline, steel, resin, and aluminum, painted with latex, 24 x 25 x 19 inches (61 x 63.5 x 48.3 cm). Collection of Mr. and Mrs. Morton L. Janklow, New York.*

291. Study for the Bottle of Notes, *1987.*
Pencil and colored pencil on paper, 30 x
25½ inches (76.2 x 64.8 cm). Collection of
Claes Oldenburg and Coosje van Bruggen,
New York.

292. Bottle of Notes (Model), *1989—90.*
Aluminum and expanded polystyrene,
painted with latex, 107 x 49 x 39 inches
(271.8 x 124.4 x 99 cm). IVAM, Instituto
Valenciano de Arte Moderno, Generalitat
Valenciana, Valencia.

293. Bottle of Notes, 1993. Steel, painted with polyurethane enamel, 30 x 16 x 10 feet (9.14 x 4.88 x 3.05 m). Central Gardens, Middlesbrough, England.

294. Clarinet Bridge, *1992. Canvas, wood, clothesline, polyurethane foam, and resin, painted with latex, 14½ x 11¼ x 98 inches (36.8 x 28.6 x 248.9 cm). Collection of Claes Oldenburg and Coosje van Bruggen, Courtesy of PaceWildenstein.*

295. Soft Harp, Scale B – Ghost Version, *1992. Canvas, steel, aluminum, clothesline, expanded polystyrene, and dacron, painted with latex, 95 x 27 x 48 inches (241.3 x 68.6 x 121.9 cm). Collection of Claes Oldenburg and Coosje van Bruggen, New York.*

298. Leaning Fork with Meatball and
Spaghetti I, *1994. Cast aluminum,
painted with urethane enamel; two parts,
97½ x 18½ x 12 inches (247.7 x 47 x
30.5 cm); 39 x 51½ x 64 inches (99.1 x 131 x
162.6 cm); 131½ x 51 x 39 inches (334 x
129.5 x 99.1 cm) overall. Collection of
Claes Oldenburg and Coosje van Bruggen,
Courtesy of PaceWildenstein.*

299. Geometric Apple Core, 1991.
*Stainless steel, steel, and polyurethane
foam, coated with resin, painted with
latex, 92 x 55 x 42 inches (233.7 x 139.7 x
106.7 cm). Collection of Claes Oldenburg
and Coosje van Bruggen, Courtesy of
PaceWildenstein.*

300. Leaf Boat with Floating Cargo, 1992. Leaf boat: canvas, steel, aluminum, cardboard, and resin, painted with latex; floating cargo: canvas, urethane foam, expanded polystyrene, cardboard, and resin, painted with latex; sail: 80 x 29 x 90¼ inches (203.2 x 73.7 x 230.5 cm); boat: 5⅜ x 49 x 76½ inches (13.7 x 124.5 x 194.3 cm). Collection of Claes Oldenburg and Coosje van Bruggen, New York.

301. Inverted Collar and Tie – Third Version, *1993. Canvas, resin, steel, and urethane foam, painted with latex, on painted wood base; 60 x 57 x 27 inches (152.4 x 144.8 x 68.6 cm); base: ¾ x 38¼ x 38¼ inches (1.9 x 97.2 x 97.2 cm). Collection of Claes Oldenburg and Coosje van Bruggen, Courtesy of PaceWildenstein.*

302. Inverted Collar and Tie, *1994. Fiberglass-reinforced plastic, painted with gelcoat; steel; and polymer concrete; 39 feet x 27 feet 9 inches x 12 feet 7½ inches (11.89 x 8.46 x 3.85 m). West End Str. 1, Mainzer Landstrasse 58, Frankfurt.*

303. The Nelson-Atkins Museum of
Art as a Net, with Shuttlecocks, *1992.*
Pastel on paper, 30⅛ x 40 inches
(76.5 x 101.6 cm). The Nelson-Atkins
Museum of Art, Kansas City, Missouri,
Gift of Claes Oldenburg and Coosje
van Bruggen, F 94-16.

304. Shuttlecock (Fabrication Model), *1994. Aluminum, cardboard, felt, resin, and urethane enamel; 27 inches (68.6 cm) high, 24½ inches (62.2 cm) in diameter; base: ½ x 18 x 18 inches (1.3 x 45.7 x 45.7 cm). Collection of Claes Oldenburg and Coosje van Bruggen, New York.*

pages 534–35:
305. Shuttlecocks, *1994. Aluminum and fiberglass-reinforced plastic, painted with polyurethane enamel; four shuttlecocks, each 17 feet 10¼ inches (5.45 m) high, 15 feet ¼ inches (4.59 m) in diameter; sited: 19 feet 2½ inches x 17 feet 5 inches x 15 feet ¼ inches (5.85 x 5.31 x 4.59 m); 20 feet x 15 feet 10 inches x 15 feet ¼ inches (6.1 x 4.83 x 4.59 m); 17 feet 10¼ inches x 15 feet ¼ inches x 15 feet ¼ inches (5.45 x 4.59 x 4.59 m); 18 feet 3½ inches x 18 feet 10 inches x 15 feet ¼ inches (5.58 x 5.74 x 4.59 m). The Nelson-Atkins Museum of Art, Kansas City, Missouri.*

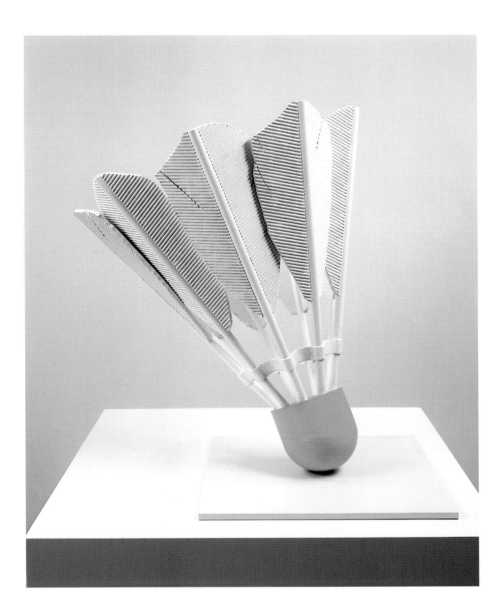

Selected Exhibition History

David Platzker

Solo and Two-Person Exhibitions

For full information about catalogues cited in this section, see "Exhibition Catalogues" in the bibliography. Exhibition entries are followed by related articles and reviews.

1954

Tally-Ho Restaurant, Evanston, Ill. *An Exhibit of Paintings and Drawings*. Nov. 1–28.

1955

The Bramson Gallery, Evanston, Ill. *A Collection of Paintings by Claes Thure Oldenburg*. Opened March 12. Brochure.

Frank Ryan Contemporary Furnishings, Chicago. *Paintings/Drawings: Claes Oldenburg*. Opened Nov. 4.

1959

Cooper Union Library, New York. *Figure Drawings*. March.

Judson Gallery, New York. *Drawings Sculptures Poems*. May 22–June 10.

Judson Gallery, New York. *Two-Man: Dine/Oldenburg*. Nov. 13–Dec. 3.
—V[entura], A[nita]. "In the Galleries." *Arts Magazine* (New York) 34, no. 3 (Dec. 1959), p. 59.

1960

Judson Gallery, New York. *Ray Gun Show* (included Oldenburg's *The Street* and Jim Dine's *The House*). March. Brochure, with statement by Oldenburg with Dine.
—Krim, Seymour. "An Art for Downtown Person's." *Village Voice* (New York), March 23, 1960, pp. 4, 6.

Reuben Gallery, New York. *The Street*. May 6–19.
—S[andler], I[rving] H[ershel]. "Reviews and Previews." *Art News* (New York) 59, no. 10 (summer 1960), p. 16.
—T[illim], S[idney]. "In the Galleries." *Arts Magazine* (New York) 34, no. 9 (June 1960), p. 53.

Sun Gallery, Provincetown, Mass. *Irene Barrell/Claes Oldenburg*. July–Aug.

1961

Ray Gun Mfg. Co., 107 East Second Street, New York (in cooperation with Green Gallery, New York). *The Store*. Dec. 1, 1961–Jan. 31, 1962.
—J[ohnston], J[ill]. "Exhibitions for 1961–62." *Art News* (New York) 60, no. 9 (Jan. 1962), pp. 47, 60.
—J[ohnston], J[ill]. "Reviews and Previews." *Art News* (New York) 61, no. 3 (May 1962), p. 55.
—Tillim, Sidney. "Month in Review." *Arts Magazine* (New York) 36, no. 5 (Feb. 1962), pp. 34–37.

1962

Green Gallery, New York. *Claes Oldenburg*. Sept. 24–Oct. 20.
—Ashton, Dore. "Exhibition at the Green Gallery." *Studio International* (London) 165 (Jan. 1963), pp. 25–26.
—Ashton, Dore. "New York Letter." *Das Kunstwerk* (Baden-Baden) 16, no. 7 (Jan. 1963), pp. 31–32.
—Fried, Michael. "New York Letter." *Art International* (Zurich) 6, no. 8 (Oct. 25, 1962), pp. 72–76.
—Johnson, Ellen H. "The Living Object." *Art International* (Zurich) 7, no. 1 (Jan. 25, 1963), pp. 42–45.

—J[ohnston], J[ill]. "Reviews and Previews." *Art News* (New York) 61, no. 3 (May 1962), p. 55.
—J[ohnston], J[ill]. "Exhibition at Green Gallery." *Art News* (New York) 61, no. 7 (Nov. 1962), p. 13.
—Preston, Stuart. "Current and Forthcoming Exhibitions: New York." *The Burlington Magazine* (London) 104, no. 716 (Nov. 1962), pp. 507–08.
—Roberts, Colette. "Les Expositions à l'étranger: Lettre de New York." *Aujourd'hui* (Paris) 7, no. 39 (Nov. 1962), pp. 50–52.
—Rudikoff, Sonya. "New York Letter." *Art International* (Zurich) 6, no. 9 (Nov. 25, 1962), pp. 60–62.
— Rudikoff, Sonya. "New Realists in New York." *Art International* (Zurich) 7, no. 1 (Jan. 25, 1963), pp. 38–41.
—Tillim, Sidney. "Month in Review." *Arts Magazine* (New York) 37, no. 2 (Nov. 1962), pp. 36–38.

1963

Dwan Gallery, Los Angeles. *Oldenburg.* Oct. 1–26.
—Nordland, Gerald. "Marcel Duchamp and Common Object Art." *Art International* (Lugano) 8, no. 1 (Feb. 15, 1964), pp. 30–32.
—Nordland, Gerald. "A Succession of Visitors." *Artforum* (San Francisco) 2, no. 12 (summer 1964), pp. 64–68.

1964

Sidney Janis Gallery, New York. *Exhibition of Recent Work by Claes Oldenburg.* April 7–May 2. Catalogue.
—Canaday, John. "Art: By Claes Oldenburg, An Exhibition of Food and Other Things at the Sidney Janis Gallery." *The New York Times*, April 7, 1964, p. 32.
—Canaday, John. "Maybe Hopeful: Symptoms in a New Pop Exhibition." *The New York Times*, April 12, 1964, section 2, p. 19.
—Genauer, Emily. "Art: The Large Oldenburgs and Small van Goghs." *The Herald Tribune* (New York), April 12, 1964, p. 39.
—J[ohnston], J[ill]. "Claes Oldenburg." *Art News* (New York) 63, no. 4 (May 1964), p. 12.
—J[udd], D[onald]. "In the Galleries." *Arts Magazine* (New York) 38, no. 10 (Sept. 1964), p. 63.
—Kozloff, Max. "New Works by Oldenburg." *The Nation* (New York), April 27, 1964, pp. 445–46.
—Roberts, Colette. "Les Expositions à l'étranger: Lettre de New York." *Aujourd'hui* (Paris) 8, no. 46 (July 1964), pp. 90–91.
—Rose, Barbara. "New York Letter." *Art International* (Lugano) 8, nos. 5–6 (summer 1964), pp. 77–81.

The Pace Gallery, Boston. *Claes Oldenburg.* May 10–June 6.

Galerie Ileana Sonnabend, Paris. *Claes Oldenburg.* Oct. 21–Nov. 30. Catalogue.
—F[rança], J[osé]-A[ugusto]. "Les Expositions à Paris: Claes Oldenburg." *Aujourd'hui* (Paris) 8, no. 48 (Jan. 1965), p. 86.
—Gassiot-Talabot, Gérald. "Lettre de Paris." *Art International* (Lugano) 8, no. 10 (Dec. 1964), pp. 55–56.
—L., M. C. "Le Sujet d'Oldenburg." *Le Monde* (Paris), Nov. 13, 1964, p. 13.
—Mégret, Frédéric. "Claes Oldenburg: Le Pop'Art au cours des Halles ou la sculpture au kilo." *Figaro littéraire* (Paris), Oct. 29, 1964.
—Ragon, Michel. "Oldenburg: Un Art alimentaire." *Arts* (Paris), Oct. 28, 1964.

Exhibition of Recent Work by Claes Oldenburg, *Sidney Janis Gallery, New York, April 7–May 2, 1964. Two views.*

Pop Tart, *1967, wall painting outside the Museum of Contemporary Art, Chicago.*

Claes Oldenburg, *The Museum of Modern Art, New York, September 25–November 23, 1969.*

1966

Sidney Janis Gallery, New York. *New Work by Oldenburg.* March 9–April 2. Catalogue.
—Adrian, Dennis. "New York." *Artforum* (Los Angeles) 4, no. 9 (May 1966), pp. 47–53.
—Ashton, Dore. "Conditioned Historic Reactions." *Studio International* (London) 171, no. 877 (May 1966), pp. 204–05.
—B[erkson], W[illiam]. "In the Galleries." *Arts Magazine* (New York) 40, no. 7 (May 1966), pp. 57–58.
—"Big City Boy." *Newsweek* (New York), March 21, 1966, p. 100.
—Canaday, John. "Gag Man Returns with a Few Bathroom Jokes: Oldenburg's 'Soft' Ware at the Janis Gallery." *The New York Times*, March 12, 1966, p. 23.
—Genauer, Emily. "Art Tour: Critical Guide to the Galleries." *New York Herald Tribune*, March 12, 1966, p. 6.
—Lippard, Lucy R. "New York and Philadelphia Letter: An Impure Situation." *Art International* (Lugano) 10, no. 5 (May 20, 1966), pp. 60–65.

Moderna Museet, Stockholm. *Claes Oldenburg: Skulpturer och teckningar, 1963–66.* Sept. 17–Oct. 30. Catalogue.
—Feuk, Douglas. "Tord Baeckströms antipatier." *Göteborgs-Tidningen* (Gothenburg), Oct. 2, 1966.
—Fridemar, Gösta. "Popkonstnären Oldenburg återskapar verkligheten." *Norrbottens-Kuriren* (Stockholm), Sept. 28, 1966. (Reprinted in *Nordstjernan-Svea* [New York], April 13, 1967, p. 4.)
—Judd, Donald. "Claes Oldenburg." In *Donald Judd: Complete Writings 1959–1975.* Halifax: The Press of the Nova Scotia College of Art and Design; New York: New York University Press, 1975, pp. 191–93.
—Malice. "Herr Oldenburg i Knäckebröholm." *Dagens Nyheter* (Stockholm), Aug. 26, 1966.

Robert Fraser Gallery, London. *Claes Oldenburg.* Nov. 22–Dec. 31. Brochure, with texts by Gene Baro and Öyvind Fahlström with Ulf Linde.
—"Claes Oldenburg's First London Exhibition." *The Times* (London), Dec. 12, 1966, p. 14.
—Gosling, Nigel. "Claes Oldenburg at Robert Fraser Gallery." *London Observer*, Nov. 12, 1966.
—Grinke, Paul. "London Fantasies." *The Financial Times* (London), Dec. 10, 1966.
—"London: Male City" (interview). *International Times* (London), Dec. 12, 1966.
—Lynton, Norbert. "London Letter." *Art International* (Lugano) 11, no. 1 (Jan. 20, 1967), pp. 50–51.
—Melville, Robert. "Common Objects." *New Statesman* (London), Nov. 25, 1966, p. 804.
—Melville, Robert. "Gallery: The Human Element." *The Architectural Review* (London) 141, no. 840 (Feb. 1967), pp. 139–42.
—Overy, Paul. "Sticklike and Drooping." *The Listener* (London), Dec. 22, 1966.
—Reichardt, Jasia. "Gigantic Oldenburgs." *Architectural Design* (London) 36, no. 11 (Nov. 1966), p. 534.
—Robertson, Bryan. "Very Lovely Home." *Spectator* (London), Dec. 2, 1966, p. 723.
—Russell, John. "London." *Art News* (New York) 65, no. 10 (Feb. 1967), p. 58.

—Spencer, Charles S. "An Artist Who Paints Objects with Souls." *The New York Times* (International edition), Dec. 12, 1966.

1967

Sidney Janis Gallery, New York. *An Exhibition of New Work by Claes Oldenburg.* April 26–May 27. Catalogue; and supplement, with text by Oldenburg, "Some Program Notes About Monuments, Mainly" (reprinted in *Chelsea* [New York], nos. 22–23 [June 1968], pp. 87–92).
—Broadwater, Bowden. "On Art: He Raises Monuments to the Commonplace." *Newsday* (New York), May 8, 1967, p. 2A.
—B[rown], G[ordon]. "In the Galleries." *Arts Magazine* (New York) 41, no. 7 (May 1967), pp. 56–57.
—Canaday, John. "Art: Some Recent History of Sculpture." *The New York Times*, April 29, 1967, p. 31.
—Mellow, James R. "New York." *Art International* (Lugano) 11, no. 6 (summer 1967), p. 49.
—Perreault, John. "Touch of the Scary." *The Village Voice* (New York), May 11, 1967, pp. 17–18.
—Rosenberg, Harold. "Artworld." *The New Yorker*, June 3, 1967, pp. 117–18.
—R[osenstein], H[arris]. "Reviews and Previews." *Art News* (New York) 66, no. 4 (summer 1967), p. 64.
—Willard, Charlotte. "In the Art Galleries: Metamorphosis." *New York Post*, May 6, 1967, p. 48.

Museum of Contemporary Art, Chicago. *Claes Oldenburg, Drawings: Projects for Monuments.* Oct. 24–Nov. 26. Traveled to Krannert Art Museum, University of Illinois, Champaign. Dec. 1–31.

1968

Irving Blum Gallery, Los Angeles. *Claes Oldenburg.* Opened June 2.
—T[erbell], M[elinda]. "Month in Review." *Arts Magazine* (New York) 42, no. 8 (summer 1968), p. 66.

1969

Richard Feigen Gallery, Chicago. *Claes Oldenburg: Constructions, Models, and Drawings.* April 30–May 31. Catalogue.
—Halstead, Whitney. "Chicago." *Artforum* (New York) 8, no. 1 (Sept. 1969), pp. 67–68.

The Museum of Modern Art, New York. *Claes Oldenburg.* Sept. 25–Nov. 23. Catalogue; and checklist, with text by Alicia Legg. Traveled to Stedelijk Museum, Amsterdam, Jan. 16–March 15, 1970 (catalogue); Städtische Kunsthalle Düsseldorf, April 15–May 24, 1970 (catalogue); and Tate Gallery, London, June 24–Aug. 16, 1970 (catalogue).
—Bourgeois, Jean-Louis. "New York: Claes Oldenburg, Museum of Modern Art." *Artforum* (New York) 8, no. 3 (Nov. 1969), pp. 74–78.
—Brett, Guy. "Nature in a Supermarket." *The Times* (London), June 25, 1970, p. 7.
—Burr, James. "London Galleries: Carnival Cakes." *Apollo* (London) 92, no. 101 (July 1970), p. 77.
—Canaday, John. "Oldenburg as the Picasso of Pop." *The New York Times*, Sept. 28, 1969, p. 33.
—Causey, Andrew. "A Man with a Primitive Urge." *The Illustrated London News*, July 11, 1970, p. 27.

—Delus, Dieter. "Bananen und Hamburger: Claes-Oldenburg-Retrospektive in der Düsseldorfer Kunsthalle." *Manheimer Morgen*, April 22, 1970, p. 36.
—Engelhard, Ernst Günter. "Claes, Hofnarr bei König Konsum: Amerikas originellster Pop-Plastiker in Deutschland." *Christ und Welt* (Bonn), April 17, 1970, p. 11.
—Finch, Christopher. "Notes for a Monument to Claes Oldenburg." *Art News* (New York) 68, no. 6 (Oct. 1969), pp. 52–56.
—Friedrichs, Yvonne. "Vermenschlichte Objekte: Claes Oldenburg's 'weiche' und 'harte' Gegenstände/Ausstellung in Düsseldorf." *Rheinische Post* (Düsseldorf), April 16, 1970, p. 8.
—Genauer, Emily. "Art and the Artist." *New York Post*, Sept. 27, 1969, p. 14.
—Glozer, Laszlo. "Blue Toilet oder: Das Ding ist Verwandlung: Große Oldenburg—Retrospektive im Stedelijk-Museum Amsterdam." *Süddeutsche Zeitung Munchen* (Munich), Feb. 18, 1970.
—Glueck, Grace. "Soft Sculpture or Hard—They're Oldenburgers." *The New York Times Magazine*, Sept. 21, 1969, pp. 28–29, 100–15.
—Gosling, Nigel. "Pop Goes Pecan Pie." *Sunday Observer* (London), July 5, 1970, p. 27.
—Gruen, John. "Art in New York: Things that Go Limp." *New York Magazine*, Sept. 1, 1969, p. 57.
—Honnef, Klaus. "Aus hart mach weich!: Zu einer Oldenburg-Retrospektive in der Düsseldorfer Kunsthalle." *Aachener Nachrichten*, April 16, 1970, p. 4.
—Kaltwasser, Gerda. "Die Mausbanner locken: Mit Bier zur Kunst in der Kunsthalle." *Rheinische Post* (Düsseldorf), April 16, 1970, p. 18.
—Kipphoff, Petra. "Der große Weichmacher: Zur Claes-Oldenburg-Retrospektive in der Kunsthalle Düsseldorf." *Die Zeit* (Hamburg), April 24, 1970, p. 16.
—Kornilov, Iu. "Sausages and van Gogh." *Izvestia* (Moscow), Jan. 24, 1970, p. 5.
—"Kultur: Oldenburg, Weicher Golem." *Der Spiegel* (Berlin), April 20, 1970, pp. 212, 215, 217.
—"The Master of the Soft Touch." *Life* (New York) 67, no. 21 (Nov. 21, 1969), pp. 58–64A.
—Mellow, James R. "On Art: Oldenburg's Scatological 'Soft Touch.'" *The New Leader* (New York), Nov. 10, 1969, pp. 26–27.
—Melville, Robert. "Softened-Up." *The New Statesman* (London), July 10, 1970.
—Mullaly, Terence. "Exhibition by Oldenburg Exalts Trivial." *Daily Telegraph* (London), July 7, 1970, p. 12.
—Rainer, Wolfgang. "Unbekanntes von Claes Oldenburg: Der Weichmacher: Ausstellung in Düsseldorf." *Stuttgarter Zeitung*, April 16, 1970, p. 34.
—Roberts, Keith. "Current and Forthcoming Exhibitions: London." *The Burlington Magazine* (London) 112, no. 809 (Aug. 1970), pp. 550, 553.
—Rosenberg, Harold. "The Art World: Marilyn Mondrian." *The New Yorker* 45 (Nov. 8, 1969), pp. 167–70, 173–76.
—Russell, David. "London." *Arts Magazine* (New York) 45, no. 1 (Sept.–Oct. 1970), p. 56.
—Schjeldahl, Peter. "New York." *Art International* (Lugano) 13, no. 9 (Nov. 1969), pp. 68–70.
—Schwartz, Fred R. "Exhibition at Museum of Modern Art." *Craft Horizons* (New York) 29 (Nov.–Dec. 1969), p. 57.
—Smith, Miles A. "'Colossal Monuments' Latest in Pop Art." *Baltimore Morning Sun*, Nov. 13, 1969, section B, p. 4.

—Sylvester, David. "Furry Lollies and Soft Machines." *The Sunday Times Magazine* (London), July 7, 1970, pp. 14–20.
—Taylor, W. S. "Art: Pomposity in Plastic from Oldenburg." *Morning Telegraph* (Sheffield), July 20, 1970, p. 4.
—Tisdall, Caroline. "Softly, Softly." *The Guardian* (London), June 25, 1970.
—Vaizey, Marina. "'Claes Oldenburg.'" *The Financial Times* (London), July 21, 1970, p. 3.
—"The Venerability of Pop." *Time* (New York) 94, no. 15 (Oct. 10, 1969), pp. 68–69.

1970
Dickson Art Center, University of California, Los Angeles. *Claes Oldenburg at Gemini.* Sept. 28–Nov. 8.
—Plagens, Peter. "Los Angeles." *Artforum* (New York) 9, no. 4 (Dec. 1970), pp. 86–88.
—Young, Joseph E. "Los Angeles." *Art International* (Lugano) 15, no. 5 (May 20, 1971), pp. 77–79.

Sidney Janis Gallery, New York. *New Work by Claes Oldenburg.* Nov. 4–28. Catalogue.
—Domingo, Willis. "Galleries." *Arts Magazine* (New York) 45, no. 3 (Dec. 1970–Jan. 1971), pp. 56–57.
—Henry, Gerrit. "New York Letter." *Art International* (Lugano) 15, no. 1 (Jan. 20, 1971), pp. 37–42.
—Marandel, J. Patrice. "Lettre de New York." *Art International* (Lugano) 15, no. 1 (Jan. 20, 1971), p. 43.
—R[osenstein], H[arris]. "Reviews and Previews." *Art News* (New York) 69, no. 8 (Dec. 1970), pp. 59–60.

1971
Pasadena Art Museum, Calif. *Claes Oldenburg: Object into Monument.* Dec. 7, 1971–Feb. 6, 1972. Catalogue. Traveled to University Art Museum, University of California, Berkeley, March 1–April 9, 1972; William Rockhill Nelson Gallery of Art and Mary Atkins Museum of Fine Arts, Kansas City, Mo., May 12–June 18, 1972; Fort Worth Art Center Museum, Tex., July 13–Aug. 20, 1972; Des Moines Art Center, Iowa, Sept. 18–Oct. 29, 1972; Philadelphia Museum of Art, Nov. 16–Dec. 27, 1972; and the Art Institute of Chicago, Jan. 17–Feb. 25, 1973.
—Adrian, Dennis. "Claes Oldenburg: No Mere Prankster." *Panorama* (magazine of *Chicago Daily News*), Jan. 20–21, 1973, p. 9.
—Albright, Thomas. "Art Based on Contradiction." *San Francisco Chronicle*, March 1, 1972, p. 46.
—Auer, James. "The World of Art: Of Saws and Scissors: Oldenburg's 'Proposals.'" *The Milwaukee Journal*, Jan. 28, 1973, section 5, p. 6.
—Baldwin, Nick. "Des Moines Exhibit Displays Oldenburg's Place in Art." *Des Moines Register*, Sept. 20, 1972, p. 9.
—Baldwin, Nick. "He Blends Realism, Fantasy." *Des Moines Register*, Sept. 22, 1972, p. 24.
—Begley, Kathy. "Oldenburg Exhibit Opens: Did You Ever See a Ten-Foot High Fan?" *The Philadelphia Inquirer*, Nov. 17, 1972, p. 35.
—Butterfield, Jan. "Oldenburg Exhibition Reveals Approach of Artist to Career" (interview). *Fort Worth Star-Telegram*, July 23, 1972, section G, p. 5.

—Carr, Jack. "New Show at the Pasadena Art Museum: Claes Oldenburg Makes Art Jumbo Sized but He Also Makes It Delightfully Humorous." *Pasadena Star-News*, Dec. 12, 1971, p. A1.
—De Shazo, Edith. "The Sensitive Eye: For Oldenburg, Art Is Bigger than Life." *Courier-Post* (Camden, N.J.), Nov. 11, 1972, p. 12.
—Donohoe, Victoria. "Art and Science: Claes Oldenburg: Monuments to the Consumer Society." *The Philadelphia Inquirer*, Nov. 19, 1972, section H, p. 8.
—Frankenstein, Alfred. "The Giant Visual Puns of a Master." *San Francisco Chronicle*, March 5, 1972, "This World," pp. 29–30.
—Fried, Alexander. "The Lively Arts: Odd Art From a Free-Wheeling Mind." *San Francisco Examiner*, March 1, 1972, p. 30.
—Forman, Nessa. "Art: Secret Language Carries Mountain of Meaning." *The Sunday Bulletin* (Philadelphia), Nov. 26, 1972.
—Genauer, Emily. "Art and the Artist." *New York Post*, Nov. 25, 1972, "Magazine," p. 14.
—Gold, Barbara. "Art Notes: A Requiem for a Noble Notion." *The Sun* (Philadelphia), Nov. 26, 1972, section D, p. 8.
—Harris, Peggy. "Claes Oldenburg's Show Is One for the Boys." *Philadelphia Daily News*, Nov. 17, 1972, p. 41.
—Hayden, Harold. "Galleries: How One Thing Led to Another for Claes Oldenburg and Grew and Grew." *Chicago Sun-Times*, Jan. 19, 1973, p. 1.
—H[ope], H[enry] R. "Public Art Museum Notes." *Art Journal* (New York) 32, no. 3 (spring 1973), pp. 328–38.
—Hughes, Robert. "Magician, Clown, Child." *Time*, Feb. 21, 1972, pp. 60–63.
—Ives, Dorothy. "Artist Gets Message Across through Humor." *The Post-Tribune* (Gary, Ind.), Jan. 28, 1973, section C, p. 3.
—Kutner, Janet. "Scene in Art: Oldenburg Dreams Colossal Visions." *The Dallas Morning News*, July 14, 1972, p. 19A.
—Levisetti, Katharine. "Heads Will Roll if Claes Has His Way." *Chicago Today*, Jan. 26, 1973, p. 26.
—M., C. N. "Claes Oldenburg Monuments." *Art Week* (Hayward, Calif.), Jan. 15, 1972, p. 1.
—Mone, Sheila. "Soft Fantasy in Pasadena." *The Highlander* (Highland Park, Calif.), Jan. 27, 1972, p. 10.
—Polley, E. M. "Art and Artists: 'Object into Monument' Opens at UAM, Berkeley." *Sunday Times Herald* (San Francisco), March 5, 1972.
—Seldis, Henry J. "Art: 'Objects' a Kaleidoscope of Fact and Fantasy." *Los Angeles Times*, Jan. 16, 1972, pp. 46, 48.
—Smith, Jack. "Claes Is Funny That Way." *Los Angeles Times*, Dec. 30, 1971, "View," p. 1.

Margo Leavin Gallery, Los Angeles. *Claes Oldenburg: Works in Edition.* Dec. 10, 1971–Jan. 25, 1972. Catalogue.

1973
M. Knoedler and Co., New York. *Claes Oldenburg: Recent Prints and Preparatory Drawings.* March 17–April 21. Catalogue.
—Masheck, Joseph. "Reviews." *Artforum* (New York) 11, no. 10 (June 1973), p. 76.

Minami Gallery, Tokyo. *Claes Oldenburg.* June 18–July 14. Catalogue.
—Nickel, Phyllis F. "Claes Oldenburg Exhibition." *The Japan Times* (Tokyo), June 27, 1973, p. 6.

Anna Leonowens Gallery, Nova Scotia College of Art and Design, Halifax. *Claes Oldenburg: Posters, 1961–1972.* Sept. 1–15.

The New Gallery, Cleveland, Ohio. *Claes Oldenburg: Standing Mitt with Ball, 1973.* Dec. 5, 1973–Jan. 4, 1974. Catalogue. Traveled to the Dayton Art Institute, Ohio, Jan. 18–Feb. 10, 1974.

1974
Hammarskjold Plaza Sculpture Garden, New York. *Claes Oldenburg: Geometric Mouse Scale X.* April–June.
—Rose, Barbara. "New York Is an Oldenburg Festival" (interview). *New York Magazine,* May 6, 1974, pp. 91–95.

Leo Castelli Gallery, New York. *Claes Oldenburg.* April 27–May 18.
—Dreiss, Joseph. "Arts Reviews." *Arts Magazine* (New York) 49, no. 1 (Sept. 1974), p. 58.
—Reese, Joanna. "Oldenburg: Man of Steel." *The SoHo Weekly News* (New York) 1, no. 30 (May 2, 1974), pp. 20–21.
—Rose, Barbara. "New York Is an Oldenburg Festival" (interview). *New York Magazine,* May 6, 1974, pp. 91–95.
—Russell, John. "Oldenburg Sees Nothing Insignificant." *The New York Times,* May 11, 1974, p. 27.
—Thomsen, Barbara. "Review of Exhibitions: New York: Claes Oldenburg at Castelli." *Art in America* (New York) 62, no. 5 (Sept.–Oct. 1974), pp. 113–14.

Yale University Art Gallery, New Haven, Conn. *The Lipstick Comes Back.* Oct. 17–Nov. 30. Catalogue.

1975
Margo Leavin Gallery, Los Angeles. *Claes Oldenburg: The Alphabet in L.A.* Feb. 5–March 29. Catalogue.
—Wortz, Melinda. "The Nation: Watching Letters Go By." *Art News* (New York) 74, no. 4 (April 1975), pp. 73–74.

Kunsthalle Tübingen. *Claes Oldenburg: Zeichnungen – Aquarelle–Collagen, 1954–1974.* March 1–April 20. Catalogue, *Zeichnungen von Claes Oldenburg.* Traveled to Kunstmuseum Basel, as *Claes Oldenburg, Zeichnungen,* May 10–July 6; Städtische Galerie im Lenbachhaus, Munich, July 17–Aug. 31; Nationalgalerie Berlin, Sept. 17–Oct. 26; Museum Haus Lange Krefeld, as *Claes Oldenburg: Unbekannte Aquarelle, Zeichnungen, Gouachen 1954–1974,* Nov. 16, 1975–Jan. 4, 1976; Museum des 20. Jahrhunderts, Vienna, Jan. 14–Feb. 29, 1976; Kunstverein im Hamburg, April 3–May 16, 1976; Städelsches Kunstinstitut und Städtische Galerie, Frankfurt, as *Claes Oldenburg: Zeichnungen, Objekte, Filme,* May 27–Aug. 22, 1976; Kestner-Gesellschaft, Hanover, Aug. 27–Sept. 26, 1976; and Louisiana Museum, Humlebaek, as *Claes Oldenburg: Tegninger fra 1954 til 1974,* Jan. 15–Feb. 13, 1977.
—Geelhaar, Christian. "Des ewigen Sinnes ewige Unterhaltung." *Neue Zürcher Zeitung* (Basel), June 6, 1975, p. 41.
—Koepplin, Dieter. "Oldenburg probt di Langeweile." *National-Zeitung Basel,* May 28, 1975, p. 27.
—Kunz, Martin. "Claes Oldenburg." *Kunst Nachrichten* (Lausanne) 11, no. 6 (Sept. 1975), pp. 152–60, 168.
—Lange, Rudolf. "Mit Claes im Wunderland: Die Oldenburg-Ausstellung in der Kestner-Gesellschaft Hannover." *Hannoversche Allgemeine Zeitung,* Sept. 2, 1976, p. 7.
—Sterk, Harald. "Mythologisches Denken der Konsumwelt im Bild." *Neue Zeit* (Vienna), Feb. 12, 1976.

Giant Ice Bag. *1969–70, installed at the Seattle Art Museum, 1971.*

Oldenburg: Six Themes, *Walker Art Center, Minneapolis, April 6–May 25, 1975. Two views.*

—Stutzer, Bee. "Zeichnungen begleiten Oldenburgs Entwicklung." *Basler Volksblatt*, May 21, 1975.
—Winter, Peter. "Claes Oldenburg." *Das Kunstwerk* (Baden-Baden) 28, no. 3 (May 1975), pp. 75–77.

Walker Art Center, Minneapolis. *Oldenburg: Six Themes.* April 6–May 25. Catalogue. Traveled to the Denver Art Museum, June 28–Aug. 24; Seattle Art Museum, Sept. 29–Nov. 9; Institute of Contemporary Art, Boston, and Hayden Gallery, Massachusetts Institute of Technology, Cambridge, Jan. 16–Feb. 25, 1976; and Art Gallery of Ontario, Toronto, April 3–May 9, 1976.
—Close, Roy M. "Six Oldenburg Themes Convert Trivial to Art." *The Minneapolis Star*, April 9, 1975, "Variety," p. 3.
—Garrett, Bob. "The Contradiction of Claes Oldenburg: What's So Unfunny about Art, Anyway?" *Boston Herald*, Jan. 25, 1976.
—Kowalenko, Al. "Six Themes Show Oldenburg's Best Sculptures." *Revue* (Toronto), April 9, 1976.
—Mills, James. "Oldenburg Transcends Pop Art in 'Six Themes' Work." *Denver Post*, July 6, 1975, p. 20.
—"Oldenburg Show Now in Toronto." *The Sault Star* (Sault Ste. Marie), April 28, 1976, section A, p. 1.
—Pollock, Duncan. "He of the Geometric Mouse." *Rocky Mountain News* (Denver), July 6, 1975, "Now," p. 10.
—Steele, Mike. "Oldenburg: Monuments from Trivia." *Picture Magazine* (Minneapolis), April 6, 1975, pp. 18–27.
—Taylor, Robert. "Oldenburg's Many Masks." *Boston Globe*, Jan. 18, 1976, section B, p. 1.

The Sable-Castelli Gallery, Toronto. *Claes Oldenburg.* May 1–22.

The Mayor Gallery, London. *Claes Oldenburg: Recent Erotic Fantasy Drawings.* Nov. 4–Dec. 6. Catalogue.
—McCorquodale, Charles. "London." *Art International* (Lugano) 19, no. 10 (Dec. 20, 1975), pp. 20–28.
—Tisdall, Caroline. "Claes Oldenburg." *The Guardian* (London), Nov. 6, 1975, p. 8.

1976
Margo Leavin Gallery, Los Angeles (in collaboration with Gemini G.E.L., Los Angeles). *The Soft Screw: Eight Lithographs and a Multiple Sculpture by Claes Oldenburg.* April 10–30. Book, *Claes Oldenburg: The Soft Screw*, with texts by Oldenburg and Melinda Wortz, published on the occasion of the exhibition by Gemini G.E.L.

Multiples, New York. *Claes Oldenburg, New Works on Paper: Etchings, Aquatints, Lithographs.* April 24–May 15.

Leo Castelli Gallery, New York. *Claes Oldenburg.* Nov. 6–27. Book by Oldenburg, *Claes Oldenburg: Log, May 1974–August 1976* (2 vols.), published on the occasion of the exhibition by Hansjörg Mayer, Stuttgart, and Store Days, New York.
—French-Frazier, Nina. "New York Reviews: Claes Oldenburg." *Art News* (New York) 76, no. 1 (Jan. 1977), p. 116.
—Hess, Thomas B. "Art: The Story of O." *New York Magazine* 9, no. 48 (Nov. 29, 1976), pp. 78, 80, 83.
—Kramer, Hilton. "More than Just a Touch of Claes at SoHo Gallery." *The New York Times*, Nov. 12, 1976, section C, pp. 1, 18.
—Zimmer, William. "Claes Oldenburg." *Arts Magazine* (New York) 51, no. 5 (Jan. 1977), pp. 29–30.

1977

Stedelijk Museum, Amsterdam. *Claes Oldenburg: Tekeningen, aquarellen en grafiek.* April 30–June 12. Catalogue. Traveled to Musée National d'Art Moderne, Centre Georges Pompidou, Paris, as *Claes Oldenburg: Dessins, aquarelles et estampes*, Aug. 24–Oct. 16 (catalogue); and Moderna Museet, Stockholm, as *Claes Oldenburg: Teckningar, akvareller och grafik*, Oct. 29–Dec. 4 (catalogue).
—Ahlström, Crispin. "Clown och Forskningsresande." *Göteborgsposten* (Gothenburg), Nov. 22, 1977.
—Beeke, Anna. "Het Formaat Van Claes Oldenburg." *Hollands Diep* (Amsterdam), May 7, 1977, pp. 44–47.
—Berthold, Christina. "Underbarnet som skapar köer till muséerna." *Damenrnas Värld* (Stockholm), Nov. 30, 1977.
—Olander, William R. "Claes Oldenburg." *Arts Magazine* (New York) 52, no. 2 (Oct. 1977), p. 2.
—Stengard, Elisabeth. "Claes Oldenburg—konstruktör i kolossalformat." *Dagen* (Stockholm), Nov. 14, 1977.
—Sydhoff, Beate. "Överväldigad av tingen." *Svenska Dagbladet* (Stockholm), Nov. 6, 1977, p. 8.
—Van Ginneken, Lily. "Tentoonstelling in Stedelijk: Vooral monumenten Oldenburg boeiend." *de Volkskrant* (Amsterdam), May 3, 1977, p. 6.

Galerie Jurka, Amsterdam. *Claes Oldenburg.* May 21–June 16.

Richard Gray Gallery, Chicago. *Claes Oldenburg: An Exhibition of Recent Small Scale Fabricated Works and Drawings.* Sept. 30–Nov. 15.
—Schulze, Franz. "Our Kind of Burg, Oldenburg Is." *Panorama* (magazine of *Chicago Daily News*), Nov. 5–6, 1977, p. 14.

Akron Art Institute, Ohio. *Claes Oldenburg: The Inverted Q.* Oct. 9–Dec. 4. Catalogue.

De volle maan, Delft, The Netherlands. *Claes Oldenburg.* Nov. 5–Dec. 11. Catalogue.

Museum of Contemporary Art, Chicago. *The Mouse Museum/The Ray Gun Wing: Two Collections/Two Buildings by Claes Oldenburg.* Nov. 18, 1977–Jan. 8, 1978. Catalogue. Traveled to Phoenix Art Museum, Ariz., Jan. 27–March 12, 1978; St. Louis Art Museum, Mo., April 20–June 11, 1978; Dallas Museum of Fine Arts, June 28–Aug. 6, 1978; Whitney Museum of American Art, New York, Sept. 28–Nov. 26, 1978; Rijksmuseum Kröller-Müller, Otterlo, June 16–July 29, 1979 (catalogue); Museum Ludwig, Cologne, Sept. 4, 1979–May 20, 1980 (catalogue).
—Artner, Alan G. "Oldenburg's New Mouse Is on the Loose at the MCA." *Chicago Tribune*, Nov. 27, 1977, section 6, p. 2.
—Auer, James. "Oldenburg Chicago Exhibit: Kitsch and Tell." *The Milwaukee Journal*, Dec. 11, 1977, part 5, p. 4.
—Haase, Amine. "Eis am Stiel im Mausekopf." *Kölner Stadt-Anzeiger*, Sept. 5, 1979, p. 7.
—Hanson, Henry. "Zap, Squeak, Pow! It's Ray the Mouse." *Panorama* (magazine of *Chicago Daily News*), Nov. 19–20, 1977, p. 4.
—Haydon, Harold. "Oldenburg's Inspirations." *Chicago Sun-Times*, Nov. 27, 1977, p. 7.
—Kutner, Janet. "Objects Become Pop Art." *The Dallas Morning News*, June 29, 1978, section A, p. 40.

Oldenburg: Six Themes, *Walker Art Center, Minneapolis, April 6–May 25, 1975.*

Oldenburg: Six Themes, *Art Gallery of Ontario, Toronto, April 3–May 9, 1976.*

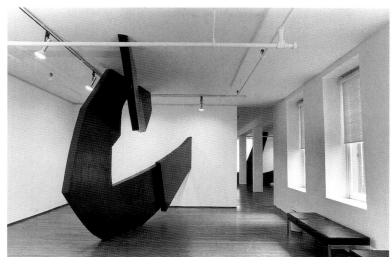

Claes Oldenburg: Large-Scale
Projects, 1977–1980, *Leo Castelli
Gallery, New York, May 24–June 14,
1980. Two views.*

—Kutner, Janet. "A Mask Here, a String There: Oldenburg's Commonplace Fills Museum." *The Dallas Morning News*, July 2, 1978, section C, p. 9.
—Marvel, Bill. "'Mouse Museum'—Sinister but Comic." *Dallas Times Herald*, June 28, 1978, section E, pp. 1, 7.
—Wallach, Amei. "Of Mice and Museums." *Newsday* (New York), Oct. 1, 1978, section 2, pp. 1, 3, 17.

1978
Margo Leavin Gallery, Los Angeles. *Claes Oldenburg: Sculptures, 1971–1977.* July 8–Aug. 19.

1980
Leo Castelli Gallery, New York. *Claes Oldenburg: Large-Scale Projects, 1977–1980.* May 24–June 14. Book, with texts by Rudi Fuchs and Oldenburg with Coosje van Bruggen, published on the occasion of the exhibition by Rizzoli, New York.
—Frank, Elizabeth. "Claes Oldenburg at Castelli." *Art in America* (New York) 68, no. 9 (Nov. 1980), pp. 138–39.
—Kramer, Hilton. "Art: Progress Report on Oldenburg Pieces." *The New York Times*, June 13, 1980, section C, p. 21.

1981
Fine Arts Gallery, University of Nevada, Las Vegas. *Models, Studies, and Plans for the Flashlight: A Large-Scale Sculpture by Claes Oldenburg for the University of Nevada, Las Vegas.* Feb. 2–20.

1982
The Bruce Museum, Greenwich, Conn. *Claes Oldenburg: Selected Prints.* Jan. 17–March 14.

Galerie Schmela, Düsseldorf. *Claes Oldenburg.* Dec. 16, 1982– Jan. 31, 1983. Brochure.

1983
Museum Boymans-van Beuningen, Rotterdam. *The Screwarch Project.* June 19–Sept. 19. Catalogue.
—Simons, Riki. "Claes Oldenburgs schroefboogproject in museum Boymans-van Beuningen: Rotterdam koopt een onuitvoerbare brug." *NRC Handelsblad* (Rotterdam), June 24, 1983.
—Tilroe, Anna. "Amuseren en presenteren." *Haagse Post* (The Hague), Aug. 13, 1983, pp. 42–43.

1984
Wave Hill, New York. *Standing Mitt with Ball: From Concept to Monument.* Sept. 16–Nov. 4. Catalogue.

1985
The Art Center, Waco, Tex. *Claes Oldenburg: Selected Posters and Announcements, 1959–1985.* Oct. 26–Dec. 1.

1986
Palacio de Cristal, Madrid. *El Cuchillo Barco de "Il Corso del Coltello": Claes Oldenburg, Coosje van Bruggen, Frank O. Gehry.* June 18–Sept. 9. Catalogue.
—"Claes Oldenburg coloca en el Retiro una navaja de 12 metros que es también un barco." *El País* (Madrid), June 19, 1986, p. 40.

Castelli Gallery, New York. *The Course of the Knife.* Dec. 13, 1986–Jan. 24, 1987. Catalogue; and book, *The Course of the Knife,* with texts by Germano Celant, Frank O. Gehry, Oldenburg, and Coosje van Bruggen, published by Electa, Milan on the occasion of the exhibition.
—Smith, Roberta. "Art: Oldenburg's Works as Props for 'Il Corso.'" *The New York Times,* Jan. 9, 1987, section C, p. 26.

Solomon R. Guggenheim Museum, New York. *The Knife Ship from "Il Corso del Coltello."* Dec. 16, 1986–Feb. 16, 1987. Catalogue; and book, *The Course of the Knife,* with texts by Germano Celant, Frank O. Gehry, Oldenburg, and Coosje van Bruggen, published by Electa, Milan on the occasion of the exhibition.
—"An Outsize Oldenburg Cuts a Wide Swath at the Guggenheim." *People Weekly* (New York), Jan. 26, 1987, pp. 102–03.
—Venant, Elizabeth. "A Ship Out of Water." *L.A. Times Magazine,* March 15, 1987, pp. 18–19.
—Wallach, Amei. "Sharp Points in Famous Curves." *Newsday* (New York), Jan. 11, 1987, part 2, p. 3.

A Bottle of Notes and Some Voyages.
Glynn Vivian Art Gallery, Swansea,
September 17–November 12, 1988.

1987

Museum Haus Esters Krefeld, Germany. *Claes Oldenburg: The Haunted House.* May 31–June 26. Catalogue.

Musée National d'Art Moderne, Centre Georges Pompidou, Paris. *Le Couteau navire: Décors, costumes, dessins, "Il Corso del Coltello" de Claes Oldenburg, Coosje van Bruggen et Frank O. Gehry.* July 7–Oct. 5. Catalogue.
—B[oissiere], O[livier]. "'J'en ai fini des partis pris du happening'" (interview). *Le Matin* (Paris), July 16, 1987, p. 13.
—B[oissiere], O[livier]. "Sponsors, mécènes, etc." *Le Matin* (Paris), July 16, 1987, p. 13.
—B[oissiere], O[livier]. "Variations autour d'un bateau-couteau." *Le Matin* (Paris), July 16, 1987, pp. 12–13.

Galerie Konrad Fischer, Düsseldorf. *Piano/Hammock 1987.* Nov. 24–Dec. 18.

1988

Margo Leavin Gallery, Los Angeles. *Claes Oldenburg: Props, Costumes and Designs for the Performance "Il Corso del Coltello" by Claes Oldenburg, Coosje van Bruggen, Frank O. Gehry.* Jan. 9–Feb. 13.
—Knight, Christopher. "Pop Icons Roll Out a Page from the Past." *Los Angeles Herald Examiner,* Jan. 22, 1988, p. 13.
—Muchnic, Suzanne. "Claes Oldenburg on a Comic Roll with 'House Ball,' Sculpture of the Commonplace." *Los Angeles Times,* Jan. 11, 1988, section 6, pp. 1, 4.

Northern Centre for Contemporary Art, Sunderland, England. *A Bottle of Notes and Some Voyages.* Feb. 2–March 26. Catalogue. Traveled to Leeds City Art Gallery, April 27–June 26; Serpentine Gallery, London, July 9–Aug. 29; Glynn Vivian Art Gallery, Swansea, Sept. 17–Nov. 12; Palais des Beaux-Arts, Brussels, Nov. 27–Dec. 30 (catalogue supplement [in French]); Wilhelm-Lehmbruck Museum, Duisburg, Germany, Jan. 22–March 27, 1989 (catalogue supplement, with texts by Christoph Brockhaus, Max Imdahl, Gottlieb Leinz, and Oldenburg [in German]); Malmö Konsthall, Sweden, April 29–Aug. 6, 1989 (catalogue supplement [in Swedish]); IVAM, Centre Julio González, Valencia, Sept. 15–Nov. 15, 1989; and Tampereen taidemuseo, Tampere, Finland, Jan. 12–March 6, 1990.

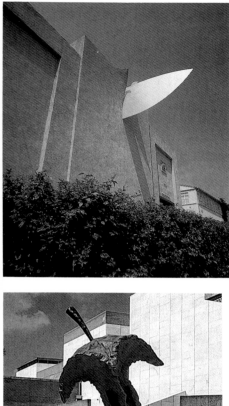

Knife Slicing Through Wall, *permanent installation at Margo Leavin Gallery, Los Angeles, installed August 17, 1989.*

Apple Core, *1993, permanent installation at the Billy Rose Art Garden, Israel Museum, Jerusalem.*

—Brähammer, Gunnar. "Djärva accenter för dagens stad." *Sydvenskan,* May 10, 1989, p. 4.
—Ericsson, Lars O. "Claes Oldenburg i Malmö: Öga mot öga med det Förbisedda." *Dagens Nyheter* (Stockholm), May 24, 1989, p. 4.
—Feaver, William. "Monumental Dummies." *Observer* (London), July 17, 1988, p. 41.
—Graham-Dixon, Andrew. "Man of the Match." *The Independent* (London), May 3, 1988, p. 16.
—Hilton, Tim. "Lost in the Third Dimension." *The Guardian* (Manchester), May 11, 1988, p. 17.
—Homila, Paula. "Claes Oldenburgin jättiläismäiset poliittis-croottis-ironiset . . ." *Uusi Suomi* (Helsinki), Jan. 13, 1990, "Kultuurilehti," pp. 22–23.
—Homila, Paula. "'Harja on Coosje, putki olen minä.'" *Uusi Suomi* (Helsinki), Jan. 13, 1990, "Kultuurilehti," pp. 1, 22–23.
—Lindgren, Bertil. "Än blander Claes Oldenburg politik med erotik och magi." *NST* (Kristianstad), May 5, 1989.
—Paananen, Erkki. "Claes Oldenburgin poptaide valtasi Tampereen Taidemuseon." *Helsingen Sanomat* (Helsinki), Jan. 13, 1990, section B, p. 1.
—Rubin, Birgitta. "Claes Oldenburg i Malmö konsthall: Monumental ironi i vardagsforemal." *Dagens Nyheter* (Stockholm), June 12, 1989, p. 28.
—Sandqvist, Tom. "Det förföriska objektet." *Hufvudstadsbladet* (Helsinki), May 11, 1989, "Kultur," p. 12.
—Söron, Camilla. "Oldenburg ser inte allt som konst." *Malmö,* April 29, 1989.

Palais des Beaux-Arts, Brussels. *Claes Oldenburg: Tekeningen/Dessins.* Nov. 27–Dec. 30. Traveled to Musée d'Art Contemporain, Nîmes, Feb. 14–April 9, 1989; and IVAM, Centre Julio González, Valencia, as *Claes Oldenburg: Dibujos/Drawings 1959–1989,* Sept. 15–Nov. 15, 1989 (catalogue).

1989

Margo Leavin Gallery, Los Angeles. *Knife Slicing Through Wall.* Sited work; installed Aug. 17.
—Garcia-Marques, Francesca. "Oldenburg/Van Bruggen: Il Coltello Affeita-Muro." *Domus* (Milan), no. 716 (May 1990), pp. 14–15.
—Muchnic, Suzanne. "Oldenburg Sculpture Cuts to the Heart of Art as Architecture." *Los Angeles Times,* Aug. 19, 1989, part 5, pp. 1, 9.

1990

Carl Solway Gallery, Cincinnati. *Claes Oldenburg: A Complete Survey of Sculptures in Edition 1963–1990.* April 20–June 9.
—Casadio, Mariuccia. "Claes Oldenburg Multiple Choice." *Interview* (New York), Aug. 1991, p. 44.
—Senaldi, Marco. "Claes Oldenburg." *Flash Art* (Italian edition) (Milan), no. 157 (summer 1990), pp. 138–39.

Galleria Christian Stein, Milan. *Claes Oldenburg: The European Desk Top.* May 3–June 20. Book by Oldenburg, *Claes Oldenburg: Sketches and Blottings toward the European Desktop,* with text by Coosje van Bruggen, published by Hopeful Monster, Florence and Galleria Christian Stein on the occasion of the exhibition.
—Iannacci, Anthony. "Claes Oldenburg." *Artforum* (New York) 19, no. 2 (Oct. 1990), p. 181.

Susan Sheehan Gallery, New York. *Claes Oldenburg: Prints and Multiples*. Sept. 4–29. Brochure.
—De Vuono, Frances. "Claes Oldenburg: Prints and Multiples." *Art News* (New York) 89, no. 9 (Nov. 1990), p. 162.

Brooke Alexander Editions, New York. *Claes Oldenburg: Multiples in Retrospect, 1964–1990*. Sept. 14–Oct. 20. Book published by Rizzoli, New York on the occasion of the exhibition.

The Mayor Gallery, London. *Claes Oldenburg: Eight Sculptures 1961–1987*. Oct. 15–Nov. 23. Catalogue.

Castelli Graphics, New York. *Claes Oldenburg: Lithographs from Gemini G.E.L. 1988–1990*. Nov. 27, 1990–Jan. 12, 1991.

Leo Castelli Gallery, New York. *Claes Oldenburg/Coosje van Bruggen*. Nov. 27, 1990–Jan. 12, 1991.
—Johnson, Ken. "Claes Oldenburg and Coosje van Bruggen at Castelli." *Art in America* (New York) 79, no. 3 (March 1991), pp. 133–34.
—MacAdam, Barbara A. "Claes Oldenburg and Coosje van Bruggen: Castelli, Castelli Graphics." *Art News* (New York) 90, no. 4 (April 1991), pp. 146–49.
—Smith, Roberta. "A Never Land Version of the Palace at Versailles." *The New York Times*, Jan. 4, 1991, section C, p. 27.
—Wallach, Amei. "The Evolution of a Team." *Newsday* (New York), Dec. 2, 1990, part 2, pp. 23–24.

1991
BP Building, Cleveland, Ohio. *Larger than Life*. Nov. 11, 1991–Jan. 31, 1992.
—Litt, Steven. "BP Exhibit Traces Oldenburg's Forty Year Career." *The Plain Dealer* (Cleveland), Nov. 14, 1991, section E, p. 16.

1992
Portikus, Frankfurt. *Claes Oldenburg: Multiples 1964–1990*. Feb. 22–March 31. Catalogue. Traveled to Städtische Galerie im Lenbachhaus, Munich, April 8–May 10; Hochschule für angewandte Kunst, Vienna, as *Claes Oldenburg: Multiples and Notebook Pages*, Nov. 6–Dec. 24; Musée Municipal, La Roche-sur-Yon, France, Jan. 16–March 8, 1993 (catalogue); Musée d'Art Moderne, Saint-Etienne, France, March 17–April 26, 1993; Neues Museum Weserburg Bremen, as *Claes Oldenburg: Geometrische Mäuse und vieles mehr . . . Multiples, Objekte, Zeichnungen*, May 16–Aug. 30, 1993.

Cleveland Center for Contemporary Art, Ohio. *Claes Oldenburg: Recent Sculpture*. March 13–May 24. Brochure, with text by Pamela R. Esch.

Museum für Gegenwartskunst, Basel. *Claes Oldenburg: Die frühen Zeichnungen*. June 5–Sept. 7. Catalogue.
—Giger, Romeo. "Claes Oldenburgs frühe Zeichnungen." *Neue Züricher Zeitung* (Basel), Aug. 7, 1992, p. 23.

Walker Art Center, Minneapolis. *Claes Oldenburg: In the Studio*. Aug. 2, 1992–Feb. 14, 1993. Traveled to Musée Cantini, Marseille, as *Claes Oldenburg: In the Studio/Dans l'atelier*, July 10–Sept. 12, 1993 (catalogue).
—Abbe, Mary. "Show Explores Oldenburg Thinking." *Minneapolis Star Tribune*, Aug. 6, 1992, section E, pp. 1, 8.

The Pace Gallery, New York. *Claes Oldenburg*. Sept. 18–Oct. 17. Catalogue.

—MacAdam, Barbara. "Claes Oldenburg: Pace." *Art News* (New York) 91, no. 10 (Dec. 1992), p. 110.
—Wallach, Amei. "Turkeys, Sinks and Saxophones." *Newsday* (New York), Oct. 16, 1992, part 2, p. 74.

The Richard F. Brush Art Gallery, St. Lawrence University, Canton, N.Y. *Claes Oldenburg, John Baldessari: (Scale/Selection/Narration)*. Oct. 6–Nov. 6.

1993
Gemini G.E.L. at Joni Moisant Weyl, New York. *Claes Oldenburg: Recent Print and Sculpture Editions*. June 2–Aug. 27. Catalogue.

Ernst A. Busche, Berlin. *The Store: Zeichnungen und Skizzen 1960–1963*. Sept. 8–Oct. 27.
—B[lechen], C[amilla]. "Claes Oldenburg: In der Berliner Galerie Busche." *Frankfurter Allgemeine Zeitung*, Oct. 9, 1993, p. 34.

1994
Tel Aviv Museum of Art. *Claes Oldenburg: Multiples and Notebook Pages*. Jan. 13–March 12. Catalogue.

Glenn Horowitz Bookseller, East Hampton, New York. *Claes Oldenburg: Books and Ephemera, 1960–1994*. July 9–Aug. 7. Traveled to Printed Matter, Inc., New York, Sept. 17–Oct. 22.
—Smith, Roberta. "Claes Oldenburg: 'Books and Ephemera, 1960–1994.'" *The New York Times*, Sept. 16, 1994, p. 29.

The Pace Gallery, New York. *Claes Oldenburg Coosje van Bruggen Large-Scale Projects: Drawings and Sculpture*. Dec. 2, 1994–Jan. 7, 1995.

I.C. Editions, New York. *Claes Oldenburg: The Geometric Mouse*. Dec. 8, 1994–Jan. 14, 1995.

Group Exhibitions
1953
Club St. Elmo, Chicago. *Robert E. Clark, C. T. Oldenburg, George Yelich*. March 9–April 11.

1955
The Evanston Art Center, Ill. *Young Artists among Us*. April 24–May 12.

1956
72 East Eleventh Street, Chicago. *Momentum 1956*. May 23–June 20. Catalogue, with artists' statement.

1958
City Gallery, New York. *Drawings*. Dec. 19, 1958–Jan. 6, 1959.

The 5721 Gallery, New York. *Momen-Toes: Selections from the Myrnann Collection*. Opened Dec. 30.

1959
Nonagon Gallery, New York. *Spring Invitational*. May 21–June 11.

Judson Gallery, New York. *Judson Group: Baer, Dine, Oldenburg, Ratliff, Stasik, Tyler, Wesselman*. Oct. 2–23.

Judson Gallery, New York. *Xmas Show: Drawings, Prints*. Dec. 4–31.

Reuben Gallery, New York. *Below Zero*. Dec. 18, 1959–
Jan. 5, 1960.

1960
Reuben Gallery, New York. *Paintings*. Jan. 29–Feb. 18.
—P[etersen], V[alerie]. "Reviews and Previews." *Art News*
(New York) 59, no. 10 (Feb. 1961), p. 16.

Area Gallery, New York. *Invitational Show: Drawings and
Sculpture*. March 11–31.

Martha Jackson Gallery, New York. *New Media — New Forms in
Painting and Sculpture*. Part I, June 6–24; Part II, Sept. 28–
Oct. 22. Catalogue, *New Forms — New Media I*, with texts by
Lawrence Alloway and Allan Kaprow and cover by Oldenburg.
—Sandler, Irving Hershel. "New York Letter: Ash Can
Revisited." *Art International* (Zurich) 4, no. 8 (Oct. 25, 1960),
pp. 28–30.

Washington Square Gallery, New York. *Paintings, Drawings,
Collages*. Oct. 26–Nov. 27.

Green Gallery, New York. *A Group of Paintings, Sculptures and
Drawings*. Dec. 13, 1960–Jan. 7, 1961.

1961
The Museum of Modern Art, New York. *Painting and Sculpture
Acquisitions*. Jan. 1–Dec. 31. Catalogue.

The Alan Gallery, New York. *New Work by New Artists*.
March 6–25.
—H[ayes], R[ichard]. "Reviews and Previews: New Names
This Month: New Work by New Artists." *Art News* (New York)
60, no. 2 (April 1961), p. 20.

The Art Institute of Chicago. *Contemporary Society*.
May 17–June 4.

Martha Jackson Gallery, New York. *Environments, Situations,
Spaces*. May 25–June 23. Catalogue, with artists' statements.
—B[urrows], C[arlyle]. "Art of Environment." *Herald Tribune*
(New York), June 4, 1961, p. 18.
—Johnston, Jill. "'Environments' at Martha Jackson's." *The
Village Voice* (New York), July 6, 1961, p. 13.
—K[roll], J[ack]. "Reviews and Previews." *Art News*
(New York) 60, no. 5 (Sept. 1961), p. 16.

Green Gallery, New York. Sept. 19–Oct. 14.

1962
The Dallas Museum for Contemporary Arts. *1961*. April 3–
May 13. Catalogue.
—Askew, Rual. "Reviews: Dallas." *Artforum* (San Francisco) 1,
no. 1 (June 1962), p. 7.
—Askew, Rual. "Reviews: Dallas." *Artforum* (San Francisco) 1,
no. 2 (July 1962), p. 44.

Wadsworth Atheneum, Hartford, Conn. *Continuity and Change:
Forty-five American Abstract Painters and Sculptors*. April 12–
May 27. Catalogue, with text by Samuel Wagstaff, Jr.

Tanager Gallery, New York. *The Closing Show: 1952–1962*.
May 25–June 14.

Arts Council of the YM/YWHA, Philadelphia. *Art 1963 —
A New Vocabulary*. Oct. 25–Nov. 7. Brochure, with artists'
statements.

Sidney Janis Gallery, New York. *New Realists*. Nov. 1–Dec. 1. Catalogue, with texts by John Ashbery, Pierre Restany, and Sidney Janis.
—Ashton, Dore. "New York Report." *Das Kunstwerk* (Baden-Baden) 16, nos. 5–6 (Nov.–Dec. 1962), pp. 68–70.
—H[ess], T[homas] B. "Reviews and Previews: 'New Realists.'" *Art News* (New York) 61, no. 8 (Dec. 1962), pp. 12–13.
—O'Doherty, Brian. "Avant-Garde Revolt, 'New Realists' Mock U.S. Mass Culture in Exhibition at Sidney Janis Gallery." *The New York Times*, Oct. 31, 1962, p. 41.
—O'Doherty, Brian. "'Pop' Goes the New Art." *The New York Times*, Nov. 4, 1962, section 2, p. 23.
—Restany, Pierre. "The World of Art: Paris Letter: The New Realism." *Art in America* (New York) 51, no. 1 (Feb. 1963), pp. 102–04.
—Restany, Pierre. "Le Nouveau Réalisme à la conquête de New York." *Art International* (Lugano) 7, no. 1 (Jan. 25, 1963), pp. 29–36.
—Rose, Barbara. "Dada Then and Now." *Art International* (Zurich) 7, no. 1 (Sept. 25, 1963), pp. 23–28.
—Rosenberg, Harold. "The Art Galleries: The Game of Illusion." *The New Yorker* 38, no. 40 (Nov. 24, 1962), pp. 161–67.
—Rudikoff, Sonya. "New Realists in New York." *Art International* (Zurich) 7, no. 1 (Jan. 25, 1963), pp. 38–41.
—Saarinen, Aline B. "Explosion of Pop Art: A New Kind of Fine Art Imposing Poetic Order on the Mass-Produced World." *Vogue* (New York), April 15, 1963, pp. 87–88, 134–35.
—Sandler, Irving. "In the Galleries." *New York Post Magazine*, Nov. 18, 1962, p. 12.
—Sandler, Irving. "In the Galleries." *New York Post*, Dec. 2, 1962, p. 12.
—Sottsass, Ettore, Jr. "Dada, New Dada, New Realists." *Domus* (Milan), no. 399 (Feb. 2, 1963), pp. 27–32.

Dwan Gallery, Los Angeles. *My Country 'Tis of Thee*. Nov. 18–Dec. 15. Catalogue, with introduction by Gerald Nordland.
—Langsner, Jules. "Los Angeles Letter." *Art International* (Lugano) 7, no. 1 (Jan. 25, 1963), pp. 81–83.

Museum of Contemporary Crafts, New York. *Cookies and Breads: The Baker's Art*. Nov. 20, 1962–Jan. 9, 1963.

The Museum of Modern Art, New York. *Recent Acquisitions*. Nov. 20, 1962–Jan. 13, 1963.

The Pace Gallery, Boston. *Pop Art: Stock Up for the Holidays*. Dec.

1963
Allen Memorial Art Museum, Oberlin College, Ohio. *Three Young Americans*. Jan. 8–29.
—Johnson, Ellen H. "Is Beauty Dead?" *Allen Memorial Art Museum Bulletin* (Oberlin) 20, no. 2 (winter 1963), pp. 56–65.

Richard Feigen Gallery, Chicago. *Pop Art Show*. Jan. 10–Feb. 23.

The Art Institute of Chicago. *Sixty-sixth Annual American Exhibition: Directions in Contemporary Painting and Sculpture*. Jan. 11–Feb. 10. Catalogue.
—Schulze, Franz. "Art News from Chicago: Electrified Annual." *Art News* (New York) 62, no. 1 (March 1963), p. 19.

Thibaut Gallery, New York. *According to the Letter*. Jan. 15–Feb. 9. Brochure, with text by Nicolas Calas.

—Fried, Michael. "New York Letter." *Art International* (Lugano) 7, no. 3 (March 25, 1963), pp. 51–52.

Dwan Gallery, Los Angeles. *Dealer's Choice*. Feb. 10–March.

The Washington Gallery of Modern Art, Washington, D.C. *The Popular Image*. April 18–June 2. Catalogue, *The Popular Image Exhibition*, with text by Alan R. Solomon and LP record with interviews with the artists by Henry Geldzahler (recorded and edited by Billy Klüver; transcripts published by Experiments in Art and Technology, New York, 1981).
—Getlein, Frank. "Modern Art Pop Show Is Strictly Dullsville." *The Sunday Star* (Washington, D.C.), April 21, 1963, section C, p. 12.

Nelson Gallery–Atkins Museum, Kansas City, Mo. *Popular Art: Artistic Projections of Common American Symbols*. April 28–May 26. Catalogue, with text by Ralph T. Coe.

Stedelijk Museum, Amsterdam. *Schrift en beeld*. May 3–June 10. Catalogue.

The Museum of Modern Art, New York. *Americans 1963*. May 22–Aug. 18. Catalogue, edited by Dorothy C. Miller, with statement by Oldenburg. Traveled to National Gallery of Canada, Ottawa, Nov. 8–Dec. 1; Artist's Guild of St. Louis, Mo., Dec. 18, 1963–Jan. 15, 1964; Toledo Museum of Art, Ohio, Feb. 3–March 2, 1964; Ringling Museum of Art, Sarasota, Fla., March 18–April 15, 1964; Colorado Springs Fine Arts Center, May 1–29, 1964; San Francisco Museum of Art, June 16–Aug. 9, 1964; Seattle Art Museum, Sept. 9–Oct. 11, 1964; and Detroit Institute of Arts, Nov. 1–29, 1964.
—Ashton, Dore. "Art." *Arts and Architecture* (Los Angeles) 80, no. 7 (July 1963), pp. 4–5.
—Baro, Gene. "A Gathering of Americans." *Arts Magazine* (New York) 37, no. 10 (Sept. 1963), pp. 28–33.
—M[onte], J[ames]. "San Francisco." *Artforum* (San Francisco) 3, no. 1 (Sept. 1964), pp. 43–44.
—Rose, Barbara. "Americans 1963.'" *Art International* (Lugano) 7, no. 7 (June 25, 1963), pp. 77–79.
—Rosenberg, Harold. "The Art Galleries: Black and Pistachio." *The New Yorker*, June 15, 1963, pp. 84–92.

Oakland Art Museum, Calif. (organized in collaboration with California College of Arts and Crafts). *Pop Art USA*. Sept. 7–29. Catalogue, with text by John Coplans.
—Coplans, John. "Notes from San Francisco." *Art International* (Lugano) 7, no. 8 (Oct. 25, 1963), pp. 91–94.

Institute of Contemporary Arts, London (organized in collaboration with Galerie Ileana Sonnabend, Paris). *The Popular Image*. Oct. 24–Nov. 23. Catalogue, with text by Alan Solomon.

Wadsworth Atheneum, Hartford, Conn. *Harvest of Plenty: De Gustibus*. Oct. 24–Dec. 1. Catalogue, with introduction by C. C. Cunningham.

Albright-Knox Art Gallery, Buffalo, N.Y. *Mixed Media and Pop Art*. Nov. 19–Dec. 15. Catalogue.

The Contemporary Arts Center, Cincinnati. *An American Viewpoint, 1963*. Dec. 4–21. Catalogue.

1964
Sidney Janis Gallery, New York. *Four Environments by Four New Realists*. Jan. 6–Feb. 1.

—Ashton, Dore. "Arts." *Arts and Architecture* (Los Angeles) 81, no. 2 (Feb. 1964), pp. 6–9.
—Brown, Gordon. "Gallery Previews." *Art Voices* (New York) 3, no. 2 (Feb. 1964), p. 29.
—Canaday, John. "Hello, Goodbye: A Question about Pop Art's Staying Power." *The New York Times*, Jan. 12, 1964, section 2, p. 17.
—Coates, Robert M. "The Art Galleries: The Passage of Time." *The New Yorker*, Jan. 18, 1964, pp. 107, 113.
—Ferebee, Ann. "Statement: On the Move." *Industrial Design* (New York) 11, no. 2 (Feb. 1964), pp. 62–64.
—Kozloff, Max. "Art." *The Nation* (New York) 198, no. 5 (Jan. 27, 1964), pp. 107–08.
—Lippard, L[ucy] R. "New York." *Artforum* (San Francisco) 2, no. 9 (March 1964), pp. 18–19.
—Oeri, Georgine. "The Object of Art." *Quadrum* (Brussels), no. 16 (1964), pp. 4–26.
—Roberts, Colette. "Les Expositions à New York." *Aujourd'hui* (Paris) 8, no. 44 (Jan. 1964), pp. 96–97.
—Rose, Barbara. "New York Letter." *Art International* (Lugano) 8, no. 3 (April 25, 1964), pp. 52–56.
—S[wenson], G[ene]. R. "Reviews and Previews." *Art News* (New York) 62, no. 10 (Feb. 1964), p. 8.

Dwan Gallery, Los Angeles. *Boxes*. Feb. 2–29. Catalogue, with text by Walter Hopps.
—Weber, John W. "Boxes." *Art in America* (New York) 52, no. 3 (June 1964), pp. 98–102.

Moderna Museet, Stockholm. *Amerikansk pop-konst*. Feb. 28–April 12. Catalogue, with text by Alan R. Solomon. Traveled to Louisiana Museum, Humlebaek, Denmark, as *Amerikansk Popkunst*, April 17–May 24 (catalogue, special issue of *Louisiana Revy* [Humlebaek], no. 4 [April 1964], with text by Solomon); and Stedelijk Museum, Amsterdam, as *American Pop Art/De Nieuwe Amerikaanse Kunst*, June 22–July 26 (catalogue, with text by Solomon).
—Dienst, Rolf-Gunter. "Porträts zwischen Expressionismus und Pop Art: Zu Ausstellungen in Den Haag, Gent und Amsterdam." *Das Kunstwerk* (Baden-Baden) 18, no. 4 (Oct. 1964), pp. 45–46.

Tate Gallery, London. *Painting and Sculpture of a Decade: 54–64*. April 22–June 28. Catalogue.

Institute of Contemporary Art, Boston. *The Eight Americans in the Venice Biennale*. June 12–July 29.

Padiglioni delle Nazioni, Italy (organized by the Jewish Museum, New York). *XXXII Esposizione Biennale Internazionale d'Arte: Quattro Artisti Più Giovani/Four Younger Artists*. June 20–Oct. 18. Catalogue, with texts by Alan R. Solomon, published by the Jewish Museum, New York.
—Chevalier, Denys. "La Sculpture à la XXXIIe Biennale de Venise." *Art International* (Lugano) 8, no. 7 (Sept. 25, 1964), pp. 42–44.
—de Marchis, Giorgio. "The Significance of the 1964 Venice Biennale." *Art International* (Lugano) 8, no. 9 (Nov. 25, 1964), pp. 21–23.
—Gendel, Milton. "Hugger-Mugger in the Giardini." *Art News* (New York) 63, no. 63 (Sept. 1964), pp. 32–35, 53.
—Keller, Heinz. "Ausstellungen: Venedig XXXII Biennale Internazionale." *Werk* (Winterthur) 51, no. 8 (Aug. 1964), supplement, pp. 188–91.

—Zahn, Leopold. "Biennale 1964." *Das Kunstwerk* (Baden-Baden) 18, nos. 1–3 (July–Sept. 1964), pp. 31–48.

Solomon R. Guggenheim Museum, New York. *American Drawings*. Sept. 17–Oct. 27. Catalogue, with text by Lawrence Alloway.

Haags Gemeentemuseum, The Hague. *Nieuwe Realisten*. June 24–Aug. 30. Catalogue. Traveled to Museum des 20. Jahrhunderts, Vienna, as *Pop etc.*, Sept. 19–Oct. 31 (catalogue, with texts by Otto A. Graff, Werner Hofmann, et al.); Akademie der Künste, Berlin, as *Neue Realisten und Pop Art*, Nov. 20, 1964–Jan. 3, 1965 (catalogue, with text by Hofmann); and Palais des Beaux-Arts, Brussels, as *Pop Art–Nouveau Réalisme–etc.*, Feb. 5–March 1, 1965 (catalogue, with texts by Jean Dypréau and Pierre Restany).

The Museum of Modern Art, New York. *Contemporary Painters and Sculptors as Printmakers*. Sept. 15–Oct. 25. Catalogue, with text by Elaine L. Johnson.

Bianchini Gallery, New York. *The American Supermarket*. Oct. 6–Nov. 7.

Museum of Art, Carnegie Institute, Pittsburgh. *1964 Pittsburgh International Exhibition of Contemporary Painting and Sculpture*. Oct. 30, 1964–Jan. 10, 1965. Catalogue.

Sidney Janis Gallery, New York. *A Selection of Twentieth Century Art of Three Generations*. Nov. 24–Dec. 26. Catalogue.
—Lippard, Lucy R. "New York Letter." *Art International* (Lugano) 9, no. 1 (Feb. 1965), pp. 34–41.

Bianchini Gallery, New York. *Yankee Doodles under $300*. Dec. 1–31.

Whitney Museum of American Art, New York. *Annual Exhibition 1964: Contemporary American Sculpture*. Dec. 9, 1964–Jan. 31, 1965. Catalogue.

The Memorial Art Gallery, University of Rochester. *In Focus: A Look at Realism in Art*. Dec. 28, 1964–Jan. 31, 1965. Catalogue.

1965
Solomon R. Guggenheim Museum, New York. *Eleven from the Reuben Gallery*. Jan. 6–28. Catalogue, with text by Lawrence Alloway.
—Lippard, Lucy R. "New York Letter." *Art International* (Lugano) 9, no. 3 (April 1965), pp. 48–64.

Dwan Gallery, Los Angeles. *Drawings by Claes Oldenburg, Jim Dine, Robert Whitman, Ben Talbert*. Feb. 9–March 6.
—F[actor], D[on]. "Los Angeles." *Artforum* (San Francisco) 3, no. 7 (April 1965), p. 9.
—Marmer, Nancy. "Los Angeles Letter." *Art International* (Lugano) 9, no. 4 (May 1965), pp. 43–46.

Bianchini Gallery, New York. *Warhol, Oldenburg, Lichtenstein*. March.
—B[erkson], W[illiam]. "In the Galleries." *Arts Magazine* (New York) 39, no. 9 (May 1965), pp. 59–60.

Milwaukee Art Center, Wis. *Pop Art and the American Tradition*. April 9–May 9. Catalogue, with introduction by Tracy Atkinson.

Whitney Museum of American Art, New York. *A Decade of American Drawing, 1955–1965*. April 28–June 6. Catalogue.

The Pace Gallery, New York. *Beyond Realism*. May 4–29. Catalogue, with text by Michael Kirby.

Sidney Janis Gallery, New York. *Recent Work by Arman, Dine, Fahlstrom, Marisol, Oldenburg, Segal at Sidney Janis*. May 5–31. Catalogue.

City-Galerie Zürich. *Pop Art*. June 15–July 10. Catalogue, with text by Otto Hahn.

Musée Rodin, Paris (organized by the Museum of Modern Art, New York). *Etats-Unis: Sculptures du XXe siècle*. June 22–Oct. 16. Catalogue. Traveled to Hochschule für Bildende Künste, Berlin, as *Amerikanische Plastik 20. Jahrhundert. Deutsche gessellschaft fur Bildende Kunst*, Nov. 20, 1965–Jan. 6, 1966; and Staatliche Kunsthalle Baden-Baden, Feb.–April 17, 1966.
—Frigerio, Simone. "Les Expositions à l'étranger: Pop Art phénomène universel." *Aujourd'hui* (Paris) 9, no. 49 (April 1965), pp. 46–47.

Sidney Janis Gallery, New York. *Pop and Op*. Dec. 1–31.

1966
The Jewish Museum, New York. *Environments: Painting and Constructions*. Jan. 12–Feb. 13.

Bianchini Gallery, New York. *Master Drawings: Pissarro to Lichtenstein*. Jan. 15–Feb. 5. Catalogue. Traveled to Contemporary Arts Center, Cincinnati, Feb. 7–26.

Institute of Contemporary Art, University of Pennsylvania, Philadelphia. *The Other Tradition*. Jan. 27–March 7. Catalogue, with text by Gene R. Swenson.
—Lippard, Lucy R. "New York and Philadelphia Letter: An Impure Situation." *Art International* (Lugano) 10, no. 5 (May 20, 1966), pp. 60–65.

Cordier and Ekstrom, New York. *Exhibition to Benefit the American Chess Foundation Organized by Marcel Duchamp*. Feb. 8–26.

Institute of Contemporary Art, Boston. *As Found: An Experiment in Selective Seeing*. March 5–April 10. Brochure, with text by Ulfert Wilke.

San Francisco Museum of Art. *The Current Moment in Art*. April 15–May 22.

Institute of Contemporary Art, Boston. *Multiplicity*. April 16–June 5. Catalogue, with introduction by Molly Rannells.

The Museum of Modern Art, New York. *The Object Transformed*. June 28–Aug. 21. Catalogue, with text by Mildred Constantine with Arthur Drexler.

Walker Art Center, Minneapolis. *Eight Sculptors: The Ambiguous Image*. Oct. 22–Dec. 4. Catalogue, with texts by Martin Friedman and Jan van der Marck.

Whitney Museum of American Art, New York. *Annual Exhibition 1966: Contemporary Sculpture and Prints*. Dec. 16, 1966–Feb. 5, 1967. Catalogue.

1967
Dwan Gallery, New York. *Scale Models and Drawings*. Jan. 7–Feb. 11.

Giant Soft Fan, *1966–67, included in* American Painting Now, *United States Pavilion, Expo '67, Montreal, April 28– October 27, 1967.*

Art Gallery of Ontario, Toronto. *Dine–Oldenburg–Segal: Painting/Sculpture.* Jan. 14–Feb. 12. Catalogue, with text on Oldenburg by Ellen H. Johnson. Traveled to Albright-Knox Art Gallery, Buffalo, N.Y., Feb. 24–March 26.
—Hale, Barrie. "Dine, Oldenburg, Segal: Who Are They? What Are They? And What Do They Want Anyway?" *Telegram* (Toronto), Jan. 17, 1967, p. 40.
—Russell, Paul. "Exhibitions: Toronto." *Artscanada* (Toronto) 24, no. 2 (Feb. 1967), supplement, p. 3.

Richard Feigen Gallery, New York. *Projects for Macrostructures.* Feb. 11–March 9.
—Goldin, Amy. "Macrostructures." *Artforum* (Los Angeles) 5, no. 8 (April 1967), pp. 59–60.
—Picard, Lil. "Ausstellungen in New York: 'Makro-Strukturen' (Richard Feigen Gallery)." *Das Kunstwerk* (Baden-Baden) 20, nos. 7–8 (April–May 1967), p. 24.

Museum of Contemporary Crafts, New York. *Monuments, Tombstones and Trophies.* March 17–May 14.

Los Angeles County Museum of Art. *American Sculpture of the Sixties.* April 28–June 25. Catalogue, with texts by Lawrence A. Alloway, Wayne V. Andersen, Dore Ashton, John Coplans, Clement Greenberg, Max Kozloff, Lucy R. Lippard, James Monte, Oldenburg, Barbara Rose, Irving Sandler, and Maurice Tuchman. Traveled to Philadelphia Museum of Art, Sept. 14–Oct. 29.
—"American Sculpture of the Sixties." *Arts and Architecture* (Los Angeles) 84, no. 6 (June 1967), pp. 6–9.
—Tuten, Frederic. "'American Sculpture of the Sixties': A Los Angeles 'Super Show.'" *Arts Magazine* (New York) 41, no. 7 (May 1967), pp. 40–44.
—Wechsler, Judith. "Why Scale?" *Art News* (New York) 66, no. 4 (summer 1967), pp. 32–34, 67–68.

United States Pavilion, Expo '67, Montreal. *American Painting Now.* April 28–Oct. 27. Catalogue.

Museu de Arte Moderna, São Paulo (organized by International Art Program, National Collection of Fine Arts, Smithsonian Institution, Washington, D.C.). *IX Bienal do Museu de Arte Moderna, São Paulo: Environment U.S.A., 1957–1967/Meio-Natural U.S.A., 1957–1967.* Sept. 22, 1967–Jan. 8, 1968. Catalogue, with texts by William C. Seitz and Lloyd Goodrich and artists' statements, published by the Smithsonian Institution Press, Washington, D.C. Traveled to Rose Art Museum, Brandeis University, Waltham, Mass., Feb. 19–March 23, 1968.

Central Park, New York (sponsored by New York City Administration of Recreation and Cultural Affairs for Cultural Showcase Festival). *Sculpture in Environment.* Oct. 1–31. Catalogue, with text by Irving Sandler.
—Baker, Russell. "Observer: On Crying 'Art!' to an Unused Grave." *The New York Times*, Oct. 10, 1967.

Museum of Art, Carnegie Institute, Pittsburgh. *1967 Pittsburgh International Exhibition of Contemporary Painting and Sculpture.* Oct. 27, 1967–Jan. 7, 1968. Catalogue.

Sidney Janis Gallery, New York. *Homage to Marilyn Monroe.* Dec. 6–30. Catalogue.
—Alloway, Lawrence. "Marilyn as Subject Matter." *Arts Magazine* (New York) 42 (Dec. 1967), p. 29.

—Pincus-Witten, Robert. "New York." *Artforum* (New York) 6, no. 6 (Feb. 1968), pp. 48–49.

1968
The Museum of Modern Art, New York. *Dada, Surrealism, and Their Heritage*. March 27–June 9. Catalogue, with text by William S. Rubin. Traveled to Los Angeles County Museum of Art, July 16–Sept. 8; and the Art Institute of Chicago, Oct. 19–Dec. 8.

Stedelijk Van Abbemuseum, Eindhoven. *Three Blind Mice/de Collecties: Visser, Peeters, Becht*. April 5–May 19. Catalogue, with texts by W. A. L. Beeren, Hubert Peeters, and Pierre Restany. Traveled to Sint Pietersabdij, Ghent, June 15–Aug. 15.

Haus der Kunst, Neue Pinakothek, Munich (organized by Galerie-Verein, Munich). *Sammlung 1968 Karl Ströher*. June 14–Aug. 9. Catalogue, with text by Jürgen Wissmann. Traveled to Kunstverein Hamburg, Aug. 24–Oct. 6; Neue Nationalgalerie, Berlin, March 1–April 14, 1969; Städtische Kunsthalle Düsseldorf, April 25–June 17, 1969; and Kunsthalle Bern, July 12–Sept. 28, 1969.

Padiglione Centrale, Venice. *XXXIV Esposizione Biennale Internazionale d'Arte Venezia: Linee della ricera: dall'informale alle nuove strutture*. June 22–Oct. 20. Catalogue.

Museum Fridericianum, Orangerie, Galerie an der Schönen Aussicht, Kassel. *Documenta 4*. June 27–Oct. 6. Catalogue (2 vols.), with texts by Arnold Bode, Max Imdahl, Jürgen Harten, J. Leering, Janni Müller-Hauch, et al.

Dwan Gallery, New York. *Earth Works*. Oct. 5–30.

Richard Feigen Gallery, Chicago. *Richard J. Daley*. Oct. Catalogue. Traveled to the Contemporary Arts Center, Cincinnati, Dec. 19, 1968–Jan. 4, 1969.
—Garino, David P. "Portrait of a Mayor: Art Show in Chicago Takes Aim at Daley." *The Wall Street Journal*, Oct. 23, 1968, p. 1.
—Halstead, Whitney. "Chicago." *Artforum* (New York) 7, no. 5 (Jan. 1969), pp. 67–68.
—"The Politics of Feeling." *Time*, Nov. 1, 1968, p. 76.

The Museum of Modern Art, New York. *The Machine as Seen at the End of the Mechanical Age*. Nov. 25, 1968–Feb. 9, 1969. Catalogue, with text by K. G. Pontus Hultén. Traveled to University of St. Thomas, Houston, March 25–May 18, 1969; and San Francisco Museum of Art, June 23–Aug. 24, 1969.
—Ashton, Dore. "The End and the Beginning of an Age." *Arts Magazine* (New York) 43, no. 3 (Dec. 1968–Jan. 1969), pp. 46–50.
—"Love, Hate and the Machine." *Time*, Dec. 6, 1968, pp. 86–89.

Whitney Museum of American Art, New York. *1968 Annual Exhibition: Contemporary American Sculpture*. Dec. 17, 1968–Feb. 9, 1969. Catalogue.

1969
Vancouver Art Gallery. *New York Thirteen*. Jan. 21–Feb. 16. Catalogue, edited by Lucy Lippard, with texts by Lippard, Oldenburg, and Doris Shadbolt. Traveled to Norman MacKenzie Art Gallery, Regina, Canada, March 10–April 21; and Musée d'Art Contemporain, Montreal, June 3–July 5.

Sidney Janis Gallery, New York. *Seven Artists: Dine, Fahlstrom, Kelly, Marisol, Oldenburg, Segal, Wesselmann*. May 1–31. Catalogue.

Hayward Gallery, London (organized by the Arts Council of Great Britain, London). *Pop Art*. July 9–Sept. 3. Catalogue, with text by John Russell with Suzi Gablik; and book, *Pop Art Redefined*, edited by John Russell and Suzi Gablik, published on the occasion of the exhibition by Thames and Hudson, London.
—Russell, John. "Pop Reappraised." *Art in America* (New York) 57, no. 4 (July–Aug. 1969), pp. 78–89.

Institute of Contemporary Art, University of Pennsylvania, Philadelphia. *The Spirit of the Comics*. Oct. 1–Nov. 9. Catalogue.

The Metropolitan Museum of Art, New York. *New York Painting and Sculpture: 1940–1970*. Oct. 18, 1969–Feb. 1, 1970. Catalogue, with text by Henry Geldzahler.
—"From the Brink, Something Grand." *Time*, Oct. 24, 1969, pp. 78–81.

Museum of Contemporary Art, Chicago. *Art by Telephone*. Nov. 1–Dec. 14. Catalogue, issued as LP record, with artists' instructions (recorded via telephone) for the realization of works in the exhibition and text by Jan van der Marck.

Richard Feigen and Co., New York. *Dubuffet and the Anticulture*. Nov. 25, 1969–Jan. 3, 1970. Catalogue, with texts by George Cohen, Jean Dubuffet, Richard L. Feigen, and Oldenburg.
—Ashton, Dore. "Dubuffet and Anticulture." *Arts Magazine* (New York) 44, no. 3 (Dec. 1969–Jan. 1970), pp. 36–38.

1970
Sidney Janis Gallery, New York. *String and Rope*. Jan. 7–31. Catalogue.

United States Pavilion, Expo '70, Osaka. *United States Pavilion, Japan World Exposition, Osaka 1970: New Arts*. March 15–Sept. 15. Catalogue.

Allen Memorial Art Museum, Oberlin College, Ohio. *Art in the Mind*. April 17–May 12. Catalogue, with text by Athena T. Spear and artists' projects.

United States Pavilion, Venice, Italy. *XXXV Esposizione Biennale Internazionale d'Arte Venezia*. June 24–Oct. 25. Catalogue.

Museum of Art, Carnegie Institute, Pittsburgh. *1970 Pittsburgh International: Exhibition of Contemporary Art*. Oct. 30, 1970–Jan. 10, 1971. Catalogue.

Kölnischer Kunstverein, Cologne. *Happening & Fluxus*. Nov. 6, 1970–Jan. 6, 1971. Catalogue.

Sidney Janis Gallery, New York. *Seven Artists: New Work by Fahlstrom, Kelly, Marisol, Oldenburg, Segal, Steinberg, Wesselmann*. Dec. 4–31. Catalogue.

Whitney Museum of American Art, New York. *1970 Annual Exhibition: Contemporary American Sculpture*. Dec. 12, 1970–Feb. 7, 1971. Catalogue.

1971
Philadelphia Museum of Art. *Multiples: The First Decade*. March 5–April 4. Catalogue, with text by John L. Tancock.

The Museum of Modern Art, New York. *Technics and Creativity: Gemini G.E.L.* May 5–June 6. Catalogue, with text by Riva Castelman.

Los Angeles County Museum of Art. *Art and Technology.* May 11–Aug. 29. Catalogue, with texts by John Forkner, Jane Livingston, Gail R. Scott, and Maurice Tuchman.
—Burnham, Jack. "Corporate Art." *Artforum* (New York) 10, no. 2 (Oct. 1971), pp. 66–71.
—Buhrman, Robert. "Portrait of the Artist as a Mad Scientist." *Los Angeles Magazine* 14, no. 11 (Nov. 1969), pp. 42–45, 68.
—Gottschalk, Jr., Earl C. "What's That Thing Resembling a Giant, Salmon-Hued Ice Bag?" *The Wall Street Journal*, May 5, 1971, p. 1.
—Kozloff, Max. "The Multi-Million Dollar Art Boondoggle." *Artforum* (New York) 10, no. 2 (Oct. 1971), pp. 72–76.
—"Man and Machine." *Time*, June 28, 1971, pp. 60–63.
—Tuchman, Maurice. "An Introduction to 'Art and Technology.'" *Studio International* (London) 181, no. 932 (April 1971), pp. 173–80.
—Young, Joseph E. "Los Angeles." *Art International* (Lugano) 14, no. 3 (March 20, 1970), pp. 83–84.

Park Sonsbeek, Arnhem, The Netherlands. *Sonsbeek 71: Sonsbeek buiten de perken.* June 19–Aug. 15. Catalogue, with text by Ton Haak.
—Blok, Cor. "Sonsbeek '71." *Art International* (Lugano) 15, no. 9 (Nov. 20, 1971), p. 47.
—Kurtz, Bruce. "Sonsbeek '71: Beyond Lawn and Order." *Arts Magazine* (New York) 46, no. 1 (Sept. 1971), pp. 50–52.
—Linville, Kasha. "Sonsbeek: Speculations, Impressions." *Artforum* (New York) 10, no. 2 (Oct. 1971), pp. 54–61.

Louisiana Museum, Humlebaek, Denmark. *Amerikansk kunst 1950–70.* Sept. 11–Oct. 24. Catalogue, special issue of *Louisiana Revy* (Humlebaek) 12, no. 1 (Sept. 1971), with texts by Öyvind Fahlström and Oldenburg.

Royal Dublin Society. *ROSC '71: The Poetry of Vision.* Oct. 24–Dec. 29. Catalogue, with text by David M. Wilson.

1972
Sidney Janis Gallery, New York. *Colossal Scale: The Appeal of Gigantic Representational Images for Today's Artist.* March 9–April 1. Catalogue.

Kassel, Germany. *Documenta 5: Maus Museum: Eine Auswahl von Objekten gesammelt von Claes Oldenburg/Mouse Museum: A Selection of Objects Collected by Claes Oldenburg.* June 30–Oct. 8. Catalogue, with text by Kasper König.
—Alloway, Lawrence. "'Reality': Ideology at D5." *Artforum* (New York) 11, no. 2 (Oct. 1972), pp. 30–36.
—Granath, Olle. "Konsten bortom det verifierbara." *Dagens Nyheter* (Amsterdam), July 22, 1972.
—Kramer, Hilton. "Documenta 5: The Bayreuth of the Neo-Dadaists." *The New York Times*, July 9, 1972, section 2, p. 15.
—Reaves, Angela Westwater. "Claes Oldenburg, An Interview." *Artforum* (New York) 11, no. 2 (Oct. 1972), pp. 36–39.
—Rose, Barbara. "Document of an Age." *New York*, Aug. 14, 1972, pp. 66–67.

—Rose, Barbara. "Oldenburg's Mouseleum at Documenta." *Vogue* (New York) 160 (Sept. 15, 1972), p. 32.

Rijksmuseum Kröller-Müller, Otterlo. *Diagrams and Drawings.* Aug. 12–Sept. 24. Catalogue, with text by R. Oxenaar. Traveled to Kunstmuseum Basel, Jan. 20–March 4, 1973.

Moderna Museet, Stockholm. *New York Collection for Stockholm.* Oct. 27–Dec. 2. Catalogue, with texts by Emile de Antonio, Pontus Hultén, and Billy Klüver.

1973
Sidney Janis Gallery, New York. *Twenty-five Years of Janis: Part 2, From Pollock to Pop, Op and Sharp-Focus Realism.* March 13–April 13. Catalogue.

Städtisches Museum Abteiberg Mönchengladbach, Germany. *Stilkunde an Beispielen: Einlehrspiel.* March 28–April 28. Catalogue.

1974
Whitney Museum of American Art, New York. *American Pop Art.* April 6–June 16. Catalogue, with text by Lawrence Alloway.
—Baldwin, Carl R. "On the Nature of Pop." *Artforum* (New York) 12, no. 10 (June 1974), pp. 34–38.
—Derfner, Phyllis. "New York Letter." *Art International* (Lugano) 18, no. 6 (summer 1974), pp. 46–51.
—Hess, Thomas B. "Up Against the Wall, Pop." *New York Magazine* 7, no. 19 (May 13, 1974), pp. 92–93.
—Hughes, Robert. "The Instant Nostalgia of Pop." *Time,* April 15, 1974, pp. 80–83.

The Vancouver Gallery. *3-D to 2-D: Drawing for Sculpture.* May 7–June 17.

Marlborough Gallery, New York. *Selected Works from the Collection of Carter Burden.* May 9–June 1. Catalogue.

Indianapolis Museum of Art. *Painting and Sculpture Today 1974.* May 22–July 14. Catalogue, with text by Richard L. Warrum. Traveled to the Contemporary Art Center and the Taft Museum, Cincinnati, Sept. 12–Oct. 26.

Dayton's Gallery 12, Minneapolis. *Prints '73–'74.* July 6–Aug. 24.

Newport, Rhode Island (organized by Monumenta Newport). *Monumenta: Sculpture in Environment.* Aug. 17–Oct. 13. Catalogue, with texts by Sam Hunter and Hugh M. Davies with Sally E. Yard.

Dallas Museum of Fine Arts and Pollock Galleries, Southern Methodist University, Dallas. *Poets of the Cities, New York and San Francisco, 1950–1965.* Nov. 20–Dec. 29. Catalogue, with texts by Neil A. Chassman, Robert Creeley, Lana Davis, John Clellon Holmes, and Robert M. Murdock, published by E. P. Dutton, New York. Traveled to San Francisco Museum of Art, Jan. 31–March 23, 1975; and Wadsworth Atheneum, Hartford, Conn., April 23–June 1, 1975.

1975
Minami Gallery, Tokyo. *Minami '75: A Selection of Twentieth Century Art.* April 14–May 2. Catalogue.

Albright-Knox Art Gallery, Buffalo, N.Y. *The Martha Jackson Collection at the Albright-Knox Art Gallery.* Nov. 21, 1975–Jan. 4, 1976. Catalogue.

1976
The New Gallery of Contemporary Art, Cleveland. *American Pop Art and the Culture of the Sixties.* Jan. 10–Feb. 21. Catalogue, with texts by Carol Nathanson, Nina Sundell, and Marjorie Talalay.

The Museum of Modern Art, New York. *Drawing Now.* Jan. 21–March 9. Catalogue, with text by Bernice Rose. Traveled to Kunsthaus Zürich, as *Zeichnung heute—Drawing Now*, Oct. 10–Nov. 14 (catalogue, with text by Rose, in German); Staatliche Kunsthalle Baden-Baden, as *Drawing Now—Zeichnung heute*, Nov. 25, 1976–Jan. 16, 1977 (catalogue, with text by Rose, published by Kunsthaus Zürich and Staatliche Kunsthalle Baden-Baden, in German); Graphische Sammlung Albertina, Vienna, Jan. 20–Feb. 28, 1977; and Sonia Henie-Niels Onstad Foundation, Oslo, March 20–April 24, 1977.

Solomon R. Guggenheim Museum, New York. *Twentieth-Century American Drawing: Three Avant-Garde Generations.* Jan. 23–March 21. Catalogue, with text by Diane Waldman. Traveled to Staatliche Kunsthalle Baden-Baden, May 27–July 11; and Kunsthalle Bremen, July 18–Aug. 29.

The Art Institute of Chicago. *Seventy-second American Exhibition.* March 13–May 9. Catalogue, with text by Anne Rorimer.

The Brooklyn Museum, New York. *Thirty Years of American Printmaking.* Nov. 20, 1976–Jan. 30, 1977. Catalogue, with text by Gene Baro.

Whitney Museum of American Art, New York. *American Master Drawings and Watercolors: A History of Works on Paper from Colonial Times to the Present.* Nov. 23, 1976–Jan. 23, 1977. Catalogue, with text by Theodore E. Stebbins, Jr.

1977
Musée National d'Art Moderne, Centre Georges Pompidou, Paris. *Paris–New York: Un Album.* June 1–Sept. 19. Catalogue.

Orangerie and Neue Galerie, Kassel. *Documenta 6: Wirklichkeit—Klischee und Reflexion und Objektkataloge.* June 24–Oct. 2. Catalogue.

Westfälisches Landesmuseum für Kunst und Kulturgeschichte, Schloßgarten, Universität, Aasee, Münster, Germany. *Skulptur: Austellung in Münster, 1977.* July 3–Nov. 13. Catalogue (2 vols.), with texts by Gottfried Boehm, Laszlo Glozer, Kurt Johnen, Bernhard Kerber, Werner Schnell, and Herbert Schöttle, and artists' statements; in German.

Museum of Contemporary Art, Chicago. *Landfall Press: A Survey of Prints (1970–1977).* Nov. 18, 1977–Jan. 8, 1978. Catalogue.

1978
Nationalgalerie Berlin. *Aspekte der 6oer Jahre: Aus der Sammlung Reinhard Onnasch.* Feb. 2–April 23. Catalogue.

Whitney Museum of American Art, New York. *Art About Art.* July 19–Sept. 24. Catalogue, with texts by Jean Lipman with Richard Marshall, and Leo Steinberg, published by E. P. Dutton, New York, in association with the Whitney Museum of American Art. Traveled to North Carolina Museum of Art, Raleigh, N.C., Oct. 15–Nov. 26; the Frederick S. Wight Art Gallery, University of California, Los Angeles, Dec. 17, 1978–Feb. 11, 1979; and Portland Art Museum, Oreg., March 6–April 15, 1979.

1980
Allen Memorial Art Museum, Oberlin College, Ohio. *From Reinhardt to Christo.* Feb. 20–March 19. Catalogue, with texts by Ellen H. Johnson and William Olander.

Kölnischer Kunstverein, Cologne. *Monumente-Denkmal.* March 18–April 20. Catalogue, with texts by Wulf Herzogenrath, Ed Kienholz, Oldenburg, Michael Sandle, and Timm Ulrichs. Traveled to Badischer Kunstverein, Karlsruhe, June 22–Sept. 14.

Institute of Contemporary Art, University of Pennsylvania, Philadelphia. *Urban Encounters: Art Architecture Audience.* March 19–April 30. Catalogue, with texts by Lawrence Alloway, Nancy Foote, Janet Kardon, and Ian L. McHarg.

Istituto di Cultura di Palazzo Grassi, Venice. *Pop Art: Evoluzione di una generazione.* March 22–July 6. Catalogue.

Wenkenpark Riehen, Basel. *Skulptur im 20. Jahrhundert: Austellung im Wenkenpark Riehen/Basel.* May 10–Sept. 14. Catalogue, with text by Reinhold Hohl, published by Werner Druck, Basel.

Museum of Contemporary Art, Chicago. *Late Entries to the Chicago Tribune Tower Competition.* May 30–July 19. Catalogue, with text by Stanley Tigerman.

National Gallery of Art, Washington, D.C. *The Morton G. Neumann Family Collection: Selected Works.* Aug. 31–Dec. 31. Catalogue (2 vols.), with texts by E. A. Carmean, Jr., Sam Hunter, Eliza E. Rathbone, and Trinkett Clark.

1981
National Gallery of Art, Washington, D.C. *Contemporary American Prints and Drawings 1940–1980.* March 22–July 19. Brochure, with text by Andrew Robison.

Museen der Stadt Köln, Cologne. *Westkunst: Zeitgenoissische Kunst seit 1939.* May 30–Aug. 10. Catalogue, with text by Laszlo Glozer.

The Brooklyn Museum, New York. *Twenty-second National Print Exhibition.* Oct. 3, 1981–Feb. 3, 1982. Catalogue, with text by Gene Baro.

Whitney Museum of American Art, New York. *American Prints: Process and Proofs.* Nov. 25, 1981–Jan. 24, 1982. Catalogue, with text by Judith Goldman.

1982
Stedelijk Museum, Amsterdam. *'60–'80: Attitudes/Concepts/ Images.* April 9–July 11. Catalogue, with texts by Wim Beeren, Cor Blok, Edy de Wilde, Gijs van Tuyl, and Antje von Graevenitz, and supplement, with texts by Dorine Mignot and Frans van Rossum; in Dutch and English.

Museum Fridericianum, Kassel. *Documenta 7.* June 19–Sept. 28. Catalogue (2 vols.), with texts by Germano Celant, Johannes Gachnang, Walter Nikkels, Oldenburg, Gerhard Stock, and Coosje van Bruggen.
—Hoelterhoff, Manuela. "What Does This 'Documenta' Document?" *The Wall Street Journal*, Sept. 17, 1982, p. 21.
—Kuspit, Donald B. "Documenta: Claes Oldenburg." *Artforum* (New York) 21, no. 2 (Oct. 1982), pp. 84–85.
—Owens, Craig. "Bayreuth '82." *Art in America* (New York) 70, no. 8 (Sept. 1982), pp. 132–39, 191.

San Francisco Museum of Modern Art. *Twenty American Artists: Sculpture 1982.* July 22–Sept. 19. Catalogue.

1983
Kunstmuseum Basel. *Neue Zeichnungen aus dem Kunstmuseum Basel.* Jan. 29–April 24. Catalogue, with text by Dieter Koepplin. Traveled to Kunsthalle Tübingen, Germany, May 21–July 10; and Neue Galerie, Staatliche und Städtische Kunstsammlungen, Kassel, Aug. 13–Sept. 25.

Whitney Museum of American Art at Philip Morris, New York. *Twentieth-Century Sculpture: Process and Presence.* April 8–May 11. Catalogue, with text by Lisa Phillips.

Sunderland Arts Centre, England. *Drawing in Air: An Exhibition of Sculptors' Drawings: 1882–1982.* July 11–Aug. 20. Catalogue, edited by Tony Knipe, with texts by Antoine Bourdelle, Terry Friedman, Knipe, and Paul Overy. Traveled to Glynn Vivian Art Gallery and Museum, Swansea, England, Sept. 3–Nov. 5; and City Art Gallery and Henry Moore Study Centre, Leeds, Jan. 13–Feb. 19, 1984.

Whitney Museum of American Art, Downtown Branch, New York. *The Comic Art Show: Cartoons in Painting and Popular Culture.* July 18–Aug. 26. Catalogue, with texts by John Carlin and Sheena Wagstaff.

1984
Hirshhorn Museum and Sculpture Garden, Washington, D.C. *Drawings: 1974–1984.* March 15–May 13. Catalogue, with texts by Frank Gettings and Oldenburg.

St. Jakob Merian-Park, Basel. *Skulptur im 20. Jahrhundert.* June 3–Sept. 30. Catalogue, with texts by Zdenek Felix, Andreas Franzke, Laszlo Glozer, Reinhold Hohl, Werner Jehle, Franz Meyer, Willy Rotzler, Martin Schwander, Karina Türr, Antje von Graevenitz, Joachim Heusinger von Waldegg, Theodora Vischer, and Alan Wilkinson.

The Museum of Contemporary Art, Los Angeles. *Automobile and Culture.* July 21, 1984–Jan. 6, 1985. Catalogue, with text by Gerard Silk.

Whitney Museum of American Art, New York. *Blam! The Explosion of Pop, Minimalism, and Performance, 1958–1964.* Sept. 20–Dec. 2. Catalogue, with texts by John G. Hanhardt and Barbara Haskell.
—Glueck, Grace. "Exploring Six Years of Pop and Minimalism." *The New York Times*, Sept. 28, 1984, section C, p. 27.
—Russell, John. "When Art Came Out of the Studio and Mingled." *The New York Times*, Oct. 28, 1984, section H, p. 33.
—Smith, Roberta. "Splat!" *The Village Voice* (New York), Oct. 16, 1984, p. 109.

National Gallery of Art, Washington, D.C. *Gemini G.E.L.: Art and Collaboration*. Nov. 18, 1984–Feb. 24, 1985. Catalogue, with texts by Bruce Davis and Ruth E. Fine.

1985

Whitney Museum of American Art, Fairfield County, Stamford, Conn. *Nine Printmakers and the Working Process*. Jan. 18–March 30. Catalogue, with text by Pamela Gruninger Perkins.

The Art Museum, Princeton University. *Selections from the Ileana and Michael Sonnabend Collection: Works from the 1950's and 1960's*. Feb. 3–June 9. Catalogue. Traveled to Arthur M. Huntington Art Gallery, University of Texas, Austin, Sept. 8–27; Walker Art Center, Minneapolis, Nov. 23, 1985–March 9, 1986; and Museum of Fine Arts, Boston, March 29–June 8, 1986.

The Fort Worth Art Museum, Tex. *On Paper: Major Paintings and Drawings from the Collection*. Feb. 3–April 7.

The Museum of Contemporary Art, Los Angeles. *The Panza Collection*. Feb. 13–Sept. 29. Catalogue.

Art Gallery of New South Wales, Sydney (organized by the International Council of the Museum of Modern Art, New York). *Pop Art: 1955–70*. Feb. 27–April 14. Catalogue, with text by Henry Geldzahler, published by the International Cultural Corporation of Australia, Sydney. Traveled to Queensland Art Gallery, Brisbane, May 1–June 2; and National Gallery of Victoria, Melbourne, June 26–Aug. 11.

Ecole Nationale Supérieure des Beaux-Arts, Paris (organized by the Menil Collection, Houston). *Cinquante ans de dessins américains: 1930–1980*. May 3–July 13. Catalogue. Traveled to Städelschen Kunstinstitut, Frankfurt, as *Amerikanische Zeichnungen: 1930–1980*, Nov. 28, 1985–Jan. 26, 1986 (catalogue, with text by Walter Hopps with Neil Pintz, in German).

Staatliche Kunsthalle Baden-Baden, Germany. *Räume heutiger Zeichnung*. Oct. 12–Dec. 1. Catalogue, with text on Oldenburg by Dieter Koepplin. Traveled to Tel Aviv Museum, Jan. 2–March 8, 1986.

1986

Museum of Art, Fort Lauderdale. *An American Renaissance: Painting and Sculpture since 1940*. Jan. 12–March 30. Catalogue, edited by Sam Hunter, with texts by Malcolm R. Daniel, Harry F. Gaugh, Hunter, Karen Koehler, Kim Levin, Robert C. Morgan, and Richard Sarnoff, published by Abbeville Press, New York.

Kent Fine Art, New York. *Reality Remade*. March 15–April 19. Catalogue, with text by Douglas Walla.

Park Sonsbeek, Arnhem, The Netherlands. *Sonsbeek 86*. June 18–Sept. 14. Catalogue (2 vols.), with texts by Saskia Bos, Marianne Brouwer, and Antje von Graevenitz, published by Veen/Reflex, Utrecht.

Musée National d'Art Moderne, Centre Georges Pompidou, Paris. *Qu'est-ce que la sculpture moderne?* July 3–Oct. 13. Catalogue, with texts by Benjamin H. D. Buchloh, Jean-Pierre Criqui, Thierry de Duve, Rosalind Krauss, Franz Meyer, Jean-Marc Poinsot, Barbara Rose, and Margit Rowell.

Tools of the Trade, *1982, included in* Documenta 7. *Museum Fridericianum. Kassel, June 19–September 28, 1982.*

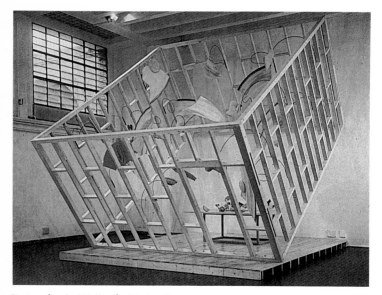

Project for the Walls of a Dining Room: Broken Plate of Scrambled Eggs, with Fabrication Model of the Dropped Bowl Fountain, *1988, included in* International Exhibition of the XVII Triennale di Milano: World Cities and the Future of the Metropolis, *Palazzo dell'Arte, Milan, September 21–December 18, 1988.*

Museum Ludwig, Cologne. *Europa/Amerika: Die Geschichte einer künstlerischen Faszination seit 1940*. Sept. 6–Nov. 30. Catalogue, with texts by Craig Adcock, Dore Ashton, Alberto Boatto, John Cage, Henning Christiansen, Rainer Crone, Andreas Franzke, Johannes Gachnang, Siegfried Gohr, Cynthia Goodman, Paul Groot, Hayden Herrera, Max Imdahl, Rafael Jablonka, Thomas Kellein, Per Kirkeby, Margot Klütsch, Barbara Lesák, Gail Levin, Mayo Thompson, and Denys Zacharopoulos.

The Museum of Contemporary Art, Los Angeles. *Individuals: A Selected History of Contemporary Art, 1945–1986*. Dec. 10, 1986–Jan. 10, 1988. Catalogue, edited by Howard Singerman, with texts by Germano Celant, Hal Foster, Sherri Geldin, Richard Koshalek, Donald Kuspit, Thomas Lawson, Kate Linker, Achille Bonito Oliva, Ronald J. Onorato, and John C. Welchman, published by Abbeville Press, New York.

1987
Institute of Contemporary Art, University of Pennsylvania, Philadelphia. *1967: At the Crossroads*. March 13–April 26. Catalogue, with texts by Hal Foster, Janet Kardon, Lucy R. Lippard, Barbara Rose, and Irving Sandler.

University Art Museum, University of California, Berkeley. *Made in U.S.A.: An Americanization in Modern Art, The '50s and '60s*. April 4–June 21. Catalogue, with texts by Ben H. Bagdikian, James E. B. Breslin, Thomas Schaub, and Sidra Stich, co-published by University of California Press, Berkeley, Los Angeles, and London. Traveled to the Nelson-Atkins Museum of Art, Kansas City, Mo., July 25–Sept. 6; and Virginia Museum of Fine Arts, Richmond, Oct. 7–Dec. 7.
—Wilson, William. "Made in the U.S.A." *Calendar* (magazine of *Los Angeles Times*), May 24, 1987, pp. 4, 72.

The Spanish Institute, New York. *The Barcelona Plazas: Preview of an Urban Experience*. April 23–June 7.

Westfälisches Landesmuseum für Kunst und Kulturgeschichte, Münster, Germany. *Skulptur Projekte in Münster*. June 14–Oct. 4. Catalogue (2 vols.), with texts by Marianne Brouwer, Benjamin H. D. Buchloh, Thomas Kellein, Hannelore Kersting, Veit Loers, Christoph Schreier, Antje von Graevenitz, and Gundolf Winter.

Padiglione d'Arte Contemporanea, Milan. *Dalla Pop Art Americana alla Nuova Figurazione: Opere del Museo d'Arte Moderna di Francoforte*. Sept. 23–Nov. 23. Catalogue, with texts by Hans Hollein, Peter Iden, and Rolf Lauter.

1988
Sidney Janis Gallery, New York. *'60s/'80s: Sculpture Parallels*. Feb. 25–March 26.

The Museum of Contemporary Art, Los Angeles. *Five Installations*. March 22–June 19.

Palazzo dell'Arte, Milan. *International Exhibition of the XVII Triennale di Milano: World Cities and the Future of the Metropolis*. Sept. 21–Dec. 18. Catalogue (2 vols.), with texts by Steve Baker, Stephen Bann, Marshall Berman, Jacques Bertin, Francesco Brambilla, Bazon Brock, Lucius Burckhardt, Victor Burgin, Germano Celant, Gianni Celati, Jonathan Crary, Marco De Michelis, Hal Foster, Luigi Ghirri, Milton Glaser, Nelson Goodman, Jacques Guillerme, Brian Hatton, Bernard Huet,

Ignasi de Solà Morales, Gaddo Morpurgo, Pierluigi Nicoli, Massimo Piattelli Palmarini, Pierre Pinon, Franco Raggi, Denis Santachiara, Richard Sennett, Georges Teyssot, Bas C. van Fraassen, Gianni Vattimo, Brian Wallis, and Richard Saul Wurman, published by Electa, Milan.

1989
Musée National d'Art Moderne, Centre Georges Pompidou, Paris, and La Grande Halle–La Villette, Paris. *Magiciens de la Terre*. May 18–Aug. 14. Catalogue, with texts by Jean-Hubert Martin, Aline Luque, Mark Francis, André Mgnin, Pierre Gaudibert, Thomas McEville, Homi Bhabha, Jacques Soulillou, and Bernard Marcadé, and statements and projects by the artists.

Helsingin Taidehalli, Helsinki. *Modern Masters '89*. May 17–July 30. Catalogue, with text by J. O. Mallander.

1990
Kunsthalle Nürnberg, Nuremberg. *Zeichnungen: Joseph Beuys, Francesco Clemente, Martin Disler, Donald Judd, Bruce Nauman, Claes Oldenburg, A. R. Penck, Frank Stella*. June 1–July 8. Catalogue, with texts by Lucius Grisebach and Dieter Koepplin.

The Museum of Modern Art, New York. *High and Low: Modern Art and Popular Culture*. Oct. 7, 1990–Jan. 15, 1991. Catalogue, with texts by Adam Gopnik and Kirk Varnedoe. Traveled to the Art Institute of Chicago, Feb. 20–May 12, 1991; and the Museum of Contemporary Art, Los Angeles, June 21–Sept. 15, 1991.
—Danto, Arthur C. "High and Low at MoMA." *The Nation* (New York), Nov. 26, 1990, pp. 654–58.
—Glueck, Grace. "Despite a Thrashing by Critics, Art Show Is Proving Popular." *The New York Times*, Dec. 3, 1990, section C, pp. 13, 15.
—Smith, Roberta. "High and Low Culture Meet on a One-Way Street." *The New York Times*, Oct. 5, 1990, section C, pp. 1, 25.

1991
Royal Academy of Arts, London. *Pop Art*. Sept. 13–Dec. 15. Catalogue, with texts by Dan Cameron, Constance W. Glenn, Thomas Kellein, Marco Livingstone, Sarat Maharaj, Alfred Pacquement, and Evelyn Weiss. Traveled to Museum Ludwig, Cologne, as *Die Pop Art Show*, Jan. 22–April 21, 1992 (catalogue); Centro de Arte Reina Sofía, Madrid, as *Arte Pop*, June 16–Sept. 14, 1992 (catalogue); and the Montreal Museum of Fine Arts, Oct. 23, 1992–Jan. 24, 1993 (catalogue).
—"Eat Better Art." *RA* (London), no. 23 (autumn 1991), pp. 42–43.
—Graham-Dixon, Andrew. "Art in the Promised Land." *The Independent Magazine* (London), Sept. 7, 1991, pp. 28–37.
—Hughes, Robert. "Wallowing in the Mass Media Sea." *Time*, Oct. 28, 1991, pp. 102–03.
—Lambirth, Andrew. "Visual Arts: Pop Icons' Blast from the Past." *The Sunday Times* (London), Sept. 15, 1991, section 5, pp. 14–15.
—Pye, Michael. "The Longest Fifteen Minutes." *The Sunday Review* (magazine of *The Independent*, London), Sept. 1, 1991, pp. 8–9.

1992
Stedelijk Museum, Amsterdam. *A Century in Sculpture*. Summer. Catalogue, with texts by Wim Beeren, Marja Bloem, Liesbeth Crommelin, Bert Jansen, Robert Jan Muller, and Jan Hein Sassen.

Museu Nacional de Belas Artes, Rio de Janeiro (organized by Servicos de Comunicación e Información Cultural, Rome). *. . . Reperti . . . O meio ambiente visto por 18 dos mais renomados artistas do mundo*. June 5–July 5. Catalogue, with texts by Ricardo Grassi and Eugenio Miccini and artists' statements, published by Das Andere, Nuremberg.

Kunst- und Ausstellungshalle der Bundesrepublik Deutschland, Bonn. *Territorium Artis*. June 19–Sept. 20. Catalogue, with texts by Pontus Hultén and Oldenburg (German and English editions).

Newport Harbor Art Museum, Newport Beach, Calif. *Both Art and Life: Gemini at Twenty-five*. Sept. 22–Nov. 29.

The Museum of Contemporary Art, Los Angeles. *Hand-Painted Pop: American Art in Transition, 1955–62*. Dec. 6, 1992–March 7, 1993. Catalogue, with texts by David Deitcher, Donna De Salvo, Stephen C. Foster, Dick Hebdige, Linda Norden, Paul Schimmel, Kenneth E. Silver, and John Yau, co-published by Rizzoli, New York. Traveled to the Museum of Contemporary Art, Chicago, April 3–June 20, 1993; and Whitney Museum of American Art, New York, July 9–Oct. 10, 1993.
—Hughes, Robert. "When the Easel Went Pop." *Time* (New York), Aug. 16, 1993, pp. 54–55.
—Kimmelman, Michael. "Explosive Painting: The Path to Pop." *The New York Times*, July 9, 1993, section C, pp. 1, 24.

1993
Guggenheim Museum SoHo, New York. *"Four Rooms" and a "House Ball": Pop and the Everyday Object*. Jan. 27–April 25.

Carré d'Art, Musée d'Art Contemporain, Nîmes. *L'Ivresse du réel: L'Objet dans l'art du XXe siècle*. May 7–Aug. 29. Catalogue, with texts by Jean-Pierre Criqui, Elisabeth Lebovici, Pierre Restany, and Guy Tosatto.

Martin-Gropius-Bau, Berlin. *American Art in the Twentieth Century: Painting and Sculpture 1913–1993*. May 8–July 25. Catalogue, with texts by Brooks Adams, David Anfam, Richard Armstrong, John Beardsley, Neal Benezra, Arthur C. Danto, Abraham A. Davidson, Wolfgang Max Faust, Mary Emma Harris, Christos M. Joachimides, Thomas Kellein, Donald Kuspit, Mary Lublin, Karal Ann Marling, Barbara Moore, Francis V. O. O'Connor, Achille Bonito Oliva, Stephen Polcari, Carter Ratcliff, Norman Rosenthal, Irving Sandler, Wieland Schmied, Peter Selz, Gail Stavitsky, and Douglas Tallack. Traveled to Royal Academy of Arts, London, Sept. 16–Dec. 12.

1994
PaceWildenstein, New York. *Sculptors' Maquettes*. Jan. 14–Feb. 12.

The Museum of Modern Art, New York. *For Twenty-five Years: Brooke Alexander Editions*. Jan. 27–May 17. Brochure, with text by Wendy Weitman.

National Gallery of Art, Washington, D.C. *Gemini G.E.L.: Recent Prints and Sculpture*. June 5–Oct. 2. Catalogue, with texts by Ruth E. Fine and Charles Ritchie.

Large-Scale Projects

David Platzker

For detailed information on the large-scale projects, see: *Claes Oldenburg: Large-Scale Projects, 1977–1980.* New York: Rizzoli, 1980; and *Claes Oldenburg Coosje van Bruggen: Large-Scale Projects.* New York: The Monacelli Press, 1994. Entries are followed by related articles, books, and reviews.

Installation of *Lipstick (Ascending) on Caterpillar Tracks*, Beinecke Plaza, Yale University, New Haven, Conn., May 15, 1969; removed March 1970. Reconstruction installed and inaugurated, Samuel F. B. Morse College, Yale University, Oct. 17, 1974. (See also Solo and Two-Person Exhibitions: Yale University Art Gallery, *The Lipstick Comes Back*, 1974; and Group Exhibitions: The Museum of Modern Art, New York, *High and Low: Modern Art and Popular Culture*, 1990.)
—Darnton, John. "Oldenburg Hopes His Art Will Make Imprint at Yale." *The New York Times*, May 16, 1969, pp. 37, 76.
—Diehl, Jackson. "Enthusiastic Crowd Welcomes Oldenburg Lipstick Erection." *Yale Daily News* (New Haven, Conn.), Oct. 18, 1974, p. 1.
—Grace Glueck. "Oldenburg Lipstick Rejoins Yale with Cosmetic Repairs." *The New York Times*, Oct. 19, 1974, section L, p. 33.
—Kroll, Jack. "A Lipstick for Yale." *Newsweek* (New York), June 2, 1969, p. 69.
—*The* Lipstick *Comes Back* (exh. cat.). New Haven, Conn.: Yale University Art Gallery, 1974.
—Oldenburg, Claes. "Notes on the Lipstick Monument." *Novum Organum* (New Haven, Conn.), no. 7 (May 15, 1969). (Poster.)
—Oldenburg, Claes. *Photo Log, May 1974–August 1976.* Stuttgart: Hansjörg Mayer; New York: Store Days, 1976.
—Price, Jonathan. "Claes Oldenburg: Or I Spent Four Very Long Years at Yale—I Can't Remember Anything About Them." *Yale Alumni Magazine* (New Haven, Conn.) 32, no. 3 (Dec. 1968), pp. 26–31.
—Rose, Barbara. "Oldenburg Joins the Revolution." *New York Magazine* 2, no. 2 (June 2, 1969), pp. 54–57.
—Shapiro, David. "Sculpture as Experience: The Monument that Suffered." *Art in America* (New York) 62, no. 3 (May–June 1974), pp. 55–58.
—"The 'Vasari' Diary: Can a Three-Story-High Lipstick on Tank Treads Find Happiness Again in a Secluded College Courtyard?" *Art News* (New York) 73, no. 10 (Dec. 1974), pp. 18–19.
—Winer, Jem. "Oldenburg Lipstick May Rise Once More at Yale." *Yale Daily News* (New Haven, Conn.), Feb. 26, 1974, p. 1.

Installation of *Trowel* as part of *Sonsbeek 71: Sonsbeek buiten de perken*, Arnhem, The Netherlands (see Group Exhibitions), June 18, 1971. Later destroyed. Installation of *Trowel I* (with Coosje van Bruggen), Rijksmuseum Kröller-Müller, Otterlo, The Netherlands, Aug. 30, 1976. Installation of *Trowel II* (with van Bruggen), Donald M. Kendall Sculpture Gardens at PepsiCo, Purchase, N.Y., July 9, 1984.
—Blok, Cor. "Sonsbeek '71." *Art International* (Lugano) 15, no. 9 (Nov. 20, 1971), pp. 47–49.
—Kurtz, Bruce. "Sonsbeek 71: Beyond Lawn and Order." *Arts Magazine* (New York) 46, no. 1 (Sept. 1971), pp. 50–52.
—Linville, Kasha. "Sonsbeek: Speculations, Impressions." *Artforum* (New York) 10, no. 2 (Oct. 1971), pp. 54–61.
—Oldenburg, Claes. *Photo Log, May 1974–August 1976.* Stuttgart: Hansjörg Mayer; New York: Store Days, 1976.

—*Sonsbeek 71: Sonsbeek buiten de perken* (exh. cat.). Arnhem: Sonsbeek Foundation, 1971, pp. 54–56.

Inauguration of *Clothespin*, Centre Square Plaza, Fifteenth and Market streets, Philadelphia, July 1, 1976.
—Donohoe, Victoria. "The Nation: Philadelphia: Clothespin and Sculptural Oratory." *Art News* (New York) 75, no. 7 (Sept. 1976), pp. 88–89.
—Donohoe, Victoria. "Claes Oldenburg: Monuments to the Consumer Society." *The Philadelphia Inquirer*, Nov. 19, 1976, section H, p. 8.
—Oldenburg, Claes. *Photo Log, May 1974–August 1976.* Stuttgart: Hansjörg Mayer; New York: Store Days, 1976.

Inauguration of *Batcolumn* (with Coosje van Bruggen), Harold Washington Social Security Center, 600 West Madison Street, Chicago, April 14, 1977. Brochure, *Batcolumn: Oldenburg—Chicago.*
—Artner, Alan G. "Oldenburg Sculpture on Baseball Set." *Chicago Tribune*, June 8, 1976, p. 4.
—Artner, Alan G. "'Simple, Pure, Suggestive Object': Oldenburg Battles 'Batcolumn' Myths." *Chicago Tribune*, April 14, 1977, section 2, pp. 1, 3.
—Artner, Alan G., and Paul Gapp. "The Species of the Spaces—Time to Go to Bat for Those Objets d'Plaza . . . that Are Sometimes Splendid Except They Don't Suit the Site." *Chicago Tribune*, April 24, 1977, section 6, pp. 2–12.
—Artner, Alan G., and Paul Gapp. "The Nation: Chicago: Fair Game." *Art News* (New York) 76, no. 6 (summer 1977), pp. 158–59.
—"Arts: The City with Big Shoulders Gets a Ten-Story Baseball Bat by Oldenburg." *People Weekly* (New York) 7, no. 17 (May 2, 1977), p. 100.
—Galloway, Paul. "A Truckload of Clout's Swinging Its Way into City." *Chicago Sun-Times*, April 8, 1977, pp. 5, 34.
—Gilbreth, Edward S., and Robert G. Schultz. "Going to Bat for U.S.-Paid Art." *Chicago Daily News*, April 19, 1977.
—Hanson, Henry. "Sculpture Home Run: One-Hundred-Foot Ball Bat Created for Us." *Chicago Daily News*, June 8, 1976, pp. 1, 14.
—Hanson, Henry. "Claes' Striking Sculpture." *Chicago Daily News*, April 2–3, 1977, p. 10.
—Haydon, Harold. "Oldenburg Goes Bananas." *Chicago Sunday Sun-Times*, May 1, 1977, "Art," p. 3.
—King, Seth S. "A Giant Baseball Bat Sculpture Dedicated in Chicago Ceremony." *The New York Times*, April 15, 1977, section A, p. 14.
—Rapoport, Ron. "The Batcolumn: Well, It Is and It Isn't." *Chicago Sun-Times*, April 14, 1977, p. 154.
—Rose, Barbara. "Public Art's Big Hit: Oldenburg Bats High in Chicago." *Vogue* (New York) 167, no. 7 (July 1977), pp. 118–19, 145.
—Tomkins, Calvin. "Profiles: Look What I've Got Here." *The New Yorker* 53, no. 43 (Dec. 12, 1977), pp. 55–88.

Installation of *Pool Balls* (with Coosje van Bruggen), Aaseeterrassen, Münster, Germany, June 6, 1977. (See also Group Exhibitions: Westfälisches Landesmuseum für Kunst und Kulturgeschichte, Münster, *Skulptur: Austellung in Münster*, 1977.)
—"Claes Oldenburg: 'rollte' Kugeln in Roxels Mitte." *Westfälische Nachrichten*, April 1, 1987.

Lipstick (Ascending) on Caterpillar Tracks, *1974 reconstruction of a 1969 original, installed at Samuel F. B. Morse College, Yale University, New Haven, Connecticut.*

—Granath, Olle. "Skulpturutställning i Münster: Från statisk heroism till social biljard." *Dagens Nyheter* (Stockholm), July 22, 1977, p. 3.
—Ippisch, Marcus. "Zweimal eine halbe: Die Kugeln am Aasee erhalten Gesellschaft." *Allgemeine Zeitung*, March 3, 1987.
—M., K. P. "Giant Pool Balls oder die Geburt der Kunst." *Münstersche Zeitung*, May 17, 1977.
—Obermeyer, Erhard. "Als wenn win Riese Billard spielte . . ." *Westfälische Nachrichten*, May 17, 1977.
—"Zur Eröffnung der Skulptur '87: Keine vierte Aasee-Kugel." *Kaufen+Sparen*, June 4, 1987.

Inauguration of *Crusoe Umbrella* (with Coosje van Bruggen), Nollen Plaza, Civic Center of Greater Des Moines, Nov. 29, 1979.
—Baldwin, Nick. "Civic Center Picks Artist for Sculpture Plan." *The Des Moines Register*, Nov. 27, 1978, section A, pp. 1, 6.
—Baldwin, Nick. "The Man and His Umbrella: Giant Downtown Umbrella Makes Homage to Defoe." *The Des Moines Register*, Feb. 20, 1979, section B, p. 10.
—Baldwin, Nick. "'Umbrella' Installation to Start Today." *The Des Moines Register*, Nov. 27, 1979, section A, p. 4.
—Baldwin, Nick. "Explorer Oldenburg." *The Des Moines Sunday Register*, Dec. 16, 1979, section C, p. 5.
—Baldwin, Nick. "How to Build an Umbrella." *Picture* (magazine of *The Des Moines Sunday Register*), March 30, 1980, pp. 18−20.
—Ballantine, Elizabeth. "Claes and His Umbrella." *The Des Moines Register*, Nov. 30, 1979, section B, p. 1.
—Brown, Dave. "'Crusoe Umbrella' Draws Early Stares." *Des Moines Tribune*, Nov. 27, 1979, pp. 1, 3.
—Doak, Richard. "Reaction to 'Umbrella': Partly Cloudy." *Des Moines Tribune*, April 17, 1979, p. 1.
—Gordon, Bill. "'Umbrella' for Nollen Plaza?" *Des Moines Tribune*, Feb. 19, 1979, p. 1.
—Graham, Diane. "D.M. Umbrella Sculpture Draws Some Puzzled Looks." *The Des Moines Register*, March 12, 1979, p. 1.
—"Opening of the Umbrella." *The Des Moines Register*, Nov. 28, 1979, section 2, p. 1.

Inauguration of *Flashlight* (with Coosje van Bruggen), University of Nevada, Las Vegas, March 12, 1981.
—Bentley, Colleen. "Famed Sculptor to 'Light Up' UNLV." *Las Vegas Sun*, Jan. 27, 1980, p. 15.
—Bouton, Ken. "UNLV Flashlight a Kooky Proposal." *The Valley Times* (Las Vegas), Feb. 5, 1980, section A, p. 2.
—Hillinger, Charles. "All of Las Vegas Turned On by the 'Flashlight.'" *Los Angeles Times*, Sept. 14, 1988, section I, pp. 3, 32.
—Kelley, Jeff. "Claes Oldenburg's 'Flashlight.'" *Arts Magazine* (New York) 55, no. 10 (June 1981), pp. 100−02.
—Kuzins, Rebecca. "UNLV Flashlight Sculpture Lighted." *Las Vegas Review-Journal*, March 13, 1981.
—Levy, Mark. "Reviews: Las Vegas: Claes Oldenburg, University of Nevada." *Artforum* (New York) 20, no. 1 (Sept. 1981), p. 82.
—Verbon, Dave. "Giant Flashlight Arrives in LV." *The Valley Times* (Las Vegas), March 11, 1981, pp. 1−2.

Installation of *Split Button* (with Coosje van Bruggen), Levy Park, University of Pennsylvania, Philadelphia, June 25, 1981; inaugurated Nov. 6, 1981.

—Seltzer, Ruth. "Button, Button, Who'll Get the Button? Why, We Will." *Philadelphia Inquirer*, March 29, 1981, section G, p. 4.

Inauguration of *Hat in Three Stages of Landing* (with Coosje van Bruggen), Sherwood Park, Salinas, Calif., March 26, 1982.
—Doty, Betty Farrell. "Art World Awaits." *Salinas Californian*, Sept. 11, 1981, p. 15.
—Doty, Betty Farrell. "Salinas Will Don Oldenburg 'Hats.'" *Salinas Californian*, March 22, 1982, pp. 1, 10.
—Doty, Betty Farrell. "Oldenburg's Hats Surprise Viewers." *Salinas Californian*, March 23, 1982, p. 1.
—Doty, Betty Farrell. "Those Big Yellow 'Hats' Bring City Touch of 'Claes.'" *Salinas Californian*, March 26, 1982, p. 1.
—Doty, Betty Farrell. "Salinas Welcomes Oldenburg 'Hats.'" *Salinas Californian*, March 27, 1982, p. 1.
—Muchnic, Suzanne. "Oldenburgs Hang Their Hats in Salinas." *Calendar* (magazine of *Los Angeles Times*), April 4, 1982, p. 88.
—Robledo, Roberto. "Claes Oldenburg's 'Hats' Finally in Place." *Salinas Californian*, March 24, 1982, p. 1.
—Schultz, Ken. "Three-Level Hat Sculpture Settles onto Site Next to Salinas Rodeo Grounds." *Monterey Peninsula Herald*, March 24, 1982, section 2, p. 19.
—Temko, Allan. "Oldenburg Tips His Hats to Salinas." *San Francisco Chronicle*, April 8, 1982, p. 43.
—Wood, Jim. "Salinas Townfolk Splitting Hairs over Three Larger-than-Life Hats." *San Francisco Sunday Examiner and Chronicle*, March 28, 1982, section A, pp. 6–7.

Installation of *Spitzhacke* (*Pickaxe*; with Coosje van Bruggen) as part of *Documenta 7*, Kassel (see Group Exhibitions), May 1982.
—Kimpel, Harald, and Johanna Werckmeister. *Aversion/Akzeptanz*. Marburg, Germany: Jonas, 1992.

Inauguration of *Gartenschlauch* (*Garden Hose*; with Coosje van Bruggen), Stühlinger Park, Freiburg im Breisgau, Germany, May 2, 1983.
—Dienst, Rolf-Gunter. "Der Gartenschlauch—ein hintergründiges Signet." *Frankfurter Allgemeine Zeitung*, May 6, 1983, p. 27.
—*Der Gartenschlauch von Claes Oldenburg und Coosje van Bruggen.* Freiburg im Breisgau, Germany: Kunstverein Freiburg, 1983.
—Gassert, Siegmar. "Mammut-Schlauch." *Basler Zeitung* (Basel), April 19, 1983, p. 43.
—H., D. P. "Werben um die Kunden." *Badische Zeitung* (Freiburg im Breisgau), May 3, 1983, p. 23.
—H., D. P. "'Gartenschlauch' soll Anziehungspunkt werden." *Badische Zeitung* (Freiburg im Breisgau), May 3, 1983.
—K., R. "Werkshalle wurde zum Riesenatelier." *Mannesmannröhren-Werke aktuell*, Feb. 10, 1983.
—M., H. J. "Oldenburgs Schlauch." *Die Zeit* (Hamburg), May 6, 1983, p. 56.
—Müller, Hans-Joachim. "Unternehmen Wasserhahn mit Gartenschlauch." *Badische Zeitung* (Freiburg im Breisgau), April 2, 1983, p. 10.
—Müller, Hans-Joachim. "Starkes Stück." *Badische Zeitung* (Freiburg im Breisgau), May 2, 1983, p. 15.
—"Der Schlauch von Freiburg." *Der Spiegel* (Frankfurt), May 9, 1983, p. 175.

Installation of *Screwarch* (with Coosje van Bruggen), Museum Boymans-van Beuningen, Rotterdam, May 1983. (See Solo and Two-Person Exhibitions: Museum Boymans-van Beuningen, Rotterdam, *The Screwarch Project*, 1983.)
—Koepplin, Dieter. "Oldenburgs Brücke." *Basler Magazin* (Basel), Feb. 19, 1983, p. 9.
—Zumbrink, Jan. "Zaal vol jonge wilden in Boymans." *Haarlem Dagblad*, Aug. 11, 1983.

Installation and inauguration of *Cross Section of a Toothbrush with Paste, in a Cup, on a Sink: Portrait of Coosje's Thinking* (with Coosje van Bruggen), Haus Esters Krefeld, Germany, Nov. 25, 1983.
—*Claes Oldenburg: Cross Section of a Toothbrush with Paste in a Cup on a Sink: Portrait of Coosje's Thinking.* Krefeld: Krefelder Kunstmuseen, 1985. Texts by Gerhard Storck and Oldenburg; in German and English.
—Franklin, Mark. "U of H Scrubs Sculpture." *The Hartford Courant* (Hartford, Conn.), March 25, 1981, section A, pp. 1, 12.
—Frese, Hans Martin. "Der Krefelder Kunstverein wird 100 Jahre alt: Zum Jubiläum eine Zahnbürste." *Rheinische Post* (Düsseldorf), March 2, 1983.
—Madden, Richard L. "School Rejects a 'Free' Oldenburg." *The New York Times*, March 28, 1981, pp. 1, 26.
—"The 'Vasari' Diary: Brushed Off." *Art News* (New York) 80, no. 6 (June 1981), pp. 11–12, 14.

Inauguration of *Stake Hitch* (with Coosje van Bruggen), Dallas Museum of Art, April 28, 1984.
—Kutner, Janet. "Dallas to Receive Oldenburg Sculpture for New Museum." *Dallas Morning News*, April 4, 1983, p. 9.
—Kutner, Janet. "DMA's Bold New 'Stake': Oldenburg Work Fills Main Gallery." *The Dallas Morning News*, April 29, 1984, section C, pp. 1, 6.
—Marvel, Bill. "Oldenburg Stakes Out His Space." *Dallas Times Herald*, March 17, 1983, pp. 1, 12.
—Marvel, Bill. "A Texas-Size 'Stake': New Sculpture Measures Up to Vast Quarters." *Dallas Times Herald*, May 2, 1984, section E, pp. 3, 5.
—"Museum Will Feature Claes Oldenburg Sculpture." *Dallas Downtown News*, March 28, 1983, p. 12.

Inauguration of *Balancing Tools* (with Coosje van Bruggen), Vitra International AG, Weil am Rhein, Germany, May 5, 1984.
—Baumann, Wolfgang. "Ein Riesentor aus Hammer, Zange, Schraubenzieher." *Mannheimer Morgen*, August 17, 1984.
—Gassert, Siegmar. "Oldenburgs unbedingte Lebensnähe." *Basler Zeitung* (Basel), May 5, 1984, section 4, p. 43.
—Gehry, Frank O. "Excerpts from the Rietveld Lecture." *Kunst & Museumjournaal* (Amsterdam) 2, no. 6 (1991), pp. 47–53.
—Schwander, Maria, and Theodora Vischer. "Skulpturen für einen Park." *Basler Magazin* (Basel), no. 36 (Sept. 8, 1984), pp. 1–2.

Inauguration of *Toppling Ladder with Spilling Paint* (with Coosje van Bruggen), Loyola Law School, Los Angeles, Sept. 26, 1986.
—Drohojowska, Hunter. "Unveiling Loyola's New Ladder of Success." *Los Angeles Herald Examiner*, Sept. 30, 1986, section B, p. 3.
—Greenwald, Robert, and Dean DeGruccio. "'The Toppling Ladder' Viewpoint #1; Viewpoint #2." *The Loyola Reporter* (Los Angeles), Nov. 3, 1986, p. 3.

—Muchnic, Suzanne. "Oldenburg 'Ladder' Has a Leg to Stand on in L.A." *Los Angeles Times*, Sept. 24, 1986, section 6, pp. 1, 6.
—"Oldenburg Sculpture Nears Completion." *Loyola Lawyer* (Los Angeles) 4, no. 2 (winter 1986), p. 1.

Inauguration of *Spoonbridge and Cherry* (with Coosje van Bruggen), Minneapolis Sculpture Garden, Walker Art Center, May 11, 1988.
—Friedman, Martin. "Growing the Garden." *Design Quarterly* (Minneapolis), no. 141 (1988), pp. 4–42.
—Gannon, Tom. "Boat Builders Venture into New Waters with Art Projects." *The Boston Sunday Globe*, March 6, 1988, p. 44.
—"Hey, Lick at This: Minneapolis is Spoon-Fed by Claes Oldenburg." *People Weekly* (New York), Nov. 21, 1988, pp. 201–02.
—Martin, Mary Abbe. "Walker Garden to Offer a Sundae Delight Served by Oldenburg." *Minneapolis Star and Tribune*, Aug. 17, 1986, section G, p. 2.
—Millet, Larry. "Museum without Walls." *St. Paul Pioneer Press Dispatch*, Sept. 4, 1988, section D, pp. 1, 3.
—Taylor, Sue. "Report from Minneapolis: Garden City." *Art in America* (New York) 76, no. 12 (Dec. 1988), pp. 28–37.
—Van Siclen, Bill. "Fifty-Foot Spoon Span Is Made Shipshape in Bristol Yard." *Providence Journal-Bulletin*, Jan. 30, 1988, section A, pp. 1, 11.
—Weber, Bruce. "Pitted Against the Sky." *The New York Times Magazine*, April 17, 1988, p. 106.
—Weber, Bruce. "So What Happened?" *The New York Times*, Jan. 1, 1989, pp. 41–43.

Inauguration of *Dropped Bowl with Scattered Slices and Peels* (with Coosje van Bruggen), Metro-Dade Open Space Park, Miami, March 30, 1990.
—Ahlander, Leslie Judd. "Oldenburgs Prepare to Bowl Miami Over." *The Miami News*, March 6, 1986, section C, p. 2.
—Bell, Maya. "Fragmented Oranges: The Essence of Miami." *The Orlando Sentinel*, April 1, 1990, section F, pp. 1, 11.
—Harper, Paula. "Public Art Is a Public Concern." *The Miami News*, May 24, 1985, section C, p. 8.
—Kohen, Helen L. "Oldenburg's Fountain a Fresh Symbol for Miami." *The Miami Herald*, June 16, 1985, section K, p. 2.
—Kohen, Helen L. "'Dropped Bowl' Makes a Splashy Debut: Playful Sculpture Captures Essence of the Big Orange." *The Miami Herald*, March 25, 1990, section I, pp. 1, 6.
—Meadows, Gail. "'Dropped Bowl' Makes a Splashy Debut: Made-for-Miami Work Is Artists' Most Complex to Date." *The Miami Herald*, March 25, 1990, section I, pp. 1, 6.
—Schwartzman, Allan. "Fruit of the Boom." *House and Garden* (New York) 162, no. 11 (Nov. 1990), pp. 202–03.

Installation of *Bicyclette Ensevelie* (*Buried Bicycle*; with Coosje van Bruggen), Parc de La Villete, Paris, Nov. 1990.
—Nuridsany, Michel. *La Commande publique*. Paris: Réunion des Musées Nationaux, 1991.

Installation of *Monument to the Last Horse* (with Coosje van Bruggen), Seagram Plaza, New York, June 1–Aug. 24, 1991. Inauguration of permanent installation, The Chinati Foundation, Marfa, Tex., Oct. 12, 1991.
—Brenson, Michael. "Cityful of Sculpture under the Sky." *The New York Times*, July 26, 1991, section C, pp. 1, 28.
—*Monument to the Last Horse*, 1991 (drawing). *Interview* (New York) 22, no. 1 (Jan. 1992), p. 6.

—Stevens, Mark. "Art Oasis." *Vanity Fair* (New York) 55, no. 7 (July 1992), pp. 106–11.

Inauguration of *Binoculars, Chiat/Day Building* (with Frank O. Gehry and Coosje van Bruggen), Chiat/Day, Inc., 340 Main Street, Venice, Calif., Sept. 23, 1991.
—"Frank Gehry in Collaboration with Claes Oldenburg and Coosje van Bruggen: *Chiat/Day Building, Venice, California.*" *Architectural Design* (London) 62, nos. 7–8 (July–Aug. 1992), pp. 56–61.
—"Frank O. Gehry and Associates: Chiat/Day Main Street, Venice, California, U.S.A." *GA Document* (Tokyo) no. 32 (March 1992), pp. 8–21.
—Garcia-Marques, Francesca. "Frank O. Gehry and Associates/Claes Oldenburg and Coosje van Bruggen: Office Building, Venice/California." *Domus* (Milan), no. 735 (Feb. 1992), pp. 29–39, XXII.
—Jencks, Charles. "Towards the Perfected Office." *Architectural Design* (London) 62, nos. 7–8 (July–Aug. 1992), pp. 63–65.
—Kaufman, Margo. "A Striped Warehouse Joins the Local Color." *The New York Times*, Aug. 18, 1988, pp. 19, 23.
—Murphy, Jim. "A Venice Collaboration." *Progressive Architecture* (Stamford, Conn.), no. 3 (March 1992), pp. 66–73.
—Steele, James. "The Myth of LA and the Reinvention of the City." *Architectural Design* (London) 62, nos. 7–8 (July–Aug. 1992), pp. 66–67.

Inauguration of *Free Stamp* (with Coosje van Bruggen), Willard Park, Cleveland, Nov. 15, 1991.
—Barron, James. "Five States: Nice Place Not to Visit." *The New York Times*, May 19, 1986, section A, p. 12.
—Cullinan, Helen. "Sohio Puts Its Stamp on City Art." *The Plain Dealer* (Cleveland), Aug. 2, 1985, section A, pp. 1, 10.
—Cullinan, Helen. "Standard Oil Seeks New Pad for Desk Stamp Sculpture." *The Plain Dealer* (Cleveland), April 25, 1986, section A, pp. 1, 16.
—Cullinan, Helen. "'Stamp' Fans Stump for Art." *The Plain Dealer* (Cleveland), May 3, 1986, section E, pp. 1, 7.
—Cullinan, Helen. "Exiled Art Welcomed to New Home." *The Plain Dealer* (Cleveland), Nov. 16, 1991, p. 2B.
—Grossman, Ron. "In Defense of Stomped Stamp Art." *Chicago Tribune*, July 29, 1986, section 5, pp. 1, 3.
—Hagan, Jeff. "Free Speech and Furrowed Brows: Will the Free Stamp Do Justice to the City." *Cleveland Edition*, Sept. 5, 1991, p. 10.
—List, S. K. "Rubbing Out the Rubber Stamp." *Rubber Stamp Madness* (New York) 29, no. 6 (Sept.–Oct. 1986), pp. 3–5.
—Litt, Steven. "'Free Stamp' Makes Its Mark." *The Plain Dealer* (Cleveland), Nov. 14, 1991, section E, pp. 9, 16.
—Litt, Steven. "At Last, the Stamp of Approval." *The Plain Dealer* (Cleveland), Nov. 16, 1991, section D, pp. 1, 3.
—Osinski, Bill. "Suffering the Stamp of Rejection: Standard Oil Enrages Artists." *Akron Beacon Journal*, Nov. 30, 1986, section A, pp. 1, 18.
—Russell, Mark. "Free Stamp Sculpture Gets Spot by City Hall." *The Plain Dealer* (Cleveland), April 23, 1991, section A, pp. 1, 6.
—"Standard Oil Chief Stomps the Forty-Eight-Foot Rubber Stamp." *The Wall Street Journal* (New York), April 25, 1986, p. 7.
—Talbott, Stephen. "Oldenburg Seeks to Put 'Stamp' on Willard Park." *The Plain Dealer* (Cleveland), Feb. 7, 1987, section A, pp. 1, 12.

—Thomas, Kate. "Sculpture Raises Ire of Big Oil." *The Houston Post*, April 26, 1986, section E, p. 1.
—Wood, James M. "Et Cetera: Why *Not* Free Stamp?" *Cleveland Magazine*, Oct. 1986, pp. 168–69, 178.

Inauguration of *Mistos* (*Match Cover*; with Coosje van Bruggen), La Vall d'Hebron, Barcelona, April 2, 1992.
—Apgar, Garry. "Public Art and the Remaking of Barcelona." *Art in America* (New York) 79, no. 2 (Feb. 1991), pp. 108–21, 159.
—*The Barcelona Plazas: Preview of an Urban Experience, Notes on the Proceedings of a Symposium Held in Conjunction with an Exhibition at the Spanish Institute, Inc.* New York: The Spanish Institute, 1987.
—Bradley, Kim. "Front Page: Public Art in Barcelona." *Art in America* (New York) 80, no. 6 (June 1992), p. 29.
—*La Vall d'Hebron: Barcelona '92.* Barcelona: HOLSA, 1992.

Inauguration of *Bottle of Notes* (with Coosje van Bruggen), Central Gardens, Middlesbrough, England, Sept. 24, 1993.
—Bickers, Patricia. "Claes Oldenburg" (interview). *Art Monthly* (London), no. 171 (Nov. 1993), pp. 3–11.
—Cork, Richard. "Positive Message in a Bottle." *The Times* (London), Sept. 22, 1993, p. 35.
—Graham-Dixon, Andrew. "Bottle of Pop." *Vogue* (London) 154, no. 8, no. 2317 (Aug. 1990), pp. 128–35.
—Graham-Dixon, Andrew. "A Lot of Bottle." *The Independent* (London), Sept. 28, 1993, p. 12.
—"Message in a Bottle." *The Shields Gazette* (South Shields), March 13, 1993, p. 1.
—"Message in a Bottle." *Middlesbrough News*, no. 51 (Oct. 1993), cover, p. 2.

Inauguration of *Inverted Collar and Tie* (with Coosje van Bruggen), West End Str. 1, Mainzer Landstrasse 58, Frankfurt, June 21, 1994.
—Mielcke, Gabriele. *Inverted Collar and Tie.* Ostfildern: Cantz, 1994.
—Y., D. "13 Tonnen Schlips im Schneckentempo." *Frankfurter Allgemeine Zeitung*, June 16, 1994, p. 39.

Inauguration of *Shuttlecocks* (with Coosje van Bruggen), The Nelson-Atkins Museum of Art, Kansas City, Mo., July 6, 1994.
—Abouhalkah, Yael T. "A Lot Is Happening Behind the Scenes in Shuttlecocks Dispute." *The Kansas City Star* (Metropolitan Edition), Feb. 25, 1993, section C, p. 5.
—Alm, Rick. "I Don't Know a Lot about Art, but Really . . ." *The Kansas City Star* (Eastern Jackson County Edition), April 8, 1993, p. 12.
—Gurley, George. "Birdies for Nelson Are Serious." *The Kansas City Star* (Metropolitan Edition), April 8, 1993, section C, p. 5.
—"The Shuttlecocks Are Coming." *The Kansas City Star*, Dec. 12, 1993, section C, p. 6.

Performance History and Selected Filmography

David Platzker

Performances

Performers' names appear as at the time of the performances or as given in performance programs. Entries are followed by related articles, books, and reviews.

Snapshots from the City, Judson Gallery, New York, Feb. 29, March 1–2, 1960. (Performed as part of *Ray Gun Spex*, a series of performances by various artists, and in conjunction with *Ray Gun Show* [see Solo and Two-Person Exhibitions].)
Performers: Pat Muschinski, Claes Oldenburg, and Lucas Samaras.
—Kiplinger, Suzanne. "Ray Gun." *The Village Voice* (New York), Feb. 17, 1960, p. 11.
—Tallmer, Jerry. "Theatre (?): Three New Happenings." *The Village Voice* (New York), Jan. 13, 1960, p. 9.
—"Up-Beats." *Time* (New York) 75, no. 11 (March 14, 1960), p. 80.

Blackouts (in four parts: "Chimneyfires," "Erasers," "The Vitamin Man," and "Butter and Jam"), Reuben Gallery, New York, Dec. 16–20, 1960. (Performed as part of *Christmas Varieties*, a program of performances by various artists.)
Performers: Claes Oldenburg and Pat Muschinski; lights and sound: Max Baker.
—P[etersen], V[alerie]. "Reviews and Previews: Varieties." *Art News* (New York) 59, no. 10 (Feb. 1961), p. 16.

Set and costume designs for performance by Aileen Passloff and Dance Company, Fashion Institute of Technology, New York, Feb. 5, 1961.

Circus (Ironworks/Fotodeath) (included *Pickpocket*, a slide presentation, during intermission), Reuben Gallery, New York, Feb. 21–26, 1961. Performers: Olga Adorno, Edgar Blakeney, Henry Geldzahler, Gloria Graves, Marilyn Jaffee, Carl Lehmann-Haupt, Chippy McKellen, Pat Muschinski, Claes Oldenburg, Lucas Samaras, Claire Selley, Clifford Smith, Judy Tirsch, and Tom Wesselmann; lights and sound: Max Baker.
—J[ohnston], J[ill]. "Art without Walls: Claes Oldenburg." *Art News* (New York) 60, no. 2 (April 1961), pp. 36, 57.
—Nichols, Robert. "Entertainment: Ironworks Fotodeath." *The Village Voice* (New York), March 2, 1961, p. 10.
—Oldenburg, Claes. "Fotodeath." *Tulane Drama Review* (New Orleans) 10, no. 2 (winter 1965), pp. 85–93.
—Restany, Pierre. "Une Tentative américaine de synthèse de l'information artistique: Les Happenings." *Domus* (Milan), no. 405 (Aug. 1963), pp. 35–42.

Designs for performance by Aileen Passloff and Dance Company, Fashion Institute of Technology, New York, Jan. 20, 1962.

Ray Gun Theater (comprised of ten performances), Ray Gun Mfg. Co., 107 East Second Street, New York (in cooperation with Green Gallery, New York; performed in *The Store* [see Solo and Two-Person Exhibitions]). *Store Days I*, Feb. 23–24, 1962; performers: Milet Andreyevich, Terry Brook, Lette Eisenhauer, Gloria Graves, Mickey Henrion, Billy Klüver, Johanna Lawrenson, Jean-Jacques Lebel, Claes Oldenburg, Pat Oldenburg, Lucas Samaras, and Carolee Schneemann.
Store Days II, March 2–3, 1962; performers: Cora Baron, Rachel Drexler, Jackie Ferrara, Henry Geldzahler, Gloria Graves, Claes Oldenburg, Pat Oldenburg, Lucas Samaras, and Charlotte Tokayer. *Nekropolis I*, March 9–10, 1962; performers: Claes

Oldenburg, Pat Oldenburg, and Lucas Samaras. *Nekropolis II*, March 16–17, 1962; performers: Milet Andreyevich, Öyvind Fahlström, Irene Fornés, Maricla Moyano, Claes Oldenburg, Pat Oldenburg, John Rublowsky, and Lucas Samaras. *Injun (N.Y.C.) I*, April 20–21, 1962; performers: Terry Brook, Lette Eisenhauer, Claes Oldenburg, Pat Oldenburg, and Lucas Samaras. *Injun (N.Y.C.) II*, April 27–28, 1962; performers: Cora Baron, Lette Eisenhauer, Edward Epstein, Claes Oldenburg, Pat Oldenburg, and Lucas Samaras. *Voyages I*, May 4–5, 1962; performers: Milet Andreyevich, Cora Baron, Barbara Dilley, Irene Fornés, Claes Oldenburg, Pat Oldenburg, and Lucas Samaras. *Voyages II*, May 11–12, 1962; performers: Dominic Capobianco, Jackie Ferrara, Claes Oldenburg, Pat Oldenburg, and Lucas Samaras. *World's Fair I*, May 18–19, 1962; performers: Nikky, Claes Oldenburg, Pat Oldenburg, Robert, and Mia Rublowsky. *World's Fair II*, May 25–26, 1962; performers: Dominic Capobianco, Lette Eisenhauer, Claes Oldenburg, Pat Oldenburg, Lucas Samaras, and John Weber.

—"A Happening." *Scene* (New York), Aug. 1962, pp. 12–15.

—"'In' Audience Sees Girl Doused: What Happened? A Happening." *The New York Times*, April 30, 1962, p. 29.

—Johnson, Ellen H. "The Living Object." *Art International* (Zurich) 7, no. 1 (Jan. 25, 1963), pp. 42–45.

—Johnston, Jill. "Off Off-B'way: 'Happenings' at Ray Gun Mfg. Co." *The Village Voice* (New York), April 26, 1962, p. 10.

—Johnston, Jill. "Reviews and Previews." *Art News* (New York) 61, no. 3 (May 1962), p. 55.

—Mayer, Robert. "Strange Things Are Just Happening." *Newsday* (New York), May 7, 1962, p. 1C.

—Oldenburg, Claes. *Injun and Other Histories (1960)*. New York: A Great Bear Pamphlet, 1966.

—Oldenburg, Claes. "*Injun*: The Script," "*Nekropolis II*: The Script," "*Store Days I*: The Script," "*Store Days II*: The Script," and "*World's Fair II*: The Script." In Michael Kirby, ed., *Happenings: An Illustrated Anthology*. New York: E. P. Dutton, 1965.

—Seckler, Dorothy Gees. "The Audience Is His Medium!" *Art in America* (New York) 51, no. 2 (April 1963), pp. 62–67.

—"What Happens at a Happening?" *Pageant* (Chicago) 18, no. 3 (Sept. 1962), pp. 122–27.

Injun, The Dallas Museum for Contemporary Arts, April 6–7, 1962. (Performed in conjunction with *1961* [see Group Exhibitions].) Performers: Russell Adams, Ronnie Cole, Jim Daugirda, Howard Doolittle, Nancy Ellison, Janie Grisham, Martha Hamm, Carolyn Higginbotham, Joseph Hobbs, Sue Jacobson, Joan Key, Paul Koeppe, Arthur McKnight, Gart McVean, Claes Oldenburg, Pat Oldenburg, Harold Pauley, Flora Reeder, Dennis Taylor, Peggy Wilson, Scott Wilson, Jim Woodson, and Edward Zelenak.

—Askew, Rual. "Reviews: Dallas." *Artforum* (San Francisco) 1, no. 1 (June 1962), p. 7.

—"In the Name of Art: A 'Happening's' Odd Appearance—Plotless, Scriptless, Formless." *National Observer* (New York), May 6, 1962, p. 4.

—Oldenburg, Claes. *Injun and Other Histories (1960)*. New York: A Great Bear Pamphlet, 1966.

—Porter, Bob. "New Yorker Brings 'Store.'" *Dallas Times Herald*, March 28, 1962, p. C11.

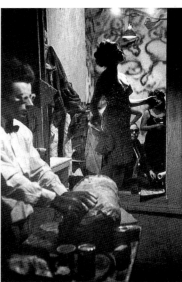

top, left and right:
Store Days II, *performed as part of* Ray Gun Theater *at Ray Gun Mfg. Co., 107 East Second Street, New York, March 2–3, 1962.*

bottom:
Nekropolis II, *performed as part of Ray Gun Theater, March 16–17, 1962.*

Injun (N.Y.C.) I, performed as part of Ray Gun Theater, *April 20–21, 1962.*

Injun, performance at the Dallas Museum for Contemporary Arts, April 6–7, 1962.

Sports, Green Gallery, New York, Oct. 5, 1962. (Performed in conjunction with *Claes Oldenburg* [see Solo and Two-Person Exhibitions].) Performers: Claes Oldenburg, Pat Oldenburg, and Lucas Samaras.

Gayety, Lexington Hall, University of Chicago, Feb. 8–10, 1963. Performers: Martha Ansara, Ann Bardacke, Harry Bouras, Lorraine Bouras, Peter Butterfield, Mary Davis, Norman Dayron, Barbara Dickerson, Ted Dickerson, Len Frazer, Kurt Hayl, George Kokines, Rosemary Kreinhofner, Dan Lyon, Pat Oldenburg, Toni Robinson, David Root, David Roth, Dan Russ, Ellen Sellenraad, Johann Sellenraad, John Snowday, Vern Zimmerman, and Roger Zoss.
—"Oldenburg Displays 'Happening.'" *Chicago Maroon*, Feb. 12, 1963, p. 1.
—Oldenburg, Claes. "*Gayety*: The Script." In Michael Kirby, ed. *Happenings: An Illustrated Anthology*. New York: E. P. Dutton, 1965.

Stars: A Farce for Objects, The Washington Gallery of Modern Art, Washington, D.C., April 24–25, 1963. (Performed in conjunction with *The Popular Image* [see Group Exhibitions].) Performers: Olga Adorno, Thomas Bartlett, Cathleen Bingham, Michael Booth, Gil Carther, Chris Denney, Jill Denney, Joan Fugazzi, Fred Goldfrank, Gloria Graves, Chris Harris, Gail Hillow, Ed Kelley, Charles Lilly, Joan Mason, Pat Oldenburg, Alan Raywid, Bette Rickerson, Thomas Roberts, Cindy Warren, and Clarence Wheat.
—Buchwald, Art. "Anything Can Happen." *New York Herald Tribune*, April 16, 1963, p. 21.
—Cheshire, Maxine. "What Happened Wasn't Too Clear." *The Washington Post*, April 25, 1963, section G, p. 3.
—C., R. L. "'A Happening.'" *The Washington Post*, April 25, 1963, section E, p. 22.
—Getlein, Frank. "Art Just 'Happens' on Pop's Night Out." *The Evening Star* (Washington, D.C.), April 25, 1963, p. 1.
—"Happenings: Pop Culture." *Time*, May 3, 1963, p. 73.
—"It Happened in Washington—But What?" *Newsweek* (New York), May 6, 1963, p. 25.
—Oldenburg, Claes. "Stars." In *Raw Notes*. Ed. Kasper König. Halifax, Canada: The Press of the Nova Scotia College of Art and Design, 1973.
—"This Happened to Be 'A Farce for Objects.'" *The Washington Post*, April 28, 1963, section F, p. 3.

Autobodys, parking lot of the American Institute of Aeronautics and Astronautics, Los Angeles, Dec. 9–10, 1963. Performers: Tony Berlant, John Daggett, Ken Dillon, Tom Etherton, Charles Frazier, Judy Gerowitz, Dejon Greene, Lloyd Hamrol, Nancy Hamrol, Jim Howell, Richard Matthews, Bobbie Neiman, Rolf Nelson, Claes Oldenburg, Pat Oldenburg, John Romeyn, Deborah Sussman, John Weber, Laurie Weber, and Santos Zuniga.
—Billeter, Erika. "Atelierbesuche bei fünf New Yorker Malern: Claes Oldenburg." *Speculum Artis* (Zurich) 17, no. 9 (Sept. 1965), pp. 34–38.
—Oldenburg, Claes. "*Autobodys*: The Script." In Michael Kirby, ed., *Happenings: An Illustrated Anthology*. New York: E. P. Dutton, 1965.
—Seidenbaum, Art. "Autobodys—Horsepowerful Art Composition on a Parking Lot." *Los Angeles Times*, Dec. 24, 1963, part 2, pp. 1–2.

Washes, Al Roon's Health Club, New York, May 22–23, 1965. (Performed as part of "First New York Theater Rally: Dance Concert III.") Performers: Richard Artschwager, Sarah Dalton, Marty Edelheit, Lette Eisenhauer, Helene Faison, Jackie Ferrara, Nancy Fish, Henry Geldzahler, Gloria Graves, Al Hansen, Alex Hay, Deborah Hay, Geoffrey Hendricks, Jon Hendricks, Michael Kirby, Barbara Lloyd, Yvonne Mulder, Anina Nosei, Pat Oldenburg, Richard Oldenburg, Dorothea Rockburne, Barbara Rose, Lucas Samaras, Raymond Saroff, Marjorie Strider, Elaine Sturtevant, David Whitney, and Rudy Wurlitzer.

—Geldzahler, Henry. "Happenings: Theater by Painters." *Hudson Review* (New York) 18, no. 4 (winter 1965–66), pp. 581–86.
—Oldenburg, Claes. "Washes." *Tulane Drama Review* (New Orleans) 10, no. 2 (winter 1965), pp. 108–18.
—Novick, Elizabeth. "Happenings in New York." *Studio International* (London) 172, no. 881 (Sept. 1966), pp. 154–59.

Piece for Telephone, Program 7, TV Studio, Eighty-first Street and Broadway, New York, May 24–26, 1965. (Performed as part of "First New York Theater Rally: Dance Concert III.") Claes Oldenburg calls from outside the theater to a phone placed on stage and speaks to anyone in the audience who gets up to answer. (No one did.)
—Novick, Elizabeth. "Happenings in New York." *Studio International* (London) 172, no. 881 (Sept. 1966), pp. 154–59.

Moveyhouse, Forty-first Street Theater, New York, Dec. 1–3, 16–17, 1965. (Performed as part of "Film-Makers' Cinematheque Festival.") Performers: Dominic Capobianco, Lette Eisenhauer, Jo Eno, John Jones, Fred Mueller, Claes Oldenburg, Pat Oldenburg, Ellen Sellenraad, and Johann Sellenraad; piano: Liz Stevens.

Gayety, *performance at the University of Chicago, February 8–10, 1963.*

Stars: A Farce for Objects, *performance at the Washington Gallery of Modern Art, Washington, D.C., April 24–25, 1963.*

—Johnston, Jill. "Three Theatre Events." *The Village Voice*, Dec. 23, 1967, p. 11.
—Mussman, Toby. "The Images of Robert Whitman." *Film Culture* (New York), no. 43 (winter 1966), p. 5.
—Oldenburg, Claes. "Moveyhouse." In *Raw Notes*. Ed. Kasper König. Halifax, Canada: The Press of the Nova Scotia College of Art and Design, 1973.

Massage, Moderna Museet, Stockholm, October 3–4, 6–7, 1966. (Performed in conjunction with *Claes Oldenburg: Skulpturer och teckningar* [see Solo and Two-Person Exhibitions].) Performers: István Almay, Gabrielle Björnstrand, Olle Granath, Six Maix, Claes Oldenburg, Pat Oldenburg, Mette Prawitz, and Rico Weber.
—Oldenburg, Claes. "Massage." In *Raw Notes*. Ed. Kasper König. Halifax, Canada: The Press of the Nova Scotia College of Art and Design, 1973.

Il Corso del Coltello (with Frank O. Gehry and Coosje van Bruggen), Campo dell'Arsenale, Venice, Sept. 6–8, 1985. Performance book by Gehry, Oldenburg, and van Bruggen, *Il Corso del Coltello: Menu*, published by Gruppo Finanziario Tessile, Turin and Gabriele Mazzotta, Milan. Produced by Gruppo Finanziario Tessile with the assistance of Germano Celant, Daniela Ferretti, Ida Gianelli, and Anna Martina. Performers: Guglielmo Aschieri, Ferruccio Bonato, Maria Grazia Calzà, Carmen Carlotta, Elena Cazzaniga, Valentina Cecchi, Germano Celant, Filippo Costi, Oscar D'Antiga, Giulio De Carli, Anna Falcone, Rossella Fossati, John Franklin, Giorgio Frisoni, Fabio Gagliardini, Federica Galbuseri, Luca

Washes, *performance at Al Roon's Health Club, New York, May 22–23, 1965.*

Gandini, Nicola Gattia, Alejo Gehry, Berta Gehry, Brina Gehry, Frank O. Gehry, Sami Gehry, Elena Giorcelli, Pontus Hulten, Angelo Jelmini, Maartje Kapteyn, Luca Locatelli, Carlo Alberto Maggiore, Gigi Mannito, Luisa Messinis, Lucia Miggiano, John Miller, Esther Musatti, Helbert Noorda, Claes Oldenburg, Mariangela Opici, Paola Pellanda, Pier Vincenzo Rinaldi, Michela Santuliana, Adilla Solazzi, Coosje van Bruggen, Sandra Varsico, and Valeria Visconti. Sound effects: Ferdinando Collico, Roberto Doati, and Paulus Kapteyn. Costumes: Marco Guglielmotto; with Alberto Frediani, Nadia Metelli, and Patrizia Monfalcone, Turin; and Cathy Lazar, Celeste Livingston, Alan Steele, and Marybeth Welch, New York. Props: Cantiere Astolfo, Murano, Venice; Yanick Castor, New York; C. W. Elmore, Tampa; John Franklin, New York; J. Robert Jennings, North Madison, Conn.; Mostrefiere, Turin; and Studio Paz, Cremona.

—Celant, Germano. "Sempre più grande." *Panorama* (Milan), Aug. 4, 1985, p. 101.
—*Il Corso del Coltello* (exh. cat.). New York: Gruppo GFT, 1986.
—*The Course of the Knife.* Milan: Electa, 1986.
—*Le Couteau navire* (exh. cat.). Milan: Electa, 1987.
—*El Cuchillo Barco* (exh. cat.). Milan: Electa, 1986.
—Dubin, Zan. "Oldenburg 'Knife' to Go on View in MOCA Plaza." *Calendar* (magazine of *Los Angeles Times*), Oct. 4, 1987, p. 105.
—Gianelli, Ida, and Umberto Allemandi. "Un cotello di 24 metri navigherà per i canali di Venezia." *Il Giornale dell'Arte* (Turin), no. 25 (July–Aug. 1985), pp. 21–22.
—van Bruggen, Coosje. "'Les Infos du Paradis': Il Corso del Coltello." *Parkett* (Zurich), no. 8 (Jan. 1986), pp. 98–109.
—van Bruggen, Coosje, Frank O. Gehry, and Claes Oldenburg. "Waiting for Dr. Coltello: A Project by Coosje van Bruggen, Frank O. Gehry, and Claes Oldenburg/Il Corso del Coltello, A Performance: Preliminary Script." *Artforum* (New York) 23, no. 1 (Sept. 1984), pp. 88–95.
—Wexler, Alice Ruth. "Venice, Sliced: Il Corso del Coltello." *High Performance* (Los Angeles) 8, no. 4 (1985), pp. 65–66.

Coltello Recalled: Reflections on a Performance (with Frank O. Gehry and Coosje van Bruggen), The Japanese American Cultural and Community Center, Los Angeles, April 8, 1988. Performers: John Baldessari, Germano Celant, James Clearwater, Maureen Dondanville, John Franklin, Frank O. Gehry, Cannon Hudson, Allan Kaprow, Gary Kornblau, James Linza, Leslie Lizotte, Claes Oldenburg, Vincenzo Rinaldi, Doug Roberts, Laura Stein, and Coosje van Bruggen.

Films

Snapshots of the City, 1960. (Film of *Snapshots from the City*, performance at Judson Gallery, New York, 1960.) 16 mm, black-and-white, sound, 5 minutes. By Stan Vanderbeek. Distributed by Film-Makers' Cooperative, New York.

Injun, 1962. (Film of *Injun*, performance at the Dallas Museum for Contemporary Arts, 1962.) 16 mm, black-and-white, silent, 12 minutes. By Roy Fridge. Produced by the Dallas Museum for Contemporary Arts. Not in circulation.

Happenings: One, 1962. (Film of *Ray Gun Theater* performances, Ray Gun Mfg. Co., 107 East Second Street, New York, 1962.) 16 mm, black-and-white, silent (sound on tape), 20 minutes 45 seconds. By Raymond Saroff. Introduction written and narrated by Brian O'Doherty.

Music by Morton Feldman. Distributed by Film-Makers' Cooperative, New York.

Happenings: Two, 1962. (Film of *Ray Gun Theater* performances, Ray Gun Mfg. Co., 107 East Second Street, New York, 1962.) 16 mm, black-and-white, silent (sound on tape), 22 minutes 30 seconds. By Raymond Saroff. Music by Morton Feldman. Distributed by Film-Makers' Cooperative, New York.

Ray Gun Theater (Store Days), 1974. (Film of *Ray Gun Theater* performances, Ray Gun Mfg. Co., 107 East Second Street, New York, 1962, including footage from *Happenings: One* and *Happenings: Two*, both 1962.) 16 mm, black-and-white, silent, 33 minutes. By Raymond Saroff. Edited by Lana Jokel. Not in circulation.

Pat's Birthday, 1962. (Film of events arranged by Oldenburg, Palisades, N.Y., June 1962.) 16 mm, black-and-white, sound, 13 minutes. By Robert Breer. Distributed by Film-Makers' Cooperative, New York.

Scarface and Aphrodite, 1963. (Film of *Gayety*, performance at Lexington Hall, University of Chicago, 1963.) 16 mm, black-and-white, sound, 15 minutes. By Vernon Zimmerman. Distributed by Film-Makers' Cooperative, New York.

Birth of the Flag I, II, 1974. (Film of events arranged by Oldenburg, New York State, June 1965.) 16 mm, black-and-white, silent, two parts, 19 minutes each. By Stan Vanderbeek, Diane Rochlin, and Sheldon Rochlin. Edited by Lana Jokel. Produced by Rudy Wurlitzer. Not in circulation.

USA: Artists—Claes Oldenburg, 1966. 16 mm, black-and-white, sound, 29 minutes. Written by Alan Solomon. Narrated by Jim Dine. Produced by Lane Slate for National Educational Television, Channel 13, New York, and broadcast June 21, 1966. Not in circulation.

Portrait of Claes Oldenburg, 1966. 16 mm, black-and-white, sound, 15 minutes. By Anders Wahlgren and Staffan Olzon. Produced by Moderna Museet, Stockholm. Unreleased.

Colossal Keepsake No. I, 1969, 1969. (Film of construction and installation of *Lipstick (Ascending) on Caterpillar Tracks*, Yale University, New Haven, Conn., 1969.) 16 mm, black-and-white and color, sound, 20 minutes. By Peter Hentschel and Bill Richardson. Distributed by Leo Castelli Gallery, New York.

Sort of a Commercial for an Icebag by Claes Oldenburg, 1969. Super-8 mm and 16 mm, color, sound, 20 minutes. Directed by Michael Hugo. Filmed by Eric Saarinen. Edited by John Hoffman. Sound by Howard Chesley. Produced by Gemini G.E.L., Los Angeles. Distributed by Gemini. G.E.L., and the Museum of Modern Art, New York.

The Great Ice Cream Robbery and *Claes Oldenburg Retrospective: Tate Gallery, London, 1970*, 1971. Two 16 mm films shown simultaneously on two screens, color, sound, 35 minutes. Directed by James Scott. Filmed by Adam B. Mill. Produced by the Arts Council of Great Britain. Not in circulation.

Possibly a Special for the Bag, 1970. Super-8 mm and 16 mm, color, sound, 30 minutes. Directed by Michael Hugo. Filmed by Eric Saarinen. Edited by John Hoffman. Sound by Howard Chesley. Produced and distributed by Gemini G.E.L., Los Angeles.

Claes Oldenburg, 1973–74. 16 mm, color, sound, 52 minutes. Directed by Michael Blackwood. Filmed by Christian Blackwood, Nicholas Proferes, and Seth Schneidman. Edited by Lana Jokel. Sound by James Musser. Production Manager: Stephen Westheimer. Produced and distributed by Blackwood Productions, New York.

Claes Oldenburg's Crusoe Umbrella, 1980. 16 mm, color, sound, 30 minutes. Directed by Martin Zell. Filmed by Neal Brown. Sound by Michael Miller and Peter Triolo. Music by Dart Brown and Marcia Miget. Narrated by Curtis Page. Produced by Martin Zell for Iowa Public Television. Not in circulation.

School Bus Yellow/Adirondack Green, 1982. 16 mm, color, sound, 49 minutes. Directed by Machteld Schrameijer and Coosje van Bruggen. Filmed by Francis Freedland, Jesper Sorensen, and Vibeke Winding. Edited by Donald George Klocek. Sound by Robert Ghiraldini. Music by Al Scotti. Produced by Machteld Schrameijer and Coosje van Bruggen. Distributed by Store Days Inc., New York.

Claes Oldenburg/Coosje van Bruggen: Large-Scale Projects, 1991. 16 mm, color, sound, 56 minutes. Directed by Lana Jokel. Filmed by Nick Doob. Produced by Nick Doob and Lana Jokel. Distributed by the Museum of Modern Art, New York.

Ein Schlips steht Kopf: Ein Film mit Claes Oldenburg und Coosje van Bruggen, 1994. 16 mm, color, sound, 21 minutes. Directed by Erwin Leiser and Vera Leiser. Filmed by Peter Warneke. Sound by Peter Warneke and Wolfgang Widmer. Edited by Werner Wullschleger. Produced by Erwin Leiser Filmproduktion, Zurich; Deutsche Genossenschaftsbank, Frankfurt; Südwestfunk, Baden-Baden; and Hessischer Rundfunk, Frankfurt. German and English editions. Distributed by Erwin Leiser Filmproduktion, Zurich.

Selected Bibliography

David Platzker

"Books by the Artist," "Writings, Statements, and Projects for Periodicals and Books by the Artist," and "Exhibition Catalogues" are arranged chronologically. All other sections in the bibliography are arranged alphabetically. Please refer to "Solo and Two-Person Exhibitions" in the exhibition history for further information about exhibitions related to catalogues listed in the bibliography.

Books by the Artist

Spicy Ray Gun. New York: Judson Gallery, 1960.

Ray Gun Poems. New York: Judson Gallery, 1960.

More Ray Gun Poems. New York: Judson Gallery, 1960.

Injun and Other Histories (1960). New York: A Great Bear Pamphlet, 1966.

Store Days: Documents from The Store (1961) and Ray Gun Theater (1962). New York: Something Else Press, 1967.

Claes Oldenburg: Notes. Los Angeles: Gemini G.E.L., 1968. Text by Barbara Rose.

Claes Oldenburg: Constructions, Models, and Drawings. Chicago: Richard Feigen Gallery, 1969.

Claes Oldenburg: Notes in Hand. New York: E. P. Dutton, 1971.

Claes Oldenburg: More Ray Gun Poems (1960). Philadelphia: Moore College of Art and Falcon Press, 1973.

Raw Notes. Ed. Kasper König. Halifax, Canada: The Press of the Nova Scotia College of Art and Design, 1973.

Claes Oldenburg: Log, May 1974–August 1976. 2 vols. Stuttgart: Hansjörg Mayer; New York: Store Days, 1976.

Oldenburg, Claes, Frank O. Gehry, and Coosje van Bruggen. *Il Corso del Coltello: Menu*. Turin: Gruppo Finanziario Tessile; Milan: Gabriele Mazzotta, 1985. In English and Italian.

Claes Oldenburg: Sketches and Blottings toward the European Desk Top. Milan and Turin: Galleria Christian Stein; Florence: Hopeful Monster, 1990. Text by Coosje van Bruggen; in English and Italian.

Writings, Statements, and Projects for Periodicals and Books by the Artist

"Portfolio and Three Poems." *Exodus* (New York), no. 3 (spring–summer 1960), pp. 73–80.

"A Statement." In Michael Kirby, ed. *Happenings: An Illustrated Anthology*. New York: E. P. Dutton, 1965.

"The Artists Say: Claes Oldenburg." *Art Voices* (New York) 4, no. 3 (summer 1965), pp. 62–63.

"Fotodeath/Washes." *Tulane Drama Review* (New Orleans) 10, no. 2 (winter 1965), pp. 85–93, 108–18.

"Extracts from the Studio Notes (1962–64)." *Artftorum* (Los Angeles) 4, no. 5 (Jan. 1966), pp. 32–33.

The Airflow—Top and Bottom, Front, Back and Sides, with Silhouette of the Inventor, to Be Folded into a Box, 1966 (artist's project). *Art News* (New York) 64, no. 10 (Feb. 1966), cover.

"Afterthoughts." *Konstrevy* (Stockholm), nos. 5–6 (Nov.–Dec. 1966), pp. 214–20.

"Egomessages about Pollock." In "Jackson Pollock: An Artist Symposium, Part 2." *Art News* (New York) 66, no. 3 (May 1967), pp. 27, 66–67.

"America: War and Sex, Etc." *Arts Magazine* (New York) 41, no. 8 (summer 1967), cover, pp. 32–38.

Statement. In Lucy Lippard, "Homage to the Square." *Art in America* (New York) 55, no. 4 (July–Aug. 1967), pp. 50–57.

"Some Program Notes about Monuments, Mainly." *Chelsea* (New York), nos. 22–23 (June 1968), pp. 87–92.

"About the Famous Toronto Drainpipe." *Arts Canada* (Toronto) 25, no. 3 (Aug. 1968), pp. 40–41.

"Claes Oldenburg: Fireplugs." *Design Quarterly* (Minneapolis), nos. 74–75 (1969), unpaginated.

"My Very Last Happening." *Esquire Magazine* (New York), May 1969, pp. 154–57.

"Notes on the Lipstick Monument." *Novum Organum* (New Haven), no. 7 (May 15, 1969), unpaginated.

"Bedroom Ensemble, Replica I." *Studio International* (London) 178, no. 913 (July–Aug. 1969), pp. 2–3.

"Claes Oldenburg: Postcard 8/23/69." *Art Now: New York* 1, no. 8 (Oct. 1969), unpaginated.

"Statements." *Museumjournaal* (Amsterdam) 15, no. 2 (April 1970), pp. 72–76.

"Chronology of Drawings." *Studio International* (London) 179, no. 923 (June 1970), cover, pp. 249–53.

Letter to Maurice Tuchman, Jan. 27, 1969. In Tuchman, "An Introduction to 'Art and Technology.'" *Studio International* (London) 181, no. 932 (April 1971), pp. 176–77.

"The Double-Nose/Purse/Punching Bag/Ashtray." *Tracks* (New York) 2, no. 1 (winter 1976), pp. 5–10.

Oldenburg, Claes, and Roy Bongartz. "Oldenburg Draws Seven New Wonders of the World." *Horizon* (New York) 14, no. 2 (spring 1972), pp. 70–71, 81.

"Claes Oldenburg Collecting Ray Guns in New York." *Vision* (Oakland), no. 3 (Nov. 1976), pp. 22–25.

Artists Call Against U.S. Intervention in Central America, 1983–84 (poster design). *Arts Magazine* (New York) 58, no. 5 (Jan. 1984), cover.

"Waiting for Dr. Coltello: A Project by Coosje van Bruggen, Frank O. Gehry and Claes Oldenburg." *Artforum* 23 (Sept. 1984), pp. 88–95.

A Bottle of Notes—Proposal for a Large-Scale Project in Middlesbrough, England, 1988 (drawing). *Artforum* (New York) 26, no. 7 (March 1988), cover, p. 1.

"Alternate Proposal for Number One Poultry: Prince's Foot in the Spaghetti." *The Independent* (London), July 7, 1988, p. 16.

Proposal for the Courtyard of the Royal Academy, London on the Occasion of the Exhibition of Pop Art: Great Fried Egg Canopy with Colossal Bacon Strips, 1991 (drawing). *RA* (London), no. 23 (autumn 1991), pp. 42–43.

Interviews with the Artist

Pincus-Witten, Robert. "The Transformation of Daddy Warbucks: An Interview with Claes Oldenburg." *Chicago Scene* 4, no. 4 (April 1964), pp. 34–38.

McDevitt, Jan. "Object: Still Life; Interview." *Craft Horizons* (New York) 25, no. 5 (Sept. 1965), pp. 31–32, 55–56.

"Waldorf Panel 2" (discussion among Isamu Noguchi, Oldenburg, Phillip Pavia, George Segal, George Sugarman, and James Wines). *It Is* (New York), fall 1965, pp. 77–80, 110–13.

Baro, Gene. "Oldenburg's Monuments." *Art and Artists* (London) 1, no. 9 (Dec. 1966), pp. 28–31.

Glaser, Bruce. "Oldenburg, Lichtenstein, Warhol: A Discussion." *Artforum* (Los Angeles) 4, no. 6 (Feb. 1966), pp. 20–24.

Schilling, Alfons. "'Bau' Interview with Claes Oldenburg." *Bau* (Vienna), no. 4 (1966), pp. 83–87; English insert, pp. 87–88A.

Fraser, Robert. "London: Male City." *International Times* (London), Dec. 12, 1966.

Gablik, Suzi. "Take a Cigarette Butt and Make It Heroic." *Art News* (New York) 66, no. 3 (May 1967), pp. 30–31, 77.

Kostelanetz, Richard. "Interview with Claes Oldenburg." In *The Theatre of Mixed Means: An Introduction to Happenings, Kinetic Environments and Other Mixed-Means Presentations.* New York: Dial Press, 1968.

Coplans, John. "The Artist Speaks: Claes Oldenburg." *Art in America* (New York) 57, no. 2 (March 1969), pp. 68–75.

Siegel, Jeanne. "How to Keep Sculpture Alive In and Out of a Museum: An Interview with Claes Oldenburg on His Retrospective Exhibition at the Museum of Modern Art." *Arts Magazine* (New York) 44, no. 1 (Sept.–Oct. 1969), pp. 24–28.

Reaves, Angela Westwater. "Claes Oldenburg, An Interview." *Artforum* (New York) 11, no. 2 (Oct. 1972), pp. 36–39.

Rose, Barbara. "New York Is an Oldenburg Festival." *New York Magazine*, May 6, 1974, pp. 91–95.

Shapiro, David. "Claes Oldenburg un colloquio a New York/ An Interview with Claes Oldenburg." *Domus* (Milan), no. 545 (April 1975), pp. 49–52.

Bach, Friedrich. "Interview mit Claes Oldenburg." *Das Kunstwerk* (Baden-Baden) 28, no. 3 (May 1975), pp. 3–13.

Brown, Kathan. "About California." *Vision* (Oakland), no. 1 (Sept. 1975), pp. 5–7.

Mesley, R. "Claes Oldenburg in Toronto." *Vie des arts* (Montreal) 21, no. 84 (autumn 1976), pp. 54–56, 93–94; in English and French.

Slavutski, Victoria. "El broche más grande del mundo." *La Opinión Cultural* (Buenos Aires), Sept. 19, 1976, pp. 2–5.

Beeke, Anna. "Het Formaat van Claes Oldenburg." *Hollands Diep* (Amsterdam) 3, no. 9 (May 7, 1977), pp. 44–47.

Bourdon, David. "Artist's Dialogue: A Conversation with Claes Oldenburg." *Architectural Digest* (Los Angeles) 39, no. 6 (June 1982), pp. 164, 168, 170, 172.

de Smecchia, Muni. "Gli artisti nel loro studio: Claes Oldenburg." *Vogue Speciale* (Milan), no. 6 (March 1984), pp. 616–21, 664.

"Claes Oldenburg parla del suo progetto spettacolo per Venezia." *Il Manifesto* (Rome), June 9–10, 1985, p. 13.

Minervino, Fiorella. "Oldenburg: 'Io, Cézanne e l'hamburger.'" *Corriere della sera* (Milan), Dec. 31, 1986, p. 13.

B[oissiere], O[livier]. "'J'en ai fini des partis pris du happening.'" *Le Matin* (Paris), July 16, 1987, p. 13.

Lebovici, Elisabeth. "Claes Oldenburg: Le matériau en action." *Art Press* (Paris), no. 116 (July–Aug. 1987), pp. 13–21.

"An Observed Conversation." In *Modern Dreams: The Rise and Fall and Rise of Pop*. New York: Institute for Contemporary Art, 1987.

Gardener, Paul. "What Artists Like About the Art They Like When They Don't Know Why." *Art News* (New York) 90, no. 8 (Oct. 1991), pp. 116–21.

Schmidt, Felix. "Neue Welt nach Regeln der Phantasie." *Art: das Kunstmagazin* (Hamburg), no. 12 (Dec. 1991), pp. 28–44.

Gross, Terry. "Interview: Out of the Ordinary." *Applause* (Philadelphia) 18, no. 8 (Aug. 1992), pp. 12–16.

Bickers, Patricia. "Claes Oldenburg." *Art Monthly* (London), no. 171 (Nov. 1993), pp. 3–11.

Exhibition Catalogues

Exhibition of Recent Work by Claes Oldenburg. New York: Sidney Janis Gallery, 1964.

Claes Oldenburg. Paris: Galerie Ileana Sonnabend, 1964. Text by Otto Hahn; in French.

New Work by Oldenburg. New York: Sidney Janis Gallery, 1966. Text by Oldenburg.

Claes Oldenburg: Skulpturer och teckningar. Stockholm: Moderna Museet, 1966. Texts by Öyvind Fahlström, Ulf Linde, and Oldenburg; in English and Swedish.

An Exhibition of New Work by Claes Oldenburg. New York: Sidney Janis Gallery, 1967.

Claes Oldenburg. New York: The Museum of Modern Art, 1970. Texts by Oldenburg and Barbara Rose. (Catalogue to the 1969 exhibition at the Museum of Modern Art.) Separate catalogues published by touring venues; Amsterdam: Stedelijk Museum, 1970, texts by Alicia Legg and Oldenburg, in English and Dutch; Düsseldorf: Städtische Kunsthalle Düsseldorf, 1970, texts by Gene Baro, Öyvind Fahlström, Legg, and Oldenburg, in German; London: The Arts Council of Great Britain, 1970, texts by Legg and Oldenburg (catalogue to exhibition at Tate Gallery).

New Work by Claes Oldenburg. New York: Sidney Janis Gallery, 1970. Text by Oldenburg.

Claes Oldenburg: Object into Monument. Pasadena, Calif.: Pasadena Art Museum; Los Angeles: The Ward Ritchie Press, 1971. Texts by Barbara Haskell and Oldenburg.

Claes Oldenburg: Works in Edition. Los Angeles: Margo Leavin Gallery, 1971.

Maus Museum: Eine Auswahl von Objekten gesammelt von Claes Oldenburg/Mouse Museum: A Selection of Objects Collected by Claes Oldenburg. Kassel: Documenta, 1972. Text by Kasper König; in German and English. (Supplement to *Documenta 5* catalogue.)

Claes Oldenburg: Recent Prints. New York: M. Knoedler and Co., 1973. Text by Barbara Mathes. (Catalogue to *Claes Oldenburg: Recent Prints and Preparatory Drawings*.)

Claes Oldenburg. Tokyo: Minami Gallery, 1973. Text by Yoshiaki Tono; in Japanese.

The Lipstick Comes Back. New Haven, Conn.: Yale University Art Gallery, 1974. Text by Susan P. Casteras.

Claes Oldenburg: The Alphabet in L.A. Los Angeles: Margo Leavin Gallery, 1975. Texts by Helen Ferulli, Margo Leavin, and Oldenburg.

Zeichnungen von Claes Oldenburg. Tübingen: Kunsthalle Tübingen; Basel: Kunstmuseum Basel, 1975. Texts by Götz Adriani, Dieter Koepplin, and Barbara Rose; in German. (Catalogue to *Claes Oldenburg: Zeichnungen—Aquarelle—Collagen, 1954–1974*.) Edition published by touring venue; Hanover: Kestner-Gesellschaft, 1976, in German.

Oldenburg: Six Themes. Minneapolis: Walker Art Center, 1975. Text by Martin Friedman and interviews with Oldenburg by Friedman.

Claes Oldenburg: An Exhibition of Recent Erotic Fantasy Drawings. London: The Mayor Gallery, 1975. Text by Richard Morphet. (Catalogue to *Claes Oldenburg: Recent Erotic Fantasy Drawings*.)

Claes Oldenburg: Tekeningen, aquarellen en grafiek. Amsterdam: Stedelijk Museum, 1977. Texts by Oldenburg and Coosje van Bruggen; in English and Dutch. Editions published by touring venues; *Claes Oldenburg: Dessins, aquarelles et estampes*, Paris: Musée National d'Art Moderne, Centre Georges Pompidou, 1977, texts by Oldenburg and van Bruggen, in French; *Claes Oldenburg: Teckningar, akvareller och grafik*, Stockholm: Moderna Museet, 1977, texts by Oldenburg and van Bruggen; in Swedish and English.

Oldenburg/The Inverted Q. Akron, Ohio: Akron Art Institute, 1977. Edited by Robert Doty, with texts by Doty and Oldenburg. (Catalogue to *Claes Oldenburg: The Inverted Q*.)

Claes Oldenburg. Delft, The Netherlands: Stedelijk Museum, 1977. Texts by Ank Leeuw-Marcar and Oldenburg; in Dutch. (Catalogue to exhibition at De volle maan, Delft.)

Mouse Museum/Ray Gun Wing: Two Collections/Two Buildings by Claes Oldenburg. Chicago: Museum of Contemporary Art, 1977. Texts by Judith Russi Kirshner and Oldenburg. Separate catalogue published by touring venues, *Claes Oldenburg: Mouse Museum/Ray Gun Wing*, Otterlo: Rijksmuseum Kröller-Müller; Cologne: Museum Ludwig, 1979, text by Coosje van Bruggen, English, German, and Dutch editions.

Claes Oldenburg: The Screwarch Project Commissioned by Museum Boymans-van Beuningen Rotterdam, 1978–1982. Rotterdam: Museum Boymans-van Beuningen, 1983. Texts by Cor Blok and Oldenburg with Coosje van Bruggen; in English and Dutch. (Catalogue to *The Screwarch Project*.)

Claes Oldenburg: Standing Mitt with Ball—From Concept to Monument. New York: Wave Hill, 1984. Text by Nina Sundell.

El Cuchillo Barco. Milan: Electa, 1986. Texts by Germano Celant and Coosje van Bruggen; in Spanish. (Catalogue to *El Cuchillo Barco de "Il Corso del Coltello": Claes Oldenburg, Coosje van Bruggen, Frank O. Gehry*, Palacio de Cristal, Madrid.)

Il Corso del Coltello. New York: Gruppo GFT, 1986. Text by Enrico Filippini. (Catalogue to *The Course of the Knife*, Castelli Gallery, New York, and *The Knife Ship from "Il Corso del Coltello,"* Solomon R. Guggenheim Museum, New York.)

Claes Oldenburg: The Haunted House. Essen: H. Gerd Margreff, 1987. Texts by Gerhard Storck and Coosje van Bruggen; in English and German. (Catalogue to exhibition at Museum Haus Esters Krefeld.)

Le Couteau navire. Milan: Electa, 1987. Texts by Germano Celant, Frank O. Gehry, and Coosje van Bruggen. (Catalogue to *Le Couteau navire: Décors, costumes, dessins, "Il Corso del Coltello" de Claes Oldenburg, Coosje van Bruggen et Frank O. Gehry*, Musée National d'Art Moderne, Centre Georges Pompidou.)

A Bottle of Notes and Some Voyages. Sunderland: Northern Centre for Contemporary Art; Leeds: The Henry Moore Centre for the Study of Sculpture, Leeds City Art Galleries, 1988. Texts by Germano Celant, Oldenburg, Gerhard Storck, and Coosje van Bruggen. Editions published for touring venues; *Eine Flasche voller Aufzeichnungen und Einige Reisen*, Basel: Wiese Verlag, 1989, in German; *A Bottle of Notes and Some Voyages*, Valencia: IVAM, Centre Julio González, 1989, in Spanish.

Claes Oldenburg: Dibujos/Drawings 1959–1989. Valencia: IVAM, Centre Julio González, 1989. Texts by Oldenburg and Coosje van Bruggen; in English and Spanish.

Claes Oldenburg. London: The Mayor Gallery, 1990. Text by John McEwen. (Catalogue to *Claes Oldenburg: Eight Sculptures 1961–1987*.)

Claes Oldenburg: Multiples 1964–1990. Frankfurt: Portikus, 1992. Text by Thomas Lawson and catalogue raisonné by David Platzker; German and French editions.

Claes Oldenburg: Die frühen Zeichnungen. Basel: Öffentliche Kunstsammlung Basel, 1992. Texts by Dieter Koepplin and Oldenburg. (Catalogue to exhibition at Museum für Gegenwartskunst, Basel.)

Claes Oldenburg. New York: The Pace Gallery, 1992. Interview with Oldenburg by Arne Glimcher.

Claes Oldenburg: Recent Print and Sculpture Editions. Los Angeles: Gemini G.E.L., 1993. Texts by Oldenburg and Jim Reid.

Claes Oldenburg: In the Studio/Dans l'atelier. Marseille: Musée Cantini, 1993. Text by Sylvie Coëllier; in French.

Claes Oldenburg. Tel Aviv: Tel Aviv Museum of Art, 1994. Text by Edna Moshenson; in Hebrew and English. (Catalogue to *Claes Oldenburg: Multiples and Notebook Pages*.)

Books About the Artist

Baro, Gene. *Claes Oldenburg: Drawings and Prints*. New York: Paul Bianchini; London and New York: Chelsea House, 1969. Reprint, Secaucus, N.J.: Wellfleet Books, 1988.

Claes Oldenburg Coosje van Bruggen: Large-Scale Projects. New York: The Monacelli Press, 1994.

Claes Oldenburg: Cross Section of a Toothbrush with Paste in a Cup on a Sink: Portrait of Coosje's Thinking. Krefeld: Krefelder Kunstmuseen, 1985. Texts by Gerhard Storck and Oldenburg; in German and English.

Claes Oldenburg: Geometric Mouse, Scale C. Los Angeles: Gemini G.E.L., [1971]. Text by Oldenburg.

Claes Oldenburg: Large-Scale Projects, 1977–1980. New York: Rizzoli, 1980. Texts by Rudi Fuchs and Coosje van Bruggen with Oldenburg.

Claes Oldenburg: Multiples in Retrospect 1964–1990. New York: Rizzoli, 1991. Texts by Thomas Lawson, Oldenburg, and Arthur Solway; catalogue raisonné by David Platzker.

Claes Oldenburg: Proposals for Monuments and Buildings, 1965–1969. Chicago: Big Table, 1969. Interview with Oldenburg by Paul Carroll.

Claes Oldenburg: The Soft Screw. Los Angeles: Gemini G.E.L., 1976. Texts by Melinda Wortz and Oldenburg.

The Course of the Knife. Milan: Electa, 1986. Texts by Germano Celant, Frank O. Gehry, Oldenburg, and Coosje van Bruggen.

Der Gartenschlauch von Claes Oldenburg und Coosje van Bruggen. Freiburg im Breisgau, Germany: Kunstverein Freiburg, 1983.

Johnson, Ellen H. *Claes Oldenburg*. Penguin New Art 4. Harmondsworth, England and Baltimore: Penguin Books, 1971.

———. *Oldenburg's Giant Three-Way Plug at Oberlin*. Oberlin, Ohio: Allen Memorial Art Museum, 1971.

Kerber, Bernhard. *Claes Oldenburg: Schreibmaschine*. Stuttgart: Philipp Reclam, 1971.

Mielcke, Gabriele. *Inverted Collar and Tie*. Ostfildern: Cantz, 1994.

Oldenburg: Tube Supported by Its Contents. Düsseldorf: Galerie Schmela, 1985. Text by Oldenburg and poem by Schuldt; in English and German.

van Bruggen, Coosje. *Claes Oldenburg: Nur Ein Anderer Raum/Just Another Room*. Frankfurt: Museum für Moderne Kunst, 1991. In English and German.

Articles and Essays About the Artist

Adams, Brooks. "Feats of Claes." *Harper's Bazaar* (New York), no. 3369 (Sept. 1992), pp. 336–39.

Altman, Jack. "Claes Oldenburg: The Super, Giant, Economy-Sized Fantasies of the King of Neubern." *Midwest* (magazine of *Chicago Sun-Times*), Feb. 18, 1968, pp. 6, 8, 10–12, 15.

Ashton, Dore. "Claes Oldenburg: 'The Store,' New York 1961." In *Die Kunst der Ausstellung*. Frankfurt: Insel Verlag, 1991, pp. 148–55.

Baro, Gene. "Claes Oldenburg, or the Things of This World." *Art International* (Lugano) 10, no. 9 (Nov. 20, 1966), pp. 41–43, 45–48.

"Big City Boy." *Newsweek* (New York), March 21, 1966, p. 100.

Billeter, Erika. "Atelierbesuche bei fünf New Yorker Malern: Claes Oldenburg." *Speculum Artis* (Zurich) 17, no. 9 (Sept. 1965), pp. 34–38.

Bourdon, David. "Claes Oldenburg." *Konstrevy* (Stockholm) 40, nos. 5–6 (Nov.–Dec. 1964), pp. 164–69.

———. "Immodest Proposals for Monuments." *New York World Journal Tribune*, Jan. 8, 1967, pp. 22–23.

———. "Claes Oldenburg's *Store Days*." *The Village Voice* (New York), Dec. 28, 1967, pp. 6–7, 23.

Downs, Linda. "Oldenburg's Profile Airflow and Giant Three-Way Plug." *Bulletin of The Detroit Institute of Arts* 50, no. 4 (1971), pp. 69–78.

Ellmann, Lucy. "Cheap and Sexy Throwaways." *The Times Literary Supplement* (London), April 3, 1992, p. 24.

Fahlström, Öyvind, and Ulf Linde. "Claes Oldenburg: Two Contrasting Viewpoints." *Studio International* (London) 172, no. 884 (Dec. 1966), pp. 326–29.

Finch, Christopher. "Notes for a Monument to Claes Oldenburg." *Art News* (New York) 68 (Oct. 1969), pp. 52–56.

Flynn, Betty. "You Can Take an Object and Change It from Small to Big to Colossal." *Panorama* (magazine of *Chicago Daily News*), July 22, 1967, pp. 2–3.

Foote, Nancy. "Oldenburg's Monuments to the Sixties." *Artforum* (New York) 15, no. 5 (Jan. 1977), pp. 54–56.

Garcia-Marques, Francesca. "Oldenburg/van Bruggen: Il Coltello Affeita-Muro." *Domus* (Milan), no. 716 (May 1990), pp. 14–15.

Glueck, Grace. "Soft Sculpture or Hard—They're Oldenburgers." *The New York Times Magazine*, Sept. 21, 1969, pp. 28–29, 100–15.

Goldman, Judith. "Sort of a Commerical for Objects." *The Print Collector's Newsletter* (New York) 2, no. 6 (Jan.–Feb. 1972), pp. 117–19.

Graham, Dan. "Oldenburg's Monuments." *Artforum* (New York) 6, no. 5 (Jan. 1968), pp. 30–35.

Graham-Dixon, Andrew. "Making Spaghetti for the Prince." *The Independent* (London), July 7, 1988, p. 16.

———. "Bottle of Pop." *Vogue* (London) 154, no. 8 (Aug. 1990), pp. 128–35.

Gruen, John. "Art in New York: Things That Go Limp." *New York Magazine*, Sept. 1, 1969, p. 57.

Hess, Thomas B. "Art: The Story of O." *New York Magazine* 9, no. 48 (Nov. 29, 1976), pp. 78, 80, 83.

Hughes, Robert. "Magician, Clown, Child." *Time*, Feb. 21, 1972, pp. 60–63.

Johnson, Ellen H. "Oldenburg's Giant Three-Way Plug." *Arts Magazine* (New York) 45, no. 3 (Dec. 1970–Jan. 1971), pp. 43–45.

———. "Oldenburg's Poetics: Analogues, Metamorphoses and Sources." *Art International* (Lugano) 14, no. 4 (April 20, 1970), pp. 42–45, 51.

Kenedy, R. C. "Oldenburg Draughtsman." *Art and Artists* (London) 5, no. 4 (July 1970), pp. 25–27.

Knight, Michael. "Twelve-Foot-High Baseball Mitt Is Safe at Home." *The New York Times*, Oct. 17, 1973, p. 49.

Kokkimen, Eila. "Books" (review of *Claes Oldenburg: Drawings and Prints*). *Arts Magazine* (New York) 44, no. 2 (Nov. 1969), pp. 12, 14.

Kunz, Martin. "Claes Oldenburg." *Kunst Nachrichten* (Lausanne) 11, no. 6 (Sept. 1975), pp. 152–60, 168.

Legg, Alicia. "Claes Oldenburg." *Art and Artists* (London) 5, no. 4 (July 1970), pp. 20–24.

Leiser, Erwin. "Claes Oldenburg and Coosje van Bruggen." *Frankfurter Allgemeine Magazin*, no. 706 (Sept. 10, 1993), pp. 10–18.

Loring, John. "Oldenburg on Multiples: Multiples as Concept and Technology in the Work of Claes Oldenburg." *Arts Magazine* (New York) 48, no. 8 (May 1974), pp. 42–45.

Marcuse, Herbert. "Commenting on Claes Oldenburg's Proposed Monuments for New York City." *Perspecta: The Yale Architectural Journal* (New Haven), no. 12 (1969), pp. 75–76.

"The Master of the Soft Touch." *Life* (New York) 67, no. 21 (Nov. 21, 1969), pp. 58–64D.

Mekas, Jonas. "Movie Journal." *The Village Voice* (New York), Feb. 3, 1966, p. 21.

Mellow, James R. "On Art: Oldenburg's Scatological 'Soft Touch.'" *The New Leader* (London), Nov. 10, 1969, p. 49.

Muchnic, Suzanne. "Oldenburg Sculpture Cuts to the Heart of Art as Architecture." *Los Angeles Times*, Aug. 19, 1989, part 5, pp. 1, 9.

O'Hara, Frank. "Art Chronicle." *Kulchur* (New York) 3, no. 9 (spring 1963), pp. 55–68.

Patton, Phil. "Oldenburg's Mouse." *Artforum* (New York) 14, no. 7 (March 1976), pp. 51–53.

Ramljak, Suzanne. "Claes Oldenburg: Lifetime Achievement Award Recipient." *Sculpture* (Washington, D.C.) 13, no. 5 (Sept.–Oct. 1994), pp. 18–19.

Rastorfer, Darl. "Engineering Oldenburg." *Architectural Record* (New York) 174, no. 3 (March 1986), pp. 146–51.

Reese, Joanna. "Oldenburg: Man of Steel." *The SoHo Weekly News* (New York) 1, no. 30 (May 2, 1974), pp. 20–21.

Reichardt, Jasia. "Gigantic Oldenburgs." *Architectural Design* (London) 36, no. 11 (Nov. 1966), p. 534.

———. "Bridges and Oldenburgs." *Studio International* (London) 173, no. 885 (Jan. 1967), pp. 2–3.

Restany, Pierre. "Une Personnalité charnière de l'art américain: Claes Oldenburg, premières oeuvres." *Metro* (Milan), no. 9 (March–April 1965), pp. 20–26.

————. "Claes Oldenburg 1965 e i disegni di 'Monumenti Giganti' per New York." *Domus* (Milan), no. 433 (Dec. 1965), pp. 50–53.

Rose, Barbara. "Claes Oldenburg's Soft Machines." *Artforum* (New York) 5, no. 10 (summer 1967), pp. 30–35.

————. "The Origins, Life and Times of Ray Gun: 'All Will See as Ray Gun Sees . . .'" *Artforum* (New York) 8 (Nov. 1969), pp. 50–57.

————. "The Airflow Multiple of Claes Oldenburg." *Studio International* (London) 179, no. 923 (June 1970), pp. 254–55.

————. "Larger than Life: Claes Oldenburg and Coosje van Bruggen Think—and Build—Big." *The Journal of Art* (New York) 4, no. 5 (May 1991), pp. 33, 40–43.

Rosenstein, Harris. "Climbing Mt. Oldenburg." *Art News* (New York) 64, no. 10 (Feb. 1966), pp. 21–25, 56–58.

Salisbury, Stephan. "The Public Views of Claes Oldenburg." *The Philadelphia Inquirer*, Nov. 21, 1986, section C, pp. 1, 10.

Schulze, Franz. "Sculptor Claes Oldenburg: A Wry View of 'the Locked Mind of Chicago' and Its Ruthless, Dominating Edifices." *Panorama* (magazine of *Chicago Daily News*), May 17, 1969, pp. 4–5.

Siegel, Jeanne. "Oldenburg's Places and Borrowings." *Arts Magazine* (New York) 44, no. 2 (Nov. 1969), pp. 48–49.

Smith, Brydon. "Claes Oldenburg." *Albright-Knox Gallery Notes* (Buffalo, N.Y.) 29, no. 2 (autumn 1966), pp. 20–21.

Solomon, Deborah. "Partners in Art." *Elle* (New York), Aug. 1988, pp. 138, 140.

Soutif, Daniel. "Claes Oldenburg ou l'autoportrait à l'objet." *Artstudio* (Paris), no. 19 (winter 1990), pp. 40–55.

Sylvester, David. "The Soft Machines of Claes Oldenburg." *Vogue* (New York) 151 (Feb. 1, 1968), pp. 166, 209, 211–12.

————. "Furry Lollies and Soft Machines." *The Sunday Times Magazine* (London), July 7, 1970, pp. 14–20.

Tomkins, Calvin. "Profiles: Look What I've Got Here." *The New Yorker* 53, no. 43 (Dec. 12, 1977), pp. 55–88.

Tuten, Frederic. "Books" (review of Claes Oldenburg, *Store Days*). *Arts Magazine* (New York) 42, no. 1 (Sept.–Oct. 1967), p. 63.

"Up-Beats." *Time* (New York) 75, no. 11 (March 14, 1960), p. 80.

Väth-Hinz, Henriette. "Bie Claes Oldenburg." *Pan* (Munich), no. 7 (1989), pp. 46–52.

Wallach, Amei. "The Evolution of a Team." *Newsday* (New York), Dec. 2, 1990, part 2, pp. 23–24.

Wilson, Martha. "Books" (review of Claes Oldenburg, *Raw Notes*). *Art and Artists* (London) 9, no. 3 (June 1974), pp. 47–51.

Wohlfert, Lee. "The Bizarre, Colossal Shapes of Oldenburg: 'My Monuments Are a Kind of Theatre.'" *People Weekly* (New York) 3, no. 25 (June 30, 1975), pp. 54–56.

Woodward, Richard B. "Pop and Circumstance." *Art News* (New York) 89, no. 2 (Feb. 1990), pp. 118–23.

General Reference Books and Articles

Alloway, Lawrence. "Art in Escalation, The History of Happenings: A Question of Sources." *Arts Magazine* (New York) 41, no. 3 (Dec. 1966–Jan. 1967), pp. 40–43.

————. "Popular Culture and Pop Art." *Studio International* (London) 178, no. 913 (July–Aug. 1969), pp. 17–21.

————. *Topics in American Art since 1945.* New York: W. W. Norton, 1975.

Amaya, Mario. *Pop as Art: A Survey of New Super Realism.* London: Studio Vista, 1965. (Reprinted as *Pop Art . . . And After.* New York: Viking Press, 1966.)

Ashton, Dore. "Conditioned Historic Reactions." *Studio International* (London) 171, no. 877 (May 1966), pp. 204–05.

Baldwin, Carl R. "On the Nature of Pop." *Artforum* (New York) 12, no. 10 (June 1974), pp. 34–38.

Boatto, Alberto. *Pop Art in U.S.A.* Milan: Lerici, 1967.

Bromberg, Craig. "That Collaborative Itch." *Art News* (New York) 87, no. 9 (Nov. 1988), pp. 160–63.

Celant, Germano. "Artspaces." *Studio International* (London) 190, no. 977 (Sept.–Oct. 1975), pp. 115–23.

————. *Roma/New York: 1948–1964.* Milan and Florence: Charta; New York: The Murray and Isabella Rayburn Foundation, 1993.

Compton, Michael. *Pop Art: Movements of Modern Art.* London: Hamlyn, 1970.

DeLynn, Jane. "Creative Coupling." *Avenue* (New York) 14, no. 7 (Feb. 1990), pp. 60–73.

Dienst, Rolf-Gunter. *Pop-Art.* Wiesbaden: Limes Verlag, 1965.

Finch, Christopher. "The Object in Art." *Art and Artists* (London) 1, no. 2 (May 1966), pp. 18–21.

————. *Pop Art: Object and Image.* London: Studio Vista; New York: E. P. Dutton, 1968.

————. "The Role of the Spectator." *Design Quarterly* (Minneapolis), no. 73 (1969), unpaginated.

Fisher, Stanley, ed. *Beat Coast East: An Anthology of Rebellion.* New York: Excelsior Press, 1960.

Flavin, Dan. "Some Other Comments . . . : More Pages from a Spleenish Journal." *Artforum* (New York) 6, no. 4 (Dec. 1967), pp. 20–25.

Forge, Andrew. "Media Crises." *Studio International* (London) 175, no. 898 (March 1968), pp. 162–63.

————. "Forces Against Object-Based Art." *Studio International* (London) 181, no. 929 (Jan. 1971), pp. 32–37.

Gablik, Suzi. "Protagonists of Pop: Five Interviews Conducted by Suzi Gablik." *Studio International* (London) 178, no. 913 (July–Aug. 1969), pp. 9–16.

Geldzahler, Henry. "Happenings: Theater by Painters." *Hudson Review* (New York) 18, no. 4 (winter 1965–66), pp. 581–86.

Glueck, Grace. "At the Whitney, It's Guerrilla Warfare." *The New York Times*, Nov. 1, 1970, section 2, p. 22.

————. "Art Notes: No Bones in Their Noses." *The New York Times* (New York), April 18, 1971, section D, p. 21.

Goldberg, RoseLee. *Performance: Live Art, 1909 to Present.* New York: Harry N. Abrams, 1979.

Goldin, Amy. "Requiem for a Gallery." *Arts Magazine* (New York) 40, no. 3 (Jan. 1966), pp. 25–29.

Graham, Dan. "Models and Monuments: The Plague of Architecture." *Arts Magazine* (New York) 41, no. 5 (March 1967), pp. 30–37.

Gray, Cleve. "Art Centers: New York: Remburgers and Hambrandts." *Art in America* (New York) 51, no. 6 (Dec. 1963), pp. 118–29.

Gustafson, Donna. "Food and Death: *Vanitas* in Pop Art." *Arts Magazine* (New York) 60, no. 6 (Feb. 1986), pp. 90–93.

Guthrie, Derek, and Jane Allen. "Wit Strikes a Balance in Schizophrenic Struggle." *Chicago Tribune*, January 14, 1973, section 6, pp. 1, 3.

Henri, Adrian. *Total Art: Environments, Happenings, and Performance.* London: Thames and Hudson, 1974.

Hughes, Robert. "The Instant Nostalgia of Pop." *Time* (New York), April 15, 1974, pp. 80–83.

H[ope], H[enry] R. "Public Art Museum Notes." *Art Journal* (New York) 32, no. 3 (spring 1973), pp. 328–38.

Irwin, David. "Pop Art and Surrealism." *Studio International* (London) 171, no. 877 (May 1966), pp. 187–91.

Isaacson, Elisa. "The 'Vasari' Diary: Artists Call." *Art News* (New York) 83, no. 3 (March 1984), p. 17.

Johnson, Ellen H. "The Living Object." *Art International* (Zurich) 7, no. 1 (Jan. 25, 1963), pp. 42–45.

————. "Is Beauty Dead?" *Allen Memorial Art Museum Bulletin* (Oberlin, Ohio) 20, no. 2 (winter 1963), pp. 56–65.

Judd, Donald. "Specific Objects." In *Arts Yearbook 8: Contemporary Sculpture.* New York: The Art Digest, 1965.

Kaprow, Allan. "'Happenings' in the New York Scene." *Art News* (New York) 60, no. 3 (May 1961), pp. 36–39, 58–62.

————. *Assemblage, Environments and Happenings.* New York: Harry N. Abrams, 1966.

————. "The Shape of the Art Environment." *Artforum* (New York) 6, no. 10 (summer 1968), pp. 32–33.

Kelly, Edward T. "Neo-Dada: A Critique of Pop Art." *The Art Journal* (New York) 23, no. 3 (spring 1964), pp. 192–201.

Kirby, Michael. "The New Theatre." *Tulane Drama Review* (New Orleans) 10, no. 2 (winter 1965), pp. 23–43.

Klüver, Billy. "Bakelsen som konst." *Vi* (Stockholm) 51, no. 9 (Feb. 29, 1964), pp. 11–13, 42, 44.

Kozloff, Max. "'Pop' Culture, Metaphysical Disgust, and the New Vulgarians." *Art International* (Zurich) 6, no. 2 (March 1962), pp. 34–36.

————. "Art." *The Nation* (New York), no. 205 (July 3, 1967), pp. 27–29.

———. "The Poetics of Softness." In *Renderings*. New York: Simon and Schuster, 1968.

———. "The Division and Mockery of the Self." *Studio International* (London) 179, no. 918 (Jan. 1970), pp. 9–15.

Kramer, Hilton. "A Symposium on Pop Art." *Arts Magazine* (New York) 37, no. 7 (April 1963), pp. 38–39.

Lahr, John, and Jonathan Price, eds. *The Great American Life Show: Nine Plays from the Avant-Garde Theater*. New York: Bantam Books, 1974.

Leider, Philip. "Gallery '68: High Art and Low Art." *Look* (New York) 32, no. 1 (Jan. 9, 1968), pp. 14–21.

Linker, Kate. "Public Sculpture: The Pursuit of the Pleasurable and Profitable Paradise." *Artforum* (New York) 19, no. 7 (March 1981), pp. 64–73.

Lippard, Lucy R., ed. *Pop Art*. New York and Washington, D.C.: Frederick A. Praeger, 1966.

Livingstone, Marco. *Pop Art: A Continuing History*. London: Thames and Hudson, 1990.

Lobell, John. "Developing Technologies for Sculptors." *Arts Magazine* (New York) 45, no. 8 (summer 1971), pp. 27–29.

Mahsun, Carol Anne. *Pop Art and the Critics*. Ann Arbor, Mich.: UMI Research Press, 1987.

Maitland, Leslie. "Factory Brings Sculptors' Massive Dreams to Fruition." *The New York Times*, Nov. 24, 1976, section L, pp. 35, 55.

Morris, Robert. "Anti Form." *Artforum* (New York) 6, no. 8 (April 1968), pp. 33–35.

Nordland, Gerald. "Marcel Duchamp and Common Object Art." *Art International* (Lugano) 8, no. 1 (Feb. 15, 1964), pp. 30–32.

O'Doherty, Brian. "Inside the White Cube, Part II: The Eye and the Spectator." *Artforum* (New York) 14, no. 8 (April 1976), pp. 26–34.

Restany, Pierre. "Le Nouveau Réalisme à la conquête de New York." *Art International* (Zurich) 7, no. 1 (Jan. 25, 1963), pp. 29–36.

Rose, Barbara. "Dada Then and Now." *Art International* (Zurich) 7, no. 1 (Sept. 25, 1963), pp. 23–28.

———. "Blowup—The Problem of Scale in Sculpture." *Art in America* (New York) 56, no. 4 (July–Aug. 1968), pp. 80–91.

———. "Problems of Criticism, V: The Politics of Art, Part II." *Artforum* (New York) 7, no. 5 (Jan. 1969), pp. 44–49.

———. "Problems of Criticism, VI: The Politics of Art, Part III." *Artforum* (New York) 7, no. 9 (May 1969), pp. 46–49.

Rosenberg, Harold. "From Pollock to Pop: Twenty Years of Painting and Sculpture." *Holiday* (New York) 39, no. 3 (March 1966), pp. 96–100, 136–40.

Rosenthal, Mark. *Artists at Gemini G.E.L.* New York: Harry N. Abrams; Los Angeles: Gemini G.E.L., 1993.

Rublowsky, John. *Pop Art*. New York: Basic Books, 1965.

Russell, John. "Pop Reappraised." *Art in America* (New York) 57, no. 4 (July–Aug. 1969), pp. 78–89.

Sandler, Irving. *American Art of the 1960s.* New York: Harper and Row, 1988.

Seckler, Dorothy Gees. "Folklore of the Banal." *Art in America* (New York) 51, no. 4 (Aug. 1963), pp. 44–48.

Seitz, William C. "Pop Goes the Artist." *Partisan Review* (New York) 30 (summer 1963), pp. 313–16.

———. "The Real and the Artificial: Painting of the New Environment." *Art in America* (New York) 60, no. 6 (Nov.–Dec. 1972), pp. 58–72.

Selz, Peter. "A Symposium on Pop Art." *Arts Magazine* (New York) 37, no. 7 (April 1963), pp. 36–45.

Skelton, Robin. "Pop Art and Pop Poetry." *Art International* (Lugano) 8, no. 8 (Oct. 1969), pp. 39–41.

Smith, C. Ray. *Supermannerism: New Attitudes in Post-Modern Architecture.* New York: E. P. Dutton, 1977.

Smith, Charles C. "The Sculpture Factory." *New England-Boston Sunday Globe,* Aug. 27, 1978, pp. 20–21, 24–28, 30, 35.

Smith, Miles A. "'Colossal Monuments' Latest In Pop Art." *Baltimore Morning Sun,* Nov. 13, 1969, section B, p. 4.

Smith, Roberta. "Splat!" *The Village Voice* (New York), Oct. 16, 1984, p. 109.

Solomon, Alan R. "The New American Art." *Art International* (Lugano) 8, no. 2 (March 20, 1964), pp. 50–55.

Sottsass, Ettore, Jr. "Dada, New Dada, New Realists." *Domus* (Milan), no. 399 (Dec. 1966), pp. 49–50.

Spear, Athena T. "Brancusi and Contemporary Sculpture." *Arts Magazine* (New York) 46, no. 2 (Nov. 1971), pp. 28–31.

Swenson, Gene R. "The New American 'Sign Painters.'" *Art News* (New York) 61, no. 5 (Sept. 1962), pp. 44–47, 60–62.

———. "New York: The Boundaries of Chaos." *Art and Artists* (London) 1, no. 1 (April 1966), pp. 60–63.

Trini, Tommaso. "At Home with Art: The Villa of Count Giuseppe Panza di Biumo." *Art in America* (New York) 58, no. 5 (Sept.–Oct. 1970), pp. 102–09.

von Zahn, Irena. "Multiple View." *Art in America* (New York) 65, no. 1 (Jan.–Feb. 1977), pp. 41–43.

Wald, Matthew L. "Palette of Steel and Brush of Fire." *The New York Times,* June 18, 1978, section 11, pp. 1, 4.

Waldman, Diane. *Collage, Assemblage, and the Found Object.* New York: Harry N. Abrams, 1992.

Wilson, Simon. *Pop.* London: Thames and Hudson, 1974.

Yates, Peter. "Music." *Arts and Architecture* (Los Angeles) 84, nos. 7–8 (July–Aug. 1967), pp. 30–32.

Table of illustrations (by figure number)

About the Artists

Claes Oldenburg
Claes Oldenburg was born in Stockholm, Sweden, on January 28, 1929.
After living in New York City; Rye, New York; and Oslo, Norway, his
family settled in Chicago in 1936. Oldenburg attended Yale University
from 1946 to 1950. He subsequently worked as an apprentice reporter at the
City News Bureau of Chicago and studied at the Art Institute of Chicago.
He became an American citizen in December 1953. In 1956, the artist
moved to New York City, where he has since lived. The performances,
sculptures, drawings, and prints he has made over the past three decades
have been the subject of numerous exhibitions around the world.

Coosje van Bruggen
Coosje van Bruggen, born in Groningen, the Netherlands, in 1942, received
a Doctorandus degree in art history from the University of Groningen.
From 1967 to 1971, she served as a member of the curatorial staff of the
Stedelijk Museum in Amsterdam and from 1971 to 1976 she taught at the
Academy of Fine Arts in Enschede. In 1982, she was a member of the
selection committee for *Documenta 7* in Kassel, Germany. She is the author
of *Claes Oldenburg: Mouse Museum/Ray Gun Wing* (Otterlo: Rijksmuseum
Kröller Müller; Cologne: Museum Ludwig, 1979); "The Realistic
Imagination and Imaginary Reality of Claes Oldenburg," in *Claes
Oldenburg: Dibujos/Drawings 1959–1989* (Valencia: IVAM, Centre Julio
González, 1989); *Claes Oldenburg: Nur Ein Anderer Raum/Just Another Room*
(Frankfurt: Museum für Moderne Kunst, 1991); *Bruce Nauman* (New York:
Rizzoli, 1990); and *John Baldessari* (New York: Rizzoli, 1990). She is also the
curator of a limited-edition artist's book by Hanne Darboven titled
Urzeit/Uhrzeit (New York: Rizzoli, 1991). Most recently, she was the project
director of *Claes Oldenburg Coosje van Bruggen: Large-Scale Projects*
(New York: The Monacelli Press, 1994). She has lived in New York City
since 1978 and in December 1993 became an American citizen.

Oldenburg and van Bruggen were married in 1977. They have collaborated
on performances and on twenty-five large-scale projects around the world.

Photo credits (by figure number)

2. Robert R. McElroy, N.Y. 3. Ellen Page Wilson. 5. David Heald. 6. Courtesy of Claes Oldenburg and Coosje van Bruggen, N.Y. 7. Courtesy of Claes Oldenburg and Coosje van Bruggen, N.Y. 8. Martha Holmes, N.Y. 9. D. James Dee, N.Y. 10. Charles Rappaport. 11. Dorothy Zeidman. 12. Courtesy of The Museum of Modern Art, N.Y. 14. David Heald. 15. Biff Henrich. 17. Robert R. McElroy, N.Y. 20. Ellen Page Wilson. 21. Sheldon C. Collins. 22. Robert R. McElroy, N.Y. 26. Douglas M. Parker Studio. 27. Philippe Migeat; courtesy of Musée National d'Art Moderne, Centre Georges Pompidou. 28. Douglas M. Parker Studio. 29. Jim Strong, Inc. 31. Courtesy of The Museum of Modern Art, N.Y. 32. Douglas M. Parker Studio. 33. Courtesy of Anne and William J. Hokin, Chicago. 34. Geoffrey Clements. 36. Geoffrey Clements. 37. Martin Bühler, Basel. 38. Douglas M. Parker Studio. 39. Ellen Page Wilson. 40. Courtesy of BlumHelman Gallery. 41. Jens Ziehe, Berlin. 42. Jens Ziehe, Berlin. 49. Robert R. McElroy, N.Y. 50. Robert R. McElroy, N.Y. 51. Robert R. McElroy, N.Y. 52. Robert R. McElroy, N.Y. 53. Robert R. McElroy, N.Y. 54. Douglas M. Parker Studio. 55. G. Lepkowski, Berlin. 57. Courtesy of Rheinisches Bildarchiv. 59. David Heald. 63. David Heald. 65. Per Bergström, Stockholm. 66. Douglas M. Parker Studio. 67. Robert R. McElroy, N.Y. 68. Robert R. McElroy, N.Y. 69. Courtesy of Walker Art Center, Minneapolis. 70. David Heald. 72. Courtesy of The Museum of Modern Art, N.Y. 74. Courtesy of The Museum of Modern Art, N.Y. 75. Robert R. McElroy, N.Y. 76. Douglas M. Parker Studio. 77. Douglas M. Parker Studio. 78. Douglas M. Parker Studio. 79. Courtesy of The Museum of Modern Art, N.Y. 80. Joe Ziolkowski. 82. Ellen Page Wilson. 83. Douglas M. Parker Studio. 84. Philip A. Charles. 85. Courtesy of The Museum of Modern Art, N.Y. 86. Robert R. McElroy, N.Y. 87. Robert R. McElroy, N.Y. 88. Courtesy of Claes Oldenburg and Coosje van Bruggen, N.Y. 89. David Heald. 90. Julian Wasser, Beverly Hills. 91. Dennis Hopper. 92. Jann and John F. Thompson. 93. Courtesy of BlumHelman Gallery. 95. David Heald. 96. David Heald. 98. Lee B. Ewing. 99. Ellen Page Wilson. 101. Jann and John F. Thompson. 102. Geoffrey Clements. 104. David Heald. 105. Ellen Page Wilson. 106. David Heald. 107. Dorothy Zeidman. 108. Robert Newcomb. 111. Geoffrey Clements. 112. Rudolf Nagel, Frankfurt. 113. David Heald. 115. Ugo Mulas, Milan. 118. Ruth Kaiser, Viersen, German.y. 120. Geoffrey Clements. 122. Geoffrey Clements. 124. Tom Haarsten, Fotografie Beeldende Kunst. 125. Rudolf Nagel, Frankfurt. 127. Jerry L. Thompson, N.Y. 128. Courtesy of Rheinisches Bildarchiv. 129. Ron Vickers, Toronto. 130. Rudolf Nagel, Frankfurt. 131. Tom Haarsten, Fotografie Beeldende Kunst. 132. Jim Mathews. 133. Lee B. Ewing. 134. Joseph Szaszfai; courtesy of Yale University Art Gallery, New Haven, Connecticut. 135. Toni Dolonski. 136. Glenn Halvorson; courtesy of Walker Art Center, Minneapolis. 137. Courtesy of Stedelijk Museum, Amsterdam. 138. Courtesy of The Museum of Modern Art, N.Y. 139. Courtesy of Sotheby's. 140. Robert R. McElroy, N.Y. 141. Robert R. McElroy, N.Y. 142. Ingemar Berlin, Stockholm. 143. Courtesy of The Museum of Modern Art, N.Y. 144. Allan Finkelman. 146. Glenn Halvorson; courtesy of Walker Art Center, Minneapolis. 147. Lee B. Ewing. 148. Allan Finkelman. 152. Paul Hester, Houston. 153. D. James Dee, N.Y. 154. Dorothy Zeidman. 156. Lee B. Ewing. 157. Courtesy of Des Moines Art Center. 158. Courtesy of Dr. and Mrs. Phillip T. George. 160. William Wilson. 163. Ellen Page Wilson. 166. Courtesy of The Museum of Modern Art, N.Y. 171. Ellen Page Wilson. 172. Philippe Migeat; courtesy of Musée National d'Art Moderne, Centre Georges Pompidou. 175. Courtesy of Philadelphia Museum of Art. 178. Ellen Page Wilson. 179. Ellen Page Wilson. 180. David Heald. 182. Courtesy of Musée National d'Art Moderne, Centre Georges Pompidou. 183. Courtesy of Stedelijk Museum, Amsterdam. 184. Graydon Wood. 185. Douglas M. Parker Studio. 186. Frank Thomas. 188. Charles Hupé. 189. Courtesy of National Gallery of Art, Washington, D.C. 190. Courtesy of Stedelijk Museum, Amsterdam. 191. Lee B. Ewing. 192. David Heald. 193. Shunk-Kender, N.Y. 195. Courtesy of The Saint Louis Art Museum. 196. Courtesy of Walker Art Center, Minneapolis. 197. Douglas M. Parker Studio. 198. John Kender. 199. Douglas M. Parker Studio. 200. Ellen Page Wilson. 201. Dorothy Zeidman. 202. Douglas M. Parker Studio. 203. Lee B. Ewing. 204. Lee B. Ewing. 205. Courtesy of Gamma One Conversions, N.Y. 207. Dorothy Zeidman. 209. Pieter Boersma. 210. Malcolm Lubliner; courtesy of Gemini G.E.L., Los Angeles. 211. Gianfranco Gorgoni. 212. David Lees. 213. Joel Conison. 214. Hans Blezen, Eindhoven. 215. Helaine Messer. 216. Gerd Kittel. 217. Attilio Maranzano. 218. Ray Andrews; courtesy of Des Moines Art Center. 219. Ellen Page Wilson; courtesy of PaceWildenstein. 220. Attilio Maranzano. 221. Attilio Maranzano. 222. Earl Ripling. 223. Douglas M. Parker Studio. 225. Attilio Maranzano. 226. Ivan dalla Tana, N.Y. 227. David Heald. 228. David Heald. 229. Attilio Maranzano. 230. Eugene Mopsik. 231. Balthasar Burkhard. 232. Attilio Maranzano. 233. Attilio Maranzano. 234. Attilio Maranzano. 235. Attilio Maranzano. 236. David Heald. 238. Attilio Maranzano. 239. Attilio Maranzano. 240. Dorothy Zeidman. 242. Attilio Maranzano. 243. Volker Döhne. 244. Dorothy Zeidman. 246. Nanda Lanfranco. 247. Nanda Lanfranco. 248. Hans Hammarskiöld. 249. Hans Hammarskiöld. 250. Hans Hammarskiöld. 251. Hans Hammarskiöld. 253. David Heald. 254. Squidds & Nunns. 255. Dorothy Zeidman. 256. Douglas M. Parker Studio. 257. Douglas M. Parker Studio. 258. Douglas M. Parker Studio. 260. Douglas M. Parker Studio. 261. Sidney B. Felsen; courtesy of Gemini G.E.L., Los Angeles. 262. Attilio Maranzano. 263. Volker Döhne. 264. Volker Döhne. 265. Volker Döhne. 267. Courtesy of Stedelijk Museum, Amsterdam. 268. Glenn Halvorson. 269. Glenn Halvorson. 270. Attilio Maranzano. 271. Photo Kleinefenn. 272. Ellen Page Wilson; courtesy of PaceWildenstein. 274. Attilio Maranzano. 275. Attilio Maranzano. 276. Attilio Maranzano. 277. David Heald. 278. Attilio Maranzano. 279. Attilio Maranzano. 280. Attilio Maranzano. 281. Attilio Maranzano. 282. Attilio Maranzano. 283. Attilio Maranzano. 284. Attilio Maranzano. 285. D. James Dee, N.Y. 287. Attilio Maranzano. 288. Ellen Page Wilson; courtesy of PaceWildenstein. 289. Ellen Page Wilson; courtesy of PaceWildenstein. 290. Ellen Page Wilson; courtesy of PaceWildenstein. 291. D. James Dee, N.Y. 292. Dorothy Zeidman. 293. Attilio Maranzano. 294. Ellen Page Wilson; courtesy of PaceWildenstein. 295. Ellen Page Wilson; courtesy of PaceWildenstein. 296. Ellen Page Wilson; courtesy of PaceWildenstein. 297. Ellen Page Wilson; courtesy of PaceWildenstein. 298. Ellen Page Wilson; courtesy of PaceWildenstein. 299. Bill Jacobson; courtesy of PaceWildenstein. 300. Ellen Page Wilson; courtesy of PaceWildenstein. 301. D. James Dee, N.Y. 302. Attilio Maranzano. 303. Ellen Page Wilson; courtesy of PaceWildenstein. 304. Robert Newcomb. 305. Attilio Maranzano.

Performers depicted in photographs (by page number)

48. Claes Oldenburg. 49, left to right: Pat Muschinski, Claes Oldenburg. 65. Pat Muschinski Oldenburg. 66 – 67, left to right: Claes Oldenburg, Gloria Graves. 68 – 69, left to right: Henry Geldzahler, Marilyn Jaffee, Chippy McKellen, Carl Lehmann-Haupt. 70 – 71, clockwise from rear left: Lucas Samaras, Olga Adorno, Claes Oldenburg, Judy Tirsch, Gloria Graves. 132, left to right: Johanna Lawrenson, Carolee Schneemann, Billy Klüver, Lette Eisenhauer. 133. Pat Muschinski Oldenburg. 134. Pat Muschinski Oldenburg. 135, left to right: Maricla Moyano, Milet Andreyevich, Lucas Samaras. 136, left to right: Lette Eisenhauer, Pat Muschinski Oldenburg, Terry Brook, Lucas Samaras. 137. Lucas Samaras. 138, left to right: Barbara Dilley, Lucas Samaras, Pat Muschinski Oldenburg. 139, left to right: Lucas Samaras, Pat Muschinski Oldenburg. 140, left to right: Lucas Samaras, Mia Rublowsky, Pat Muschinski Oldenburg. 176 – 77, left to right: Pat Muschinski Oldenburg, Rolf Nelson. 178 – 79, left to right: Dejon Greene, Santos Zuniga. 180 – 81, Rolf Nelson. 247, left to right: Lette Eisenhauer, Anita Nosei, David Whitney. 248 – 49, clockwise, from within balloons: Lette Eisenhauer, Elaine Sturtevant, Martha Edelheit, Michael Kirby. 250 – 51, left to right: Fred Mueller, Ellen Sellenraad, Pat Muschinski Oldenburg. 252 – 53, center left: Olle Granath. 419. Sami Gehry, Claes Oldenburg, Alejo Gehry. 421. Coosje van Bruggen. 423. Frank O. Gehry. 427, left to right: John Franklin (in costume), Luisa Messinis. 434 – 35, left to right: Frank O. Gehry, Sami Gehry, Alejo Gehry, Coosje van Bruggen, Germano Celant, Claes Oldenburg. 430. Berta Gehry. 431. Pontus Hulten. 428 – 29. Oscar D'Antiga.

Photo credits (by page number)

13, bottom: Courtesy of The Museum of Modern Art, N.Y. 20, top: Robert R. McElroy. 20, bottom: Jack Mitchell. 257, Fred W. McDarrah. 259, top: Courtesy of The Museum of Modern Art, N.Y. 365, top and bottom: Courtesy of Art Resource, N.Y. 368. Geoffrey Clements, Inc., N.Y.

Front cover: Detail of *Giant Soft Drum Set*, 1967 (fig. 171).
Back cover: *Spoonbridge and Cherry*, 1988 (fig. 270).